ELEMENTS OF
DISTRIBUTED COMPUTING

ELEMENTS OF DISTRIBUTED COMPUTING

VIJAY K. GARG

Department of Electrical and Computer Engineering
University of Texas at Austin

WILEY-INTERSCIENCE

A John Wiley & Sons, Inc., Publication

For ordering and customer service, call 1-800-CALL WILEY.

Library of Congress Cataloging-in-Publication Data is available.

ISBN 0-471-03600-5

Transferred to Digital Printing 2006

10 9 8 7 6 5 4 3 2 1

To
my parents (Shri Saran Lal and Shrimati Laxmi Devi),
my wife (Meenakshi),
and my children (Sonika and Rohan)

Contents

Foreword

Distributed computing arises as soon as one has to solve a problem in terms of processes that individually have only a partial knowledge of the several parameters associated with the problem. Thus, distributed computing appears everywhere (even in everyday life!) and is consequently at the heart of lots of applications. The difficulty in designing a distributed algorithm comes from the fact that each of the processes cooperating in the achievement of the common goal cannot have instantaneous knowledge of the current state of the other processes; it can only know their past states. Moreover, because of the possibility of process or communication failures, this knowledge can become very difficult or even impossible to obtain.

Whereas parallel computing is mainly concerned with efficiency, distributed computing addresses uncertainty created by the multiplicity of control flows, the absence of shared memory and global time, and the occurrence of failures. Although it is true that distributed algorithms are often made up of only a few lines, their behaviors can be difficult to understand and their properties hard to state and prove. Hence, distributed computing is not only a fundamental topic but also a challenging topic where simplicity, elegance, and beauty are first-class criteria.

In this book, Vijay K. Garg provides a comprehensive and timely treatment of all these challenges. In a clear and consistent way, he addresses the fundamental problems, issues, and solutions that define the core of distributed computing. The book is both versatile and complete. While each chapter (designed to correspond to one lecture) addresses a basic issue of distributed computing, the examination of chapters addressing several facets of the same topic provides the reader with a deep insight into the subject and a good understanding of the subtleties one has to cope with when solving distributed computing problems. Moreover, the exercises accompanying each chapter can help the reader test her acquaintance with the subject concerned.

The book is addressed to all those who are concerned with algorithms, distributed computing, and distributed systems. It will provide software engineers with provably correct distributed protocols, researchers with a large collection of up-to-date results, teachers with a solid foundation for a course on distributed computing, and students with an introduction to distributed algorithms for distributed computing.

Professor Michel Raynal
IRISA,
Université de Rennes 1
Campus de Beaulieu, Rennes
France

18 February 2002

Preface

The existing books on distributed computing have mainly been developed as reference books on distributed algorithms. They are more useful to researchers than to students. The present book was designed keeping students in mind. Simplicity has been chosen at the cost of completeness whenever that choice was required.

The topics have been selected very carefully. No book, short of a thick encyclopedia, can cover all topics in distributed systems. I have chosen topics that have practical usefulness as well as aesthetic beauty. Because usefulness and beauty are only in the eyes of the beholder, the selection was necessarily subjective. In my defense, I will only give a brief rationale behind the choice of topics. My rule for selecting topics was simple: I have chosen algorithms over arguments for lower bounds and general mechanisms over special case optimized algorithms—the former choice for usefulness and the latter for beauty. For the sake of usefulness or beauty, I violated my general rule whenever necessary; for example, the result on impossibility of consensus in presence of failures (a negative result) and the algorithm for termination detection (a special case of stable property detection) have been included.

Most proofs in the book are rigorous but not completely formal. I have avoided proofs by contradiction. To quote Royden from his book on Real Analysis: "All students are enjoined in the strongest possible terms to eschew proof by contradiction! There are two reasons for this prohibition: First, such proofs are very often fallacious, the contradiction on the final page arising from an erroneous deduction on an earlier page,... Second, even when correct, such a proof gives little insight into connection between A and B (antecedent and consequent)."

The book is organized as a large number of small chapters rather than a small number of large chapters. Besides the obvious advantage of providing more occasions for satisfaction gained on finishing a chapter, this organization provides more flexibility to the instructor. Assuming that there is little dependency across chapters, as is the case for the present book, the instructor can substitute his or her own handouts and papers for some chapters.

The book is designed for a graduate level course on distributed systems. Several examples and exercise problems are included in each chapter to facilitate classroom teaching. My treatment is based on the graduate courses given at The University of Texas at Austin.

The list of known errors and the supplementary material for the book will be maintained on my home page:

http://www.ece.utexas.edu/~garg

I would like to thank the following people for working with me on various projects discussed in this book. These people include Craig Chase (weak predicates), Om Damani (message logging), Eddy Fromentin (predicate detection), Joydeep Ghosh (global computation), Richard Kilgore (channel predicates), Roger Mitchell (channel predicates), Neeraj Mittal (predicate detection and control, slicing, self-stabilization, distributed shared memory), Venkat Murty (synchronous ordering), Michel Raynal (control flow properties, distributed shared memory), Alper Sen (slicing), Chakarat Skawratonand (vector clocks), Ashis Tarafdar (message logging, predicate control) Alexander Tomlinson (global time, mutual exclusion, relational predicates, control flow properties) and Brian Waldecker (weak and strong predicates). I owe special thanks to Alper Sen for helping me with figures and his meticulous review of an early draft of this book. Ajay Kshemkalyani and Michel Raynal provided valuable feedback on the contents of the book.

I thank the Department of Electrical and Computer Engineering at The University of Texas at Austin, where I was given the opportunity to develop and teach courses on distributed systems. Students in my course gave me very useful feedback. I was supported in part by many grants from the National Science Foundation over the last twelve years. Many of the results reported in this book would not have been discovered by me and my research group without that support. I also thank John Wiley & Sons, Inc. for supporting the project.

Finally, I thank my wife Meenakshi, whose love, support, and understanding kept me inspired in accomplishing this goal.

Chapter 1

Introduction

Distributed System: You know you have one when the crash of a computer you've never heard of stops you from getting any work done.
— *Leslie Lamport*

1.1 Introduction

This book is on distributed systems. We define distributed systems as those computer systems that contain multiple processors connected by a communication network. In these systems processors communicate with each other using messages that are sent over the network. Such systems are increasingly available because of decreases prices of computer processors and the availability of high-bandwidth links to connect them. Despite the availability of hardware for distributed systems, there are few software applications that exploit the hardware. One reason is that distributed software requires a different set of tools and techniques than that required by the traditional sequential software. The focus of this book is on these techniques.

1.2 Distributed Systems Versus Parallel Systems

In this book, we make a distinction between distributed systems and parallel systems. A parallel system consists of multiple processors that communicate with each other using shared memory. This distinction is only at a logical level. Given a physical system in which processors have shared memory, it is easy to simulate messages. Conversely, given a physical system in which processors are connected by a network, it is possible to simulate shared memory. Thus a parallel hardware system may run distributed software and vice versa.

This distinction raises two important questions. Should we build parallel hardware or distributed hardware? Should we write applications assuming shared memory or not? At the hardware level, we would expect that the prevalent model would be multiprocessor workstations connected by a network. Thus the system is both parallel and distributed. Why would the system not be completely parallel? There are many reasons.

- *Scalability*: Distributed systems are inherently more scalable than parallel systems. In parallel systems shared memory becomes a bottleneck when the number of processors is increased.

- *Modularity and heterogeneity*: A distributed system is more flexible because a single processor can be added or deleted easily. Furthermore, this processor can be of a completely different type than the existing processors.

- *Data sharing*: Distributed systems provide data sharing as in distributed databases. Thus multiple organizations can share their data with each other.

- *Resource sharing*: Distributed systems provide resource sharing. For example, an expensive special purpose processor can be shared by multiple organizations.

- *Geographical structure*: The geographical structure of an application may be inherently distributed. The low communication bandwidth may force local processing. This is especially true for wireless networks.

- *Reliability*: Distributed systems are more reliable than parallel systems because the failure of a single computer does not affect the availability of others.

- *Low cost*: Availability of high-bandwidth networks and inexpensive workstations also favors distributed computing for economic reasons.

Why would the system not be purely a distributed one? The reasons for keeping a parallel system at each node are mainly of a technological nature. With the current technology it is generally faster to update a shared memory location than to send a message to some other processor. This is especially true when the new value of the variable must be communicated to multiple processors. Consequently, it is more efficient to get fine grain parallelism from a parallel system than from a distributed system.

So far our discussion has been at the hardware level. As mentioned earlier, the interface provided to the programmer can actually be independent of the underlying hardware. So which model would then be used by the programmer? At the programming level, we expect that programs will be written using multithreaded distributed objects. In this model, an application consists of multiple heavy-weight processes that communicate using messages (or remote method invocations). Each heavy-weight process consists of multiple light-weight processes called threads. Threads communicate through the shared memory. This software model mirrors the hardware that is (expected to be) widely available. By assuming that there is at most one thread per process (or by ignoring the parallelism within one process), we get the usual model of a distributed system. By restricting our attention to a single heavy-weight process, we get the usual model of a parallel system. Why would the system have aspects of distributed objects? The main reason is the logical simplicity of the distributed object model. A distributed program is more object oriented because data in a remote object can only be accessed through an explicit message (or a remote procedure call). The object orientation promotes reusability as well as design simplicity. Conversely, threads are also useful to provide efficient objects. For many applications such as servers, it is useful to have a large shared data structure. It is a programming burden to split the data structure across multiple heavy-weight processes.

In summary, we will see aspects of both parallel processing and distributed processing in hardware as well as software. This book is mainly about techniques and tools for distributed software.

1.3 Characteristics of Distributed Systems

We take the following characteristics as the defining ones for distributed systems.

- *Absence of a shared clock*: In a distributed system, it is impossible to synchronize the clocks of different processors precisely because of uncertainty in communication delays between them. As a result, it is rare to use physical clocks for synchronization in distributed systems. In this book we will see how the concept of causality is used instead of time to tackle this problem.

- *Absence of shared memory*: In a distributed system, it is impossible for any one processor to know the global state of the system. As a result, it is difficult to observe any global property of the system. In this book we will see how efficient algorithms can be developed for evaluating a suitably restricted set of global properties.

- *Absence of accurate failure detection*: In an asynchronous distributed system (a distributed system is asynchronous if there is no upper bound on the message communication time), it is impossible to distinguish between a slow processor and a failed processor. This leads to many difficulties in developing algorithms for consensus, election, etc. In this book we will see how failure detectors can be built to alleviate some of these problems.

1.4   Scope of the Book

This book discusses fundamental concepts in distributed computing systems such as time, state, simultaneity, order, knowledge, failure, and agreement in distributed systems. The emphasis of the book is on developing general mechanisms that can be applied to variety of problems. Examples are clocks, locks, cameras, sensors, controllers, slicers, and synchronizers. The topics have been carefully chosen so that they are fundamental yet useful in practical contexts. The emphasis is on positive results (algorithms) rather than on negative results (lower bounds and impossibility).

The book is based on an *asynchronous* model of distributed computing. Thus it does not deal with shared memory models or network computing with bounded delays on messages and bounded delay between consecutive steps of a processor. An algorithm developed for an asynchronous model of distributed computing will work correctly on all communication networks. In contrast, a *synchronous* algorithm may not work correctly when message delays exceed the upper bound or when processors do not provide hard real-time guarantees.

1.5 Overview of the Book

This book is intended for a one-semester advanced undergraduate or an introductory graduate course on distributed systems. Each chapter can be covered in one 75-minute lecture. There are exactly thirty chapters in the book, making it sufficient for a fifteen-week semester.

There is very little dependence across chapters so that the instructor can pick and choose chapters that he or she wants to cover in the course.

Chapter 1 provides the motivation for distributed systems. It compares advantages of distributed systems with those of parallel systems. It also gives the defining characteristics of distributed systems and the fundamental difficulties in designing algorithms for such systems.

The rest of the chapters are organized as shown in Figure 1.1.

Chapter 2 discusses models of a distributed computation. It describes three models. The first model, called the *interleaving model*, totally orders all the events in the system; the second model, called the *happened before model*, totally orders all the events on a single process; and the third model, called the *potential causality mode*, assumes only a partial order on events even within a single process. This chapter is fundamental to the entire book and should be read before all other chapters.

Chapters 3–22 assume that there are no faults in the system whereas Chapters 23–30 describe solutions (or impossibility thereof) for various problems under various kinds of faults.

Chapters 3–5 discuss mechanisms called clocks used to timestamp events in a distributed computation such that order information between events can be determined with these clocks. Chapter 3 discusses logical and vector clocks. Chapter 4 gives a formal proof of correctness of a vector clock algorithm. This chapter may be skipped without any loss of continuity. Chapter 5 describes clocks of different dimensions, such as matrix clocks.

Chapters 6–9 discuss problems that arise in coordinating resources. Chapters 6 and 7 discuss one of the most studied problems in distributed systems—mutual exclusion. Chapter 6 presents mutual exclusion algorithms based on timestamping, whereas Chapter 7 presents token-based mutual exclusion algorithms. The goal of Chapter 6 is

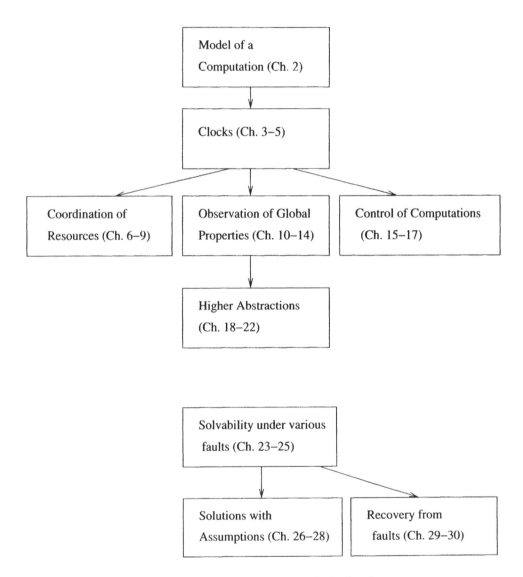

Figure 1.1: Organization of the book

to give the reader a flavor of methods in specification and verification of properties of distributed algorithms. In particular, Chapter 6 emphasizes a method for specification and verification that is based on the structural induction on the partially ordered set generated by a distributed program. The goal of Chapter 7 is to show how a centralized algorithm can be decentralized based on the notion of tokens. It also presents quorum-based algorithms for mutual exclusion. Chapter 8 discusses a generalization of the mutual exclusion problem called the drinking philosophers problem. Chapter 9 describes algorithms for leader election. Leader election is useful for resource coordination problems to implement a centralized coordinator scheme.

Chapters 10–14 discuss observation of global properties. In Chapter 10, we describe Chandy and Lamport's algorithm to compute the global state of a distributed system. Our proof of correctness of Chandy and Lamport's algorithm is based on the structure of the poset of the distributed computation. This proof is different from the original proof based on execution sequence, as provided by Chandy and Lamport. This algorithm can be used for detecting stable global properties— properties that remain true once they become true. Chapter 11 discusses the main techniques for detecting unstable predicates. The general problem of detecting unstable predicates is shown to be NP-complete; however, if the given predicate satisfies certain properties, then it can be efficiently detected. Chapter 12 and 13 discuss two important classes of unstable predicates—conjunctive predicates and channel predicates. Chapter 14 presents a variant of Dijkstra and Scholten's algorithm for termination detection. Chapters 13 and 14 can be skipped without any loss of continuity.

Chapters 15–17 discuss issues in controlling distributed computations. Chapter 15 discusses a method of off-line control in which appropriate control messages are inserted in a computation to guarantee invariance of a given predicate such as nonviolation of mutual exclusion. Chapter 16 describes methods to provide the causal ordering of messages, and Chapter 17 describes the synchronous and total ordering of messages.

Chapters 18–22 describe various higher-level abstractions and tools that can be used to build distributed applications. Chapter 18 and 19 discuss methods to compute a global function in a network either just once or repeatedly. By using various methods to gather and disseminate data, these abstractions hide the fact that data is distributed. The intent is to develop a framework that can be applied to a variety of problems in a distributed system. For example, the techniques presented in this chapter can be used to compute centers of a network, to compute fixed points of equations, and to solve problems using branch-and-bound techniques. Chapter 20 discusses synchronizers, a method to abstract out asynchrony in the system. A synchronizer allows a synchronous algorithm to be simulated on top of an asynchronous system. Chapter 21 discusses slicing, a tool to combat computational complexity of analysis of distributed computations. Chapter 22 describes methods to build distributed shared memory, thereby allowing parallel algorithms to be simulated on top of distributed systems.

Chapters 23–25 analyze possibility (or impossibility) of solving problems in the presence of various types of faults. Chapter 23 discusses self-stabilizing systems. We discuss solutions of the mutual exclusion problem when the state of any of the processors may change arbitrarily because of a fault. We show that it is possible to design algorithms that guarantee that the system converges to a legal state in a finite number of moves irrespective of the system execution. Chapter 24 discusses the ability to solve problems in the absence of reliable communication. The two-generals problem shows that agreement on a bit (gaining common knowledge) is impossible in a distributed system. Chapter 25 discusses the ability to solve problems when processors may crash. It includes the fundamental impossibility result of Fischer, Lynch and Patterson that shows that consensus is impossible to solve in the presence of even one unannounced failure.

Chapters 26–28 solve problems in the presence of faults either by making stronger assumptions on the environment or by weakening the requirements of the problem. Chapter 26 shows that the consensus problem can be solved in a synchronous environment under crash and Byzantine faults. Chapter 27 shows that it can be solved assuming the presence of failure detectors. Chapter 28 shows some problems that can be solved in an asynchronous environment.

Chapters 29 and 30 discuss methods of recovering from failures when failure detection is perfect.

Finally, the Appendix gives a concise introduction to the concepts in partially ordered sets and lattices.

There are a large number of starred and unstarred problems at the end of each chapter. A student is expected to solve unstarred problems with little effort. The starred problems may require the student to either spend more effort or read the cited paper.

1.6 Notation

We use the following notation for quantified expressions:

$$(op \text{ free-var-list} : \text{range-of-free-vars} : \text{expression})$$

where op is a universal or an existential quantifier, free-var-list is the list of variables over which the quantification is made, and the range-of-free-vars is the range of the variables. For example, $(\forall i : 0 \leq i \leq 10 : i^2 \leq 100)$ means that for all i such that $0 \leq i \leq 10$, $i^2 \leq 100$ holds. If the range of the variables is clear from the context, then we simply use:

$$(op \text{ free-var-list} : \text{expression})$$

For example, if it is clear that i and j are integers then we may write

$$\forall i : (\exists j : j > i)$$

We use a calculational style of proofs for many of our theorems. For example, a proof that $[A \equiv C]$ is rendered in our format as

$$A$$
$$\equiv \quad \{ \text{ hint why } [A \equiv B] \}$$
$$B$$
$$\equiv \quad \{ \text{ hint why } [B \equiv C] \}$$
$$C.$$

We use implication ($\Rightarrow$) instead of equivalence when proving $A \Rightarrow C$.

A predicate with free variables is assumed to be universally quantified for all possible values of free variables. We use the usual convention for binding powers of operators. In order of increasing binding powers, the operators are:

$$\equiv$$
$$\Rightarrow$$
$$\vee, \wedge$$
$$\neg$$
$=, \neq, <, \leq$, and other relational operators over integers and sets,
arithmetic operators, and
function applications.

Operators that appear on the same line have the same binding power, and we use parentheses to show the order of application. We sometimes omit parentheses in expressions when they use operators from different lines. Thus

$$s \to t \Rightarrow C(s) < C(t)$$

is equivalent to

$$\forall s, t : ((s \to t) \Rightarrow (C(s) < C(t))).$$

1.7   Problems

1.1. Give advantages and disadvantages of a parallel programming model over a distributed system (message based) model.

1.2. Compare the mechanisms for *synchronization* and *communication* in parallel programming languages and distributed programming languages.

1.8   Bibliographic Remarks

Many books are available on distributed systems. The reader is referred to books by Attiya and Welch [AW98], Barbosa [Bar96], Chandy and Misra [CM89], Garg [Gar96], Lynch [Lyn96], Raynal [Ray88], and Tel [Tel94] for the range of topics in distributed algorithms. Couloris, Dollimore, and Kindberg [CDK94] and Chow and Johnson [CJ97] cover some practical aspects of distributed systems, such as distributed file systems, that are not covered in this book. Goscinski [Gos91] and Singhal and Shivaratri [SS94] cover concepts in distributed operating systems. Some edited books are also available. The book edited by Yang and Marsland [YM94] includes many papers that deal with global time and state in distributed systems. The book edited by Mullender [Mul94] covers many other topics such as protection, fault tolerance, and real-time communications. The proof format adopted for many theorems in this book is taken from Dijkstra and Scholten [DS90].

Chapter 2

Model of a Computation

Do not quench your inspiration and your imagination; do not become the slave of your model. — Vincent van Gogh

2.1 Introduction

In this chapter, we describe models for capturing behavior of a distributed system. The rest of the book uses these models for reasoning about correctness of our programs as well as for analysis of distributed computations.

Our model for a distributed system is based on message passing, and all of our algorithms are based around that concept. Many of these algorithms have analogs in the shared memory world but will not be discussed in this book. Moreover, our algorithms do not assume any upper bound on the message delays. Thus we assume loosely coupled systems. An advantage is that all the algorithms developed in this model are also applicable to tightly coupled systems.

One of the important issues in reasoning about a distributed program is the model used for a *distributed computation*. It is clear that when a distributed program is executed, at the most abstract level, a set of events is generated. Some examples of events are the beginning of the execution of a function, the end of its execution, sending of a message, and receiving of that message. This set alone does not characterize the behavior. We also impose an ordering relation on this set. The first relation is based on the physical time model. Assuming that all events are instantaneous, that no two events are simultaneous, and that a shared physical clock is available, we can totally order all the events in the system. This is called the *interleaving* model of computation. If there is no shared physical clock, then we can observe a total order among events on a single processor but only a partial order between events on different processors. The order for events on different processors is determined on basis of the information flow from one processor to another. This is the *happened before* model of computation. The last model is based on the idea of causality. Even if two events happened one after another on the same processor they may not be causally related. In this model, called the *potential causality* model, events within a single process may not be totally ordered.

Depending on the application, sometimes it is more useful to talk of states (local and global) rather than events. A state is characterized by the value of all the variables including the program counter. We will discuss models based on states as well as events.

This chapter is organized as follows. Section 2.2 gives our model of a distributed system in greater detail. Sections 2.3, 2.4, and 2.5 give three models for distributed computations mentioned earlier. Section 2.6 discusses the appropriateness of these models for a given application. Section 2.7 describes state-based models.

The notation used in this chapter is summarized in Figure 2.1.

2.2   Model of a Distributed System

We model a distributed system as a loosely coupled message-passing system without any shared memory or a global clock. A *distributed program* consists of a set of N processes denoted by $\{P_1, P_2, \ldots, P_N\}$ and a set of unidirectional channels. A channel connects two processes. Thus the topology of a distributed system can be viewed as a directed graph in which vertices represent the processes and the edges represent the channels. Figure 2.2 shows the topology of a distributed system with three processes and four channels. Observe that a bidirectional channel can simply be modeled as two unidirectional channels.

A channel is assumed to have infinite buffer and to be error free. We do not make any assumptions on the ordering of messages. Any message sent on the channel may experience arbitrary but finite delay. The state of the channel at any point is defined to be the sequence of messages sent along that channel but not received.

N	The number of processes
$P_1, P_2, \ldots, P_N$	Processes
G	Global state
E	Set of events
e, f, g	Events
s, t, u	Local states
$\prec_{im}$	Immediately precedes relation
$\prec$	Locally precedes relation
$\leadsto$	Remotely precedes relation
$\rightarrow$	Happened before relation
$\xrightarrow{p}$	Potential causality relation
$\|$	Concurrency relation
S_i	Sequence of states on P_i
$next(e)$	Event immediately after e
$prev(e)$	Event immediately before e
$e.p$	Process on which event e is executed

Figure 2.1: Notation

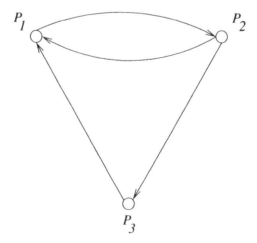

Figure 2.2: An example of topology of a distributed system

A process is defined as a set of states, an initial condition (i.e., a subset of states), and a set of events. Each event may change the state of the process and the state of at most one channel incident on that process. The behavior of a process with finite states can be described visually with state transition diagrams. Figure 2.3 shows the state transition diagram for two processes. The first process P_1 sends a token to P_2 and then receives a token from P_2. Process P_2 first receives a token from P_1 and then sends it back to P_1. The state s_1 is the initial state for P_1, and the state t_1 is the initial state for P_2.

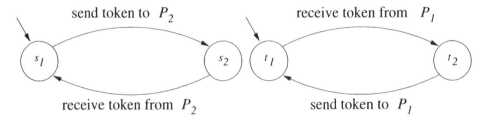

Figure 2.3: A simple distributed program with two processes

2.3   Interleaving Model

In this model of a distributed computation, a *run* is simply a *global sequence of events*. Thus all events in a run are interleaved. For example, consider a system with two processes: a bank server and a bank customer. The program of the bank customer process sends two request messages to the bank server querying the savings and the checking accounts. On receiving the response, it adds up the total balance. In the interleaving model, a run may be given as:

> P_1 sends "what is my checking balance" to P_2
> P_1 sends "what is my savings balance" to P_2
> P_2 receives "what is my checking balance" from P_1
> P_1 sets total to 0
> P_2 receives "what is my savings balance" from P_1
> P_2 sends "checking balance = 40" to P_1
> P_1 receives "checking balance = 40" from P_2
> P_1 sets total to 40 (total + checking balance)
> P_2 sends "savings balance = 70" to P_1
> P_1 receives "savings balance = 70" from P_2

P_1 sets total to 110 (total + savings balance)

To formally define which sequences are *computations in the interleaving model*, we first define a global state. The set of global states is defined as the cross product of local states of processes and the states of the channels. An initial global state is one in which all local states are initial and all the channel states are empty. It is sometimes advantageous to assume that processes record messages sent and received as part of their local state. In this case, the state of the channel can be determined using local states and therefore a global state may simply be viewed as a cross product of local states. We use the latter definition of the global state whenever convenient.

The next global state function $next(G, e)$ gives the next global state when the event e is executed in the global state G. Figure 2.4 gives an example of a transition from one global state to the other. In the first global state, P_1 is in state s_1, P_2 is in state t_1 and both the channels are empty. When P_1 sends a token to P_2, the state of P_1 changes to s_2 and the channel from P_1 to P_2 has the token.

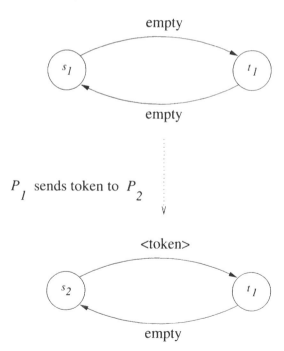

Figure 2.4: An example of a global state and a transition

Definition 2.1 (Interleaving Model) *A sequence of events seq =* $(e_i : 0 \leq i \leq m)$ *is a computation of the system in the interleaving model if there exists a sequence of global states* $(G_i : 0 \leq i \leq m + 1)$ *such that* G_0 *is an initial state and*

$$G_{i+1} = next(G_i, e_i), for \ 0 \leq i \leq m$$

2.4 Happened Before Model

In the interleaving model, there is a total order defined on the set of events. Leslie Lamport has argued that in a true distributed system only a partial order, called happened before relation, can be determined between events. In this section we define this relation formally.

As before, we will be concerned with a single computation of a distributed program. Each process P_i in that computation generates a sequence of local *states* and *events*: $s_{i,0}e_{i,0}s_{i,1}\ldots e_{i,l-1}s_{i,l}$. The initial state of P_i is $s_{i,0}$. After executing $e_{i,j}$ on state $s_{i,j}$, the state of P_i changes to $s_{i,j+1}$. We focus only on the sequence of events; the model based on states is discussed in Section 2.7.

We define a relation *immediately precedes* denoted by $\prec_{im}$ between events in the trace of a single process P_i as follows: $e \prec_{im} f$ if and only if e immediately precedes f in the sequence of events at P_i. We also say that $next(e) = f$ or $prev(f) = e$ whenever $e \prec_{im} f$. We use $\prec$ (*locally precedes*) for irreflexive transitive closure and $\preceq$ for reflexive transitive closure of $\prec_{im}$. Similar definitions hold for states. We also use $e.p$ to denote the process in whose trace e occurs. Thus, $e.p = i$ if and only if e occurs at the process P_i.

We say that event e at P_i *remotely precedes* event f at P_j if e is the send event of a message and f is the receive event of the same message. This is denoted by $e \rightsquigarrow f$. Similarly, states s and t are related by $\rightsquigarrow$ if and only if a message is sent after the state s that is received by the receiver, resulting in the state t.

Now the *happened before* relation, denoted by $\rightarrow$, can be defined as the transitive closure of the union of $\prec_{im}$ and $\rightsquigarrow$. In other words,

Definition 2.2 (Happened Before Relation) *The happened before relation* $(\rightarrow)$ *is the smallest relation that satisfies:*

1. $(e \prec_{im} f) \vee (e \rightsquigarrow f) \Rightarrow (e \rightarrow f)$, *and*

2. $\exists g : (e \rightarrow g) \wedge (g \rightarrow f) \Rightarrow (e \rightarrow f)$.

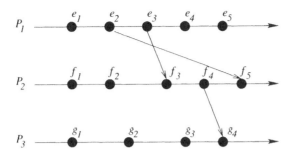

Figure 2.5: A run in the event-based happened before model

A *run* or a *computation* in the happened before model is defined as a tuple $(E, \rightarrow)$ where E is the set of all events and $\rightarrow$ is a partial order on events in E such that all events within a single process are totally ordered. Figure 2.5 illustrates a run. Such figures are usually called *space-time diagrams*, *process-time diagrams*, or *happened before diagrams*. In a process-time diagram, $e \rightarrow f$ iff it contains a directed path from the event e to event f. Intuitively, this relation captures the order that can be determined between events (or states). The important thing here is that the happened before relation is only a partial order on the set of local states. Thus two events e and f may not be related by the happened before relation. We say that e and f are *concurrent* (denoted by $e||f$) if $\neg(e \rightarrow f) \wedge \neg(f \rightarrow e)$.

2.5 Potential Causality Model

In the happened before model it was assumed that all events within a process are totally ordered. Although it is true that the order of events within a single process can be accurately determined, it is not true that all of these events have cause and effect relationship. For many applications, we are more interested in the cause and effect relationship between events. This relation called the *causality relation* is a partial order even within a single process. Because the causality relation between two events on a process may be difficult or expensive to determine, we instead use the *potential causality* relation. Our requirement of the potential causality relation is that it respect the causality relation, i.e., if event e causes event f, then e must also potentially cause event f. The converse may not be true: e may potentially cause f but not cause f. Observe that the happened before model is a valid potential causality model because if e causes f, then e must have happened before f. The happened before model satisfies an additional property: all events within a process are totally ordered. In a general potential causality model this may not be true. Formally,

Definition 2.3 (Potential Causality Relation) *The potential causality relation on the event set is the smallest relation satisfying*

- *If an event e potentially causes another event f on the same process then $e \xrightarrow{p} f$.*

- *If e is the send of a message and f is the corresponding receive, then $e \xrightarrow{p} f$.*

- *If $e \xrightarrow{p} f$ and $f \xrightarrow{p} g$, then $e \xrightarrow{p} g$.*

We say that events e and f are *independent* if $\neg(e \xrightarrow{p} f)$ and $\neg(f \xrightarrow{p} e)$.

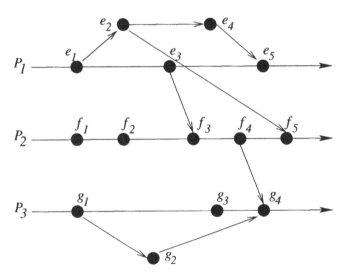

Figure 2.6: A run in the event-based potential causality model

A potential causality diagram is defined as a partially ordered set $(E, \xrightarrow{p})$, where E is the set of all events in the system and $\xrightarrow{p}$ is the potential causality relation. Figure 2.6 shows a potential causality diagram. Observe that $\xrightarrow{p}$, unlike $\rightarrow$, may not impose a total order on all events on a single process. Events on processes P_1 and P_3 are not totally ordered.

Given a potential causality diagram $(E, \overset{p}{\to})$, a happened before diagram $(E, \to)$ is consistent with it if $\overset{p}{\to} \subseteq \to$. Figure 2.5 is consistent with Figure 2.6. Observe that $e_2 \to f_4$ but $\neg(e_2 \overset{p}{\to} f_4)$. A potential causality diagram is equivalent to the set of happened before diagrams that are consistent with it.

The above definition is crucially dependent on the potential causality relation on one process. We give some examples of where this relation can be determined to be a partial order.

- A process receives two messages from different ports and updates different objects based on these two messages. The receives of these messages do not potentially cause each other, although one may have happened before the other.

- A process consists of two threads that access mutually disjoint sets of objects.

2.6 Appropriate Model

We have seen that three models can be used for capturing the behavior of a distributed program—interleaving, happened before, and potential causality. A distributed program can be viewed as a set of potential causality diagrams that it can generate. A potential causality diagram, in turn, is equivalent to a set of happened before diagrams. Each happened before diagram is equivalent to a set of global sequences of events (or states).

The following table summarizes the three models.

Model	Basis	Type
Interleaving	Physical time	Total order on all events
Happened before	Logical order	Total order on one process
Potential causality	Causality	Partial order on a process

Now that we have seen three models of behaviors of a distributed program, the natural question is which of these models is appropriate. The answer depends on the application for which this model is being used. We now give examples of three applications in which different models are appropriate. All three applications relate to checking a global property of a distributed program but in slightly different settings. By global property we mean a boolean predicate on a global state.

First consider an application in the area of verification of distributed programs. We are given a program and are required to prove certain properties about it. It may be easier to specify (or prove) the required properties of the program by modeling the behavior of a program as a global sequence. A global sequence cannot be observed in a distributed system, but for this application we are not required to observe it. We are only required to prove that all global sequences satisfy a certain property.

Now consider a second application in which we are required to capture the behavior of a program and are asked whether some property became true in it. Because a global sequence cannot be observed (in absence of perfectly synchronized clocks), the appropriate model to use here is the happened before model. Nothing more can be observed in a distributed system. Once a happened before diagram of the behavior is constructed, questions regarding the properties of that diagram can be analyzed.

Finally, consider the application of distributed debugging in which we are again required to capture the behavior but are asked whether some global property *could have* become true in a behavior of that program. In this case, even though we can observe the total order of events in the system, it is to our advantage if we capture only the partial order corresponding to the (potential) causality. By analyzing the potential causality diagram, we can detect whether the global property could have become true in any happened before diagram consistent with the potential causality diagram.

2.7 Models Based on States

For many applications such as distributed debugging, it may be more natural to model a distributed computation based on states rather than events. For example, the happened before diagram based on events in Figure 2.7 is equivalent to the diagram in Figure 2.8, which is based on states. An event such as execution of $x := x + 2$ gets translated into an edge between two states. We show the values of variables next to each state. Note that the state includes the value of the program counter pc.

From now on, we restrict ourselves to states generated during an execution of the program. Although most definitions carry over from events to states, there are a few differences. For example, any partially

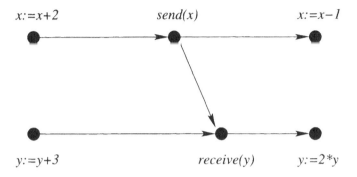

Figure 2.7: A run in the event-based model

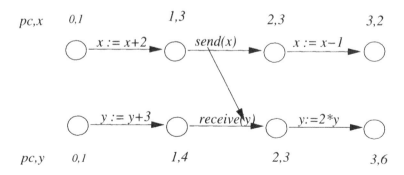

Figure 2.8: A run in the state-based model

ordered set of events in which all events on a process are totally ordered is a distributed computation in the happened before model. However, not every poset of states is a valid distributed computation. Consider the examples in Figure 2.9. In both the examples, although the states form partial orders, the induced graphs on events have cycles $((e, f)$ in the first example and (e, f, g) in the second example). Thus we can allow only those partial orders on states that do not induce cycle on the order on events. To avoid checking for cycles in the induced graph, we introduce the notion of *deposet*, which guarantees that the induced graph on events is a valid partial order.

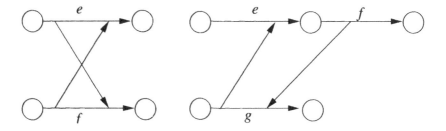

Figure 2.9: Posets on states with no valid event based posets

2.7.1 Deposet

Let S_i be the sequence of local states in P_i. With a slight abuse of notation, let

$$S = \bigcup_i S_i.$$

Then, an execution of a distributed program that consists of processes $P_1, \ldots, P_N$ can be modeled with a tuple $(S_1, \ldots S_N, \rightsquigarrow)$. We call such a structure a *deposet* (decomposed partially ordered set) provided that $(S, \rightarrow)$ is a partial order and that it satisfies the following two natural conditions. First, it is assumed that no message is received before the initial state or sent after the final state in any sequence S_i. Second, we assume that each event is a send event, in which one or more messages are sent, a receive event, in which one or more messages are received, or an internal event, in which messages are neither sent nor received. Thus we do not allow messages to be sent as well as received between two states.

To formalize, we define the initial and final states: $initial(i) \overset{\text{def}}{=}$

$min\ S_i$ and $final(i) \overset{\text{def}}{=} max\ S_i$. We also use $initial(s)(final(s))$ to denote that s is an initial (final) state.

Thus a deposet can be defined as follows.

Definition 2.4 (Deposet) *A deposet is a tuple* $(S_1, \ldots S_N, \rightsquigarrow)$ *such that* $(S, \rightarrow)$ *is an irreflexive partial order that satisfies:*

(D1) $\forall i : \neg(\exists u : u \rightsquigarrow initial(i))$ *(no messages before the initial state)*

(D2) $\forall i : \neg(\exists u : final(i) \rightsquigarrow u)$ *(no messages after the final state)*

(D3) $s \prec_{im} t \Rightarrow \neg(\exists u : s \rightsquigarrow u) \vee \neg(\exists u : u \rightsquigarrow t)$ *(cannot both send and receive between two consecutive states)*

We use the deposet as the formal model of an execution of a distributed program. We leave it for the reader to verify that every deposet induces a valid happened before diagram on events (Problem 2.3).

2.7.2   Global Sequence of States

A deposet, or a *run* of a distributed program, defines a partial order ($\rightarrow$) on the set of states and events. In general, there are many total orders that are consistent with (or linearizations of) this partial order. A *global sequence* corresponds to a single linearization of the run. A global sequence is a sequence of *global* states where a global state is a vector of local states. We denote the set of global sequences consistent with a run $r = (S_1, \ldots S_N, \rightsquigarrow)$ as $linear(r)$. A *global sequence* g is a finite sequence of global states denoted as $g = g_1 \ldots g_l$, where g_k is a global state for $1 \leq k \leq l$. A global sequence of a run is defined as:

Definition 2.5 (Sequence of Global States) *g is a global sequence of a run r (denoted by $g \in linear(r)$) if and only if the following constraints hold:*

(Q1) $\forall i : g$ *restricted to* $P_i = S_i$ *(or a stutter of S_i, defined later)*

(Q2) $\forall k : g_k[i] \| g_k[j]$ *where $g_k[i]$ is the state of P_i in the global state g_k.*

(Q3) $\forall k : g_k$ *and g_{k+1} differ in the state of exactly one process.*

The constraint (Q1) models that if the observer restricted his attention to a single process P_i, then he would observe S_i or a stutter of S_i. A *stutter* of S_i is a finite sequence where each state in S_i may be repeated a finite number of times. The constraint (Q2) requires that local states that are part of a global state are mutually pairwise concurrent. Finally, the constraint (Q3) models the *interleaving* assumption of events. Thus execution of two concurrent events, say e and f, is equivalent to assuming that there are two behaviors possible: e followed by f and f followed by e. We do not model *simultaneous* execution of e and f. If the constraint (Q3) is dropped, then the resulting model is called the *noninterleaving model of concurrency*. In this book, we use the interleaving model of concurrency for its simplicity.

Example 2.6 Consider the following distributed program:

P_1::	P_2::
var x:integer initially 7;	**var** y, z:integer initially $(0,0)$;
$\quad l_0$: $send(x)$ to P_2;	$\quad m_0$: $receive(y)$ from P_1;
$\quad l_1$: $x := x - 1$;	$\quad m_1$: $receive(z)$ from P_1;
$\quad l_2$: $send(x)$ to P_2;	$\quad m_2$:
$\quad l_3$:	

Labels $l_0, \ldots, l_3$ and $m_0, \ldots, m_2$ denote possible values of program counters. The state of a process is given by the value of its program counter and local variables. Thus $(l_0, 7)$ denotes that the process P_1 is at location l_0 and the value of x is 7. We use the event $send(i,j,m)$ to denote the sending of the message m from P_i to P_j. The event $receive(i,j,m)$ denotes the receiving of that message. A distributed run r can be specified by the sequence of states and events $r[i]$ at each process P_i.

$$r[1] = ((l_0, 7), send(1, 2, 7), (l_1, 7), internal, (l_2, 6), send(1, 2, 6), (l_3, 6))$$
$$r[2] = ((m_0, 0, 0), receive(1, 2, 7), (m_1, 7, 0), receive(1, 2, 6), (m_2, 7, 6))$$

Another run r' can be constructed when two messages sent by the process P_1 are received in the reverse order.

$$r'[1] = ((l_0, 7), send(1, 2, 7), (l_1, 7), internal, (l_2, 6), send(1, 2, 6), (l_3, 6))$$
$$r'[2] = ((m_0, 0, 0), receive(1, 2, 6), (m_1, 6, 0), receive(1, 2, 7), (m_2, 6, 7))$$

Some global sequences consistent with the run r are given below. Each item in the sequence is a global state.

$$g = [(l_0, 7, m_0, 0, 0), (l_1, 7, m_0, 0, 0), (l_2, 6, m_0, 0, 0), (l_2, 6, m_1, 7, 0),$$

$(l_3, 6, m_1, 7, 0), (l_3, 6, m_2, 7, 6)]$

$h = [(l_0, 7, m_0, 0, 0), (l_1, 7, m_0, 0, 0), (l_2, 6, m_0, 0, 0), \ (l_3, 6, m_0, 0, 0),$
$\quad (l_3, 6, m_1, 7, 0), (l_3, 6, m_2, 7, 6)]$

Our model of a distributed run and global sequences assumes that the system computation can always be specified as some interleaving of events. This assumption is convenient in reasoning of such systems. It is easy to verify that every valid interleaving of events results in a sequence of global states and vice versa.

2.8   Problems

2.1. Show that "concurrent with" is not a transitive relation.

2.2. Give a run in the happened before model that is consistent with the run in the potential causality model in Figure 2.6 and satisfies $\neg(e_2 \rightarrow f_4)$.

2.3. Show that a deposet generates a valid happened before diagram on events.

2.4. Show that every deposet has at least one global sequence.

2.5. Consider a distributed computation modeled by a poset $(E, <)$ and let X be the set of all down-sets of $(E, <)$. A sequence of down-sets is called a global sequence of states if (1) it starts with the empty down-set, (2) every two successive down-sets in the sequence differ by exactly one event, and (3) it ends with the down-set E. Show that there is a one-to-one correspondence between the set of total orders consistent with $(E, <)$ and the set of global sequences.

*2.6. In a potential causality model, events within a process may not be totally ordered. Give an efficient algorithm to decompose events of a process into a minimum number of *tasks* such that all events within a task are totally ordered.

2.9   Bibliographic Remarks

The most influential paper in this area is by Lamport, who first gave the definition of the happened before relation [Lam78]. The discussion of the model of a distributed system is taken from Chandy and Lamport [CL85]. Although the model based on events has been more popular (for example, see the book edited by Mulleneder [Mul94]), the state-based model has been used more for distributed breakpoints (see Garg and Waldecker [GW94]). The discussion of the potential causality model is taken from Ahuja [Ahu93] and Tarafdar and Garg [TG98a].

Chapter 3

Logical Clocks

Logic is the art of going wrong with confidence. — Joseph Wood Krutch

3.1 Introduction

We have defined three relations between events based on the global total order of events, the happened before order, and the potential causality order. In this chapter we discuss mechanisms called *clocks* that can be used for tracking these relations.

The first relation we discussed on events imposes a total order on all events. Because this total order cannot be observed we give a mechanism to generate a total order that could have happened in the system (rather than that actually happened in the system). This mechanism is called a *logical clock*. The second relation, happened before, can be accurately tracked by a *vector clock*. A vector clock assigns timestamps to states (and events) such that the happened before relationship between states can be determined by using the timestamps.

Tracking potential causality relations requires a mechanism within a process to determine which events are independent of each other. Because such a mechanism would depend on the model of the programming language used, we will not discuss potential causality clocks. Given any mechanism to track local independence, the ideas in the vector clocks can be used to design potential causality clocks.

In this chapter, we will use the state-based model to describe algorithms for tracking various relations. However, the theory and algo-

27

rithms are equally applicable to an event-based model. A computation is simply modeled as a partial order $(S, \rightarrow)$ that may be on the set of states or on the set of events.

This chapter is organized as follows. Section 3.2 describes logical clocks, and Section 3.3 describes vector clocks. The notation used in this chapter is summarized in Figure 3.1.

N	The number of processes
S	The set of all local states
s, t, u	Local states
$s.p$	The process on which state s occurred
$s.c$	The logical clock value in state s
$s.v$	The vector clock value in state s
C, D	Logical clocks
$\mathcal{C}$	The set of all logical clocks

Figure 3.1: Notation

3.2 Logical Clocks

When the behavior of a distributed computation is viewed as a total order, it is impossible to determine the actual order of events in the absence of accurately synchronized physical clocks. If the system has a shared clock (or equivalently, precisely synchronized clocks), then timestamping the event with the clock would be sufficient to determine the order. Because in the absence of a shared clock the total order between events cannot be determined, we will develop a mechanism that gives a total order that *could have* happened instead of the total order that did happen.

The purpose of our clock is only to give us an order between events and not any other property associated with clocks. For example, based on our clocks one could not determine the time elapsed between two events. In fact, the number we associate with each event will have no relationship with the time we have on our watches.

3.2.1 Definition

As we have seen before, there are only two kinds of order information that can be determined in a distributed system—the order of events on a single process and the order between the send and the receive event of a message. On the basis of these considerations, we get the following definition.

Definition 3.1 (Logical Clock) *A logical clock C is a map from S to $\mathcal{N}$ (the set of natural numbers) with the following constraint:*

$$\forall s, t \in S : s \prec_{im} t \ \vee \ s \leadsto t \Rightarrow C(s) < C(t)$$

Figure 3.2 gives two examples of logical clocks. We use $\mathcal{C}$ to denote the set of all logical clocks that satisfy the above constraint. The interpretation of $C(s)$ for any $s \in S$ is that the process $s.p$ enters the state s when the clock value is $C(s)$. Thus the constraint for logical clocks models the sequential nature of execution at each process and the physical requirement that any message transmission requires a nonzero amount of time. From the definition of $\rightarrow$, this constraint is equivalent to

$$\forall s, t \in S : s \rightarrow t \Rightarrow \forall C \in \mathcal{C} : C(s) < C(t) \qquad \textbf{(CC)}$$

The condition (CC) is widely used as the definition of a *logical clock* or *Lamport's clock*, since its proposal by Lamport.

We have not shown yet that $\mathcal{C}$, the set of all logical clocks, is a nonempty set. Because the run is assumed to be generated from a physical execution, by assigning the physical time to each state we derive a possible logical clock. The nonemptiness of $\mathcal{C}$ is equivalent to the condition that $\rightarrow$ is an irreflexive partial order. This is shown in the next lemma.

Lemma 3.2 $\mathcal{C}$ *is nonempty iff* $(S, \rightarrow)$ *is an irreflexive partial order.*

Proof: ($\Rightarrow$) Let $D \in \mathcal{C}$. This implies that $\forall s \in S : \neg(s \rightarrow s)$, otherwise by (CC) $D(s) < D(s)$. Thus $\rightarrow$ is irreflexive. By definition, $\rightarrow$ is transitive. It follows that $(S, \rightarrow)$ is an irreflexive partial order.

($\Leftarrow$) We are given that $(S, \rightarrow)$ is an irreflexive partial order. We define a map D from S to $\mathcal{N}$ as follows. For any $s \in S$, $D(s)$ is the length of the longest sequence $s_0, s_1, \ldots, s_n$, where $s_0 = initial(i)$ for some i, $s_n = s$, and $s_k \rightarrow s_{k+1}$ for $0 \le k \le n - 1$. D satisfies (CC) because for any s and t such that $s \rightarrow t$, the length of the longest path from some initial state to t must be longer than the longest path from some initial state to s.

∎

From now on we assume that $(S, \rightarrow)$ is an irreflexive partial order or, equivalently, that $\mathcal{C}$ is a nonempty set. We now show that the set $\mathcal{C}$ also satisfies the converse of (CC), that is,

$$\forall s, t \in S : s \not\rightarrow t \Rightarrow \exists C \in \mathcal{C} : \neg(C(s) < C(t))$$

To this end, it is sufficient to show that

$$\forall u, v \in S : u||v \Rightarrow \exists C \in \mathcal{C} : (C(u) = C(v))$$

Thus, if two local states are concurrent, then there exists a logical clock such that both states are assigned the same timestamp. We show this result for any subset X of S which contains only pairwise concurrent states.

Lemma 3.3 *For any $X \subseteq S$,*
$(\forall u, v \in X : u||v) \Rightarrow \exists C \in \mathcal{C} : (\forall u, v \in X : C(u) = C(v))$.

Proof: Because $\mathcal{C}$ is a nonempty set, let $D \in \mathcal{C}$. D satisfies the clock condition but may not assign the same value to all states in X, that is, $D(u)$ may be different from $D(v)$ for two states u and v in X. From D, we construct another logical clock C as follows:

(L1) For all $s \in X : C(s) := max\{D(u) \mid u \in X\}$;

(L2) For all $s \in S - X$ such that $\forall u \in X : u \not\rightarrow s$, we set $C(s) := D(s)$;

(L3) For all other s, we set $C(s) := D(s) + max\{C(u) - D(u) \mid u \in X \wedge u \rightarrow s\}$

For an illustration of this assignment see Figure 3.2. In this assignment, the new timestamp of all states in X is equal to the maximum of all the previous timestamps. In our example, we assign $C(u)$ as 10 because that is the maximum of $D(u)$ and $D(v)$. States that do not depend on states in X retain their old timestamps. Other states have their timestamp increased by the amount given by (L3). For example, the state s with the timestamp $D(s)$ as 15 gets $C(s)$ as 16 because u happened before that state and the timestamp of u increased by 1.

From (L1), all states in X are assigned the same value by C. We need to show that C satisfies the condition (CC). Let $s \rightarrow t$. Since D satisfies (CC), $D(s) < D(t)$. We now do a case analysis.

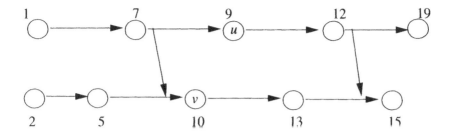

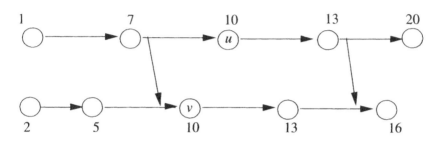

Figure 3.2: An illustration of a clock assignment that sets $C(u) = C(v)$.

Case 1: $s \in X$
Since X consists of pairwise concurrent states $t \notin X$. By (L3),

$$C(t) \geq D(t) + C(s) - D(s).$$

Since $D(s) < D(t)$, we get that $C(t) > C(s)$.

Case 2: $s \in S - X$ and $\neg(\exists u \in X : u \rightarrow s)$
By (L2), $C(s) = D(s)$. This implies that $C(s) < D(t)$, because
$D(s) < D(t)$. Since D is uniformly less than or equal to C, we get
that $C(s) < C(t)$.

Case 3: $s \in S - X$ and $\exists u \in X : u \rightarrow s$
By (L3),

$$C(s) = D(s) + max\{(C(u) - D(u)) \mid u \in X \land u \rightarrow s\}$$

Since $D(s) < D(t)$, it follows that

$$C(s) < D(t) + max\{(C(u) - D(u)) \mid u \in X \land u \rightarrow s\}$$

Furthermore, $u \to s$ implies that $u \to t$. Therefore,

$$C(s) < D(t) + max\{(C(u) - D(u)) \mid u \in X \wedge u \to t\}$$

Hence, $C(s) < C(t)$ by (L3).

    Thus C satisfies (CC).

                                                                  ■

    Combining Lemma 3.3 with (CC), we get the following pleasant characterization of $\to$:

$$\forall s, t \in S : (s \to t \Leftrightarrow \forall C \in \mathcal{C} : C(s) < C(t))$$

    Intuitively, if we consider any logical clock as an observer, then the above formula says that s happened before t in a run r if and only if all possible observers of the run agree that s occurred before t. Note that the *happened before* relation is a subset of the *occurred before* relation observed by any single observer. Moreover, from the above characterization the *happened before* relation is independent of the observation. This property of the *happened before* relation makes it more useful than the *occurred before* relation based on a single observer (such as using physical clocks).

3.2.2 Implementation

Availability of a logical clock during distributed computation makes it easier to solve many distributed problems. Recall that C is a logical clock iff it satisfies the following:

$$\forall s, t \in S : s \to t \Rightarrow C(s) < C(t)$$

An accurate physical clock clearly satisfies the above condition and therefore is also a logical clock. However, by definition of a distributed system there is no shared clock in the system. Figure 3.3 shows an implementation of a logical clock that does not use any shared physical clock or shared memory.

    It is not required that message communication be ordered or reliable. The algorithm is described by the initial conditions and the actions taken for each event type. The notation $(s, send, t)$ denotes a send event that takes the process from state s to state t; $(s, internal, t)$ denotes an internal event; and $(s, receive(u), t)$ denotes that a message is received in state s that was sent from the state u (by a different process) and the resulting state is t. The algorithm uses the variable c to assign the logical clock. The notation $s.c$ denotes the value of c in the state s.

For any send event, the value of the clock is sent with the message and then incremented. On receiving a message, a process takes the maximum of its own clock value and the value received with the message. After taking the maximum, the process increments the clock value. On an internal event, a process simply increments its clock.

P_i::
var
    c: integer initially 0;

send event $(s, send, t)$:
    // $s.c$ is sent as part of the message
    $t.c := s.c + 1$;

receive event $(s, receive(u), t)$:
    $t.c := max(s.c, u.c) + 1$;

internal event $(s, internal, t)$:
    $t.c := s.c + 1$;

Figure 3.3: A logical clock algorithm

The following claim is easy to verify:

$$\forall s, t \in S : s \rightarrow t \Rightarrow s.c < t.c$$

In some applications it is required that all events in the system be ordered totally. If we extend the logical clock with process number, then we get a total ordering on events. Recall that for any state s, $s.p$ indicates the identity of the process to which it belongs. Thus the timestamp of any event is a tuple $(s.c, s.p)$ and the total order $<$ is obtained as:

$$(s.c, s.p) < (t.c, t.p) \stackrel{\text{def}}{=} (s.c < t.c) \vee ((s.c = t.c) \wedge (s.p < t.p)).$$

For example, the second logical clock in Figure 3.2 assigns the same value 10 to u and v. If the total ordering is required, then u would be timestamped as $(10, 1)$ and v would be timestamped as $(10, 2)$.

3.3   Vector Clocks

3.3.1   Definition

We saw that logical clocks satisfy the following property:

$$s \to t \Rightarrow s.c < t.c.$$

However, the converse is not true; $s.c < t.c$ does not imply that $s \to t$. The computation $(S, \to)$ is a partial order, but the domain of logical clock values (the set of natural numbers) is a total order with respect to $<$. Thus logical clocks do not provide complete information about the *happened before* relation. In this section, we describe a mechanism called a vector clock.

Definition 3.4 (Vector Clock) *A vector clock v is a map from S to $\mathcal{N}^k$ (vectors of natural numbers) with the following constraint:*

$$\forall s, t : s \to t \Leftrightarrow s.v < t.v.$$

where $s.v$ is the vector assigned to the state s.

Because $\to$ is a partial order, it is clear that the timestamping mechanism should also result in a partial order. Thus the range of the timestamping function cannot be a total order like the set of natural numbers used for logical clocks. Instead, we use vectors of natural numbers. Given two vectors x and y of dimension N, we compare them as follows.

$$
\begin{aligned}
x < y \quad &= \quad (\forall k : 1 \le k \le N : x[k] \le y[k]) \; \wedge \\
&\qquad (\exists j : 1 \le j \le N : x[j] < y[j]) \\
x \le y \quad &= \quad (x < y) \vee (x = y)
\end{aligned}
$$

It is clear that this order is only partial for $N \ge 2$. A vector clock timestamps each event with a vector of natural numbers.

3.3.2   Implementation

Our implementation of vector clocks uses vectors of size N, the number of processes in the system. The algorithm presented in Figure 3.4 is described by the initial conditions and the actions taken for each event type. A process increments its own component of the vector clock after each event. It also includes a copy of its vector clock in every outgoing message. On receiving a message, it updates its vector clock by taking a componentwise maximum with the vector clock included in the message. It is not required that message communication be ordered or reliable. A sample execution of the algorithm is given in Figure 3.5.

P_j::
  var
      v: array$[1..N]$ of integer
          initially $(\forall i : i \neq j : v[i] = 0) \wedge (v[j] = 1)$;

  send event $(s, send, t)$:
      $t.v := s.v$;
      $t.v[j] := t.v[j] + 1$;

  receive event $(s, receive(u), t)$:
      for $i := 1$ **to** N **do**
          $t.v[i] := \max(s.v[i], u.v[i])$;
      $t.v[j] := t.v[j] + 1$;

  internal event $(s, internal, t)$:
      $t.v := s.v$;
      $t.v[j] := t.v[j] + 1$;

Figure 3.4: A vector clock algorithm

We now show some properties of the above program.

Lemma 3.5 *Let* $s \neq t$. *Then,*

$$s \not\rightarrow t \Rightarrow t.v[s.p] < s.v[s.p]$$

Proof: If $t.p = s.p$, then it follows that $t \prec s$. Because, the local component of the vector clock is increased after each event, $t.v[s.p] < s.v[s.p]$. So, we assume that $s.p \neq t.p$. Since $s.v[s.p]$ is the local clock of $P_{s.p}$ and $P_{t.p}$ could not have seen this value as $s \not\rightarrow t$, it follows that $t.v[s.p] < s.v[s.p]$.

■

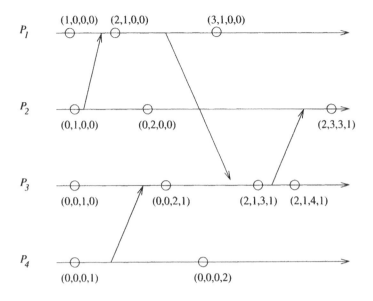

Figure 3.5: A sample execution of the vector clock algorithm

Theorem 3.6 *Let s and t be states in processes P_i and P_j with vectors $s.v$ and $t.v$, respectively. Then, $s \rightarrow t$ iff $s.v < t.v$.*

Proof: We first show that $(s \rightarrow t)$ implies $(s.v < t.v)$. If $s \rightarrow t$, then there is a message path from s to t. Since every process updates its vector on receipt of a message and this update is done by taking the componentwise maximum, we know the following holds:

$$\forall k : s.v[k] \leq t.v[k].$$

Furthermore, since $t \not\rightarrow s$, from lemma 3.5

$$t.v[j] > s.v[j].$$

Hence,

$$(\forall k : s.v[k] \leq t.v[k]) \wedge (s.v[j] < t.v[j])$$

Thus $(s \rightarrow t) \Rightarrow (s.v < t.v)$.

The converse follows from Lemma 3.5. $\blacksquare$

It can be shown that if we know the processes the vectors came from, the comparison between two states can be made in constant time.

Lemma 3.7

$$s \to t \Leftrightarrow (s.v[s.p] \le t.v[s.p]) \wedge (s.v[t.p] < t.v[t.p])$$

Proof: Left for the reader (see Problem 3.5).

■

3.4 Problems

3.1. Show that for any two distinct local states s and t, $s \not\to t$ implies that there exists a logical clock C such that $C(t) < C(s)$.

3.2. We discussed a method by which we can totally order all events within a system. If two events have the same logical time, we broke the tie using process identifiers. This scheme always favors processes with smaller identifiers. Suggest a scheme that does not have this disadvantage. (Hint: Use the value of the logical clock in determining the priority.)

3.3. Assume that you are given traces of each process as sequences of vector times. Can you draw a "process-time" diagram using these traces? A process-time diagram shows receives and sends of all the messages in the computation.

3.4. Let there be two groups of processes in a distributed system, each with its own leader. Processes in different groups communicate with each other only through their leaders. How can this feature be exploited in constructing vector clocks?

3.5. Prove the following for vector clocks: $s \to t$ iff

$$(s.v[s.p] \le t.v[s.p]) \wedge (s.v[t.p] < t.v[t.p]).$$

3.6. (**due to [SK92]**) Suppose that the underlying communication system guarantees FIFO ordering of messages. How will you exploit this feature to reduce the communication complexity of the vector clock algorithm? Give an expression for overhead savings if your scheme is used instead of the traditional vector clock algorithm. Assume that any process can send at most m messages.

3.7. Assume that you have implemented the vector clock algorithm. However, some application needs Lamport's logical clock. Write a function *convert* that takes as input a vector timestamp and outputs a logical clock timestamp.

3.8. Give a distributed algorithm to maintain clocks for a distributed program that has a dynamic number of processes. Assume that there are the following events in the life of any process: start-process, internal, send, receive, fork, join processid, terminate. It should be possible to infer the *happened before relation* using your clocks.

*3.9. Show that for all N there exists a computation $(E, \rightarrow)$ on N processes such that any mapping V from E to $\mathcal{N}^k$ that satisfies

$$\forall e, f \in E : e \rightarrow f \equiv V(e) < V(f)$$

has $k \geq N$.

3.5 Bibliographic Remarks

The idea of logical clocks is from Lamport [Lam78]. The idea of vector clocks in its pure form first appeared in Fidge [Fid89] and Mattern [Mat89]. However, vectors had been used before in some earlier papers such as Strom and Yemini [SY85]. In Charron-Bost [CB91], it was shown that there exists a computation on N processes such that the dimension of a vector clock must be at least N (the number of processes) for it to capture concurrency in that computation. In Garg and Skawratonand [GS01], it was shown that the number of coordinates equal to the string dimension of the poset corresponding to the computation are necessary and sufficient to capture concurrency. Moreover, any vector clock that captures relationships between global states must have at least N coordinates. The use of vector clocks in algorithms for distributed debugging (Fidge [Fid89], Garg and Waldecker [GW94]), distributed simulation (Mattern [Mat93], Damani, Wang and Garg [DWG97]), distributed mutual exclusion, and distributed recovery (Strom and Yemini [SY85]) is now well-known.

Chapter 4

Verifying Clock Algorithms

The longer I live the more I see that I am never wrong about any-thing, and that all the pains that I have so humbly taken to verify my notions have only wasted my time. — George Bernard Shaw

4.1 Introduction

In this chapter, we discuss a method to verify distributed algorithms. We illustrate the method by providing a formal proof of correctness of a variant of the vector clock algorithm. The original vector clock algorithm (VC1) assigns a vector $s.v$ to every local state s such that $s.v < t.v$ if and only if $s \to t$. We now present a different version of the algorithm, VC2, in which clocks preserve the happened before relation when s and t are on different processes. We use this version because it conserves state space because the vector components are incremented less frequently, and in general, one is interested in happened before relationships between states on different processes. The version we use maintains the following property:

$$(\forall s, t : s.p \neq t.p : s \to t \Leftrightarrow s.v < t.v)$$

The algorithm shown in Figure 4.1 is described by the initial conditions and the actions taken for each event type. This is the first step in proving the correctness of a distributed algorithm. A sample execution of the algorithm is given in Figure 4.2.

In our proof, we use properties of the algorithm given as comments in the text (within the braces). Their validity is clear from the al-

P_j::
var

    v: array$[1..N]$ of integer
        initially $(\forall i : i \neq j : v[i] = 0) \wedge (v[j] = 1)$;
    $\{initial(s) \Rightarrow (\forall i : i \neq s.p : s.v[i] = 0) \wedge (s.v[s.p] = 1) \}$

send event $(s, send, t)$:
    $t.v := s.v$;
    $t.v[t.p] := t.v[t.p] + 1$;
    $\{(\forall i : i \neq t.p : t.v[i] = s.v[i]) \wedge t.v[t.p] > s.v[t.p])\}$

receive event $(s, rcv(u), t)$:
    for $i := 1$ to N **do**
        $t.v[i] := \max(s.v[i], u.v[i])$;
    $\{(\forall i : t.v[i] = \max(s.v[i], u.v[i])) \}$

internal event $(s, internal, t)$:
    $t.v := s.v$;
    $\{t.v = s.v\}$

Figure 4.1: The vector clock algorithm VC2

gorithm text. Thus the proof is valid for any algorithm that satisfies these properties. For example, in the send rule of the algorithm, $t.v[t.p]$ could be increased by any positive amount and our proof would still be valid.

This chapter is organized as follows. Section 4.2 defines a relation $\xrightarrow{k}$ that is useful in proving program properties with $\rightarrow$ relation. Section 4.3 gives a formal proof of the correctness of the VC2 algorithm.

The notation used in this chapter is summarized in Figure 4.3.

4.2 Using Induction on $\rightarrow$

Induction is usually the principal technique for verifying distributed algorithms. For example, to prove that property B is an invariant, we can establish that B is initially true and all events in the system maintain B. Clock properties generally use the happened before rela-

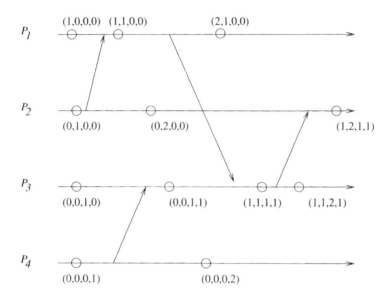

Figure 4.2: A sample execution of the vector clock algorithm VC2

N	The number of processes
S	Set of local states
$s.p$	Process on which state s occured
$s.v$	Vector clock value in state s
$\xrightarrow{k}$	Happened before relation with index k

Figure 4.3: Notation

tion, $\rightarrow$, and its complement, $\nrightarrow$. In this section, we define $\overset{k}{\rightarrow}$ (read as k-happened before) relation so that properties based on $\rightarrow$ can be shown by induction.

A chain in $(S, \rightarrow)$ is a sequence of states $s_0, s_1, \dots s_n$ such that $s_i \prec_{im} s_{i+1}$ or $s_i \rightsquigarrow s_{i+1}$. For any pair of states s and t such that $s \rightarrow t$, we define the maximum length function, $ml(s, t)$, as the length of the longest chain between s and t. If $s = t$, then $ml(s, t) = 0$, and if $s \nrightarrow t$, then $ml(s, t)$ is defined to be -1.

We use $ml(Init, t)$ to denote the length of the longest chain from some initial state to t.

The following statement is true by definition of ml.

$$ml(s, t) > 0 \Leftrightarrow (\exists u : ml(s, u) = ml(s, t) - 1 \ \wedge \ ml(u, t) = 1)$$

We define the $\overset{k}{\rightarrow}$ relation, which is used for induction on $\rightarrow$.

Definition 4.1 ($\overset{k}{\rightarrow}$ relation) *For $k > 0$,*

$$s \overset{k}{\rightarrow} t \overset{\text{def}}{=} ml(s, t) = k$$

Thus $s \overset{k}{\rightarrow} t$ if and only if $s \rightarrow t$ and the longest chain from s to t has length k.

This new relation can be used to prove claims that are expressed in terms of $\rightarrow$. For example, suppose we wish to prove the claim $s \rightarrow t \Rightarrow B(s, t)$, where $B(s, t)$ is some predicate on the local variables in s and t. We note that it is sufficient to prove $s \overset{k}{\rightarrow} t \Rightarrow B(s, t)$ for all $k > 0$. The proof can proceed by induction on k. The base case, $s \overset{1}{\rightarrow} t$, implies that either states s and t are consecutive states in a process, or a message was sent in s and received in t. Generally, the base case can be easily proven from the program text because it involves only one state transition or one message.

4.3   Proof of the Vector Clock Algorithm

In this section we prove the property stated earlier:

$$(\forall s, t : s.p \neq t.p : s \rightarrow t \Leftrightarrow s.v < t.v).$$

This is accomplished by proving the following claims:

$$s.p \neq t.p \ \wedge \ s \rightarrow t \Rightarrow s.v < t.v \tag{4.1}$$

$$s.p \neq t.p \ \wedge \ s.v < t.v \Rightarrow s \rightarrow t \tag{4.2}$$

Lemma 4.2 that follows states that if there is a chain of events from s to t then $s.v \leq t.v$. Note that the proof of Lemma 4.2 does not use the initial conditions. Thus it holds independent of the initial values of the vectors.

Lemma 4.2 $s \to t \Rightarrow s.v \leq t.v$.

Proof: It is sufficient to show that for all $k > 0$: $s \xrightarrow{k} t \Rightarrow s.v \leq t.v$. We use induction on k.

Base $(k = 1)$:

$s \xrightarrow{1} t$
$\Rightarrow$ { definition of ml }
$s \prec_{im} t \ \lor \ s \leadsto t$
$\Rightarrow$ { expand $s \prec_{im} t$ and $s \leadsto t$ }
$(s, internal, t) \ \lor \ (s, send, t) \ \lor \ (\exists u : (s, rcv(u), t))$
$\lor \ (\exists u : (u, rcv(s), t))$
$\Rightarrow$ { send, rcv, and internal rules }
$(s.v = t.v) \ \lor \ (s.v < t.v) \ \lor \ (s.v \leq t.v)$
$\lor \ (s.v \leq t.v)$
$\Rightarrow$ { simplify }
$s.v \leq t.v$

Induction: $(k > 1)$

$s \xrightarrow{k} t \ \land \ (k > 1)$
$\Rightarrow$ { definition of ml }
$(\exists u : s \xrightarrow{k-1} u \ \land \ u \xrightarrow{1} t)$
$\Rightarrow$ { induction hypothesis }
$(\exists u : s.v \leq u.v \ \land \ u.v \leq t.v)$
$\Rightarrow$ { simplify }
$s.v \leq t.v$

■

Lemma 4.4 states that if two states s and t are on different processes, and s does not happen before t, then $t.v[s.p] < s.v[s.p]$. Our formal proof of this lemma is nontrivial. We first define the notion of rank of a state t.

Definition 4.3 (Rank of a state) *The rank of a state t is equal to the length of the longest chain from an initial state to t.*

$$rank(t) = ml(Init, t).$$

Lemma 4.4 $(\forall s, t : s.p \neq t.p : s \not\rightarrow t \Rightarrow t.v[s.p] < s.v[s.p])$.

Proof: The proof is by induction on $k = rank(t)$.
Base $(k = 0)$:

$$s \not\rightarrow t \;\wedge\; s.p \neq t.p$$
$\Rightarrow \quad \{\; rank(t) = 0 \;\}$
$$initial(t) \;\wedge\; s.p \neq t.p$$
$\Rightarrow \quad \{\; \text{let } u \text{ be initial state in } s.p \;\}$
$$initial(t) \;\wedge\; s.p \neq t.p \;\wedge$$
$$(\exists u : initial(u) \;\wedge\; u.p = s.p : u = s \;\vee\; u \rightarrow s)$$
$\Rightarrow \quad \{\; \text{lemma } 4.2 \;\}$
$$initial(t) \;\wedge\; s.p \neq t.p \;\wedge$$
$$(\exists u : initial(u) \;\wedge\; u.p = s.p : u.v = s.v \;\vee\; u.v \leq s.v)$$
$\Rightarrow \quad \{\; \text{rule for initial states} \;\}$
$$t.v[s.p] = 0$$
$$\wedge \;\; (\exists u : u.v[s.p] = 1 : u.v = s.v \;\vee\; u.v \leq s.v)$$
$\Rightarrow \quad \{\; \text{simplify} \;\}$
$$t.v[s.p] < s.v[s.p]$$

Induction: $(k > 0)$

$$s \not\rightarrow t \;\wedge\; s.p \neq t.p \;\wedge\; rank(t) > 0$$
$\Rightarrow \quad \{\; \text{let } u \text{ satisfy } u \prec_{im} t, \; u \text{ exists because } \neg initial(t) \;\}$
$$s \not\rightarrow t \;\wedge\; s.p \neq t.p \;\wedge\; u.p = t.p \;\wedge\; u \prec_{im} t$$
$\Rightarrow \quad \{\; \text{definition of rank} \;\}$
$$s \not\rightarrow u \;\wedge\; rank(u) < k \;\wedge\; u.p \neq s.p \;\wedge\; u \prec_{im} t$$
$\Rightarrow \quad \{\; \text{inductive hypothesis} \;\}$
$$u.v[s.p] < s.v[s.p] \;\wedge\; u \prec_{im} t$$
$\Rightarrow \quad \{\; \text{expand } u \prec_{im} t \;\}$
$$u.v[s.p] < s.v[s.p]$$
$$\wedge \;\; ((u, internal, t) \;\vee\; (u, send, t) \;\vee\; (u, rcv(w), t))$$

Consider each disjunct separately:

Case 1: $(u, internal, t)$

$$u.v[s.p] < s.v[s.p] \ \wedge \ (u, internal, t)$$
$\Rightarrow$ { internal event rule }
$$u.v[s.p] < s.v[s.p] \ \wedge \ t.v = u.v$$
$\Rightarrow$ { simplify }
$$t.v[s.p] < s.v[s.p]$$

Case 2: $(u, send, t)$

$$u.v[s.p] < s.v[s.p] \ \wedge \ (u, send, t)$$
$\Rightarrow$ { Send rule, $s.p \neq t.p$ }
$$u.v[s.p] < s.v[s.p] \ \wedge \ t.v[s.p] = u.v[s.p]$$
$\Rightarrow$ { simplify }
$$t.v[s.p] < s.v[s.p]$$

Case 3: $(u, rcv(w), t)$

$$u.v[s.p] < s.v[s.p] \ \wedge \ (u, rcv(w), t)$$
$\Rightarrow$ { *rcv* rule }
$$u.v[s.p] < s.v[s.p] \ \wedge \ (u, rcv(w), t)$$
$$\wedge \ (t.v[s.p] = u.v[s.p] \ \vee \ t.v[s.p] = w.v[s.p])$$
$\Rightarrow$ { simplify }
$$t.v[s.p] < s.v[s.p]$$
$$\vee \ ((u, rcv(w), t) \ \wedge \ t.v[s.p] = w.v[s.p])$$

For case 3, it suffices to prove the following two cases.
Case 3A: $w.p = s.p$

$$t.v[s.p] = w.v[s.p] \ \wedge \ (u, rcv(w), t) \ \wedge \ w.p = s.p$$
$\Rightarrow$ $\left\{ \begin{array}{l} \text{let } x \text{ satisfy } w \prec_{im} x, \ x \text{ exists because} \\ w \rightsquigarrow t \text{ implies } \neg final(w) \end{array} \right\}$
$$t.v[s.p] = w.v[s.p] \ \wedge \ (w, send, x) \ \wedge \ w.p = s.p$$
$\Rightarrow$ { otherwise $s \rightarrow t$ }
$$t.v[s.p] = w.v[s.p] \ \wedge \ (w, send, x) \ \wedge \ w.p = s.p$$
$$\wedge \ w \rightarrow s$$
$\Rightarrow$ { because $w \prec_{im} x$ }
$$t.v[s.p] = w.v[s.p] \ \wedge \ (w, send, x) \ \wedge \ w.p = s.p$$
$$\wedge \ (x = s \ \vee \ x \rightarrow s)$$
$\Rightarrow$ { send rule }
$$t.v[s.p] = w.v[s.p] \ \wedge \ w.v[s.p] < x.v[s.p]$$
$$\wedge \ (x = s \ \vee \ x \rightarrow s)$$
$\Rightarrow$ { Lemma 4.2 }
$$t.v[s.p] = w.v[s.p] \ \wedge \ w.v[s.p] < x.v[s.p]$$

$$\land \; x.v \leq s.v$$
$\Rightarrow$ { simplify }
$$t.v[s.p] < s.v[s.p]$$

Case 3B: $w.p \neq s.p$

$$t.v[s.p] = w.v[s.p] \; \land \; (u, rcv(w), t) \; \land \; w.p \neq s.p$$
$\Rightarrow$ { definition of rank }
$$t.v[s.p] = w.v[s.p] \; \land \; w.p \neq s.p \; \land \; s \not\to w$$
$$\land \; rank(w) < k$$
$\Rightarrow$ { inductive hypothesis }
$$t.v[s.p] = w.v[s.p] \; \land \; w.v[s.p] < s.v[s.p]$$
$\Rightarrow$ { simplify }
$$t.v[s.p] < s.v[s.p]$$

∎

Lemma 4.5 is a refinement of Lemma 4.2 for the case when $s.p \neq t.p$, in which case $s.v < t.v$.

Lemma 4.5 $(\forall s, t : s.p \neq t.p : s \to t \Rightarrow s.v < t.v)$

Proof: From Lemma 4.2, we get that $s.v \leq t.v$. Furthermore, $s \to t$ implies that $t \not\to s$. From $t \not\to s$, $s.p \neq t.p$ and Lemma 4.4, we get that $s.v[t.p] < t.v[t.p]$. Combining this with $s.v \leq t.v$, we get the desired result.

∎

Theorem 4.6 states the property that we set out to prove at the beginning of this section.

Theorem 4.6 $(\forall s, t : s.p \neq t.p : s \to t \Leftrightarrow s.v < t.v)$

Proof: Immediate from Lemmas 4.4 and 4.5.

∎

4.4 Problems

4.1. Explain why, in the proof of Lemma 4.4, the rank of a state s has been defined as the length of the longest chain from any initial state to s rather than the length from the initial state in $s.p$ to s.

4.2. Specify and prove properties of the following algorithm:

> For any initial state s:
> $$(\forall i : i \neq s.p : s.v[i] = 0) \ \wedge \ (s.v[s.p] = 1)$$
> $(s, send, t)$:
> $$t.v[t.p] := s.v[t.p] + 1;$$
> $(s, internal, t)$:
> $$t.v[t.p] := s.v[t.p] + 1;$$
> $(s, rcv(u), t)$:
> $$t.v := s.v;$$
> $$t.v[u.p] := \max(u.v[u.p], s.v[u.p]);$$

In the above algorithm, a message sent from the state s does not include the entire vector, $s.v$, but just the component for process $s.p$, i.e., $s.v[s.p]$.

4.5 Bibliographic Remarks

Induction is a standard method for proving correctness of distributed programs (see Tel [Tel94] for example). The inductive proof of vector clocks discussed in this chapter is taken from Tomlinson and Garg [GT93].

Chapter 5

Clocks of Different Dimensions

Man's mind stretched to a new idea never goes back to its original dimensions. — Oliver Wendell Holmes, Jr.

5.1 Introduction

So far we have seen two kinds of clocks—logical clocks and vector clocks. These clocks give the main principles behind the design and use of clocks; but, a distributed algorithm designer must be aware of the fact that different applications may need clocks with different dimensions. In this chapter, we give two examples. Our first example is that of a direct-dependency clock, in which although each process maintains a $O(N)$ clock, it communicates only $O(1)$ information with each message. If the ordering information required between two events can be weakened from $\rightarrow$ to $\rightarrow_d$ defined in this chapter, then direct-dependency clocks can be used instead of vector clocks. For example, direct-dependency clocks are used to solve mutual exclusion (see Chapter 6) and to detect global properties in distributed systems (see Chapter 12).

In some other applications, even more information than $\rightarrow$ order is required. Our second example is that of a matrix clock in which each process maintains and sends $O(N^2)$ information with each message. In this chapter we show that whereas a vector clock keeps information about predecessors of any event with respect to other processes,

a matrix clock keeps information about predecessors of predecessors of
an event (or a state). A matrix clock is useful in applications such as
garbage collection in a distributed system.

This chapter is organized as follows. Section 5.2 describes direct-
dependency clocks, and Section 5.3 describes matrix clocks.

The notation used in this chapter is summarized in Figure 5.1.

$\rightarrow_d$	Directly precedes relation
(i, n)	n^{th} interval on process P_i
$\perp$	Null interval
$pred.u.i$	Predecessor of state u on process P_i
$succ.u.i$	Successor of state u on process P_i
M_k^n	Matrix on n^{th} interval in process P_k
$W[i, \cdot]$	i^{th} row of the matrix W

Figure 5.1: Notation

5.2   Direct-Dependency Clocks

One drawback with the vector clock algorithm is that it requires $O(N)$
integers to be sent with every message. For many applications, a weaker
version of the clock suffices. We now describe a clock algorithm that is
used by many algorithms in distributed systems. These clocks require
only one integer to be appended to each message. We call these clocks
direct-dependency clocks.

5.2.1   Algorithm

The algorithm shown in Figure 5.2 is described by the initial conditions
and the actions taken for each event type. On a send event, the process
sends only its local component in the message. It also increments its
component as in vector clocks. The action for internal events is the
same as that for vector clocks. When a process receives a message, it
updates two components—one for itself, and the other for the process
from which it received the message. It updates its own component in
a manner identical to logical clocks. It also updates the component for
the sender by taking the maximum with the previous value.

P_j::
  var
       v: array$[1..N]$ of integer
            initially $(\forall i : i \neq j : v[i] = 0) \land (v[j] = 1)$;

  send event $(s, send, t)$:
       $t.v[t.p] := s.v[t.p] + 1,$

  receive event $(s, rcv(u), t)$:
       $t.v[t.p] := \max(s.v[t.p], u.v[u.p]) + 1;$
       $t.v[u.p] := \max(u.v[u.p], s.v[u.p]);$

  internal event $(s, internal, t)$:
       $t.v[t.p] := s.v[t.p] + 1;$

Figure 5.2: A direct-dependency clock algorithm

An example of a distributed computation and its associated direct-dependency clock is given in Figure 5.3.

5.2.2 Properties

We first observe that if we retain only the ith component for the ith process, then the above algorithm is identical to the logical clock algorithm. We provide a direct proof of the logical clock property of direct-dependency clocks.

Lemma 5.1 $s \rightarrow t \Rightarrow s.v[s.p] < t.v[t.p]$.

Proof: It is sufficient to show that for all $k > 0$: $s \xrightarrow{k} t \Rightarrow s.v[s.p] < t.v[t.p]$. We use induction on k.

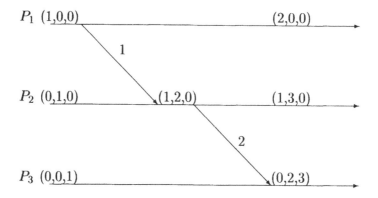

Figure 5.3: A sample execution of the direct-dependency clock algorithm.

Base $(k = 1)$:

$$s \xrightarrow{1} t$$

$\Rightarrow$ { Base case for $\rightarrow$ }

$$s \prec_{im} t \ \lor \ s \rightsquigarrow t$$

$\Rightarrow$ { expand $s \prec_{im} t$ and $s \rightsquigarrow t$ }

$$(s, internal, t) \ \lor \ (s, send, t) \ \lor \ (\exists u : (s, rcv(u), t))$$
$$\lor \ (\exists u : (u, rcv(s), t))$$

$\Rightarrow$ { send, rcv, and internal event rules }

$$s.v[s.p] < t.v[t.p]$$

Induction: $(k > 1)$

$$s \xrightarrow{k} t \ \land \ (k > 1)$$

$\Rightarrow$ { lemma induction $\rightarrow$ }

$$(\exists u : s \xrightarrow{k-1} u \ \land \ u \xrightarrow{1} t)$$

$\Rightarrow$ { induction hypothesis }

$$(\exists u : s.v[s.p] < u.v[u.p] \ \land \ u.v[u.p] < t.v[t.p])$$

$\Rightarrow$ { simplify }

$$s.v[s.p] < t.v[t.p]$$

∎

However, our interest in a direct-dependency clock is not due to its logical clock property (Lamport's logical clock is sufficient for that), but to its ability to capture the notion of direct-dependency. We first define a relation *directly precedes* $\rightarrow_d$, a subset of $\rightarrow$.

Definition 5.2 ($\rightarrow_d$)

$$s \rightarrow_d t \stackrel{\text{def}}{=} s \prec t \ \lor \ \exists q, r : s \preceq q \ \land \ q \rightsquigarrow r \ \land \ r \preceq t$$

Intuitively, $s \rightarrow_d t$ iff there is a path from s to t that uses at most one message in the happened before diagram of the computation. The following property makes direct-dependency clocks useful for many applications.

Theorem 5.3 $\forall s, t : s.p \neq t.p : (s \rightarrow_d t) \Leftrightarrow (s.v[s.p] \leq t.v[s.p])$.

Proof: To prove this theorem formally in the forward direction, we use induction on the length of the chain between s and t as we did for $\rightarrow$. However, for $\rightarrow_d$ we restrict our attention to those chains that go only through processes $s.p$ and $t.p$. It is easy to see that each link in this chain (say, from state q to r) satisfies $q.v[q.p] \leq r.v[q.p]$. We leave the details to the reader.

To prove the converse formally, we use induction on the rank of t (See Chapter 4). Let k be the rank of t.

Base $(k = 0)$:

$\quad rank(t) = 0$

$\Rightarrow \quad \{$ definition of rank $\}$

$\quad initial(t)$

$\Rightarrow \quad \{$ let u be initial state in $s.p$ $\}$

$\quad initial(t) \ \land$

$\quad (\exists u : initial(u) \ \land \ u.p = s.p : u = s \ \lor \ u \rightarrow s)$

$\Rightarrow \quad \{$ lemma 5.1 $\}$

$\quad initial(t) \ \land$

$\quad (\exists u : initial(u) \ \land \ u.p = s.p : u.v = s.v \ \lor \ u.v[u.p] < s.v[u.p])$

$\Rightarrow \quad \{$ initialization $\}$

$\quad t.v[s.p] = 0$

$\quad \land \ (\exists u : u.v[s.p] = 1 : u.v[s.p] \leq s.v[s.p])$

$\Rightarrow \quad \{$ simplify $\}$

$\quad \neg(s.v[s.p] \leq t.v[s.p])$

Induction $(k > 0)$:

$$s \not\rightarrow_d t \;\wedge\; k > 0$$
$\Rightarrow$ { let u satisfy $u \prec_{im} t$, u exists because $k = rank(t) > 0$ }
$$s \not\rightarrow_d t \;\wedge\; u \prec_{im} t$$
$\Rightarrow$ { $s \rightarrow_d u$ implies $s \rightarrow_d t$ }
$$s \not\rightarrow_d u \;\wedge\; rank(u) < k \;\wedge\; u \prec_{im} t$$
$\Rightarrow$ { inductive hypothesis }
$$\neg(s.v[s.p] \leq u.v[s.p]) \;\wedge\; u \prec_{im} t$$
$\Rightarrow$ { expand $u \prec_{im} t$ }
$$\neg(s.v[s.p] \leq u.v[s.p])$$
$$\wedge \;((u, internal, t) \;\vee\; (u, send, t) \;\vee\; (u, rcv(w), t))$$

Consider each disjunct separately:

Case 1: $(u, internal, t) \;\vee\; (u, send, t)$
$$(s.v[s.p] > u.v[s.p]) \;\wedge\; ((u, internal, t) \;\vee\; (u, send, t))$$
$\Rightarrow$ { internal and send event rules }
$$(s.v[s.p] > u.v[s.p]) \;\wedge\; t.v[s.p] = u.v[s.p]$$
$\Rightarrow$ { simplify }
$$(s.v[s.p] > t.v[s.p])$$

Case 2: $(u, rcv(w), t), w.p = s.p$
$$s \not\rightarrow_d t, s.p = w.p, w \rightsquigarrow t$$
$\Rightarrow$ { $s \prec w$ or $s = w$ imply $s \rightarrow_d t$ }
$$w \prec s$$
$\Rightarrow$ { from program, local component incremented after send }
$$w.v[s.p] < s.v[s.p]$$
$\Rightarrow$ { rcv rule }
$$(s.v[s.p] > w.v[s.p]) \;\wedge\; ((w.v[s.p] = t.v[s.p]) \;\vee\; (u.v[s.p] = t.v[s.p]))$$
$\Rightarrow$ { $(s.v[s.p] > u.v[s.p])$ }
$$(s.v[s.p] > t.v[s.p])$$

Case 3: $(u, rcv(w), t), w.p \neq s.p$
$$(s.v[s.p] > u.v[s.p]) \;\wedge\; (u, rcv(w), t) \;\wedge\; w.p \neq s.p$$
$\Rightarrow$ { rcv rule }
$$(s.v[s.p] > u.v[s.p]) \;\wedge\; t.v[s.p] = u.v[s.p]$$
$\Rightarrow$ { simplify }
$$(s.v[s.p] > t.v[s.p])$$

■

The following is an easy corollary.

Corollary 5.4 $(\forall s, t : s.p \neq t.p : s \not\rightarrow t \Rightarrow (s.v[s.p] > t.v[s.p]))$

Proof: Observe that $s \not\rightarrow t$ implies $s \not\rightarrow_d t$.

■

5.3   Higher-Dimensional Clocks

It is natural to ask whether using higher-dimensional clocks can give processes additional knowledge. The answer is yes. Assume that "knowledge" is a collection of facts. By proper encoding, any finite amount of knowledge can be represented by an integer. So, now assume that the knowledge function K returns the knowledge that the process has about itself as a natural number, that is, $K(s) \in \mathcal{N}$ for any s.

We assume that a process never forgets, that is, the knowledge increases with time for any process. Also, the only way knowledge can be communicated to a different process is through a message. If we ensure that any process includes all it knows in the message, and on receiving any message from P_j, the process P_i updates its own knowledge; then its knowledge is greater than the knowledge sent by P_j and its own previous knowledge. The above can be concisely stated as "knowledge is monotonic with respect to $\rightarrow$." Formally, $s \rightarrow t \Rightarrow K(s) < K(t)$ where $<$ denotes the ordering between knowledges. The alert reader would notice the similarity between these rules and those of logical clocks.

Now let us say that for some reason, it is important for a process to know not only what it knows but also what other processes know. A vector clock can be alternatively viewed as a knowledge vector. In this interpretation, $s.v[i]$ denotes what process $s.p$ knows about process i in the local state s. If processes include their entire vector in their messages, we retain monotonicity with respect to $\rightarrow$.

In some applications it may be important for the process to know a still higher level of knowledge. The value $s.v[i, j]$ could represent what process $s.p$ knows about what process i knows about process j. For example, if $s.v[i, s.p] > k$ for all i, then process $s.p$ can conclude that everybody knows that its state is strictly greater than k. It may be important to discard some information which has now been broadcast to everyone (despite uncertain communication).

Next, we discuss a matrix clock that encodes a higher level of knowledge than a vector clock. The discussion of properties of a matrix clock, however, requires the notion of intervals, the predecessor and the successor function.

5.3.1   State Interval

A state interval is just a sequence of states between two external events. Formally, the nth interval in P_i (denoted by (i, n)) is the subchain of $(S_i, \rightarrow)$ between the $(n-1)^{th}$ and n^{th} external events. For a given interval (i, n), if n is out of range, then (i, n) refers to $\perp$, which represents a sentinel value (or a "null" interval). The notion of intervals is useful because the relation of two states belonging to the same interval is a congruence with respect to $\rightarrow$. Thus the relation of two states being in the same interval is an equivalence relation and for any two states s and s' in the same interval and any state u from a different interval:
$$(s \rightarrow u \Leftrightarrow s' \rightarrow u) \text{ and } (u \rightarrow s \Leftrightarrow u \rightarrow s').$$

We exploit this congruence in our algorithms by assigning a single timestamp to all states belonging to the same interval. An example of a distributed computation and its state intervals is shown in Figure 5.4.

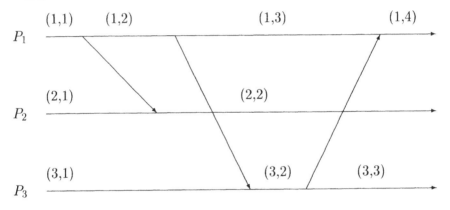

Figure 5.4: State intervals

5.3.2   Predecessor and Successor Functions

The predecessor and successor functions are defined as follows for $u \in S$ and $1 \leq i \leq N$:

$$pred.u.i = \max\{v \in S_i : v \rightarrow u\}$$

$$succ.u.i = \min\{v \in S_i : u \rightarrow v\}$$

Consider a state $u \in S$. The predecessor of u in S_i, denoted $pred.u.i$, is the latest state in S_i that causally precedes u. Thus if $(pred.u.i = v)$, then v is the maximum element in $(S_i, \rightarrow)$ that causally precedes u. If no element in S_i causally precedes u, then $pred.u.i = \perp$. Notice that the predecessor of a state (i, n) on S_i is just the previous state $(i, n-1)$.

Because of the congruence for states belonging to the same interval, the *pred* and *succ* functions and the $\parallel$ relation are well defined on intervals.

5.3.3   Algorithm for Matrix Clock

P_k::

var

   M_k: array$[1..N, \, 1..N]$ of integer
      initially $(\forall i, j : (i \neq k) \vee (j \neq k) : M_k[i, j] = 0) \wedge$
      $(M_k[k, k] = 1)$;

To send a message:
      Tag message with $M_k[\cdot, \cdot]$;
      $M_k[k, k] := M_k[k, k] + 1$; // increment local clock

Upon receipt of a message tagged with $W[\cdot, \cdot]$ from process $w.p$:
      for $i := 1$ **to** $N, \, (i \neq k)$ **do**
         $M_k[i, \cdot] := max(M_k[i, \cdot], W[i, \cdot])$;
      for $j := 1$ **to** N **do**
         $M_k[k, j] := max(M_k[k, j], W[w.p, j])$;
      $M_k[k, k] := M_k[k, k] + 1$; // increment local clock

Figure 5.5: Algorithm for maintaining matrix clock $M_k[\cdot, \cdot]$ at P_k.

Just as a vector clock allows us to compute the *pred* function (see Problem 5.7), a matrix clock allows us to compute $pred(pred())$ function. The matrix clock algorithm is presented in Figure 5.5. Let M_k^n denote the value of the matrix clock in interval (k, n). The following description applies to an $N \times N$ matrix clock in a system with N processes. The algorithm is easier to understand by noticing the vector clock algorithm embedded within it. If we focus only on row k for process P_k, the above algorithm reduces to the vector clock algorithm. Consider the update of the matrix in the algorithm in Figure 5.5 when a message is received. The first step affects only rows different from k and can be ignored. When a matrix is received from process $w.p$, then we use only the row given by the index $w.p$ of the matrix W for updating row k of P_k. Thus from our discussion of vector clock algorithms, it is clear that,

$$\forall s, t : s.p \neq t.p : s \to t \equiv s.M[s.p, \cdot] < t.M[t.p, \cdot]$$

We now describe the information contained in a matrix clock M_k^n at interval (k, n) in three steps. First we explain the meaning of the kth diagonal element. Then we explain the meaning of the kth row, followed by the entire matrix.

The kth diagonal element, $M_k^n[k, k]$, is an interval counter at P_k. Thus for any interval (k, n), the following is true: $M_k^n[k, k] = n$. As mentioned earlier, row k of M_k^n is equivalent to a traditional vector clock. In fact, when we say "P_k's vector clock" we are referring to row k of P_k's matrix clock. Since the vector clock implements the $pred$ function, row k of M_k^n can be used to find predecessors of $(k, n) = (k, M_k^n[k, k])$ as follows: the predecessor of $(k, M_k^n[k, k])$ on process j is the interval $(j, M_k^n[k, j])$. In fact, this applies to all rows: the predecessor of $(i, M_k^n[i, i])$ on process j is the interval $(j, M_k^n[i, j])$. This property explains the meaning of other rows. In other words, we can use row k to find the $pred.(k, n).j$ for $j \neq k$, and then use row j to find $pred.(pred.(k, n).j).i$ for $i \neq j$.

The matrix clock can be summarized in three simple rules. First, the kth diagonal element corresponds to some interval on P_k. Second, row i is the value of P_i's vector clock in interval $(i, M_k[i, i])$, which gives interpretation to nondiagonal elements. Third, row k of M_k equals the diagonal. The meaning of a matrix clock is formally stated and proven in Lemma 5.5.

Lemma 5.5

(M1) $M_k^n[k, k] = n$
(M2) $i \neq j \Rightarrow (j, M_k^n[i, j]) = pred.(i, M_k^n[i, i]).j$
(M3) $M_k^n[i, i] = M_k^n[k, i]$

Proof: Each part is proven by induction on the rank of the interval (k, n). In the base case, (k, n) is an initial interval.

(M1) *Base rank$(k, n) = 0$:* Initial value of $M_k^n[k, k] = 1$.
    Induction (rank$(k, n) > 0$): We assume that $M_k^n[k, k] = n$ and

show that $M_k^{n+1}[k,k] = n+1$. P_k enters interval $(k, n+1)$ only after sending or receiving a message. From the program text, the kth diagonal element is incremented after sending a message, and therefore our claim holds for the send event. For a receive event, from vector clock properties, $W[k,k] < M[k,k]$. Therefore, the net result is that $M[k,k]$ gets incremented. Thus $M_k^{n+1}[k,k] = M_k^n[k,k] + 1 = n+1$.

(M2) *Base* $rank(k,n) = 0$: For this case, M_k^n is the initial value of the matrix clock in P_k. Thus, $i \neq j$ implies that $M_k^n[i,j] = 0$, and hence $(j, M_k^n[i,j]) = (j,0) = \bot$. Thus we need to show $pred.(i, M_k^n[i,i]).j = \bot$ also. Suppose $i \neq k$, then by initial value of M_k^n, we know $(i, M_k^n[i,i]) = (i,0)$, thus $pred.(i, M_k^n[i,i]).j = pred.(i,0).j = \bot$. Now suppose $i = k$, then by initial value of $M_k^n[i,i]$ we know that $(i, M_k^n[i,i]) = (i,1)$. Since no interval precedes $(i,1)$, we know $pred.(i,1).j = \bot$.

Induction $(rank(k,n) > 0)$: Assume the claim to be true for (k,n) and every interval in the past of (k,n). Suppose the event initiating $(k, n+1)$ is a message send, then $M_k^{n+1} = M_k^n$ except for $M_k^{n+1}[k,k] = M_k^n[k,k] + 1$. Since the event is a message send, (k,n) and $(k, n+1)$ have the exact same predecessors. Thus $pred.(i, M_k^{n+1}[i,i]).j$ equals $pred.(i, M_k^n[i,i]).j$, which by induction hypothesis, equals $(j, M_k^n[i,j])$, which is equal to $(j, M_k^{n+1}[i,j])$ because $i \neq j$ and only element $M_k^n[k,k]$ changes.

Suppose the event initiating $(k, n+1)$ is a message receive tagged with matrix clock W. By the induction hypothesis, W satisfies M2.

Case 1: $(i \neq k)$
From the program text, $M_k^{n+1}[i,i] = max(M_k^n[i,i], W[i,i])$. Consider the case when $M_k^{n+1}[i,i] = M_k^n[i,i]$. From induction hypothesis $(j, M_k^n[i,j]) = pred.(i, M_k^n[i,i]).j$. Furthermore, from induction hypothesis $(j, W[i,j]) = pred.(i, W[i,i]).j$. Since $W[i,i] \leq M_k^n[i,i]$, it follows from the properties of the *pred* function that $W[i,j] \leq M_k^n[i,j]$. This implies from the program text that $M_k^{n+1}[i,j] = M_k^n[i,j]$. Thus the claim follows from the induction hypothesis. The case when $M_k^{n+1}[i,i] = W[i,i]$ is similar.

Case 2: $(i = k)$
This case corresponds to the vector clock embedded in the matrix and the claim holds from the properties of vector clocks. The

reader is encouraged to supply the formal proof for this case (see Problem 5.7).

(M3) *Base $rank(k, n) = 0$:* True by initial assignment to matrix.
   Induction ($rank(k, n) > 0$): We assume that $diag(M_k^n) = M_k^n[k, \cdot]$, and show that $diag(M_k^{n+1}) = M_k^{n+1}[k, \cdot]$. P_k enters interval $(k, n+1)$ only after sending or receiving a message. In the case of a send, $M_k^n[k, k]$ is incremented by 1. Thus the diagonal is still equal to row k. In the case of a message receive, $M_k^{n+1}[k, i] = max(M_k^n[k, i], W[w.p, i])$ and $M_k^{n+1}[i, i] = max(M_k^n[i, i], W[i, i])$ (from program text). Since, by induction hypothesis $M_k^n[k, i] = M_k^n[i, i]$ and $W[w.p, i] = W[i, i]$, the result follows.

■

Figure 5.6 shows values of the matrix clock and message tags on an example run. In this example, we have assumed that only processes P_1 and P_2 are concerned with the causality information. We leave it to the reader to derive a matrix clock algorithm for the case when we are concerned with causality information of events only on a subset of processes in the system. Note that row 1 of P_1's matrix is a traditional vector clock restricted to indices 1 and 2, and row 2 equals the value of P_2's vector clock at a state in the "past" of P_1. Similar properties hold for P_2's matrix clock.

5.3.4   Application: Garbage Collection

From the above discussion, it can be observed that a matrix of dimension k lets us compute k compositions of the *pred* function. Thus, when $k = 1$, the algorithm reduces to the vector clock, and $pred(s).i = s.v[i]$ when $s.p \neq i$. When $k = 2$, we get the two-dimensional matrix, and $pred(pred(s).i).j = s.M[i, j]$. This can be extended to any dimension.

Computing the *pred* function multiple times can be useful in many situations. For example, the following theorem says that if process $s.p$ finds that its $s.p$ column is uniformly bigger than $r.M[s.p, s.p]$ (that is, its local clock in some previous state r), then the information at r has been received by all processes.

Theorem 5.6 *Let $s.p = r.p$. If $(\forall i : r.M[r.p, r.p] \leq s.M[i, s.p])$, then $\forall t : t \| s : r \to t$.*

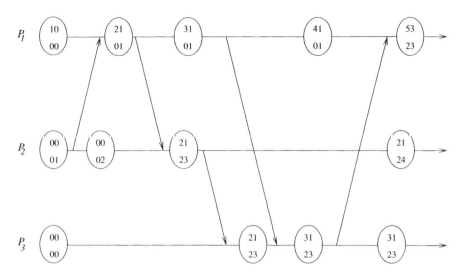

Figure 5.6: Matrix clock example.

Proof:

$$t \| s \quad \Rightarrow \quad pred.s.i \to t \tag{5.1}$$

$$(\forall i : r.M[r.p, r.p] \le s.M[i, s.p]) \quad \Rightarrow \quad r \preceq pred.(pred.s.i).(s.p) \tag{5.2}$$

From the above two equations: $r \to t$.

■

5.4 Problems

5.1. Show the following property for direct-dependency clocks.

$$\forall j : j \ne s.p : s.v[s.p] > s.v[j],$$

that is, every process has its own component bigger than everybody else's component in the vector.

5.2. Assume that a distributed program has used direct-dependency clocks to timestamp the set of local states. Given a global cut G of such a computation, a matrix $G.M$ can be formed by using a direct-dependency vector of the state $G[i]$ as the ith row of the matrix. We define G to be consistent if

$$\forall i, j : G[i] \not\rightarrow G[j]$$

(1) How can you check given $G.M$, whether G is consistent or not?

(2) How will your answer change if G is not a global cut, but a cut defined on a proper subset of the processes?

5.3. Let $s.v$ be the vector clock for the local state s. Given N vectors one from each state, one can form a matrix to represent the cross product of the local states, which can be viewed as the global state. Give a suitable condition on the matrix for this global state to be consistent (see Problem 5.2).

5.4. Show that for matrix clocks, the row corresponding to the index $s.p$ is bigger than any other row in the matrix $s.M$ for any state s.

5.5. Let two states s and s' on the same process be *send-interval* congruent if there is no message sent between them. Show that send-interval congruence is an equivalence relation and satisfies:

$$\forall u : u.p \neq s.p : s \rightarrow u \equiv s' \rightarrow u.$$

Similarly, define *receive-interval* congruence. Show that the interval congruence is the intersection of send-interval and receive-interval congruence.

5.6. Assume that states of processes are colored green, yellow, or blue. It is up to a process to define the color of its state. Design a distributed algorithm that detects whether there exists a blue state s and a green state t in the computation such that $s \rightarrow t$. Make your algorithm as decentralized and as efficient as possible.

5.7. Consider the vector clock algorithm in Figure 5.7.

Show that it computes the *pred* function, i.e.,

$$(j, V_k[j]) = pred(k, V_k[k]).j$$

To initialize:
$$V_k[\cdot] := 0;$$
$$V_k[k] := V_k[k] + 1;$$

To send a message:
Tag message with $V_k[\cdot]$;
$V_k[k] := V_k[k] + 1;$ // increment local clock

Upon receipt of a message tagged with $W[\cdot]$ from process $w.p$:
for $j := 1$ **to** N **do**
$V_k[j] := max(V_k[j], W[j]);$
endfor
$V_k[k] := V_k[k] + 1;$ // increment local clock

Figure 5.7: An algorithm for maintaining vector clock $V_k[\cdot]$ at P_k.

5.8. Give a matrix clock algorithm to track causality of events on a *subset* of all processes in the system. For example, in Figure 5.6, we are tracking causality for events on processes P_1 and P_2, but not on P_3.

*5.9. Assume that some of the states in a distributed computation are colored blue. All other states are colored white. Given two blue states s and t, we are interested in determining whether there exists a blue state u such that $s \rightarrow u$ and $u \rightarrow t$. Give an algorithm to "timestamp" each state so that given two timestamps of blue states it can be determined whether there exists a blue state that lies between them.

5.5 Bibliographic Remarks

Direct-dependency clocks have been used in mutual exclusion algorithms (e.g., [Lam78]), global property detection (e.g., [Gar96]) and recovery in distributed systems. Matrix clocks have been used for discarding obsolete information in Sarin and Lynch [SL87] and for detecting relational global predicates in Tomlinson and Garg [TG93].

Chapter 6

Mutual Exclusion: Using Timestamps

Between two evils, choose neither; between two goods, choose both.
— *Tryon Edwards*

6.1   Introduction

In a distributed system, mutual exclusion is often necessary for accessing shared resources such as data. For example, consider a table that is replicated on multiple sites. Assume that operations on the table can be issued concurrently. For their correctness we require that all operations appear *atomic* in the sense that the effect of the operations must appear indivisible to the user. For example, if an update operation requires changes to two fields x and y, then another operation should not read the old value of x and the new value of y. Observe that in a distributed system, there is no shared memory and therefore one could not use shared objects such as semaphores to implement the mutual exclusion.

Mutual exclusion is one of the most studied topics in distributed systems. It reveals many important issues in distributed algorithms such as safety and liveness properties. We will study three classes of algorithms—timestamp-based algorithms, token-based algorithms and quorum-based algorithms. The timestamp-based algorithms resolve conflict in use of resources based on timestamps assigned to requests of resources. The token-based algorithms use auxiliary resources such as tokens to resolve the conflicts. The quorum-based algorithms use a subset of processes to get permission for accessing the shared resource.

In this chapter, we will study two timestamp-based algorithms— Lamport's algorithm and Ricart and Agrawala's algorithm. Ricart and Agrawala's algorithm can be seen as an optimization of Lamport's algorithm. Both algorithms assume that there are no faults in the distributed system, that is, processors and communication links are reliable.

One of the underlying themes of this chapter is to illustrate the use of the *happened before* model to specify and verify distributed programs. For example, the property of mutual exclusion is formalized as the requirement that no two processes access a shared resource in *concurrent* states. This is different from the requirement that no two processes access the critical section *simultaneously*. Thus we avoid the notion of global time for specification and verification of a distributed algorithm.

This chapter also illustrates formal specification of safety and liveness properties of distributed programs. Informally, a safety property states that nothing "bad" will happen in the program whereas a liveness property states that something "good" will eventually happen in the program. The meanings of "good" and "bad" are application specific and the mutual exclusion problem will serve as one example application.

The chapter is organized as follows. Section 6.2 describes the mutual exclusion problem. Section 6.3 presents Lamport's algorithm and its proof of correctness. Section 6.4 presents a modification of Lamport's algorithm by Ricart and Agrawala.

The notation used in this chapter is summarized in Figure 6.1.

$\prec$	Locally precedes relation
$\rightarrow$	Happened before relation
$\rightsquigarrow$	Remotely precedes relation
$\rightarrow_d$	Directly precedes
r, s, t, u, v	Local states
$s.p$	The process that contains s
$prev(s)$	The state immediately before s

Figure 6.1: Notation

6.2 Specifications of the Problem

Let a system consist of a fixed number of processes and a shared resource called the *critical section*. An example of a critical section is the operation performed on the replicated table introduced earlier. The algorithm to coordinate access to the critical section must satisfy the following properties, which are stated informally in the interleaving model. They will be given in the happened before model when formalized.

Safety: Two processes should not have permission to use the critical section simultaneously.

Liveness: Every request for the critical section is eventually granted.

Fairness: Different requests must be granted in the order they are made.

There are many algorithms for mutual exclusion in a distributed system. However, the least expensive algorithm for the mutual exclusion is a centralized algorithm. If we are required to satisfy just the safety and liveness properties, then a simple queue-based algorithm works. One of the processes is designated as the coordinator for the critical section. Any process that wants to enter the critical section sends a request to the coordinator. The coordinator simply puts these requests in a queue in the order it receives them. It also grants permission to the process that is at the head of the queue.

The above algorithm does not satisfy the notion of fairness, which says that requests should be granted in the order they are made and not in the order they are received. Assume that the process P_i makes a request for the shared resource to the coordinator process P_k. After making the request, P_i sends a message to the process P_j. Now, P_j sends a request to P_k that reaches P_k earlier than the request made by the process P_i. This example shows that it is possible for the order in which requests are received by the coordinator process to be different from the order in which they are made.

Before we present algorithms that satisfy the fairness constraint, we formalize the problem in the happened before model. To start, we state our assumptions on the underlying communication model. We assume that all channels are reliable, that is, no message is ever lost, changed, or spuriously introduced. In addition, some algorithms such as Lamport's algorithm assume that all channels are first-in-first-out (FIFO), that is, all messages within a channel are received in the order they are sent. This assumption can be stated formally as follows:

$$s \prec t \land s \rightsquigarrow u \land t \rightsquigarrow v \Rightarrow \neg(v \prec u) \quad \textbf{(FIFO)}$$

We now introduce some predicates on the set of states. For any state s, we define $req(s)$ to be true if and only if the process $P_{s.p}$ has requested the critical section and has not yet released it and $cs(s)$ to be true if and only if the process $P_{s.p}$ has permission to enter the critical section in the state s. Note that $req(s)$ and $cs(s)$ are predicates, not program variables. They are a function of process states and will be defined formally in the algorithm.

Both req and cs are false in an initial state. Now suppose $t \prec u \prec v$ and a request for the critical section was made in t, access was granted in u, and it was released in v. Then $req(s)$ is true for all states s such that $t \preceq s \prec v$, and $cs(s)$ is true for $u \preceq s \prec v$. It is assumed that a process that is granted access to the critical section eventually releases it:

$$cs(s) \Rightarrow (\exists t : s \prec t : \neg req(t)) \quad \textbf{(cooperation)}$$

The task is to develop a distributed algorithm to ensure the required safety, liveness, and fairness properties. The safety and liveness properties can be stated formally in the happened before model as follows:

$$(s\|t) \land (s \neq t) \Rightarrow \neg(cs(s) \land cs(t)) \quad \textbf{(safety)}$$

$$req(s) \Rightarrow (\exists t : s \preceq t \land cs(t)) \quad \textbf{(liveness)}$$

The safety property ensures that mutual exclusion is not violated because no two distinct concurrent states can be in the critical section. The liveness property ensures that every request is eventually fulfilled. Before presenting the fairness property based on the happened before relation, a little ground work is needed. First, let

$$next\_cs(s) \stackrel{\text{def}}{=} min\{t \mid s \preceq t \land cs(t)\}$$

Informally, $next\_cs(s)$ is the first local state after s in which the process $P_{s.p}$ has access to the critical section. Also, let

$$req\_start(s) \stackrel{\text{def}}{=} req(s) \land \neg req(prev(s))$$

Thus $req\_start(s)$ is true if and only if $P_{s.p}$ first made a request for the critical section in state s. Then, the fairness property can be stated as:

$$(req\_start(s) \wedge req\_start(t) \wedge s \to t) \Rightarrow next\_cs(s) \to next\_cs(t) \textbf{(fairness)}$$

The fairness property ensures that requests are granted in the order they are made. Note that the formal specification uses the happened before relation for ordering requests. Also note that $next\_cs(s)$ and $next\_cs(t)$ exist because of liveness. and are not concurrent because of safety. Therefore,

$$next\_cs(s) \to next\_cs(t)$$

is equivalent to

$$\neg(next\_cs(t) \to next\_cs(s))$$

6.3 Lamport's Algorithm

In this section, we first present an informal description of Lamport's algorithm for mutual exclusion and then its formal description in the happened before model. In the informal description, each process maintains a logical clock (used for timestamps) and a queue (used for storing requests for the critical section). Lamport's algorithm ensures that processes enter the critical section in the order of timestamp of their requests. The rules of the algorithm are as follows:

- To request the critical section, a process sends a timestamped message to all other processes and adds a timestamped request to the queue.

- On receiving a request message, the request and its timestamp are stored in the queue and an acknowledgment is sent back.

- To release the critical section, a process sends a release message to all other processes.

- On receiving a release message, the corresponding request is deleted from the queue.

- A process determines that it can access the critical section if and only if:

    1. It has a request in the queue with timestamp t, and

2. t is less than all other requests in the queue, and

3. It has received a message from every other process with timestamp greater than t (the request acknowledgments ensure this).

We now present a formal version of Lamport's algorithm as shown in Figure 6.2.

P_i::

var
    v: depclock; // direct-dependency clock
    q: array$[1..N]$ of integer initially $(\infty, \infty, \ldots, \infty)$;

$request$:
    $q[i] := v[i]$;
    send $(q[i])$ to all processes; // request messages

$release$:
    $q[i] := \infty$;
    send $(q[i])$ to all processes; // release messages

$receive(u)$:
    $q[u.p] := u.q[u.p]$;
    if $event(u) = request$ **then**
        send ack to process $u.p$; // acknowledge "request"

Figure 6.2: Lamport's algorithm for mutual exclusion

In this version of Lamport's algorithm every process maintains two vectors. These two vectors simulate the queue used in the informal description given earlier. The interpretations of these vectors are:

$s.q[j]$: the timestamp of the request by process P_j. The value ∞ signifies that P_i does not have any record of outstanding request by process P_j.

$s.v[j]$: the timestamp of the last message seen from P_j if $j \neq i$. The component $s.v[i]$ represents the value of the logical clock in state s.

We describe each of the events in the program. To request the critical section, P_i simply records its clock in $q[i]$. Because all other processes also maintain this information, "request" messages are sent to all processes indicating the new value of $q[i]$. To release the critical section, P_i simply resets $q[i]$ to ∞ and sends "release" messages to all processes. Finally, we also require processes to acknowledge any request message. Note that every message is timestamped and when it is received, the vector v is updated according to the direct-dependency clock rules as discussed in Chapter 5. Thus in Figure 6.2, when an *ack* message is received, v is changed according to direct-dependency clock rules.

It is clear from the above description that state s has received a request from P_i if $s.q[i] \neq \infty$, in which case the timestamp of the request is the value of $s.q[i]$. State s has permission to access the critical section when there is a request from $P_{s.p}$ with its timestamp less than all other requests and $P_{s.p}$ has received a message from every other process with a timestamp greater than the timestamp of its own request. We use the predicates $req(s)$ and $cs(s)$ to denote that a request has been made and access has been granted, respectively. In the definitions shown below, the $<$ relation on tuples is a lexicographic ordering, that is, if two requests have the same timestamp, then the request by the process with the smaller process number is considered smaller.

$$
\begin{aligned}
req(s) &\overset{\text{def}}{=} s.q[s.p] \neq \infty \\
cs(s) &\overset{\text{def}}{=} (\forall j : j \neq s.p : \\
&\quad (s.q[s.p], s.p) < (s.v[j], j) \quad \wedge \\
&\quad (s.q[s.p], s.p) < (s.q[j], j) \ )
\end{aligned}
$$

From now on, we write $(s.q[s.p] < s.v[j])$ instead of $(s.q[s.p], s.p) < (s.v[j], j)$ for notational simplicity.

6.3.1 Proof of Correctness

Let us now prove that the above algorithm indeed satisfies all required properties.

We first note that the q vector in the algorithm is initially identical for all processes. Moreover, whenever any process changes any component it immediately sends a message to all other processes informing them of the update. When these processes receive that message, they record the change in their own vectors. This mechanism is useful for keeping a consistent state of the entire system. We refer to the vectors maintained in this manner as *active vectors*. Intuitively, if there are no pending update messages from P_i to P_j, then P_j will have the correct information about P_i. Note that this requires FIFO ordering of messages; otherwise, two update messages may arrive out of order and result in a correct value getting replaced by an obsolete one. To formalize this property of active vectors, we need the following definition. We define the predicate $msg(s, t)$ as

$$msg(s, t) \equiv \exists q, r : q \prec s \land q \rightsquigarrow r \land t \prec r$$

that is, there exists a message that was sent before s but has not been received by the process $t.p$ until after the state t.

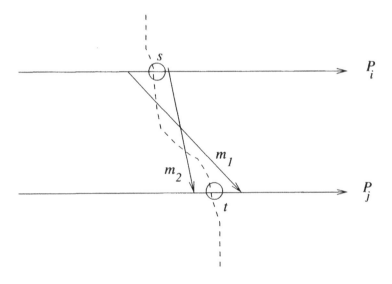

Figure 6.3: Messages crossing a cut

The next lemma describes the property of active vectors that makes them useful. Roughly speaking, it says that if there are no update messages from state s to t that cross the cut containing s and t, then t has the correct value of $s.q[s.p]$. In Figure 6.3, $\neg msg(s, t)$ implies that there cannot be any message of type m_1 and $s \not\rightarrow_d t$ implies that there cannot be any message of type m_2.

Lemma 6.1 *Assume FIFO message delivery.*
$\forall s, t : s.p \neq t.p : s \not\rightarrow_d t \land \neg msg(s, t) \Rightarrow t.q[s.p] = s.q[s.p].$

Proof: We use induction on k = rank of t.

Base Case: $(k = 0) \equiv initial(t)$

If $initial(s)$, then the result follows from the initial assignment. Otherwise, let u be the initial state in the process $s.p$. From $\neg msg(s, t)$ and the rule that any change requires send of a message, it follows that $s.q[s.p] = u.q[s.p]$. From the initial assignment, it again follows that $t.q[s.p] = s.q[s.p]$.

Induction Case: $k > 0$

Let $u = prev(t)$. Let $event(u) \neq receive$, then $\neg msg(s, t)$ implies $\neg msg(s, u)$. Using the induction hypothesis, we get that $u.q[s.p] = s.q[s.p]$ and by using program text, we conclude that $t.q[s.p] = u.q[s.p]$. Now let $event(u) = receive(w)$. If $w.p \neq s.p$, the previous case applies.

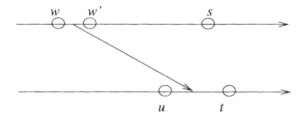

Figure 6.4: Proof for the induction case

So, let $w.p = s.p$. Since $s \not\to_d t$, it follows that $w \prec s$. Let $w' = next.w$. From the program, $w'.q[s.p] = t.q[s.p]$. We now claim that $s.q[s.p] = w'.q[s.p]$ from which the result follows. If not, the value changed between w' and s. However, this implies that a message was sent at that state. This message cannot be received before t because that violates FIFO. It cannot be received after t because that violates $\neg msg(s, t)$. We conclude that such a message cannot exist; therefore, $s.q[s.p] = w'.q[s.p]$.

∎

We note here that $\neg msg(s, t)$ only states that there are no pending *update* messages (request or release messages) in the cut containing s and t; it is okay for other messages, such as acknowledgments, to cross the cut and $\neg msg(s, t)$ to still hold.

The following lemma is crucial in proving the safety property. It says that if t in process $P_{t.p}$ has knowledge of the time at $P_{s.p}$ which is later than the time s made a request, then t has the correct value of s's request timestamp. Intuitively, because knowledge of process $P_{t.p}$

about $P_{s.p}$ can increase only through messages, some message that was sent after the request message has been received by $P_{t.p}$ before t. Using FIFO, we note that the request message must have also been received.

Lemma 6.2 $\forall s, t : s.p \neq t.p : s \not\rightarrow t \land s.q[s.p] < t.v[s.p] \Rightarrow t.q[s.p] = s.q[s.p]$

Proof: From the property of active vectors (Lemma 6.1), it is sufficient to show that $\neg msg(s, t)$ is true, that is, there is no "update" (request or release) message sent before s and received after t. Let $u \prec s$ be such that $u.v[s.p] = s.q[s.p]$, that is, the request was made in the state u. Let the message sent at u be received by $P_{t.p}$ in state w. From the event description it follows that there is no request or release message sent after u and before s. (1)

Since $u.v[u.p] < t.v[u.p]$, from the property of dependency clocks, we get that $u \rightarrow_d t$. Therefore, there exists a message sent at u or after u and received before t. Note that a message sent after u and before s can only be of type ack. From FIFO, it follows that $w \preceq t$. From FIFO, and that the message sent at u is received before t, it follows that $\neg msg(u, t)$. (2)

From (1) and (2), we get $\neg msg(s, t)$.

∎

The remaining theorems prove that the algorithm satisfies the required properties: safety, liveness, and fairness.

Theorem 6.3 (Safety) $s.p \neq t.p \land s\|t \Rightarrow \neg(cs(s) \land cs(t))$.

Proof: We show that $(s\|t) \land cs(s) \land cs(t)$ implies false. Since the predicate is symmetric with respect to s and t, we assume without loss of generality that

    0. $(s.q[s.p], s.p) < (t.q[t.p], t.p)$.

The proof now proceeds as follows:

    1. $(t.q[t.p], t.p) < (t.v[s.p], s.p)$; from $cs(t)$
    2. $(s.q[s.p], s.p) < (t.v[s.p], s.p)$; from 0 and 1
    3. $t.q[s.p] = s.q[s.p]$; from Lemma 6.2, $s \not\rightarrow t$
    4. $(t.q[t.p], t.p) < (t.q[s.p], s.p)$; Since $cs(t)$.
    5. $(t.q[t.p], t.p) < (s.q[s.p], s.p)$; from 3 and 4
    6. false ; from 0 and 5

■

Theorem 6.4 (Liveness) $req(s) \Rightarrow \exists t : s \preceq t \wedge cs(t)$

Proof: $req(s)$ implies that there exists $s_1 \in P_{s.p}$ such that $s_1.v[s.p] = s.q[s.p] \wedge event(s_1) = request$.

Wo show oxistonco of the required t with the following two claims:

Claim 1: $\exists t_1 : \forall j \neq s.p : t_1.v[j] > s.q[s.p] \wedge s.q[s.p] = t_1.q[s.p]$

Claim 2: $\exists t_2 : \forall j \neq s.p : t_2.q[j] > s.q[s.p] \wedge s.q[s.p] = t_2.q[s.p]$

By choosing $t = max(t_1, t_2)$ and verifying that $cs(t)$ holds we get the desired result.

Claim 1 is true because the message sent at s_1 will eventually be acknowledged. By rules of dependency clocks, the value of $v[j]$ for any process P_j will be greater than $s_1.v[s.p]$.

To show claim 2, we show that the number of requests smaller than $s.q[s.p]$ eventually decreases. In particular, the process with the least timestamp will eventually acquire the critical section. When that process releases the critical section, the number of requests smaller than $s.q[s.p]$ will decrease by 1.

To see that the deadlock is not possible, it is sufficient to note that a process waits only for processes with requests that have timestamps smaller than its own and that timestamps have a total order.

■

Theorem 6.5 (Fairness) $(req\_start(s) \wedge req\_start(t) \wedge s \rightarrow t) \Rightarrow (next\_cs(s) \rightarrow next\_cs(t))$

Proof: Left for the reader (see Problem 6.1).

■

Lamport's algorithm requires $3(N-1)$ messages per invocation of the critical section: $N-1$ request messages, $N-1$ acknowledgement messages and $N-1$ release messages. There is a time delay of two serial messages to get permission for the critical section—a request message followed by an acknowledgment. The space overhead per process is the vectors q and v which is $O(N \log m)$ where m is the maximum number of times any process enters the critical section.

6.4   Ricart and Agrawala's Algorithm

Ricart and Agrawala's algorithm uses only $2(N-1)$ messages per invocation of the critical section. It does so by combining the functionality of ack and release messages. Furthermore, it works even when the channels do not satisfy the FIFO property. In this algorithm, a process does not always send back an acknowledgement on receiving a request. It may defer the reply for a later time. The algorithm is stated by the following rules:

- To request a resource, the process sends a timestamped message to all processes.

- On receiving a request from any other process, the process sends an *okay* message if either the process is not interested in the critical section or its own request has a higher timestamp value. Otherwise, that process is kept in a pending queue.

- To release a resource, the process P_i sends *okay* to all the processes in the pending queue.

- Process P_i is granted the resource when it has requested the resource and it has received the *okay* message from every other process in response to its *request* message.

The algorithm is presented formally in Figure 6.5. There are two kinds of messages in the system—*request* messages and *okay* messages. Each process maintains the logical time of its request in the variable *myts*. On receiving any request with a lower timestamp than its own, it replies immediately with *okay*. Otherwise, it adds that process to *pendingQ*. The variable *numOkay* counts the number of *okay* messages received since the request was made.

The above algorithm satisfies safety, liveness, and fairness properties of mutual exclusion. To see the safety property, assume that P_i and P_j are in the critical section concurrently and P_i has the smaller value of the timestamp for its request. P_j can enter the critical section only if it received *okay* for its request. The request made by P_j can only reach P_i after P_i has made its request; otherwise, the timestamp of P_i's request would have been greater because of the rules of the logical clock. From the algorithm, P_i cannot send *okay* unless it has exited from the critical section contradicting our earlier assumption that P_j received *okay* from P_i. Thus the safety property is not violated. The

P_i::
  var
     pendingQ: list of process ids initially *null*;
     myts: integer initially ∞;
     numOkay: integer initially 0;

request:
     $myts := logical\_clock$;
     send *request* with *myts* to all other processes;
     $numOkay := 0$;

receive($u, request$):
     if ($u.myts < myts$) **then**
         send *okay* to process $u.p$;
     else $append(pendingQ, u.p)$;

receive($u, okay$):
     $numOkay := numOkay + 1$;
     if ($numOkay = N - 1$) **then**
         enter_critical_section;

release:
     $myts := \infty$;
     for $j \in pendingQ$ **do**
         send *okay* to the process j;
     $pendingQ := null$;

Figure 6.5: Ricart and Agrawala's algorithm

process with the least timestamp for its request can never be deferred by any other process, and therefore the algorithm also satisfies liveness. Because processes enter the critical section in the order of the timestamps of the requests, the fairness is also true. We leave the formal proof of correctness for the reader.

It is easy to see that every critical section execution requires $N - 1$ *request* messages and $N - 1$ *okay* messages.

6.5   Problems

6.1. Prove Theorem 6.5.

6.2. The mutual exclusion algorithm by Lamport requires that any request message be acknowledged. Under what conditions does a process not need to send an *acknowledgement* message for a *request* message?

6.3. Let there be N processes in a system. Assume that your friend has implemented a mutual exclusion algorithm for this system. Describe an algorithm that will detect violation of the mutual exclusion for any run. Assume that the underlying computation can be modified so that vector clocks are available. Also assume that a process enters the critical section at most m times. What is the number of comparisons of vectors required by your algorithm? Make your algorithm as efficient as possible in terms of the number of comparisons required.

6.4. In this chapter, we have used the happened before model for specification and verification of Lamport's algorithm. Give formal specification of the properties and their proofs using the interleaving model.

6.5. Prove the correctness of Ricart and Agrawala's algorithm formally.

6.6. Some applications require two types of accesses to the critical section—*read* access and *write* access. For these applications, it is reasonable for two *read* accesses to happen concurrently. However, a *write* access cannot happen concurrently with either a *read* access or a *write* access. Modify algorithms presented in this chapter for such applications.

6.7. Show that you can use Lamport's algorithm to build a fault-tolerant distributed server as follows. Each server is modeled as a *deterministic* state machine. All machines start from the same initial state. Then, Lamport's algorithm can be used to ensure that all machines perform all actions in the same order. For this problem, assume that the message channels are FIFO and reliable. The processes may fail; however, failure detection of processes is perfect. Specify the safety and liveness conditions satisfied by your algorithm formally.

*6.8. Extend the algorithm in Problem 6.7 to the case when failure detection is not perfect, that is, the failure detector may declare a process to be failed even when it is alive. Assume that the failure detector never declares a process to be alive when it is dead.

6.6   Bibliographic Remarks

Lamport's algorithm for mutual exclusion first appeared in [Lam78]. The algorithm was presented there as an application of logical clocks. We have followed Garg and Tomlinson [GT94] for proof of correctness of Lamport's algorithm. The number of messages per invocation of the critical section in Lamport's algorithm can be reduced as shown by Ricart and Agrawala [RA81].

Chapter 7

Mutual Exclusion: Tokens and Quorums

Would ye both eat your cake and have your cake? — John Heywood

7.1 Introduction

In this chapter, we present two more methods to resolve conflicts in distributed systems. Token-based algorithms use the auxiliary resource *token* to resolve conflicts in a resource coordination problem. The issue in these algorithms is how the requests for the token are made, maintained, and served. A centralized algorithm is an instance of a token-based algorithm in which the coordinator is responsible for keeping the token. All the requests for the token go to the coordinator. In this chapter, we first discuss such a centralized algorithm for mutual exclusion. A centralized algorithm can usually be converted to a *decentralized* token-based algorithm. We show this conversion for the mutual exclusion problem.

Yet another method to resolve conflicts is via *quorum*. Any process that wants to access the critical section is required to collect a quorum. A simple example is that of majority voting—any process that can collect $\lceil (N + 1)/2 \rceil$ votes is allowed to enter the critical section. We present the notion of *coteries* that can be used to specify and analyze quorum-based systems.

This chapter is organized as follows. Section 7.2 describes a centralized algorithm, and Section 7.3 describes a decentralized algorithm for mutual exclusion. Section 7.4 presents quorum-based systems. The notation used in this chapter is summarized in Figure 7.1.

$Q_1, Q_2, \ldots$	Quorums
C, D	Coteries
V	The total number of votes
R	The size of a read quorum
W	The size of a write quorum
p	The probability of failure of a process
α	Access strategy for a quorum

Figure 7.1: Notation

7.2   Centralized Algorithm

We first motivate the design of the centralized algorithm. As mentioned earlier, the safety and liveness properties are easy to guarantee in a centralized algorithm. The fairness constraint requires that if s and t are two local states corresponding to request events and $s \to t$, then the request s must be honored before the request t. Thus, even if the request t reaches the coordinator before s, the coordinator should be able to infer that there is a pending request from the process $P_{s.p}$ and thus wait for that request to arrive. Because $s \to t$, the state t has the information about the request s. Thus, the process $P_{t.p}$ only needs to relay to the coordinator all the requests that it knows. The coordinator can delay receiving the message t until all requests before t are received. The information about requests known at the state s can be concisely captured using a vector $s.v$ where $s.v[j]$ represents the number of requests made by the process P_j that causally precede the state s.

The algorithm for a client process is shown in Figure 7.2. To request the token, the client simply increments its component in v vector and sends the request with its v vector to P_0, the coordinator process. On receiving the token, the client process is eligible to enter the critical section. To release the critical section, it simply returns the token to P_0. To ensure fairness, processes cooperate by piggybacking v vector on all outgoing messages. When a process receives a program message, it updates its v vector with the componentwise maximum of its old value and the vector received with the message.

The algorithm for the coordinator process is given in Figure 7.3. It maintains a vector $reqdone$ with the interpretation that $reqdone[i]$ equals the number of requests made by P_i that have been fulfilled. It also maintains $reqlist$, which is the list of requests received by P_0 that have not been fulfilled yet. On receiving a request, P_0 appends it to $reqlist$. If it has the token, then it checks for eligible requests and sends the token to one of the eligible processes. A request w is eligible if $w.v$ is at most $reqdone$, that is, there is no request that happened before w and has not been fulfilled yet.

```
P_i::
  var
      v: array[1..N] of integer initially ∀j : v[j] = 0;
      inCS: boolean initially false;

  To request:
      v[i] := v[i] + 1;
      send (request, v) to P_0;

  Upon receive(token) from P_0:
      inCS := true;

  To release:
      send token to P_0;
      inCS := false;

  Upon receive(u): // program message
      v := max(v, u.v);
```

Figure 7.2: A centralized algorithm for client processes

The centralized algorithm is quite economical in terms of the number of messages. It requires only three messages per invocation of the critical section. The algorithm also requires no special action if a client process that does not hold the token fails. However, if the coordinator fails, then a new process is required to be elected to play the role of the coordinator.

P_0::
var
    $reqdone$: array$[1..N]$ of integer initially 0;
    $reqlist$: list of $(pid, reqvector)$ initially $null$;
    $havetoken$: boolean initially $true$;

Upon $receive(u, request)$:
    $append(reqlist, u)$;
    if $havetoken$ **then** $checkreq()$;

Upon $receive(u, token)$:
    $havetoken := true$;
    $checkreq()$;

$checkreq()$:
    $eligible := \{w \in reqlist \mid \forall j : j \neq w.p : w.v[j] \leq reqdone[j]\}$;
    if $eligible \neq \{\}$ **then**
        $w := first(eligible)$;
        $delete(reqlist, w)$;
        $reqdone[w.p] := reqdone[w.p] + 1$;
        send $token$ to $P_{w.p}$
        $havetoken := false$;
    endif

Figure 7.3: A centralized algorithm for the coordinator process

7.2.1 Proof of Correctness

The centralized algorithm is based on a token mechanism. A process can enter the critical section in state s only if $s.hastoken$ is true. We leave it to the reader to verify that

$$(s \neq t) \wedge (s||t) \Rightarrow \neg(s.inCS \wedge t.inCS)$$

To verify liveness, we need to show that

$$s.req \Rightarrow \exists t : s \preceq t \wedge t.inCS$$

If all processes cooperate, then all requests that happened before state s will eventually be satisfied and s will become eligible. This implies that eventually $P_{s.p}$ will be granted the token. Finally, to show fairness, we need to prove that

$$(req\_start(s) \wedge req\_start(t) \wedge s \rightarrow t) \Rightarrow next\_cs(s) \rightarrow next\_cs(t)$$

We leave the proof to the reader.

7.3 An Exercise in Decentralization

In the above algorithm, there is one fixed process P_0 that acts as the coordinator process. In many algorithms, we can replace a coordinator process by a token that moves around in the system. The token carries in it all the data structures required by the coordinator process in the centralized algorithm. The computation that is carried out by the coordinator process is done by the process holding the token. Thus we assume that the token has the following variables.

> $reqdone$: array$[1..N]$ of integer initially 0;
> $reqlist$: list of $(pid, reqvector)$ initially empty;

One difficulty in the above scheme is that in the centralized algorithm, every process knows which process to send the request and release messages. For the token-based algorithm, a process may not know the current location of the token. We handle this problem by requiring a process requesting the token to send the message to all the processes. Releasing a token is simpler because only the process possessing the token can release the token.

Another difficulty in simulating a coordinator by a token is that a message sent to the coordinator is guaranteed to reach the coordinator if channels are reliable. However, a request broadcast may never reach the token if it was made when the token was in transit between two processes. Assume that the token was initially at P_i and then sent to P_j. Also assume that P_k makes a request when the token is in transit. Thus P_i receives the request after it has sent the token and P_j receives the request before it receives the token. We solve this problem by ensuring that the records of the requests made are also maintained by processes. Thus, each process maintains

$myreqlist$: list of ($pid, reqvector$) initially empty;

Whenever the token is received, it is updated with all the entries in the $myreqlist$ that denotes some request that has not been fulfilled yet. The algorithm is shown in Figure 7.4.

The decentralized algorithm takes N messages per critical section invocation—$(N - 1)$ request messages and one token message. Even though the algorithm is decentralized, it is vulnerable to failure of a single process, the one that holds the token.

7.4   Quorum-Based Algorithms

Both centralized and decentralized token-based algorithms are vulnerable to failures of processes holding the token. We now present quorum-based algorithms, which do not have such single points of failure. The main idea behind a quorum-based algorithm is that instead of asking permission to enter the critical section from either just one process as in token-based algorithms, or from all processes, as in timestamp-based algorithms in Chapter 6, the permission is sought from a subset of processes called the $request\ set$. If any two request sets have nonempty intersection, then we are guaranteed that at most one process can have permission to enter the critical section. A simple example of this strategy is that of requiring permission from a majority of processes. In this case, a request set is any subset of processes with at least $\lceil N + 1/2 \rceil$ processes.

Quorum-based algorithms are best studied using the notion of coteries. Let $U = \{u_1, u_2, \ldots, u_n\}$ be a ground set and C be a nonempty family of subsets, called quorums, of U.

P_i::

var

    v: array$[1..N]$ of integer initially $\forall j : v[j] = 0$;

    $inCS$: boolean initially $false$;

    $havetoken$: boolean initially $false$ except for P_0;

    $myreqlist$: list of $(pid, reqvector)$ initially $null$;

To $request$:

    $v[i] := v[i] + 1$;

    send $(request, v)$ to all processes (including itself);

Upon $receive(request, u)$:

    $v := max(v, u.v)$;

    if $(havetoken)$ **then**

        $append(token.reqlist, u)$;

        if not $inCS$ **then** $checkreq()$;

    else $append(myreqlist, u)$;

$receive(u, token)$:

    $inCS := true$;

    $havetoken := true$;

    $append(token.reqlist, \{u \mid (u \in myreqlist) \wedge (u > token.reqdone)\})$;

    $myreqlist := null$;

$release$:

    $inCS := false$;

    $checkreq()$;

$receive(u)$: //program message

    $v := max(v, u.v)$;

$checkreq()$:

    $eligible := \{w \in token.reqlist$ such that

           $\forall j : j \neq w.p : w.v[j] \leq token.reqdone[j]\}$;

    if $eligible \neq \{\}$ **then**

        $w := first(eligible)$;

        $delete(token.reqlist, w)$;

        $token.reqdone[w.p] := token.reqdone[w.p] + 1$;

        send $token$ to $P_{w.p}$;

        $havetoken := false$;

    endif

Figure 7.4: A decentralized token-based algorithm for mutual exclusion

Definition 7.1 (Coterie) $C = \{Q_1, Q_2, \ldots, Q_m\}$ *where for all* $1 \leq i \leq m : Q_i \subseteq U$ *is a coterie under* U *if*

- (Minimality) *No quorum is a subset of another quorum.*

$$\forall i, j : i \neq j : \neg(Q_i \subseteq Q_j)$$

- (Intersection property) *Every two quorums intersect.*

$$\forall i, j : Q_i \cap Q_j \neq \emptyset$$

Let C and D be coteries. C *dominates* D if $C \neq D$ and

$$\forall Q \in D : (\exists Q' \in C : Q' \subseteq Q)$$

A coterie C is *nondominated* if no coterie dominates C. Intuitively, nondominated coteries are in some sense optimal because they cannot be improved by reducing the number of elements in one of the quorums.

There are generally three metrics to compare various quorum systems.

1. *Quorum size:* A small quorum size directly translates into a smaller number of messages for collecting the quorum.

2. *Availability:* This metric is useful in measuring the fault tolerance of a coterie. Even if some processes have failed, the unfailed processes can still function correctly if there is at least one live quorum in the coterie. Availability is defined as the probability that there is at least one quorum in the coterie assuming that each process fails independently with probability p.

3. *Load:* This metric is useful in measuring load on processes due to access by other processes for constructing quorums. Let us define a *strategy* α as the rule that assigns access probability to each quorum. Let $load(i, \alpha, C)$ represent the load on process P_i when strategy α is used for coterie C. Then,

$$load(i, \alpha, C) = \sum_{i \in Q, Q \in C} \alpha(Q).$$

The load of a strategy is defined to be the load on the busiest process and the load of a coterie is the load of the strategy with the smallest load, i.e.,

$$load(C) = \min_{\alpha} \max_{i} load(i, \alpha, C).$$

These metrics are conflicting so that there is no quorum system that is optimal for all metrics. We now give some examples of quorum systems.

7.4.1 Voting Systems

In these quorum systems, each process is assigned a number of votes. Let the total number of votes in the system be V. A quorum is defined to be any subset of processes with a combined number of votes exceeding $V/2$. If each process is assigned a single vote, then such a quorum system is also called a majority voting system.

When applications require *read* or *write* accesses to the critical section, then the voting systems can be generalized to two kinds of quorums—*read* quorums and *write* quorums. These quorums are defined by two parameters R and W such that $R+W > V$ and $W > V/2$. For a subset of processes if the combined number of votes exceeds R, then it is a *read* quorum and if it exceeds W, then it is a *write* quorum.

7.4.2 Crumbling Walls

A crumbling wall is a logical arrangement of processes in rows of possibly different widths. A quorum in a crumbling wall is the union of one full row and a representative from every row below the full rows. For example, consider a system with 9 processes such that P_1 to P_3 are in row 1, P_4 to P_6 are in row 2 and P_7 to P_9 are in row 3. In this system, $\{P_4, P_5, P_6, P_9\}$ is a quorum because it contains the entire second row and a representative, P_9, from the third row. Let $CW(n_1, n_2, \ldots, n_d)$ be a wall with d rows of width n_1, n_2, ..., n_d, respectively. We assume that processes in the wall are numbered sequentially from left to right and top to bottom. Our earlier example of the crumbling wall can be concisely written as $CW(3, 3, 3)$. $CW(1)$ denotes a wall with a single row of width 1. This corresponds to a centralized algorithm. The crumbling wall $CW(1, N-1)$ is called the wheel coterie because it has $N-1$ "spoke" quorums of the form $\{1, i\}$ for $i = 2, \ldots, N$ and one "rim" quorum $\{2, \ldots, N\}$. In a triangular quorum system, processes are arranged in a triangle such that the ith row has i processes. If there are d rows, then each quorum has exactly d processes. In a grid quorum system, $N(= d^2)$ processes are arranged in a grid such that there are d rows each with d processes. A quorum consists of the union of one full row and a representative from every row below the full rows.

Crumbling walls provide a method for analyzing many kinds of quorum systems. The reader is invited to analyze various quorums for availability and load (see Problems 7.9 and 7.10).

It is important to recognize that the simple strategy of getting permission to enter the critical section from one of the quorums can result in a deadlock. In the majority voting system, if two requests gather $N/2$ votes each (for an even value of N), then neither of the requests will be granted. Quorum-based systems require additional messages to ensure that the system is deadlock free. The details of ensuring deadlock freedom are left to the reader (see Problem 7.3).

7.5   Problems

7.1. Simplify the decentralized algorithm for the case when the fairness property is not required.

7.2. **(due to [Ray89])** In the decentralized algorithm, a process is required to send the message to everybody to request the token. Design an algorithm in which all processes are organized in the form of a logical binary tree. The edges in the tree are directed as follows. Each node except the one with the token has exactly one outgoing edge such that if that edge is followed it will lead to the node with the token. Give the actions required for requesting and releasing the critical section. What is the message complexity of your algorithm?

7.3. **(due to [Mae85])** Let all processes be organized in a rectangular grid. We allow a process to enter the critical section only if it has permission from all the processes in its row and its column. A process grants permission to another process only if it has not given permission to some other process. What properties does this algorithm satisfy? What is the message complexity of the algorithm? How will you ensure deadlock-freedom?

7.4. Compare all the algorithms for mutual exclusion discussed in this book using the following metrics: the response time and the number of messages.

7.5. Discuss how you will extend each of the mutual exclusion algorithms to tolerate failure of a process. Assume perfect failure detection of a process.

7.6. Extend all algorithms discussed in this chapter and Chapter 6 to solve k-mutual exclusion problem, in which at most k processes can be in the critical section concurrently.

7.7. **(due to [AA91])** In the tree-based quorum system, processes are organized in a rooted binary tree. A quorum in the system is defined recursively to be either the union of the root and a quorum in one of the two subtrees, or the union of quorums of subtrees. Analyze this coterie for availability and load.

7.8. A crumbling wall $CW(n_1, n_2, \ldots, n_d)$ is a Lovasz coterie iff $n_1 = 1$ and $n_i \geq 2$ for all $i \geq 2$. Show that $CW(n_1, n_2, \ldots, n_d)$ is a nondominated coterie iff it is a Lovasz coterie.

7.9. Assuming that each process fails with probability p, compute the probability that there is no quorum left in a crumbling wall $CW(n_1, n_2, \ldots, n_d)$ with $n_1 = 1$.

7.10. Show that the majority quorum system has load greater than $1/2$ and the triangular quorum system has load of $O(1/\sqrt{N})$.

*7.11. Show that the number of nonisomorphic nondominated crumbling walls over a universe of size $N \geq 3$ is $(N-3)^{th}$ Fibonacci number.

7.6   Bibliographic Remarks

The decentralized token-based algorithm is an extension of an algorithm due to Suzuki and Kasami [SK85]. Suzuki and Kasami's algorithm does not provide fairness. The tree-based algorithm in the problem set is due to Raymond [Ray89]. The use of majority voting systems for distributed control is due to Thomas [Tho79], and the use of weighted voting systems with R and W parameters is due to Gifford [Gif79]. The term *coterie* and the concept of nondominated coteries were introduced by Garcia-Molina and Barbara [GMB85]. Maekawa [Mae85] introduced grid-based quorums and quorums based on finite projective planes. The tree-based quorum in the problem set is due to Agrawal and El-Abbadi [AA91]. The triangular quorum systems are due to Lovasz [Lov73] and Lovasz coteries (problem 7.8) are due to Neilsen [Nei92]. The notion of *crumbling walls* is due to Peleg and Wool [PW95].

Chapter 8

Drinking Philosophers Problem

Bad men live that they may eat and drink, whereas good men eat and drink that they may live. — Socrates

8.1 Introduction

In this chapter, we discuss the dining and the drinking philosophers problems, which are abstractions of many resource allocation problems in a network. The dining problem consists of multiple philosophers who spend their time thinking and eating spaghetti. However, a philosopher requires shared resources, such as forks, to eat spaghetti. We are required to devise a protocol to coordinate access to the shared resources. A computer-minded reader may substitute processes for philosophers and files for forks in this chapter. The task of eating would then correspond to an operation that requires access to shared files.

There are two requirements on the solution of the dining philosophers problem. First, we require mutually exclusive use of shared resources, that is, a shared resource should not be used by more than one process at a time. Second, we want freedom from starvation. Every philosopher (process) should be able to eat (perform its operation) infinitely often.

The crucial problem in resource allocation is that of resolving conflicts. If a set of processes require a resource and only one of them can use it at a time, then there is a conflict that must be resolved in

93

favor of one of these processes. It is clear that if the processes are indistinguishable and the conflict resolution method is completely deterministic, then a conflict resolution is not possible. Hence, we would insist that in every conflicting set of processes, there is at least one distinguished process. This requirement alone is not enough in a realistic system where we would like the conflict resolution to be fair so that every process that needs a resource eventually gets it.

We have already studied one conflict resolution method via logical clocks in Lamport's mutual exclusion algorithm. The processes used logical clocks to resolve access to mutual exclusion. If two requests had the same logical clock value, then process identity was used to break ties. In this chapter, we study another mechanism that resolves conflicts based on location of auxiliary resources. The auxiliary resources are used only for conflict resolution and are not actual resources.

This chapter is organized as follows. We first describe a solution to the dining philosophers problem under the assumption that philosophers are always willing to eat when the resources are available. This solution corresponds to the case when there is heavy load on resource usage. In Section 8.3 we relax this assumption and allow philosophers to think for undetermined amounts of time. Finally, Section 8.4 discusses the drinking philosophers problem, which is a generalization of the dining philosophers problem.

The notation used in this chapter is summarized in Figure 8.1.

H	The conflict graph
v, w	Vertices
x, y	Resources
f	Fork
b	Bottle

Figure 8.1: Notation

8.2 Dining Philosophers—Heavy Load

We describe a simple algorithm called the edge-reversal algorithm that guarantees mutual exclusion and starvation freedom.

We model the problem as an undirected graph called a *conflict graph* in which each node represents a process and an edge between process P_i and P_j denotes that one or more resources are shared between P_i and P_j. Figure 8.2(a) shows the conflict graph for five philosophers. If a process needs all the shared resources for performing its operation, then only one of any two adjacent nodes can perform its operation in any step.

Observe that the conflict graph for a simple mutual exclusion algorithm is a complete graph. Now consider the problem of five dining philosophers sitting around a table such that two adjacent philosophers share a fork. The conflict graph of this problem is a ring on five nodes.

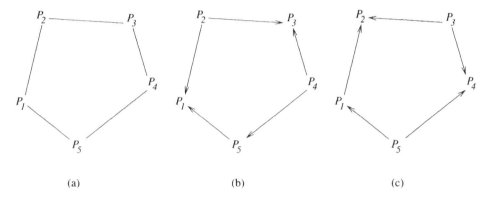

Figure 8.2: (a) Conflict graph (b) An acyclic orientation with P_2 and P_4 as sources (c) Orientation after P_2 and P_4 finish eating

An *orientation* of an undirected graph consists of providing direction to all edges. The edge between P_i and P_j points from P_i to P_j if P_i has precedence over P_j. We say that an orientation is acyclic if the directed graph that results from the orientation is acyclic. Figure 8.2(b) shows an acyclic orientation of the conflict graph. In a directed graph, we call a node a *source* if it does not have any incoming edge. Any finite-directed acyclic graph must have at least one source (see Problem 8.1). In Figure 8.2 processes P_2 and P_4 are sources.

To maintain orientation of an edge, we use the notion of an auxiliary resource, a fork, associated with each edge. Process P_i is considered to have the fork associated with the edge (i, j), if it has precedence over P_j in any conflict resolution.

The algorithm for dining philosophers under the heavy load can be specified by the following two rules.

- **(Eating rule)** A process can eat only if it has all the forks for the edges incident to it, i.e., a process can eat only when it is a source.

- **(Edge reversal)** On finishing the eating session, a process reverses orientations of all the outgoing edges to incoming edges by sending forks to its neighbors.

We have the following lemmas.

Lemma 8.1 *Edge reversal of a source maintains acyclicity of a directed graph.*

Proof: Assume that the vertex v was a source in the original graph, which is acyclic. Any directed cycle created must pass through the vertex v because only the edges connected to v have their orientation changed. But a cycle in the new graph cannot include vertex v because it does not have any outgoing edge in the new graph.

■

As a result, the following theorem holds.

Theorem 8.2 *All properties of resource allocation are satisfied by the edge reversal algorithm.*

Proof:

- *Mutual Exclusion:* If a resource is shared by processes P_i and P_j then there is an edge between P_i and P_j Only one of these processes can be a source in the graph. Hence, a resource is not used by more than one process at a time.

- *Starvation Freedom:* From Lemma 8.1, the graph is always acyclic. This implies that there is always at least one source in the graph. Therefore, there is always at least one process that can perform its operation.

  Let $numsource(i)$ denote the number of times process P_i becomes a source. We show that if process P_i and P_j are connected by a path of length k, then

  $$|numsource(i) - numsource(j)| \leq k$$

  The proof is by induction on k, the length of the shortest path between P_i and P_j. When k is 1, the assertion is clearly true, because once process P_i has become a source, it can become a source only when the edge between P_i to P_j points to P_j again. This can happen only after P_j has become a source and reversed the edges. Assume that the claim is true for all nodes at distance less than k. Now assume that the distance between processes P_i and P_j is k. Consider any intermediate node P_h on the shortest path between P_i and P_j. From the induction hypothesis,

$$|numsource(i) - numsource(h)| \leq dist(i, h)$$

$$|numsource(h) - numsource(j)| \leq dist(h, j)$$

Since $dist(i, j) = dist(i, h) + dist(h, j)$, we get that

$$|numsource(i) - numsource(j)| \leq k$$

∎

8.3 Dining Philosophers—Light Load

In the above algorithm, a process that becomes a source is required to reverse all of its outgoing edges even if it was not interested in eating (using the shared resource). In other words, a process is obligated to perform actions even when it is not interested in eating. We now present a solution that avoids this problem.

The state of a philosopher is determined by the following boolean variables

$$\{thinking, hungry, eating\}.$$

The transition from *thinking* to *hungry* is determined by the philosopher, and the philosopher may stay in the thinking state for an arbitrary amount of time. Once a philosopher is in *hungry* state, it is the responsibility of the algorithm to ensure the transition from the hungry state to the eating state. Once a process is in eating state, it should return to thinking state in a finite amount of time.

There are two main differences from the heavily loaded case. First, we do not require that once a philosopher has finished eating it sends all the forks to its neighbors. This is because its neighbors may be thinking and therefore not interested in eating. Thus we require that if a philosopher is hungry (interested in eating) and does not have the fork, then it should explicitly request the fork. To request the fork,

---

var
    $hungry, eating, thinking$: boolean;
    $fork(f)$, $request(f)$,$dirty(f)$: boolean;
initially
    1. All forks are dirty.
    2. Every fork and request token are held by different philosophers.
    3. H is acyclic.

To request a fork:
    if $hungry$ **and** $request(f)$ **and** $\neg fork(f)$ **then**
        send request token for fork f;
        $request(f) := false$;

Releasing a fork:
    if $request(f)$ **and** $\neg eating$ **and** $dirty(f)$ **then**
        send fork f;
        $dirty(f) := false$;
        $fork(f) := false$;

Upon receiving a request token for fork f:
    $request(f) := true$;

Upon receiving a fork f:
    $fork(f) := true$;

Figure 8.3: An algorithm for dining philosophers problem

we use a request token associated with each fork. Second, we need to distinguish the case when a philosopher has a fork but has not used it from the case when the philosopher has the fork and has used it for eating. This is done conveniently by associating a boolean variable *dirty* with each fork. Once a philosopher has eaten from a fork, it becomes dirty. Before a fork is sent to the neighbor, it is cleaned.

We use the following boolean variables for each process P_i.

- $fork(f)$: Process P_i holds fork f

- $request(f)$: Process P_i holds the request token for fork f

- $dirty(f)$: $fork(f)$ and f is dirty

Our solution is based on keeping an acyclic conflict resolution graph as in the previous section. The philosopher u has priority over the philosopher v if the edge between u and v points to v. The direction of the edge is from u to v if (1) u holds the fork and it is clean, (2) v holds the fork and it is dirty, or (3) the fork is in transit from v to u.

The forks are initially placed so that the conflict resolution graph is initially acyclic. The algorithm ensures that the graph stays acyclic. Observe that when a fork is cleaned before it is sent, the conflict graph does not change. The change in the conflict graph occurs only when a philosopher eats, thereby reversing all edges incident to it. The algorithm for the dining philosophers problem is given in Figure 8.3.

The following lemma shows that the conflict resolution graph is always acyclic.

Lemma 8.3 *Consider the graph H defined by the location of forks and whether they are clean or dirty. H is always acyclic.*

Proof: H is acyclic initially. The only action that changes direction of any edge in the graph is eating (which dirties the fork). A philosopher can eat only when she has all the forks corresponding to the edges that she shares with other philosophers. By the act of eating, all those forks are dirtied and therefore all those edges point toward the philosopher after eating. This transformation cannot create a cycle.

Observe that when a fork is transmitted, it is cleaned before transmission and thus does not result in any change in H.

∎

Lemma 8.4 *A nonhungry philosopher can hold only dirty forks.*

Proof: Initially, all forks are dirty. A philosopher gets a clean fork only when she is hungry. When a philosopher eats, she makes all forks dirty.

■

Theorem 8.5 *Every hungry philosopher eats.*

Proof: First note that a hungry philosopher requesting a fork that is dirty will receive it because of the rule for releasing a fork. Once a philosopher gets the fork, it will continue to hold the fork until it is dirtied by eating.

If a hungry philosopher, say v, makes a request for a clean fork, then we use induction to show that she will get the fork eventually. We use induction on the depth of v, defined as the length of the longest path from a "source" philosopher to v.

The base case is when the depth of v is 0. In this case, v has all the forks and is hungry and therefore will eventually eat and thus make the fork dirty. Assume that our assertion holds for philosophers of depth less than k. Now consider any philosopher v at depth k. Consider any fork that it does not have. If that fork is dirty, then the philosopher holding it will release it (after finishing its eating if necessary). If the fork is clean, then the philosopher holding it, say w, has precedence over v. This implies, by the definition of depth of a process, that w has less depth than v. Therefore, our induction case applies for w. Furthermore, the philosopher w must be hungry, from Lemma 8.4. The philosopher, w, will eventually eat, from the induction hypothesis, and thus make the fork dirty.

■

The above solution is completely symmetric with respect to philosophers. The asymmetry exploited in conflict resolution is due to forks. Also note that a perpetually thinking philosopher will never be disturbed once she is dispossessed of her forks.

8.4   Drinking Philosophers

Now consider a generalization of the dining philosophers problem in which a philosopher does not always require all the resources that it shares with its neighbors. A philosopher may need only a subset of these resources. Moreover, the set of resources required may change from one session to the other. For example, consider the case when processes P_i and P_j share files x and y. First assume that process P_i needs access to x and P_j needs access to y. Because these operations are independent (the intersection of the set of resources used is empty), they can go on concurrently. Assume that after these operations are performed, both processes P_i and P_j need access to both the resources x and y. At this point we need conflict resolution. We will show that by using the solution to the dining philosophers problem we can resolve the conflict.

Note that if philosophers need different sets of resources in different sessions, then it is inefficient to model each shared resource as a fork. In our example, if we had used forks for x and y, processes P_i and P_j would not have been able to do their first operation concurrently even when that is clearly possible. This problem is better modeled as a drinking philosophers problem where each philosopher cycles through the states

$$\{tranquil, thirsty, drinking\}.$$

As in the diners problem, we assume that a philosopher may be tranquil for an arbitrary amount of time but drinking takes a finite amount of time. A philosopher requires a set of resources modeled as bottles for a drinking session, possibly different from one session to the other.

To resolve conflicts for resources we use the solution to the diners problem. We introduce forks as auxiliary resources that are used only for conflict resolution. Only the bottles are real resources. In the algorithm presented below, a philosopher uses forks to eat and bottles to drink. Because in the diners problem, the state transitions thinking-to-hungry and eating-to-thinking are decided by the dining philosopher, we need to specify when these transitions take place. The rules are:

(D1) A thinking, thirsty philosopher becomes hungry in finite time.
(D2) An eating, nonthirsty philosopher starts thinking.

We will later show that each eating period is finite. For that purpose, we will use the following conflict resolution rule.

(D3) The philosopher u, on receiving a request for a bottle by philosopher v, sends the bottle iff

    1. u does not need the bottle, or

var
    $thirsty, drinking, tranquil$: boolean;
    $bot(b)$, $request(b), need(b)$: boolean;
    initially
        bottle and its request token are held by different philosophers.

To request a bottle b:
    if $thirsty$, $request(b)$, $need(b)$, $\neg bot(b)$ **then**
        send request token for bottle b;
        $request(b) := false$;

To release a bottle b:
    if $request(b), bot(b)$ **then**
        if $\neg$ [$need(b)$ and $((state = drinking)$ or $fork(f))$] **then**
            send bottle b;
            $bot(b) := false$;

Upon receiving a request token for bottle b:
    $request(b) := true$;

Upon receiving a bottle b:
    $bot(b) := true$;

Figure 8.4: An algorithm for drinking philosophers problem

2. u is not drinking and does not hold the fork for the edge (u, v).

Thus the decision to send the bottle can be made locally by u. Observe that the decision to release the bottle does not depend on the precedence in the acyclic graph, but only on the presence of a fork. Despite this, the algorithm is fair. This is because if u is thirsty, then she will request the fork from v. After u gets the fork, the algorithm ensures that the conflict between u and v is resolved in u's favor. The algorithm is shown in Figure 8.4.

We first show that the state transitions of the dining philosophers problem are maintained by our rules.

Lemma 8.6 *Every eating period is finite.*

Proof: If an eating philosopher is nonthirsty, she completes eating. If philosopher u is eating, she holds all forks. If she has a bottle that she needs, she will not release it until she completes drinking. This follows from the conflict resolution rule. If she does not have any bottle, her request for the bottle will always be honored because she holds the fork. Thus she will get all the bottles in finite time. This means she can drink (for a finite time), after which she must become tranquil. Then, from (D2), philosopher u must stop eating in finite time.

∎

It follows that the diners algorithm is applicable and therefore every hungry philosopher starts eating in finite time. Now the following is easy.

Theorem 8.7 *Every thirsty philosopher drinks in finite time.*

Proof: A thirsty philosopher is either thinking, hungry, or eating. A thinking, thirsty philosopher becomes hungry in finite time. From the diners problem, we know that a hungry philosopher will eat in finite time. Because every eating period is finite and is terminated only after drinking, the result follows.

∎

Note that, in the above algorithm, eating is not necessary before drinking. A philosopher who has all the necessary bottles is free to drink from them whenever she is thirsty. Eating is required only when a philosopher needs bottles from other philosophers, that is, when there is a conflict. Also note that a tranquil philosopher is never disturbed once she has relinquished all her forks and bottles.

8.5 Problems

8.1. Show that any finite directed acyclic graph has at least one source.

8.2. When can you combine the request token message with a fork message? With this optimization, show that a philosopher with d neighbors needs to send or receive at most $2d$ messages before making transition from hungry state to eating state.

8.3. Consider the following synchronous version of the edge reversal algorithm. At time step 0, the graph of processes has an acyclic orientation. At each time step, all sources reverse all outgoing edges to incoming. Since there are only finite orientations, the orientation repeats after a period. (a) Show that every node becomes a source an equal number of times in a period. (b) An orientation is considered periodic if on following the synchronous algorithm it is repeated. Define the concurrency measure of a periodic acyclic orientation ω as the ratio of the number of times every node becomes a source and the length of the period. Give the best and the worst values for a ring.

*8.4. Show that the problem of determining periodic acyclic orientation (see Problem 8.3) that maximizes concurrency is NP-hard.

8.5. For the drinking philosophers algorithm show that (a) A bottle b can travel at most twice between neighbors before one of them drinks from it. (b) There are at most $4qd$ message transmissions for q drinking sessions among all philosophers, where d is the maximum number of neighbors for any philosopher.

8.6. Show that the solution to the dining problem does not deny the possibility of simultaneous eating from different forks by different philosophers. Similarly, show that the the solution to the drinking philosophers problem does not deny the possibility of simultaneous drinking from different bottles by different philosophers.

8.6 Bibliographic Remarks

The problem of determining initial acyclic orientation that maximizes concurrency is NP-hard [BG89]. The discussion of the drinking philoso-

pher algorithm is from Chandy and Misra [CM84]. Other work on re-
source allocation based on the drinking philosopher problem includes
Styer and Peterson [SP98], Choy and Singh [CS92], and Awerbuch and
Saks [AS90].

Chapter 9

Leader Election

To lead the people, walk behind them. — Lao-Tzu

9.1 Introduction

Many distributed systems superimpose a logical ring topology on the underlying network to execute control functions. An important control function is that of electing a leader process. The leader can serve as a coordinator for centralized algorithms for problems such as mutual exclusion. Electing a leader in a ring can also be viewed as the problem of breaking symmetry in a system. For example, once a deadlock is detected in the form of a cycle we may wish to remove one of the nodes in the cycle to remove the deadlock. This can be achieved by electing the leader.

The leader election problem is similar to the mutual exclusion problem discussed in Chapters 6 and 7. In both problems we are interested in choosing one of the processes as a privileged process. Coordinator-based or token-based solutions for mutual exclusion are not applicable for the leader election problem, because deciding which process can serve as the coordinator or has the token is precisely the leader election problem. If processes have unique identifiers and the underlying communication network is completely connected, then we can apply Lamport's mutual exclusion algorithm to determine the leader—the first process to enter the critical section is deemed as the leader. However, this algorithm requires every process to communicate with every other process in the worst case. We will explore more efficient algorithms for the ring topology. In Chapter 18, we discuss leader elections in general graphs.

Formally, the leader election problem can be stated as follows. There is a ring of N processes. Each process has boolean variables *done* and *leaderflag*, which are initially false for all processes. The *done* variable is set when the process knows that the leader election has finished. The *leaderflag* variable is set when the process knows that it is the leader. The safety property required is that at most one process has its *leaderflag* set to true, i.e.,

$$\forall i, j : i \neq j : \neg(leaderflag(i) \land leaderflag(j))$$

The liveness property required is that eventually all processes should have their *done* variable set to true and at least one process has its *leaderflag* variable set to true, i.e.,

$$\forall i : done(i) \land \exists j : leaderflag(j)$$

This chapter is organized as follows. Section 9.2 shows that there is no deterministic algorithm to elect the leader in an anonymous ring. Section 9.3 gives a $O(N^2)$ algorithm due to Chang and Roberts, and Section 9.4 gives a $O(N \log N)$ algorithm due to Hirschberg and Sinclair for election in a ring.

The notation used in this chapter is summarized in Figure 9.1.

N	The number of processes
$P_1, \ldots, P_N$	Processes
i, j	Process ids
r	The round number

Figure 9.1: Notation

9.2 Anonymous Rings

A ring is considered anonymous if processes in the ring do not have unique identifiers. Furthermore, every process has an identical state machine with the same initial state.

It is not difficult to see that there is no deterministic algorithm for leader election in an anonymous ring. The reason is that we have complete symmetry initially—no process is distinguishable from other processes. Formally,

Theorem 9.1 *There is no deterministic algorithm for leader election in an anonymous ring with $N > 1$ processes.*

Proof: For any algorithm that maintains the safety property, we show an infinite execution in which liveness is violated. Initially the system is in a symmetric state. Since the conjunction of the safety and liveness properties implies asymmetry because there is a unique leader, we know that the system can never terminate in a symmetric state. Thus the algorithm has not terminated in the initial state. We now show an execution that moves the system from one symmetric state to the other. Assume that any process in the ring takes a step. By symmetry, this step is possible at all processes. Thus in the adversarial execution all processes take the same step. Since the algorithm is deterministic, the system must again reach a symmetric state. Therefore, the system could not have terminated (i.e., the leader could not have been elected yet). We can repeat this procedure forever.

■

Observe that our proof uses the fact that the algorithm is deterministic. A randomized algorithm can solve the leader election problem in expected finite time (see Problem 9.1).

9.3 Chang-Roberts Algorithm

Now assume that each process has a unique identifier. In such a system a leader can be elected by a very simple algorithm due to Chang and Roberts. The algorithm ensures that the process with the maximum identifier gets elected as the leader. In the algorithm shown in Figure 9.2, every process sends messages only to its left neighbor and receives messages from right neighbors. A process can send *election* message along with its identifier to its left, if it has not seen any message with a higher identifier than its own identifier. It also forwards any message that has an identifier greater than its own; otherwise, it swallows that message. If a process receives its own message, then it declares itself as the leader by sending a *leader* message.

In the algorithm, one or more processes may spontaneously wake up and initiate the election. When a process wakes up, either spontaneously or on receiving a message, it first executes the wake up procedure before receiving the message. A process knows that the election is done when *leaderid* is not *null*. It is left for the reader to verify that the algorithm satisfies the safety and liveness properties with the following definitions.

$$done(i) \equiv (P_i.leaderid \neq null)$$

$$leaderflag(i) \equiv (P_i.leaderid = i).$$

```
P_i::
  var
        myid: integer ;
        awake: boolean initially false;
        leaderid: integer initially null;

  To initiate election:
        send (election, myid) to P_{i-1};
        awake := true;

  Upon receiving a message (election, j):
        if (j > myid) then
            send (election, j) to P_{i-1};
        else if (j = myid) then
            send (leader, myid) to P_{i-1};
        else if ((j < myid) ∧ ¬awake) then
            send (election, myid) to P_{i-1};
        awake := true;

  Upon receiving a message (leader, j):
        leaderid := j;
        if (j ≠ myid) then send(leader, j) to P_{i-1};
```

Figure 9.2: The leader election algorithm at P_i

The worst case of the above algorithm is when N processes with identifiers $1 \ldots N$ are arranged clockwise in decreasing order (see Figure 9.3). The message initiated by process j will travel j processes before

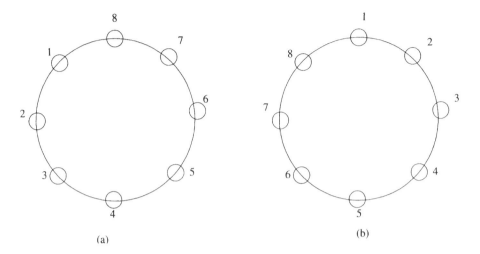

Figure 9.3: (a) The configuration for the worst case (b) The configuration for the best case

it is swallowed by a larger process. Thus the total number of *election* messages in the worst case is

$$\sum_{j=1}^{j=N} j = O(N^2).$$

In addition, there are N *leader* messages. The best case is when the same identifiers are arranged clockwise in the increasing order. In that case, only $O(N)$ election messages are required. On an average, the algorithm requires $O(N \log N)$ messages (see Problem 9.2).

9.4 Hirschberg-Sinclair Algorithm

In this section we assume that the ring is bidirectional so that messages can be sent to the left or the right neighbor. The main idea of the algorithm is to carry out elections on increasingly larger sets. The algorithm works in asynchronous rounds such that a process P_i tries to elect itself in round r. Only processes that win their election in round r can proceed to round $r + 1$. The invariant satisfied by the algorithm is that process P_i is a leader in round r iff P_i has the largest identifier of all nodes that are at distance 2^r or less from P_i. It follows that any two leaders after round r must be at least 2^r distance apart. In other words, after round r, there are at most $N/(2^r + 1)$ leaders. With each round, the number of leaders decreases, and in $O(\log N)$ rounds there is exactly one leader. It can be shown by using induction that there are at most $O(N)$ messages per round, which gives us a bound of $O(N \log N)$. The details of the algorithm and its proof of correctness are left as exercises.

9.5   Problems

9.1. An algorithm on a ring is considered *nonuniform* if every process knows the total number of processes in the ring. Show that there exists a randomized nonuniform algorithm to elect a leader on an anonymous ring that terminates with probability 1. (Hint: Consider an algorithm with rounds in which initially all processes are eligible. In each round, an eligible process draws at random from $0 \ldots m$ (where $m > 0$). The subset of processes that draw the maximum element from the set selected is eligible for the next round. If there is exactly one eligible process, then the algorithm terminates. Analyze the expected number of rounds as a function of N and m).

9.2. Show that the Chang-Roberts algorithm requires $O(N \log N)$ messages on average.

9.3. Modify the Chang-Roberts algorithm such that a process keeps track of *maxid*, the largest identifier it has seen so far. It swallows any message with any identifier that is smaller than *maxid*. What are the worst and the expected number of messages for this variant of the algorithm?

9.4. Give an $O(N \log N)$ algorithm for leader election on a bidirectional ring.

*9.5. Give an $O(N \log N)$ algorithm for leader election on a unidirectional ring.

*9.6. Show that any comparison-based algorithm that elects a leader in a ring of size N has an execution that takes $\Omega(N \log N)$ messages.

9.6 Bibliographic Remarks

The impossibility result on anonymous rings is due to Angluin [Ang80]. The $O(N^2)$ algorithm is due to Chang and Roberts [CR79]. The $O(N \log N)$ algorithm discussed in the chapter is due to Hirschberg and Sinclair [HS80]. Dolev, Klawe and Rodeh [DKR82] and Peterson [Pet82] have presented an $O(N \log N)$ algorithm for unidirectional rings. For lower bounds of $\Omega(N \log N)$ see Burns [Bur80] and Pachl, Korach, and Rotem [PKR82].

Chapter 10

Global State

We know what we are, but know not what we may be. — *William Shakespeare*

10.1 Introduction

One of the difficulties in a distributed system is that no process has access to the global state of the system, that is, it is impossible for a process to know the current global state of the system (unless the computation is frozen). For many applications, it is sufficient to capture a global state that happened in the *past* instead of the *current* global state. For example, in case of a failure the system can restart from such a global state. As another example, suppose that we were interested in monitoring the system for the property that the token in the system has been lost. This property is *stable*, that is, once it is true it stays true forever; therefore, we can check this property on an old global state. If the token is found to be missing in the old global state, then we can conclude that the token is also missing in the current global state. An algorithm that captures a global state is called a *global snapshot algorithm*.

A global snapshot algorithm provides us a useful tool in building distributed systems. Computing a global snapshot is beautifully exemplified by Chandy and Lamport as the problem of taking a picture of a big scene such as a sky filled with birds. The scene is so big that it cannot be captured by a single photograph, and therefore multiple photographs must be taken and composed together to form the global picture. The multiple photographs cannot be taken at the same time instant because there is no shared physical clock in a distributed system. Furthermore, the act of taking a picture cannot change the behavior of the underlying process. Thus birds may fly from one part of the sky to the other while the local pictures are being taken. Despite these problems, we require that the composite picture should be meaningful. For example, it should give us an accurate count of the number of birds. We first need to define what is meant by "meaningful" global state.

Consider the following definition of a global state: A *global state* is a set of local states that occur simultaneously. This definition is based on physical time. We use the phrase "time-based model" to refer to such a definition. A different definition of a global state is possible based on the "happened before model." In the happened before model, a global state is a set of local states that are all concurrent with each other. By concurrent, we mean that no two states have a happened before relationship with each other. A global state in the time-based model is also a global state in the happened before model; if two states occur simultaneously, then they cannot have any happened before relationship. However, the converse is not true; two concurrent states may or may not occur simultaneously in a given execution.

We choose to use the definition for the global state from the happened before model for two reasons. First, it is impossible to determine whether a given global state occurs in the time-based model without access to perfectly synchronized local clocks. For example, the statement "there exists a global state in which more than two processes have access to the critical section" cannot be verified in the time-based model. In the happened before model, however, it is possible to determine whether a given global state occurs. Second, program properties that are of interest are often more simply stated in the happened before model than in the time-based model, which makes them easier to understand and manipulate. This simplicity and elegance is gained because the happened before model inherently accounts for different execution schedules. For example, an execution that does not violate mutual exclusion in the time-based model may do so with a different execution schedule. This problem is avoided in the happened before model.

It is instructive to observe that a consistent global state is not simply a product of local states. To appreciate this, consider a distributed database for a banking application. Assume for simplicity that there

are only two sites which keep the accounts for a customer. Also assume
that the customer has $500 at the first site and $300 at the second site.
In the absence of any communication between these sites, the total
money of the customer can be easily computed to be $800. However,
if there is a transfer of $200 from site A to site B, and a simple pro-
cedure is used to add up the accounts, we may falsely report that the
customer has a total of $1000 in his accounts (to the chagrin of the
bank). This happens when the value at the first site is used before the
transfer and the value at the second site after the transfer. It is easily
seen that these two states are not concurrent. Note that $1,000 cannot
be justified even by the messages in transit (or, that "the check is in
the mail").

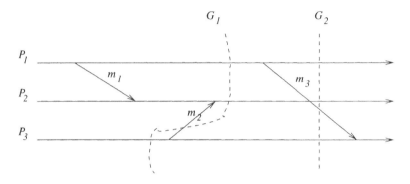

Figure 10.1: Consistent and inconsistent cuts

Figure 10.1 depicts a distributed computation. The dashed lines
labeled G_1 and G_2 represent global states that consist of local states
where G_1 and G_2 intersect P_1, P_2, and P_3. Because a global state
can be visualized in such a figure as a *cut* across the computation,
the term "cut" and "global snapshot" are used interchangeably with
"global state." The cut G_1 in this computation is not consistent because it records the message m_2 as having been received but not sent.
This is clearly impossible. The cut G_2 is consistent. The message m_3
in this cut has been sent but not yet received. Thus it is a part of the
channel from process P_1 to P_3. Our example of the distributed database
illustrates the importance of recording only the consistent cuts.

This chapter is organized as follows. Section 10.2 defines the concept of consistent cuts and shows that the set of consistent cuts forms a
distributive lattice. Section 10.3 shows that any consistent subcut can
be extended to a consistent cut in a deposet. Section 10.4 describes

Chandy and Lamport's algorithm for computing a consistent cut or a global snapshot. Finally, Section 10.5 gives application of the global snapshot algorithm.

The notation used in this chapter is summarized in Figure 10.2.

S	The deposet
S_i	The set of states on P_i
$D(S)$	The set of all cuts
$C(S)$	The set of all consistent cuts
G, H, K	Cuts
s, t	Local states

Figure 10.2: Notation

10.2 Consistent Cuts

We use the model of deposet discussed earlier. An important concept for deposets is that of a consistent cut. A *cut* is a subset of the deposet S containing exactly one state from each sequence S_i. We now define the relation $\leq$ for cuts. Let $D(S)$ be the set of all cuts for deposet S. We use the index i to range over all processes in the system, i.e., $i \in \{1 \ldots N\}$. For two cuts $G, H \in D(S)$, we say that $G \leq H$ iff $\forall i : G[i] \preceq H[i]$ where $G[i] \in S_i$ and $H[i] \in S_i$ are the states from process P_i in cuts G and H, respectively. The following theorem is an easy consequence of the definitions.

Theorem 10.1 *For any deposet S, $(D(S), \leq)$ is a distributive lattice.*

Proof: Let G and H be two cuts. Consider the cut K defined by

$$\forall i : K[i] = min(G[i], H[i]).$$

It is easy to see that K is well defined and always exists. It can be verified that it is the infimum of G and H. Similarly, the supremum of G and H can be defined as the componentwise maximum. Furthermore, it can be verified that the infimum distributes over the supremum (and vice versa) for this lattice.

■

Definition 10.2 (Consistent subcut) *A subset $G \subset S$ is a consistent subcut if and only if $\forall s, t \in G : s \| t$.*

Definition 10.3 (Consistent cut) *A subset $G \subset S$ is a consistent cut (or a consistent global state) if and only if $\forall s, t \in G : s \| t$ and $|G| = N$.*

A consistent cut G includes exactly one state from each S_i.

The following theorem says that given two consistent cuts, their least upper bound and their greatest lower bound are also consistent.

Theorem 10.4 *For any deposet S, let $C(S)$ be the set of consistent cuts of S. Then, $(C(S), \leq)$ is a sublattice of $(D(S), \leq)$.*

Proof: Consider K defined as

$$\forall i : K[i] = min(G[i], H[i]).$$

To show that K is consistent, it is sufficient to show that $K[i] \| K[j]$ for any two distinct process indices i and j. By symmetry it is sufficient to show that $K[i] \not\rightarrow K[j]$. Without loss of generality, let $K[i] = G[i]$. If $K[j] = G[j]$, then $K[i] \not\rightarrow K[j]$ follows from consistency of G. If $K[j] = H[j]$, then $K[i] \not\rightarrow K[j]$ follows from $H[j] \leq G[j]$ and $G[i] \not\rightarrow G[j]$.

Similarly, it can be verified that the supremum cut of G and H is consistent.

∎

10.3   Consistent Subcuts

We now study the properties of a consistent subcut of a deposet. A consequence of the definition of a deposet is the following.

Lemma 10.5 *For any state s and any process P_i, there exists a nonempty sequence of consecutive states called the " interval concurrent to s on P_i" and denoted by $I_i(s)$ such that:*

1. *$I_i(s) \subseteq S_i$ — i.e., the interval consists of only states from process P_i, and*

2. *$\forall t \in I_i(s) : t \| s$ — i.e., all states in the interval are concurrent with s.*

Proof: If s is on P_i, then the lemma is trivially true. The interval consists of exactly the set $\{s\}$ (which is concurrent with itself). So we assume that s is not on P_i. Define $I_i(s).lo = \min\{v \mid v \in S_i \wedge v \not\to s\}$. This is well-defined since $final(i) \not\to s$ due to (D2) (see Definition 2.4 of a deposet in Chapter 2). Similarly, on account of (D1), we can define $I_i(s).hi = \max\{v \mid v \in S_i \wedge s \not\to v\}$.

We show that $I_i(s).lo \preceq I_i(s).hi$. If not, we do a case analysis.

Case 1: There exists $v : I_i(s).hi \prec v \prec I_i(s).lo$.

Since $v \prec I_i(s).lo$ implies $v \to s$ and $I_i(s).hi \prec v$ implies $s \to v$, we get a contradiction $(v \to v)$.

Case 2: $I_i(s).hi \prec_{im} I_i(s).lo$.

From the definition of $I_i(s).lo$, it is easy to see that there must be a message sent from the state previous to $I_i(s).lo$. Similarly, from the definition of $I_i(s).hi$, there exists a message received just after $I_i(s).hi$. However, (D3) prohibits both sending and receiving messages between two successive states. Thus this case is also not possible.

From the above discussion it follows that $I_i(s).lo \preceq I_i(s).hi$. Furthermore, for any state t such that $I_i(s).lo \preceq t \preceq I_i(s).hi$, $t \not\to s$ and $s \not\to t$ holds.

■

The above lemma is used in proving the following property of subcuts.

Theorem 10.6 *Any consistent subset $G \subset S$ can be extended to a consistent cut, that is, $\forall G : G \subset S : consistent(G) \Rightarrow (\exists H : G \subseteq H : consistent(H) \wedge |H| = N)$.*

Proof: It is sufficient to show that when $|G| < N$, there exists a cut $H \supset G$ such that $consistent(H)$ and $|H| = |G| + 1$. Consider any process P_i that does not contribute a state to G. We will show that there exists a state in S_i that is concurrent with all states in G. Let s and t be two distinct states in G. We show that $I_i(s) \cap I_i(t) \neq \emptyset$. If not, without loss of generality assume that $I_i(s).hi \prec I_i(t).lo$. As in the proof of Lemma 10.5, it follows that there exists at least one state, say v, between $I_i(s).hi$ and $I_i(t).lo$ (due to (D3)). This implies that $s \to v$ (because $I_i(s).hi$ precedes v) and $v \to t$ (because v precedes $I_i(t).lo$). Thus $s \to t$, a contradiction with $consistent(G)$. Therefore, $I_i(s) \cap I_i(t) \neq \emptyset$.

Because any interval $I_i(s)$ is a total order, it follows that:

$$\bigcap_{s \in G} I_i(s) \neq \emptyset$$

We now choose any state in $\bigcap_{s \in G} I_i(s)$ to extend G.

∎

The above property allows us to restrict our attention to a consistent *subcut* rather than a consistent *cut*. We call the above theorem the *subcut extension theorem*.

10.4 Global Snapshot Algorithm

In this section, we describe an algorithm to take a global snapshot of a distributed system. The algorithm computes a consistent cut or a consistent subcut as desired. The computation of the snapshot is initiated by one or more processes. We assume that all channels are unidirectional and satisfy the FIFO property. Assuming that channels are unidirectional is not restrictive because a bidirectional channel can simply be modeled by using two unidirectional channels. The assumption that channels are FIFO is essential to the correctness of the algorithm as explained later.

The algorithm is shown in Figure 10.4. We associate with each process a variable called *color* that is either white or red. Intuitively, the computed global snapshot corresponds to the state of the system just before the processes turn red. All processes are initially white. After recording the local state, a process turns red. Thus the state of a local process is simply the state just before it turned red.

There are two difficulties in the design of rules for changing the color for the global snapshot algorithm. First, we need to ensure that the recorded local states are mutually concurrent. Second, we also need a mechanism to capture the state of the channels. To address these difficulties, the algorithm relies on a special message called a *marker*. Once a process turns red, it is required to send a *marker* along all its outgoing channels before it sends out any message. A process is required to turn *red* on receiving a marker if it has not already done so. Since channels are FIFO, the above rule guarantees that no white process ever receives a message sent by a red process. This in turn guarantees that local states are mutually concurrent.

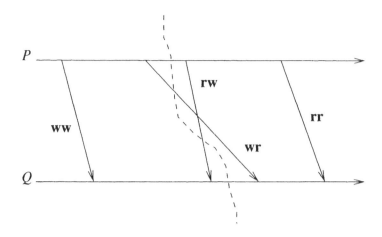

Figure 10.3: Classification of messages

Now let us turn our attention to the problem of computing states of the channels. Figure 10.3 shows that messages in the presence of colors can be of four types:

1. (**ww messages**) These are the messages sent by a white process to a white process. These messages correspond to the messages sent and received before the global snapshot.

2. (**rr messages**) These are the messages sent by a red process to a red process. These messages correspond to the messages sent and received after the global snapshot.

3. (**rw messages**) These are the messages sent by a red process received by a white process. In the figure, they cross the global snapshot in the backward direction. The presence of any such message makes the global snapshot inconsistent. The reader should verify that such messages are not possible if a *marker* is used.

4. (**wr messages**) These are the messages sent by a white process received by a red process. These messages cross the global snapshot, or cut, in the forward direction and form the state of the channel in the global snapshot because they are in transit when the snapshot is taken.

To record the state of the channel, P_j starts recording all messages it receives from P_i after turning red. Since P_i sends a marker to P_j

on turning red, the arrival of the marker at P_j from P_i indicates that there will not be any further white messages from P_i sent to P_j. It can, therefore, stop recording messages once it has received the marker.

The program shown in Figure 10.4 uses $chan[k]$ to record the state of the kth incoming channel and $closed[k]$ to stop recording messages along that channel. In the program, we say that P_j is a *neighbor* of P_i if there is a channel from P_i to P_j.

```
P_i::
  var
      color: {white, red} initially white;
      // assume k incoming channels
      chan: array[1..k] of queues of messages initially null;
      closed: array[1..k] of boolean initially false;

  turn_red() enabled if (color = white):
      save_local_state;
      color := red;
      send (marker) to all neighbors;

  Upon receive(marker) on incoming channel j:
      if (color = white) then
          turn_red();
      closed[j] := true;

  Upon receive(program_message) on incoming channel j:
      if (color = red) ∧ ¬closed[j] then // append the message
          chan[j] := append(chan[j], program_message);
```

Figure 10.4: Chandy and Lamport's snapshot algorithm

We show some elementary properties of the above program. We first define an ordering between the colors white and red by defining the color white to be less than the color red. Now observe that all events maintain the monotonicity of *color*. Thus

Lemma 10.7 (Monotonicity of *color***)** $\forall s, t : s \rightarrow t \Rightarrow s.color \leq t.color$.

Proof: Use induction on $\rightarrow$ and FIFO.

$\blacksquare$

Moreover, any change in the value of *color* must be reported to all neighbors. On receiving any such notification, a process is required to update its own color. This may result in additional messages because of the semantics of the event *turn_red*. The net result is that if one process turns red, all processes that can be reached directly or indirectly from that process also turn red. Thus if any process turns red, all other processes will also eventually turn red.

We now show that the recorded states are concurrent. For any state s such that $s.color = red$, let $rstate(s)$ represent the maximum state in that process that is colored white. This state corresponds to the recorded state of the process $s.p$. Thus

$$rstate(s) = max\{t \mid t \preceq s, t.color = white\}$$

We use $next(u)$ to represent the state immediately following u. Recall that $\rightarrow_d$ represents direct dependency.

Theorem 10.8 (Safety)
$\forall s, t : s.color = red \wedge t.color = red \Rightarrow rstate(s)\|rstate(t)$.

Proof: Let $u = rstate(s)$ and $v = rstate(t)$. States u and v are well-defined because $s.color$ and $t.color$ are red. Note that it is sufficient to show that $u \rightarrow v \Rightarrow false$. We now do a case analysis:
Case 1: $next(u) \rightarrow v$
By definition of u, $next(u).color = red$. By monotonicity of color, we get that $v.color = red$, a contradiction.
Case 2: $\exists w : u \rightarrow_d w \wedge w \rightarrow v$.
Because $u.color < next(u).color$, from the program text we know that the marker message is sent from u. Thus from FIFO it follows that $w.color = red$. This again implies that $v.color = red$.

$\blacksquare$

The following lemma shows that the state of the channel recorded between process P_i and process P_j contains exactly those messages that are sent by P_i in the white state and received by P_j in the red state.

Theorem 10.9 (Safety) *If both s and t are red, and the channel k from $P_{s.p}$ to $P_{t.p}$ is closed at t, then $t.chan[k]$ contains precisely those messages that are sent before the recorded state in $P_{s.p}$ and are received after the recorded state in $P_{t.p}$.*

Proof: A process begins recording messages only after turning red; therefore, all messages recorded in $t.chan[k]$ must have been received after the recorded state in $P_{t.p}$. A process stops recording messages on receiving a marker along the channel. Since the marker is sent on recording the local state and channels are FIFO, only those messages are recorded that are sent before the recorded state in $P_{s.p}$.

■

The program also satisfies the following liveness property. We use the notation:

$$s.done \stackrel{\text{def}}{=} \forall k : s.closed[k] \ \wedge \ s.color = red.$$

Theorem 10.10 (Liveness) *Assume that the graph corresponding to the neighbor relation is strongly connected.*
$\exists s : s.color = red \Rightarrow \forall j : (\exists t \in P_j : t.done).$

Proof: Left for the reader.

■

The above algorithm requires that a marker be sent along all channels. Thus it has an overhead of E messages where E is the number of unidirectional channels in the system. We have not discussed the overhead required to combine local snapshots into a global snapshot. A simple method would be for all processes to send their local snapshots to a predetermined process, say P_0.

10.5 Application: Detecting Stable Properties

Computation of a global snapshot is useful in many contexts. It can be be used to detect a stable property of a distributed computation. To define stable predicates we use the notion of the reachability of one global state from another. For two global states G and H, we say that $G \leq H$ if H is reachable from G.

Definition 10.11 (stable predicates) *Let $C(S)$ be the set of all consistent global states of computation. A predicate B defined on $C(S)$ is called stable iff $\forall G, H \in C(S) : G \leq H$ implies $B(G) \Rightarrow B(H)$.*

In other words, a property B is stable if once it becomes true, it stays true. Some examples of stable properties are deadlock, termination, and loss of a token. Once a system has deadlocked or terminated, it remains in that state. A simple algorithm to detect a stable property is as follows. Compute a global snapshot G. If the property B is true in the state G, then we are done. Otherwise, we repeat the process after some delay. It is easily seen that if the stable property ever becomes true, the algorithm will detect it. Conversely, if the algorithm detects that some stable property B is true, then the property must have become true in the past (and is therefore also true currently).

The following theorem precisely captures the property of the recorded state.

Theorem 10.12 *If the global snapshot computation was started in the global state G_i, the algorithm finished by the global state G_f, and the recorded state is G_*, then the following is true.*

1. $B(G_*) \Rightarrow B(G_f)$

2. $\neg B(G_*) \Rightarrow \neg B(G_i)$

Proof: From stability of B and that $G_i \leq G_* \leq G_f$.

∎

Note that the converse of (1) and (2) may not hold.

The global snapshot algorithm can also be used for providing fault tolerance in distributed systems. On failure, the system can be restarted from the last snapshot. Finally, snapshots can also be used for distributed debugging. Inspection of intermediate snapshots may sometimes reveal the source of an error.

At this point it is important to observe some limitations of the snapshot algorithm for detection of global properties.

- The algorithm is not useful for unstable predicates. An unstable predicate may turn true only between two snapshots.

- In many applications (such as debugging), it is desirable to compute the least global state that satisfies some given predicate. The snapshot algorithm cannot be used for this purpose.

- The algorithm may result in an excessive overhead depending on the frequency of snapshots. A process in Chandy and Lamport's algorithm is forced to take a local snapshot upon receiving a marker even if it knows that the global snapshot that includes its local snapshot cannot satisfy the predicate being detected. For example, suppose that the property being detected is termination. Clearly, if a process is not terminated then the entire system could not have terminated. In this case, computation of the global snapshot is a wasted effort.

10.6 Problems

10.1. In an event-based model of a computation $(E, \rightarrow)$, with total order $\prec$ on events in a single process, we define a *cut* as any subset $F \subseteq E$ such that

$$f \in F \land e \prec f \Rightarrow e \in F.$$

Let a *consistent cut* be any subset $F \subseteq E$ such that

$$f \in F \land e \rightarrow f \Rightarrow e \in F.$$

Show that the set of cuts and consistent cuts form distributive lattices under the $\subseteq$ order between two cuts.

10.2. Prove Lemma 10.7.

10.3. Prove Theorem 10.10.

10.4. Let $(S, \prec_{im}, \rightsquigarrow)$ be a distributed computation. For any state s, we associate two vectors: $s.send$ and $s.recv$. $s.send[i]$ is the total number of messages sent to process i. Similarly, $s.recv[i]$ is the total number of messages received from process i. Let $G \subseteq S$ be a global state, that is, G contains exactly one state $G[i]$ from each process i. Prove or disprove:
(a) $\forall i, j : G[i].recv[j] \leq G[j].send[i] \Rightarrow G$ is a consistent global state.
(b) $(G[i].send[j] < G[j].recv[i]) \Rightarrow (G[i] \rightarrow G[j])$.

10.5. Chandy and Lamport's algorithm requires the receiver to record the state of the channel. Since messages in real channels may get lost, it may be advantageous for senders to record the state of the channel. Give an algorithm to do so. Try to make your algorithm as practical as possible. Assume that control messages can be sent over unidirectional channels even in the reverse direction.

10.6. The original algorithm proposed by Chandy and Lamport does not require FIFO but a condition weaker than that. Specify the condition formally.

10.7. (**due to [CL85]**) Assume that the computation is modeled using the interleaving model. The snapshot algorithm by Chandy and Lamport is initiated from global state S_i and completes its snapshot when the global state is S_f. Let S^* be the snapshot recorded.

(a) List all the properties of S^*.

(b) Let h be any sequence of events that take the system from S_i to S_f. Show that there is a valid sequence of events h' that also takes the system from S_i to S_f via S^*. (Hint: h' is a permutation of h with all prerecording events before all postrecording events)

10.8. A boolean function is called *strongly stable* if it is monotonic with respect to the set of all cuts of a computation, that is, not just consistent cuts. How can this property be exploited to compute a strongly stable boolean function?

10.9. How can you use Lamport's logical clock to compute a consistent global snapshot?

*10.10. Give an algorithm to compute a global snapshot when the channels are not FIFO. (Hint: Include in each message its color and the number of white messages sent.)

*10.11. Show that any snapshot algorithm uses at least $O(E)$ messages where E is the number of unidirectional channels.

10.7   Bibliographic Remarks

Chandy and Lamport [CL85] were the first to give an algorithm for computation of a meaningful global snapshot. For a colorful description of Chandy and Lamport's algorithm see [Dij85]. Spezialetti and Kearns have given efficient algorithms to disseminate a global snapshot to processes initiating the snapshot computation [SK86]. Bouge [Bou87] has given an efficient algorithm for repeated computation of snapshots for synchronous computations. In the absence of the FIFO assumption, as shown by Taylor [Tay89], any algorithm for a snapshot is either inhibitory (that is, it may delay actions of the underlying application) or requires piggybacking of control information on basic messages. Lai and Yang [LY87] and Mattern [Mat93] have given snapshot algorithms that require only the piggybacking of control information. Helary [Hel89] has proposed an inhibitory snapshot algorithm.

Chapter 11

Observing Global Predicates

Dear Watson, you see but you do not observe ... — Arthur Conan Doyle

11.1 Introduction

Many problems in distributed systems can be viewed as special cases of the problem of observing a distributed computation. Deadlock detection, termination detection, and breakpoint detection are some specific instances of the observation problem. This chapter presents problems and solutions associated with observing a distributed computation.

There are three fundamental characteristics of distributed systems— the lack of a shared clock, the lack of a shared state, and the presence of multiple processes. The lack of a shared clock implies that the order of events in a distributed system can only be partial. The lack of a shared state implies that the computation of global functions must incur overhead of message passing. Finally, due to the presence of multiple processes, there is an exponential number of possible global states in a distributed computation and therefore we frequently face the problem of combinatorial explosion in the analysis of distributed systems. These three characteristics make the observation of distributed programs difficult.

What can we do to alleviate these problems? For observation of a distributed computation, three ideas have been used in the literature

to effectively solve these problems—happened before relation, monotonicity, and linearity. The happened before relation is used instead of
real time in defining global states. Monotonicity is used as a restriction
on the predicates so that at most one value is required to be communicated per external event of a process. Finally, linearity is used to
avoid exploring all possible global states. On the basis of these ideas,
efficient algorithms can be developed for observation.

This chapter is organized as follows. Section 11.2 formalizes the
meaning of evaluation of a global predicate on a distributed computation. Section 11.3 discusses the key ideas in observation of global
predicates in greater detail. Section 11.4 discusses the notion of linear
predicates. Linear predicates have the advantage that they can be detected efficiently in a distributed computation under certain conditions.
Finally, Section 11.5 discusses the notion of regular predicates. The set
of consistent cuts satisfying a regular predicate forms a sublattice of
the lattice of all consistent cuts. This makes the analysis of regular
predicates easier, as shown in Chapter 21.

The notation used in this chapter is summarized in Figure 11.1.

S	The deposet
$C(S)$	The lattice of consistent global states
G, H	Consistent global states
B	Global boolean predicate
m	The number of state intervals per process
N	The number of processes

Figure 11.1: Notation

11.2   Modalities of Observation

A *local predicate* is defined as any boolean-valued formula on a local
state. For any process P_i, a local predicate is written as l_i. A process
can obviously detect a local predicate on its own.

As before, we use the notion of a deposet $S = (S_1, S_2, \ldots, S_N, \leadsto)$
to model an execution. During an execution, each state $s \in S_i$ defines
a value for each variable $x \in X_i$. Each pair of states $s \in S_i$ and $t \in S_j$
defines a queue of messages in transit for channel C_{ij}, the channel from
process P_i to P_j. We define a global predicate as any boolean-valued

function B of the variables in X_i and messages in C_{ij} for all values of i and j. Let $B(G)$ denote the value of predicate B in a global state defined by a cut $G = \{s_1, \ldots, s_N\}$.

We have defined the meaning of truthness of a global predicate given a consistent cut G. We need to extend this definition to truthness of a global predicate B given a computation. Recall that a computation may be modeled as a poset of events in the system or as a deposet of local states in the system. We use deposet of states without loss of generality. For the definition of truthness of B, it is convenient to consider the lattice of consistent cuts generated by the computation. Let $C(S)$ denote the lattice on the deposet S. Figure 11.2 shows the execution lattice for a deposet. The execution lattice does not have a global state (s_3, t_0) because that is an inconsistent global state due to a message sent from t_0 to s_3.

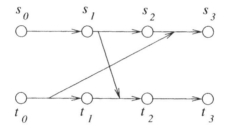

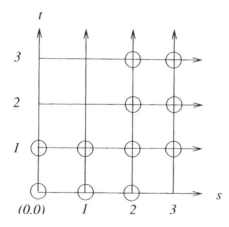

Figure 11.2: A deposet and the lattice of its consistent cuts

Now we define the following *modalities* for truthness of a boolean predicate B.

Definition 11.1 (possibly: B) *A global predicate B is possibly true for a deposet S (denoted by possibly : B) iff there exists a path from the initial state to the final state in the lattice $C(S)$ along which B is true on some state.*

In Figure 11.2, if the predicate is true on any consistent cut, then it is possibly true.

Definition 11.2 (definitely: B) *A global predicate B is definitely true for a deposet S (denoted by definitely : B) iff for all paths from the initial state to the final state in the lattice $C(S)$ B is true on some state.*

In Figure 11.2, if B is true at states (s_0, t_1) and (s_1, t_0), then it is definitely true. As another example, if B is true at (s_2, t_1), then it is also definitely true.

Possibly true predicates are useful for detecting bad conditions such as violations of mutual exclusion, whereas definitely true predicates are useful to verify occurrence of good predicates such as commit points on transaction systems.

The duals of these two modalities are also useful.

Definition 11.3 (invariant: B) *invariant* $: B \stackrel{\text{def}}{=} \neg possibly : \neg B$.

In other words, a global predicate B is invariant for a deposet S iff it is true on all the consistent cuts in the lattice $C(S)$.

Definition 11.4 (controllable: B) *controllable* $: B \stackrel{\text{def}}{=} \neg definitely : \neg B$.

In other words, a global predicate B is controllable for a deposet S iff there exists a path from the initial consistent cut in $C(S)$ to the final cut in $C(S)$ such that B is true at all consistent cuts along that path.

In this chapter, we focus on the possibly modality. The following lemma can be easily verified.

Lemma 11.5 *possibly : B for a computation S iff there exists a consistent cut G in $C(S)$ such that B is true in G.*

Thus, to detect whether a global predicate is possibly true in a computation, it is sufficient to determine whether there exists a consistent cut in which it is true. The difficulty arises because there is a large number of consistent cuts. In the worst case, there can be as many as m^N consistent cuts in a deposet $(S_1, S_2, \ldots, S_N, \leadsto)$ with each S_i containing at most m states.

11.3 Key Problems in Observation of Global Properties

Consider a distributed debugging system. Suppose that our task is to implement the most basic command of a debugging system: "stop the program when the predicate B is true." To stop the program, it is necessary to detect the predicate B; a nontrivial task if B requires access to the global state. Each of the difficulties mentioned in Section 11.1 needs to be addressed to develop algorithms for detecting B. We discuss each one of them next. Figure 11.3 summarizes problems and solutions outlined in this section.

Characteristic	Problem	Idea
No shared clock	Ordering events	Happened before
No shared memory	Message/state change	Monotonicity
Multiple processes	Combinatorial explosion	Linearity

Figure 11.3: Problems and their solutions for observation

11.3.1 Lack of Shared Clock

Our first difficulty is defining the meaning of predicates in a global system. For a simple example, consider the predicate $B = CS_1 \wedge CS_2$, where CS_1 and CS_2 are predicates local on processes P_1 and P_2, respectively. One natural way of defining truthness of this predicate is that B is true in a computation if and only if there exists an instant of time in which both CS_1 and CS_2 are true. Although this definition is adequate for sequential systems, it presents many problems in distributed systems. Since clocks are impossible to synchronize perfectly, it is impossible to ascertain whether two events happened simultaneously in a distributed system. This problem is solved by substituting the happened before relation for time (and therefore concurrency for simultaneity). Thus we define B to be true if there exist two states s and t such that CS_1 is true in s, CS_2 is true in t, and s and t are concurrent. More generally, the predicate *possibly: B* is true if in the lattice of consistent global states there is a path from the initial global state to the final global state in which B is true in some intermediate consistent global state.

An advantage of the definition based on happened before is that we can evaluate truthness of the predicate using vector clocks. Besides, for many applications, such as distributed debugging, this definition is more useful. For example, even if CS_1 and CS_2 are not true simultaneously, but there exist two concurrent states in which CS_1 and CS_2 are true, then there is an error in the program. This is because there exists a way of running the same program in which CS_1 and CS_2 are true simultaneously.

11.3.2 Lack of Shared Memory

Our second difficulty stems from the fact that there is no shared memory. Thus, there is an inherent communication complexity for observing a global property of the system. For example, consider a global predicate $B(x_1, x_2)$, where x_1 and x_2 are variables in P_1 and P_2, respectively. If evaluation of this predicate at P_2 requires communication of all values of x_1 from P_1 to P_2, and evaluation at P_1 requires communication of all values of x_2 from P_2 to P_1, the function is clearly impractical to evaluate in a distributed system. In particular, if evaluation of a function requires communication for every change in the value of a variable, then that function is impractical. To capture a class of functions that requires at most one value to be communicated per external event, we use the notion of monotonicity.

Informally, a predicate is monotone with respect to a variable x_1 if replacing the variable by a larger value while keeping all other variables the same preserves the truthness of the predicate. Formally, assume that x_1 takes its value from a set totally ordered with respect to a relation $<$. We say that B is monotone with respect to the first argument (x_1) if it satisfies the following equation:

$$\forall a, b, x_2 : (a < b) \wedge (B(a, x_2) \Rightarrow B(b, x_2)).$$

For example, consider the predicate $B = (x_1 > x_2)$, where x_1 and x_2 are integers. Then B is monotone with respect to x_1, because if $B(x_1, x_2)$ holds for a certain value of x_1, then it would continue to do so for any larger value of x_1. The predicate B is also monotone with respect to x_2 because for x_2 we can use the domain of integers with the relation $<$ defined as the greater than relation defined on natural numbers. As another example, consider the conjunctive predicate $x_1 \land x_2 \ldots \land x_n$, where each x_i is a boolean variable. By viewing the boolean domain as a totally ordered set with *false* to be defined as smaller than *true*, it can be easily seen that the conjunctive predicate is also monotone with respect to all variables. An example of a predicate that is not monotone with respect to either x_1 or x_2 is $(x_1 = x_2)$.

Monotonicity of a predicate allows us to restrict our attention to *state intervals* rather than states. A state interval is a sequence of states between two *external* events, where an external event is the sending or receiving of a message, the beginning of the process and the termination of the process. For each state interval it is sufficient to record and communicate the extremal value of the variable rather than all values taken by the variable in that interval. Since the number of state intervals is equal to the number of external events for a process, it is usually a much smaller number than the total number of events in the system. For example, if we are detecting $(x_1 > x_2)$ and x_1 takes values $2, 9, 4$ and 7 between two external events, then it is sufficient to communicate the value 9. From now on we use the term state and state interval interchangeably.

11.3.3 Combinatorial Explosion

Now assume that we have overcome limitations due to lack of shared clock and shared memory, for example, by using happened before and monotonicity. This implies that we have the poset corresponding to the computation available at one process. So now, the problem is not even of distributed computing because all the required data is at one process. The problem we may face at this point is that of computation complexity. Since there are N processes, the total number of global states possible is m^N, where m is the number of state intervals at any process. Consider a boolean predicate B. Even when B is a boolean expression, and processes do not communicate, the problem of detecting *possibly*: B is NP-complete.

We show in this section that the problem of global predicate detection is NP-complete. In fact, we show that it is NP-complete even in the absence of messages between processes.

The global predicate detection problem is a decision problem. It can be written as:

> **Input instance**: a deposet S of N sequences, a set of variables X partitioned into N subsets $X_1, \ldots, X_N$, and a predicate B defined on X.
>
> **Problem:** Determine whether there exists a consistent cut $G \in S$ such that $B(G)$ has the value true.

We now show:

Theorem 11.6 *The global predicate detection problem is NP-complete.*

Proof: First note that the problem is in NP. The verification that the cut is consistent can easily be done in polynomial time (for example, using vector clocks and examining all pairs of states from the cut). Therefore, if the predicate itself can be evaluated in polynomial time, then the detection of that predicate belongs to the set NP.

We show NP-completeness of the simplified predicate detection problem where all program variables are restricted to taking the values "true" or "false", and at most one variable from each X_i can appear in B. We reduce the satisfiability problem of a boolean expression (SAT) to the global predicate detection problem by constructing an appropriate deposet.

The deposet is constructed as shown in Figure 11.4. For each variable $u_i \in U$, we define a process P_i that hosts variable x_i (i.e., $X_i = \{x_i\}$). Let the sequence S_i consist of exactly two states. In the first state, x_i has the value false. In the second state, x_i has the value true. No messages are exchanged during the computation (i.e., $\forall s \in S_i, \forall t \in S_j : i \neq j : s||t$).

It is easily verified that the predicate B is true for some cut in S if and only if the expression is satisfiable.

■

The above result shows that detection of a general global predicate is intractable even for simple distributed computations. This implies that the class of predicates must be restricted to allow for efficient detection.

In Chapter 10, we discussed detection of stable predicates. A stable predicate is one that remains true once it becomes true. More formally, B is stable if and only if:

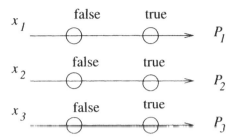

Figure 11.4: Transformation from SAT to global predicate detection

$$\forall G, H : B(G) \wedge H \text{ reachable from } G \Rightarrow B(H)$$

Well-known examples of stable predicates are termination and garbage collection. It must be noted that stability depends on the system. Some properties are stable in some systems but not stable in others. For example, the formula,

$$\min_i x_i > k$$

is a stable predicate in distributed simulation environments when the x_i are the timestamps in every process and every message. It is not stable for arbitrary systems.

Stable predicates are a subclass of *observer-independent* predicates. This class includes all predicates B such that

$$\forall G, H : possibly : B \text{ in } L(G, H) \equiv definitely : B \text{ in } L(G, H).$$

where $L(G, H)$ denote the sublattice of execution lattice that starts in the consistent global state G and ends with the global state H. The name "observer independent" stems from the notion of a set of observers, where each witnesses a different sequential execution of the system. Each observer can determine if B became true in any of the cuts witnessed by them. If the predicate is observer independent, then all observers will agree on whether B ever became true. We leave it to the reader to show that stable predicates, and disjunction of local predicates are observer independent (see Problem 11.9).

Detection of observer-independent predicates does not suffer from combinatorial explosion because a single path in the execution lattice can be traversed for detection of the global predicate B. If B is true for any global state in the path, then $possibly : B$ is clearly true. On the other hand, if B is false along that path, we know that *definitely* : B is false. Because predicates *possibly* : B is equivalent to *definitely* : B for observer-independent, we conclude that *possibly* : B is also false for the lattice.

In rest of the chapter, we discuss two more classes of predicates for which efficient algorithms are known. These classes are linear predicates and regular predicates. The relationship between various classes of predicates is shown in Figure 11.5.

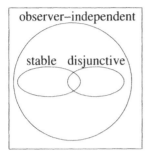
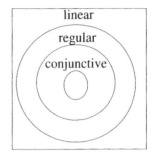

Figure 11.5: Predicate classes and relationship between them

11.4   Linear Predicates

In this section, we describe a class of global predicates for which efficient detection algorithms can be derived. We use $C(S)$ to denote the set of cuts (not necessarily consistent) of the deposet S.

A key concept in deriving an efficient algorithm is that of a *forbidden* state. Given a deposet S, a predicate B, and a cut $G \subset S$, a state $G[i]$ is called forbidden if its inclusion in any cut $H \in C(S)$, where $G \leq H$, implies that B is false for H. Formally,

Definition 11.7 (Forbidden State) *Given any predicate B, we define*

$$forbidden(G,i) \stackrel{\text{def}}{=} \forall H \in C(S) : G \leq H : (G[i] \neq H[i]) \vee \neg B(H)$$

We define a predicate B to be linear with respect to deposet S if for any cut G in the deposet, the fact that B is false in G implies that G contains a forbidden state. Formally,

Definition 11.8 (Linear Predicate) *A boolean predicate B is linear with respect to a deposet S iff:*

$$\forall G \in C(S) : \neg B(G) \Rightarrow \exists i : forbidden(G, i)$$

Observe that the linearity of a boolean predicate also depends on the set $C(S)$ and, therefore, on the deposet S. We would typically be interested in predicates that are linear for all deposets consistent with a program. Lemma 11.9 is an easy consequence of the definition of linearity.

Lemma 11.9 *The following are properties of linear predicates:*

1. *If B_1 and B_2 are linear, then so is $B_1 \wedge B_2$.*

2. *If B is defined using variables of a single process, then B is linear.*

3. *The predicate "the cut is consistent" is linear, i.e., if $B(G) \equiv \forall i, j : G(i) \| G(j)$ then B is a linear predicate.*

Proof: We just show the third part. $\neg B(G)$ implies $\exists i, j : G[i] \to G[j]$. This implies that for all $H \geq G$, $G[i] \to H[j]$. Thus we get $(G[i] \neq H[i]) \vee \neg B(H)$. Therefore, B is a linear predicate.

∎

Observe that as a consequence of Lemma 11.9, predicates that are a conjunction of local predicates are linear.

11.4.1 The Least Cut Satisfying a Linear Predicate

Note that any global predicate, B, defines a (possibly empty) subset of cuts $C_B(S) \subseteq C(S)$, where B holds for all cuts in $C_B(S)$. We now show that if B is linear then $C_B(S)$ is closed under infimum. An implication of this result is that the *least* cut satisfying B is well-defined.

Lemma 11.10 *Let $C_B(S) \subseteq C(S)$.*
$C_B(S)$ is closed under infimum operation iff B is linear with respect to $C(S)$.

Proof: ($\Rightarrow$) We prove the contrapositive. Assume that B is not linear. This implies that there exists a cut G such that $\neg B(G)$, and $\forall i : \exists H_i \geq G : (G[i] = H_i[i])$ and $B(H_i)$. Consider

$$Y = \bigcup_i \{H_i\}.$$

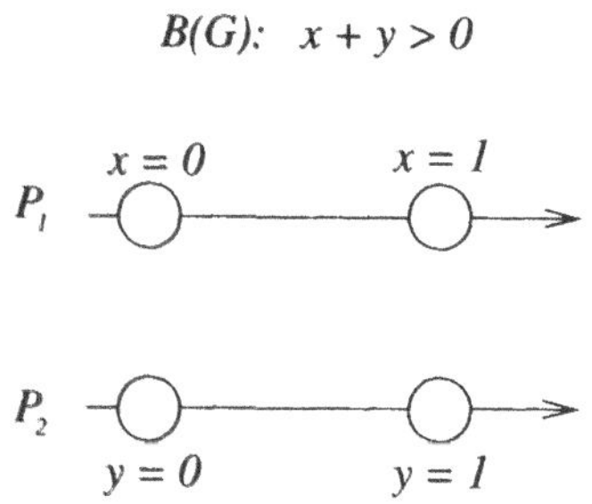

$B(G)$: $x + y > 0$

Figure 11.6: Example of a nonlinear predicate

Note that all elements of $Y \in C_B(S)$. However, $inf\ Y$ which is in G is not an element of $C_B(S)$. This implies that $C_B(S)$ is not closed under the infimum operation.

($\Leftarrow$) We again show the contrapositive. Let $Y = \{H_1, H_2, \ldots, H_k\}$ be any subset of $C_B(S)$ such that its infimum G does not belong to $C_B(S)$. Since G is infimum of Y, for any i, there exists $j \in \{1 \ldots k\}$ such that $G[i] = H_j[i]$. Since $B(H_j)$ is true for all j, it follows that there exists a G for which linearity does not hold.

■

Example 11.11 Consider the predicate $x + y \geq k$ where x and y are variables on processes P_1 and P_2 and k is some constant. In general, this predicate is not linear. Figure 11.6 illustrates this. The consistent cut with $(x = 0)$ and $(y = 1)$ satisfies the predicate and the consistent cut with $(x = 1)$ and $(y = 0)$ also satisfies the predicate, but the infimum of these two cuts does not satisfy the predicate. However, assume that x is known to be monotonically decreasing. In this case, $x + y \geq k$ is linear. Given any cut, if $x + y < k$, then the state with y variable is forbidden.

We now discuss detection of linear global predicates. We assume that given a cut, G, it is efficient to determine whether B is true for G or not. On account of linearity of B, if B is evaluated to be false in some cut G, then we know that there exists a forbidden state in G. We now make an additional assumption called the efficient advancement property.

(**Efficient Advancement Property**) There exists an efficient (polynomial time) function to determine the forbidden state.

It is easy to determine the forbidden states for all examples of linear predicates we have discussed so far. As another example, consider the predicate "Channel C_{ij} is empty". If this predicate is false for some cut C, that is, the channel is not empty, then sending more messages is guaranteed to leave the predicate false. Thus the state of the receiver is forbidden in G. With these assumptions, we get:

Theorem 11.12 *If B is a linear predicate with the efficient advancement property, then there exists an efficient algorithm to determine the least cut that satisfies B (if any).*

Proof: An efficient algorithm to find the *least* cut in which B is true is given in Figure 11.7. We search for the least cut starting from the initial state. If the predicate is false in the current state, then we find the process with the forbidden state using the efficient advancement property. If this is the last state on the process, then we return false or else we advance along the process that has the forbidden state.

∎

```
var
    G: array[1..N] of integer initially ∀i : G[i] := initial(i);

while ¬B(G) do
    Let i be such that forbidden(G, i);
    if (G[i] = final(i)) then return false
    else G[i] := next(G[i]);
endwhile;
return true;
```

Figure 11.7: An efficient algorithm to detect a linear predicate

The efficient algorithm can be visualized as searching for the first cut that satisfies the predicate in the lattice of all cuts by advancing with the help of the forbidden state. Thus, even though there are an exponential number of cuts in the lattice, we explore at most mN cuts, where m is the maximum number of states along any process in the deposet.

11.5   Regular Predicates

Informally, a global predicate is a regular predicate if the set of consistent cuts satisfying the predicate forms a sublattice of the lattice of consistent cuts, that is, the set of consistent cuts that satisfy the predicate is closed under infimum (meet) and supremum (join) operations. A regular predicate is also *linear* and hence easy to detect when the efficient advancement property holds. In practice, most linear predicates are also regular predicates; therefore, regular predicates form a useful class of predicates. We first define a regular predicate formally. In this section, we use the event-based model for a computation rather than the state-based model.

Definition 11.13 (Regular Predicate) *Let $C(E)$ be the lattice of consistent cuts of a computation $(E, \rightarrow)$. A predicate B is regular iff for any $G, H \in C(E)$:*

$$B(G) \wedge B(H) \Rightarrow B(G \cap H) \wedge B(G \cup H).$$

Some examples of regular predicates are:

- Consider the predicate B as "there is no outstanding message in the channel." We show that this predicate is regular. Observe that B holds on a consistent cut G iff for all send events in G the corresponding receive events are also in G. It is easy to see that if $B(G)$ and $B(H)$, then $B(G \cup H)$. To see that it holds for $G \cap H$, let e be any send event in $G \cap H$. Let f be the receive event corresponding to e. From $B(G)$, we get that $f \in G$ and from $B(H)$, we get that $f \in H$. Thus $f \in G \cap H$. Hence, $B(G \cap H)$. Similarly, the following predicates are also regular.

  - There is no token message in transit.
  - No token message is in transit between processes P_1 and P_5.
  - Every "request" message has been "acknowledged" in the system.

- Consider any local predicate. It can be shown that any local predicate is regular. Thus the following predicates are regular.

  - The leader has sent all "prepare to commit" messages.

– Process P_i is in a "red" state.

- Channel predicates such as "there are at most k messages in transit from P_i to P_j" and "there are at least k messages in transit from P_i to P_j" are also regular.

We now show that the class of regular predicates is closed under conjunction.

Lemma 11.14 *If B_1 and B_2 are regular predicates, then so is $B_1 \wedge B_2$.*

Proof: Given two consistent cuts G and H, let $K = G \cup H$. Since B_1 is a regular predicate $B_1(K)$ holds. Similarly, $B_2(K)$ holds. Hence, $B_1 \wedge B_2$ holds for K. A similar proof can be given when $K = G \cap H$.

∎

The closure under conjunction implies that the following predicates are also regular:

- No process has the token, and no channel has the token.

- Any conjunction of local predicates.

The closure is not true for disjunction as can be readily verified by taking B_1 and B_2 to be local predicates.

Let $C_B(E)$ be the set of consistent cuts satisfying the predicate B. From the definition of regular predicates, it follows that the $C_B(E)$ is a sublattice of $C(E)$. Since a sublattice of a distributive lattice is also distributive, we conclude that $C_B(E)$ is also distributive.

11.6 Problems

11.1. Prove or disprove the following:

   (a) If B is linear, then $\neg B$ is also linear.
   (b) If B_1 and B_2 are linear, then $B_1 \vee B_2$ is also linear.
   (c) The following channel predicate is linear: "The number of green messages in the channel is equal to the number of red messages."
   (d) The following channel predicate is linear: "Every request message has been acknowledged."

(e) If $\neg B$ is a stable predicate, then B is a linear predicate.

11.2. Assume that a distributed computation is modeled as a partially ordered set of *events* $(E, \rightarrow)$. Assume that predicates are boolean functions defined on set of cuts of E. We define e is *forbidden* in G as

$$forbidden(G, e) \stackrel{\text{def}}{=} \forall H \supseteq G : \neg B(H) \vee (succ(e) \in H).$$

Define a predicate B to be linear iff for all cuts G,

$$\neg B(G) \Rightarrow \exists e \in G : forbidden(G, e).$$

Prove that the set of cuts satisfying B are closed under $\cap$ iff B is linear.

11.3. Define a predicate B to be postlinear iff for all cuts G, H,

$$B(G) \wedge B(H) \Rightarrow B(G \cup H)$$

Show that B is stable implies that B is postlinear.

11.4. Give an example of a predicate that is linear but not regular.

11.5. Give an equivalent characterization of regular predicates using the notion of forbidden states (in the deposet model).

11.6. Monotonicity of a global predicate allowed us to communicate at most one value per state interval. Generalize the notion to *k-bounded* predicates that can be detected by communicating at most k values per state interval. Give an example of such a predicate.

11.7. (**due to [CM91]**) Give an algorithm to detect *possibly* : B when B is arbitrary predicate. Your algorithm should have the time complexity linear in the number of global states in the computation. (Hint: Define a notion of level of execution lattice. Design an algorithm that explores the lattice in the level order.)

11.8. (**due to [CM91]**) Give an algorithm to detect *definitely* : B when B is arbitrary predicate. (Hint: The final global state is reachable from the initial global state while traversing only those global states that satisfy $\neg B$ iff *definitely* : B is false.)

11.9. Show that stable predicates and disjunction of local predicates are observer independent.

*11.10. Give an example of a predicate B such that the set of consistent cuts that satisfy B form a lattice, but B is not regular. (Hint: Although the set of consistent cuts that satisfy B is a lattice, it may not be a sublattice of the lattice of all consistent cuts.)

*11.11. (**due to [CG95]**) Give an efficient algorithm for off-line detection of

$$possibly : \sum_i x_i \leq k$$

where x_i is a variable on P_i and k is a constant. (Hint: Use max-flow techniques.)

*11.12. (**due to [TG97]**) Give an efficient algorithm for off-line detection of

$$possibly : \sum_i x_i \geq k$$

where x_i is a *boolean* variable on P_i, and k is a constant. (Hint: Consider the poset formed by states when x_i equals 1. Check if that poset has any antichain of size at least k.)

*11.13. Show that it is NP-complete to detect

$$possibly : \sum_i x_i = k$$

when x_i can increase or decrease by arbitrary amount in any step. Give an efficient algorithm when x_i can increase or decrease by at most 1 in each step. (Hint: For NP-completeness use the subset sum problem. For the algorithm, first compute the value of $\sum_i x_i$ in the initial global state. If it is strictly greater than k, then check $possibly : \sum_i x_i \leq k$. If it is strictly less than k, then check $possibly : \sum_i x_i \geq k$. See Problem 11.11.)

*11.14. (**due to [MG01a]**) A predicate $B(x_1, x_2, \ldots, x_n)$ of n boolean variables is *symmetric* iff it is invariant under any permutation of its variables. Give an efficient algorithm to detect any symmetric predicate. (Hint: Use the fact that a predicate is symmetric iff it can be specified by a set of numbers $\{a_1, a_2, \ldots, a_m\}$, where $0 \leq a_i \leq n$, $m \leq n+1$ such that the predicate is true only when exactly $a_i (1 \leq i \leq m)$ of the variables are true.)

*11.15. (**due to [MG01a]**) Show that detecting conjunctions of clauses of the form $x_i \leq x_j$, where x_i is an integer variable, is NP-complete. Show that the NP-completeness holds when $<$ or $\neq$ is used instead of the $\leq$ relational operator.

11.7 Bibliographic Remarks

The discussion on difficulties in observing global properties is taken from Garg [Gar97]. The notion of *possibly* and *definitely* is taken from Cooper and Marzullo [CM91]. Similar notions were defined in Garg and Waldecker [GW91]. Observer-independent predicates were introduced by Charron-Bost, Delporte-Gallet, and Fauconnier [CBDGF95]. Linear predicates were introduced by Chase and Garg [CG98], and regular predicates were introduced by Garg and Mittal [GM01]. Other algorithms for predicate detection include relational predicates [TG97], atomic sequences [HPR93], linked predicates [MC88], dynamic properties [BR95], regular patterns [FRGT94], general control flow patterns [GTFR95], event normal form predicates [CK94], and recursive poset logic predicates [TG95].

Chapter 12

Observing Conjunctive Predicates

In the field of observation chance favors only the prepared mind. —
Louis Pasteur

12.1   Introduction

In Chapter 11, we gave an off-line algorithm for detection of linear
predicates. In this chapter we consider on-line detection of conjunctive
predicates that are special cases of linear predicates. A conjunctive
predicate B under the modality *possibly* : B is also called a weak
conjunctive predicate (WCP).

A weak conjunctive predicate (WCP) is true for a given run if and
only if there exists a consistent global cut in that run in which all
conjuncts are true. Intuitively, detecting a weak conjunctive predicate
is generally useful when one is interested in detecting a combination
of states that is unsafe. For example, violation of mutual exclusion for
a two process system can be written as: "P_1 is in the critical section
and P_2 is in the critical section." Conjunctive predicates also form
an interesting class of predicates because their detection is sufficient
for detection of any global predicate that can be written as a boolean
expression of local predicates. This observation is shown in Section
12.2.

This chapter is organized as follows. Section 12.3 gives a vector
clock-based centralized algorithm. This algorithm is the best when

149

a small latency of detection (the time between a predicate turning true and its detection) is desired and the predicate is defined on a small subset of the total number of processes in the system. When the predicate to be detected spans the entire system, then a direct dependency-based algorithm is better. This algorithm is described in Section 12.4. Finally, we discuss a distributed token-based algorithm in Section 12.5. This algorithm imposes equal load on all processes.

The notation used in this chapter is summarized in Figure 12.1.

B	Global boolean predicate
l_i	A predicate local to P_i
m	The number of state intervals per process
N	The number of processes
n	The number of local predicates in the conjunctive predicate
s, t, u	Local states
x, y, z	Variables

Figure 12.1: Notation

12.2 Boolean Expressions of Local Predicates

We first show the following.

Lemma 12.1 *Let B be any predicate constructed from local predicates using boolean connectives. Then, B can be detected using an algorithm that can detect q, where q is a pure conjunction of local predicates.*

Proof: The predicate B can be rewritten in its disjunctive normal form. Thus,

$$B = q_1 \vee \ldots \vee q_k \qquad k \geq 1$$

where each q_i is a pure conjunction of local predicates. Next, observe that a global cut satisfies B if and only if it satisfies at least one of the q_i's. Thus the problem of detecting B is reduced to solving k problems of detecting q, where q is a pure conjunction of local predicates.

∎

As an example, consider a distributed program in which x, y and z are in three different processes. Then,

$$even(x) \wedge ((y < 0) \vee (z > 6))$$

can be rewritten as

$$(even(x) \wedge (y < 0)) \vee (even(x) \wedge (z > 6))$$

where each disjunct is a weak conjunctive predicate.

Note that even if the global predicate is not a boolean expression of local predicates, but is satisfied by a finite number of possible global states, then it can also be rewritten as a disjunction of weak conjunctive predicates. For example, consider the predicate $(x = y)$, where x and y are in different processes. $(x = y)$ is not a *local* predicate because it depends on both processes. However, if we know that x and y can only take values $\{0, 1\}$, then the above expression can be rewritten as

$$((x = 0) \wedge (y = 0)) \vee ((x = 1) \wedge (y = 1)).$$

Each of the disjuncts in this expression is a weak conjunctive predicate.

We have emphasized conjunctive predicates and not disjunctive predicates. The reason is that disjunctive predicates are quite simple to detect. To detect a disjunctive predicate $l_1 \vee l_2 \vee \ldots \vee l_n$, where l_i denotes a local predicate in the process P_i, it is sufficient for the process P_i to monitor l_i. If any of the processes finds its local predicate true, then the disjunctive predicate is true.

We first give a necessary and sufficient condition for a weak conjunctive predicate to be true in a computation $(S_1, S_2, \ldots, S_N, \rightsquigarrow)$ where S_i is the set of states on process P_i. Let $l_i(s)$ denote that the predicate l_i is true in the state s.

Our aim is to detect whether $(l_1 \wedge l_2 \wedge \ldots l_n)$ holds for a given computation. We can assume $n \leq N$ (the total number of processes in the system) because $l_i \wedge l_j$ is just another local predicate if l_i and l_j belong to the same process. From the definition of the consistent state, we get the following.

Theorem 12.2 $(l_1 \wedge l_2 \wedge \ldots l_n)$ *is possibly true for a computation iff for all $1 \leq i \leq n$, $\exists s_i \in S_i$ such that l_i is true in state s_i, and s_i and s_j are concurrent for $i \neq j$.*

Proof: From the definition of possibly true for a global predicate.

∎

12.3   A Vector Clock-Based Centralized Algorithm

Theorem 12.2 shows that it is necessary and sufficient to find a set of incomparable states in which local predicates are true to detect a weak conjunctive predicate. In this section, we present a centralized algorithm to do so. Later, we will see how the algorithm can be decentralized. This algorithm finds the *first* consistent cut for which a WCP is true. Indeed, because a WCP is a linear predicate, if there exists a cut for which the WCP is true, then there exists a first such cut.

In this algorithm, one process serves as a checker. All other processes involved in detecting the WCP are referred to as application processes.

12.3.1   Application Process

Each application process checks for local predicates. It also maintains the vector clock algorithm. Whenever the local predicate of a process becomes true for the *first* time since the most recently sent message (or the beginning of the trace), it generates a debug message containing its local timestamp vector and sends it to the checker process.

The above algorithm is practical because a process is not required to send its vector clock every time the local predicate is detected. Observe that if two local states, say s and t, on the same process are separated only by internal events, then they are indistinguishable to other processes so far as consistency is concerned, that is, if u is a local state on some other process, then $s||u$ if and only if $t||u$. Thus it is sufficient to consider at most one local state between two external events and the vector clock need not be sent if there has been no message activity since the last time the vector clock was sent.

12.3.2   Checker Process

The checker process is responsible for searching for a consistent cut that satisfies the WCP. Its pursuit of this cut can be most easily described as considering a sequence of candidate cuts. If the candidate cut either is not a consistent cut or does not satisfy some term of the WCP, the checker can efficiently eliminate one of the states along the cut. The eliminated state can never be part of a consistent cut that satisfies the WCP. The checker can then advance the cut by considering the successor to one of the eliminated states on the cut. If the checker finds a cut for which no state can be eliminated, then that cut satisfies the WCP and the detection algorithm halts. The algorithm for the checker process is shown in Figure 12.2.

```
var
      cut: array[1..n] of struct
          v: array[1..n] of integer;
          color: {red, green};
      endstruct initially (∀i : cut[i].color = red);
      detect: boolean initially false;

      while (∃i : (cut[i].color = red)) do
          if (q[i] = null) and Pᵢ terminated then return false;
          else cut[i].v := receive(q[i]);// advance the cut
          paintState(i);
      endwhile;

detect := true;
```

Figure 12.2: WCP detection algorithm—checker process.

The checker receives local snapshots from the other processes in the system. These messages are used by the checker to create and maintain data structures that describe the global state of the system for the current cut. The data structures are divided into two categories: queues of incoming messages and those data structures that describe the state of the processes.

The queue of incoming messages is used to hold incoming local snapshots from application processes. We require that messages from an individual process be received in FIFO order. We abstract the message passing system as a set of n FIFO queues, one for each process. We use the notation $q[1\ldots n]$ to label these queues in the algorithm.

The checker also maintains information describing one state from each process P_i. The collection of this information is organized into a vector *cut* which is an array of structure consisting of the vector v and *color*. The color of a state is either red or green and indicates whether the state has been eliminated in the current cut. A state is green only if it is concurrent with all other green states. A state is red only if it cannot be part of a consistent cut that satisfies the WCP.

The aim of advancing the cut is to find a new candidate cut. However, we can advance the cut only if we have eliminated at least one state along the current cut and if a message can be received from the corresponding process. The data structures for the processes are updated to reflect the new cut. This is done by the procedure *paintState*. This procedure is shown in Figure 12.3. The parameter i is the index of the process from which a local snapshot was most recently received. The color of $cut[i]$ is temporarily set to green. It may be necessary to change some green states to red to preserve the property that all green states are mutually concurrent. Hence, we must compare the vector clock of $cut[i]$ to each of the other green states. Whenever the states are comparable, the smaller of the two is painted red.

$paintState(i)$
  $cut[i].color := green;$
  for $j := 1$ **to** n **do**
      if $(cut[j].color = green)$ **then**
          if $(cut[i].v < cut[j].v)$ **then** $cut[i].color := red;$
          else if $(cut[j].v < cut[i].v)$ **then** $cut[j].color := red;$
  endfor

Figure 12.3: Procedure *paintState*.

12.3.3 Proof of Correctness

Now we show correctness of the WCP algorithm. First, some properties of the program are given that will be used in demonstrating soundness and completeness.

Lemma 12.3 *The following is an invariant of the program assuming that the function paintState is atomic.*

$$\forall i, j : (cut[i].color = green) \land (cut[j].color = green) \Rightarrow cut[i] \| cut[j]$$

Proof: Initially, the invariant is true because $cut[i].color = red$ for all i. The color of $cut[i]$ is set to green only in the *paintState* function. In that function, $cut[i]$ is compared with all $cut[j]$ whose *color* are green. If $cut[i]$ is not concurrent with $cut[j]$, then one of them is painted red, preserving the invariant assertion after the *paintState* function.

■

The following lemma is crucial in making the detection algorithm efficient. It enables the algorithm to discard any red-colored state.

Lemma 12.4 *For all i, if $cut[i].color$ is red for any global state G, then there does not exist any global cut $H \geq G$ that satisfies the WCP and includes $cut[i]$, that is, $cut[i]$ is a forbidden state.*

Proof: The variable $cut[i]$ is painted red only in the function *paintState*. This implies that there exists j such that $cut[i] < cut[j]$. We show that there is no state in process P_j that is a part of a global cut with $cut[i]$ satisfying the WCP. States $cut[j]$ and $cut[i]$ cannot be part of any global state because $cut[i] < cut[j]$. Furthermore, by our assumption of FIFO between application processes and the checker process, all states later than $cut[j]$ in the queue for P_j are greater than $cut[j]$ and so are also greater than $cut[i]$. This implies that no other candidate state from P_j that is at least $cut[j]$ can be concurrent with $cut[i]$. Therefore, $cut[i]$ can be eliminated.

■

We are now ready to prove that the algorithm is sound and complete. The next theorem says that the algorithm never makes a false detection. If the detect flag is true, then the current cut indeed satisfies the WCP.

Theorem 12.5 (Soundness) *If the detect flag is true, then there exists a cut in which the WCP is true. Moreover, the cut produced by the algorithm is the first cut for which the WCP is true.*

Proof: The *detect* condition evaluating to true is equivalent to

$$(\forall i : cut[i].color = green).$$

By the algorithm of the application process, $l_i(cut[i])$ holds. From Lemma 12.3, $\forall i, j : cut[i]||cut[j]$. Thus the cut satisfies the WCP.

We now show that this is the first such cut. Observe that the cut is advanced only when $cut[i]$ is red. From Lemma 12.4, $cut[i]$ cannot be part of any cut that makes the WCP true. Since all cuts previous to the current cut have at least one red state, it follows that the detected cut is the first cut in which the WCP is true.

■

Theorem 12.6 (Completeness) *Let G be the first cut that satisfies the WCP. Then the WCP algorithm sets the detect flag to be true with G as the cut.*

Proof: Because G is the first cut that satisfies the WCP, all the earlier states cannot make the WCP true. We show that all earlier states are painted red. The proof is by induction on the number of total states that are before this cut. If there are no states, then the claim is true. Assume that k states have been painted red. Consider the last state painted red. There is at least one more state ahead of it. This makes the while condition true, and the cut is advanced to the next state. If this next cut is not equal to the cut G, then there exists at least one violation of the concurrency relation in the current cut. Therefore, for all cuts preceding G, at least one state is painted red, and because of this, the cut will be advanced. Eventually, the checker will advance the cut to G. By Lemma 12.4, all states must be green. At this point, the checker will exit the repeat loop, and the detect flag will be set to true.

∎

12.3.4   Overhead Analysis

We use N for the total number of processes in the system, n for processes involved in the WCP ($n \leq N$), and m for the maximum number of messages sent or received by any process.

We first analyze the complexity of application processes. The space complexity is given by the vector clock v and is $O(n)$. Note that strictly speaking, each vector clock timestamp may require $O(n \log m)$ bits, but we assume that storage and manipulation of each component is a constant time/space overhead. This is true in practice because one word containing 32 bits would be sufficient to capture a computation with 2^{32} messages. The main time complexity is involved in detecting the local predicates and time required to maintain vector clocks. In the worst case, one debug message is generated for each program message sent, so the worst case message complexity is $O(m)$. In addition, program messages have to include time vectors. Every process sends $O(m)$ local snapshots to the checker process. With the same assumptions as made for space complexity, it follows that $O(mn)$ bits are sent by each process.

The main space requirement of the checker process is the buffer for the local snapshots. Each local snapshot consists of a vector clock that requires $O(n)$ space. Since there are at most $O(mn)$ local snapshots, $O(n^2m)$ total space is required to hold the component of local snapshots devoted to vector clocks. Therefore, the total amount of space required by the checker process is $O(n^2m)$.

We now discuss the time complexity of the algorithm. Note that it takes only two comparisons to check whether two vectors are concurrent. Hence, each invocation of $paintState$ requires at most n comparisons. This function is called at most once for each state, and there are at most mn states. Therefore, at most n^2m comparisons are required by the algorithm.

Can the number of comparisons be reduced? It can be shown that the complexity of the above problem is at least $\Omega(n^2m)$; thus the algorithm is optimal. We first show an intermediate lemma that handles the case when the size of each queue is exactly one, i.e., $m = 1$.

Lemma 12.7 *Let there be n elements in a set S. Any algorithm that determines whether all elements are incomparable must make at least $n(n-1)/2$ comparisons.*

Proof: The adversary will give to the algorithm a set in which either zero or exactly one pair of elements are incomparable. The adversary also chooses to answer "incomparable" to the first $n(n-1)/2 - 1$ questions. Thus the algorithm cannot determine whether the set has a comparable pair unless it asks about all the pairs.

■

We use the above lemma to show the desired result.

Theorem 12.8 *Let $(S, <)$ be any partially ordered finite set of size mn. We are given a decomposition of S into n sets $P_0, \ldots, P_{n-1}$ such that P_i is a chain of size m. Any algorithm that determines whether there exists an anti-chain of size n must make at least $mn(n-1)/2$ comparisons.*

Proof: Let $P_i[k]$ denote the kth element in P_i^{th} chain. The adversary will give the algorithm S and P_i's with the following characteristic:

$$\forall i, j, k : P_i[k] < P_j[k+1]$$

Thus the above problem reduces to m instances of the problem that checks whether any of the n elements is incomparable. The algorithm for the adversary is shown in Figure 12.4.

```
var
    // number of questions asked for each level
    num: array[1..m] of integer initially 0;

On being asked to compare P_i[k] and P_j[l]
    if (k < l) then return P_i[k] < P_j[l];
    if (l < k) then return P_j[l] < P_i[k];
    if (l = k) then
        num[k] := num[k] + 1;
        if (num[k] = n * (n - 1)/2) then return P_i[k] < P_j[l];
        else return P_j[l]||P_i[k];
    endif
```

Figure 12.4: The algorithm for the adversary

If the algorithm does not completely solve one instance, then the adversary chooses that instance to show a poset consistent with all its answers but different in the final outcome.

∎

12.4   A Direct Dependency-Based Algorithm

In this section we describe a WCP detection algorithm that does not use vector clocks. The algorithm is based on satisfying only direct dependencies between states. Hence, it is necessary for all N processes to participate in the algorithm. Recall that the vector clock-based algorithm required participation by only the n processes for which local predicates are defined. The direct dependency-based algorithm has $O(Nm)$ time, space and message complexity and is more efficient when n^2 is large relative to N. At first, this seems to contradict our adversary argument, which says that that any algorithm based on comparison of vectors requires at least n^2m steps. However, this is not the case, because the second algorithm uses additional information sent by the application processes to reduce the number of comparisons.

There are three main differences from the previous algorithm. First, we do not use vector clocks. We only require the processes to include their own components in outgoing messages. This reduces communication overhead and improves message sending and receive time. Second, a message sent to the checker process includes a list of dependencies in addition to the value of the local clock. This list contains the set of all processes that have sent messages to process P_i since the last local snapshot. This list is used to check for consistency of the current cut. Observe that because there are at most $O(mN)$ messages in the system, the total number of dependencies can only be $O(mN)$. Finally, we require that all processes participate in the algorithm. This is because if vector clocks are used, then even indirect dependencies are accounted for; however, if only local clocks are used, then an indirect dependency may be missed if all processes do not check for consistency.

12.4.1 Application Process

In this algorithm, we do not incur the overhead of a vector clock. To uniquely identify a state, we use a logical counter. We use the notation (i, k) to represent the kth state on process P_i. We simply use k to represent this state when the identity of process P_i is obvious from the context. A logical counter is maintained by each application process. The process increments the counter each time a message is sent. Since there are at most m messages sent by any process, this establishes at most m distinguishable local states on each of the N processes.

The application process is responsible for creating local snapshots and sending them to the checker process. A local snapshot is created every time the local predicate is true for the first time since the local clock was last changed. This snapshot consists of the current value of the local clock and a list of dependencies. The dependencies are local state identifiers from remote processes and are used to determine concurrency between states. Dependencies are encoded as pairs (i, k). A dependency (i, k) is included in a local snapshot if it has not already appeared in the dependency list of previous local snapshots. The sequence of local snapshots is delivered to the checker process in FIFO order.

12.4.2 Checker Process

We now describe the algorithm for the checker process shown in Figure 12.5. G represents the current global cut that is being considered. The array *color* has the same interpretation as in the previous algorithm. The variable *candidate* represents the local snapshot. The checker process simply keeps receiving local snapshots from red processes until all

```
var
    candidate: struct
        myindex : 1..m;
        depend: list of (pid : 1..N, stateindex : 1..m) ;
    endstruct;
    G: array[1..N] of stateindex initially 0;
    color: array[1..N] of {red, green} initially red;
    q_1 ... q_N: queue of candidate;
    detect: boolean initially false;

    while (∃i : color[i] = red) do
        if (q[i] = null) and P_i terminated then return false;
        candidate := receive(q[i]) ;
        if (candidate.myindex > G[i]) then
            G[i] := candidate.myindex;
            color[i] := green;
        endif
        for (j, k) ∈ candidate.depend do
            if (k > G[j]) then
                G[j] := k;
                color[j] := red;
            endif
        endfor
    endwhile

detect:=true;
```

Figure 12.5: Checker process algorithm

processes become green. On receiving the snapshot, the checker process checks whether $G[i]$ has some dependency (j, k) such that $G[j] < k$. In this case, the process P_j is colored red.

12.4.3 Proof of Correctness

In this section we show that finding a global consistent cut with respect to indirect dependency is equivalent to finding a global consistent cut with respect to direct dependency when all processes are involved. Direct dependency, denoted $s \rightarrow_d t$, means that s and t are on the same process and s happens before t, or there exists a single message sent after s and received before t. Now, we can state the result that consistency can be checked with respect to direct dependency.

Lemma 12.9 *Let G be any global cut. Then, G is a consistent cut (i.e. $\forall i, j : G[i] \not\rightarrow G[j]$) if and only if $\forall i, j : G[i] \not\rightarrow_d G[j]$.*

Proof: ($\Rightarrow$) Since $s \rightarrow_d t$ implies that $s \rightarrow t$, it follows that $s \not\rightarrow t$ implies $s \not\rightarrow_d t$. Thus the right hand side follows.
($\Leftarrow$) It is sufficient to show that $(\exists i, j : G[i] \rightarrow G[j])$ implies $(\exists k, l : G[k] \rightarrow_d G[l])$. The proof is using induction on the number of processes in the causality chain from $G[i]$ to $G[j]$, that is, on the level of indirect dependency from $G[i]$ to $G[j]$. The base case is trivially true because if there are no processes in the causality chain, then $G[i] \rightarrow_d G[j]$ and we are done.

Now consider the case when the indirect dependency goes through K processes. Let the first process in the chain be $P_{i'}$, that is, there exists a message sent after $G[i]$ that is received by $P_{i'}$. There are two cases. If this message is received before $G[i']$, then we are done because $G[i] \rightarrow_d G[i']$ and the right-hand side is true. The second case is when this message is received after $G[i']$. However, this implies that $G[i'] \rightarrow G[j]$ and from the induction hypothesis the right-hand side is true again.

■

12.4.4 Overhead Analysis

There are two main components of the computation—elimination of local states (done in the *while* loop) and determination of the dependencies of the local state on other processes (done in the *for* loop). Note that one iteration of any of these loops requires $O(1)$ work. Since there are at most $O(mN)$ local states and at most $O(mN)$ dependencies in the entire system, it follows that the entire computation takes $O(mN)$ time.

12.5 A Vector Clock-Based Distributed Algorithm

Up to this point we have described detection of WCP based on a checker process. The checker process in the vector clock-based centralized algorithm requires $O(n^2m)$ time and space, where m is the number of messages sent or received by any process and n is the number of processes over which the predicate is defined. We now introduce token-based algorithms that distribute the computation and space requirements of the detection procedure. The distributed algorithm has $O(n^2m)$ time, space, and message complexity, distributed such that each process performs $O(nm)$ work.

We introduce a new set of n *monitor processes*. One monitor process is mated to each application process. The application processes interact according to the distributed application. In addition, the application processes send local snapshots to monitor processes. The monitor processes interact with each other but do not send any information to the application processes.

The distributed WCP detection algorithm uses a unique token. The token contains two vectors. The first vector is labeled G. This vector defines the current candidate cut. If $G[i]$ has the value k, then state k from process P_i is part of the current candidate cut. Note that all states on the candidate cut satisfy local predicates. However, the states may not be mutually concurrent, that is, the candidate cut may not be a consistent cut. The token is initialized with $\forall i : G[i] = 0$.

The second vector is labeled *color*, where *color*$[i]$ indicates the color for the candidate state from application process P_i. The color of a state can be either *red* or *green*. If *color*$[i]$ equals *red*, then the state $(i, G[i])$ and all its predecessors have been eliminated and can never satisfy the WCP. If *color*$[i] = green$, then there is no state in G such that $(i, G[i])$ happened before that state. The token is initialized with $\forall i : color[i] = red$.

The token is sent to monitor process M_i only when *color*$[i] = red$. When it receives the token, M_i waits to receive a new candidate state from P_i and then checks for violations of consistency conditions with this new candidate. This activity is repeated until the candidate state does not causally precede any other state on the candidate cut, that is, the candidate can be labeled green. Next, M_i examines the token to see if any other states violate concurrency. If it finds any j such that $(j, G[j])$ happened before $(i, G[i])$, then it makes $color[j]$ red. Finally, if all states in G are green, that is, G is consistent, then M_i has detected the WCP. Otherwise, M_i sends the token to a process whose color is red. The algorithm for these actions is given in Figure 12.6. Note that the token can start on any process.

```
var
     // vector clock from the candidate state
     candidate: array[1..n] of integer initially 0;

Upon receiving the token (G, color)
     while (color[i] = red) do
          receive candidate from application process P_i;
          if (candidate[i] > G[i]) then
               G[i] := candidate[i];
               color[i] := green;
          endif;
     endwhile;
     for j := 1 to  n, (j ≠ i) do
          if (candidate[j] ≥ G[j]) then
               G[j] := candidate[j];
               color[j] := red;
          endif
     endfor
     if (∃j : color[j] = red) then send token to M_j;
     else detect := true;
```

Figure 12.6: Monitor process algorithm

12.5.1   Overhead Analysis

We first analyze the time complexity for computation. It is easy to see that whenever a process receives the token, it deletes at least one local state, that is, it receives at least one message from the application process. Every time a state is eliminated, $O(n)$ work is performed by the process with the token. There are at most mn states; therefore, the total computation time for all processes is $O(n^2m)$. The work for any process in the distributed algorithm is at most $O(nm)$. The analysis of message and space complexity is left as an exercise (see Problem 12.8).

12.6   Problems

12.1. Show that it is sufficient to send the vector clock once after each message is sent irrespective of the number of messages received. Formally, let $first(s)$ be true if and only if the local predicate is true for the first time since the most recently sent message (or the beginning of the trace). We say $wcp(s_1, s_2, \ldots, s_n)$ is true if $s_1, s_2, \ldots, s_n$ are the states in different processes making the WCP true (as in Theorem 12.2). Prove the following claim:
$$\exists s_1, \ldots, s_n : wcp(s_1, s_2, \ldots, s_n) \Leftrightarrow$$
$$\langle \exists s'_1, \ldots, s'_n : wcp(s'_1, s'_2, \ldots, s'_n) \wedge \forall i : 1 \le i \le n : first(s'_i) \rangle$$

12.2. Assume that the given global predicate is a simple conjunction of local predicates. Further assume that the global predicate is stable. In this scenario, both Chandy and Lamport's algorithm and the weak conjunctive algorithm can be used to detect the global predicate. What are the advantages and disadvantages of using each of them?

12.3. The main drawback of the single-token WCP detection algorithm is that it has no concurrency—a monitor process is active only if it has the token. Design an algorithm that uses multiple tokens in the system. (Hint: Partition the set of monitor processes into g groups and use one token-algorithm for each group. Once there are no longer any red states from processes within the group, the token is returned to a predetermined process (say P_0). When P_0 has received all the tokens, it merges the information in the g tokens to identify a new global cut. Some processes may not satisfy the consistency condition for this new cut. If so, a token is sent into each group containing such a process.)

12.4. Design a hierarchical algorithm to detect WCP based on ideas in the previous exercise.

12.5. Show the following properties of the vector clock-based algorithm for WCP detection. For any i,

1. $G[i] \neq 0 \wedge color[i] = red \Rightarrow \exists j : j \neq i : (i, G[i]) \rightarrow (j, G[j])$;
2. $color[i] = green \Rightarrow \forall k : (i, G[i]) \not\rightarrow (k, G[k])$;
3. $(color[i] = green) \wedge (color[j] = green) \Rightarrow (i, G[i]) \| (j, G[j])$.
4. If $(color[i] = red)$, then there is no global cut satisfying the WCP which includes $(i, G[i])$.

12.6. Show the following claim for the vector clock-based distributed WCP detection algorithm: The flag *detect* is true with G if and only if G is the first cut that satisfies the WCP.

12.7. Design a distributed version of the direct dependency-based algorithm for detecting WCP.

12.8. Show that the message complexity of the vector clock-based distributed algorithm is $O(mn)$, the bit complexity (number of bits communicated) is $O(n^2m)$, and the space complexity is $O(nm)$ entries per process.

*12.9. Let $(S, <)$ be any partially ordered finite set of size mn. We are given a decomposition of S into n sets $P_1, \ldots, P_n$ such that P_i is a chain of size m. Each chain is accessed through a queue. Only the head element of each queue may be examined at any instant. When the head element has been removed from the queue, it is lost from further consideration. Let the steps of a parallel algorithm consist of any of the following:

(S1) compare all heads of the queues in parallel

(S2) delete the heads of any number of queues in parallel.

Let A be any parallel algorithm that determines if there exists an antichain of size n in such a poset of size mn. If A is restricted to steps (S1) and (S2), then show that it takes at least $\Omega(nm)$ steps to determine the correct answer.

*12.10. **(due to [SS95])** Consider the global predicate $B = (x_1 < x_2) \wedge (x_3 < 20)$ where x_i is on process P_i. Your task is to design an algorithm to detect this predicate in an off-line fashion. In an off-line algorithm, a trace is generated for each process. After the computation is finished all the traces are sent to a checker process. The checker process is responsible for detecting the predicate.

You need to show what information should be kept as part of the trace. Also, give the algorithm for the checker process. What is the time complexity of the checker process if a process has at most m state intervals?

*12.11. **(due to [HMRS98])** Assume that every process communicates with every other process directly or indirectly infinitely often. Design a distributed algorithm in which information is piggybacked on existing program messages to detect a conjunctive predicate under the above assumption, i.e., the algorithm does not use any additional messages for detection purposes.

*12.12. **(due to [TG98a])** Consider the problem of predicate detection in the potential causality model (in which events with in a single process may not be totally ordered). Show that detecting a conjunctive predicate is NP-complete under this model. Also show that the problem can be efficiently solved if all receive events in a process are totally ordered.

12.7 Bibliographic Remarks

Detection of conjunctive properties was first discussed by Garg and Waldecker in [GW92]. Distributed on-line algorithms for detecting conjunctive predicates were first presented in Garg and Chase [GC95]. Hurfin, Mizuno, Raynal and Singhal [HMRS98] were the first to give a distributed algorithm that does not use any additional messages for predicate detection. Their algorithm piggybacks additional information on program messages to detect conjunctive predicates. Distributed algorithms for off-line evaluation of global predicates are also discussed in Venkatesan and Dathan [VD92]. Stoller and Schneider [SS95] have shown how Cooper and Marzullo's algorithm can be integrated with that of Garg and Waldecker to detect conjunction of global predicates. Garg and Mitchell discuss use of computational geometric techniques for detecting conjunction of global predicates in [GM97]. Lower bounds on these algorithms were discussed in Garg [Gar92].

Chapter 13

Channel Predicates

It is the theory that decides what can be observed. — *Albert Einstein*

13.1   Introduction

We earlier presented algorithms for efficient detection of global predicates that could be specified as a boolean formula of local predicates. Many properties in distributed systems, however, use the state of channels. For example, the property "there is no token in the system" is equivalent to "no process has the token" and "no channel has the token." We now present an efficient algorithm to detect any boolean formula of local and channel predicates.

A channel predicate is any boolean function of the state of the channel. The channel state is defined as the set difference of the send events and the receive events on that channel. Since a channel is defined as the unidirectional connection between two processes, one process performs all send events and the other all receive events, that is, the messages that are in transit. It should be noted that channels have no memory. Hence, any channel state that can be constructed by a combination of both send events and receive events can also be produced by some other sequence of just send events. For efficiency reasons, the channel predicates must be linear.

This chapter is organized as follows. Section 13.2 gives many examples of linear predicates, and Section 13.3 gives a centralized algorithm for detecting channel predicates.

The notation used in this chapter is summarized in Figure 13.1.

l_i	A predicate local to P_i
c	A channel predicate
m	The number of messages per process
N	The number of processes
n	The number of distinct processes referenced in GCP
S	Send events
R	Receive events

Figure 13.1: Notation

13.2 Linear Channel Predicates

We use the symbol S and S' to represent arbitrary sequences of send events from a process and the symbol R to represent an arbitrary sequence of receive events. Let c denote the channel predicate. Then, the requirement for linearity is:

$$\forall S : \neg c(S) \Rightarrow (\forall S' : \neg c(S \cup S')) \vee (\forall R : \neg c(S - R))$$

Thus, given any channel state, S, in which the predicate is false, then either sending more messages is guaranteed to leave the predicate false or receiving more messages is guaranteed to leave the predicate false. We assume that when the channel predicate is evaluated in some state S, it is also known which of these two cases applies. To model this assumption, we define linear channel predicates to be 3-valued functions. The predicate can evaluate to:

1. T—The channel predicate is true for the current channel state.

2. F_s—The channel predicate is false for the current channel state. Furthermore, the predicate will remain false when an arbitrary set of additional messages is sent on the channel in the absence of receives. We call the predicate send monotonic when this condition holds.

3. F_r—The channel predicate is false for the current channel state. Furthermore, the predicate will remain false when an arbitrary set of messages is received from the channel in the absence of sends. We call the predicate receive monotonic when this condition holds.

Example 13.1 Some examples of linear channel predicates are given below.

- *Detection of empty channels:* $c(S) \equiv (S = \emptyset)$: It is obvious that if this predicate is not currently true, sending more messages will not make it true. This linear predicate can be used in termination detection where termination is equivalent to the condition that all processes are idle and all channels are empty.

- *Detection of at least k messages in a channel:* $c(S) \equiv$ (number of messages in $S \geq k$): This is similar to the detection of empty channels. This linear predicate can be used in buffer overflow detection.

- *Detection of exactly k messages in a channel:* $c(S) \equiv$ (length of $S = k$): In any state where there are more than k messages in the channel, the predicate cannot be made true by sending more messages. In any state when there are less than k messages in a channel, the predicate cannot be made true by receiving more messages. The only other possible state is when the channel has exactly k messages in it, and in this state the predicate is true.

From now on, we assume that all channel predicates are linear. Our goal is to develop an algorithm that can detect a generalized conjunctive predicate (GCP) of the form

$$(l_1 \wedge l_2 \wedge \ldots l_n \wedge c_1 \wedge c_2 \wedge \ldots c_e)$$

where l_i's are local predicates and c_i's are channel predicates. From linearity of GCP, we know that the set of all global cuts in which the GCP is true is closed under the infimum operation. This property does not hold for arbitrary channel predicates, as shown by the next example.

Example 13.2 Consider the distributed computation shown in Figure 13.2. Consider the channel predicate—"There is an odd number of messages in the channel." Note that this channel predicate is not linear. Assume that the local predicates are true only at points $C[1]$ and $D[1]$ for P_1 and $C[2]$ and $D[2]$ for P_2. It is easily verified that the GCP is true in the cut C and D but not in their greatest lower bound.

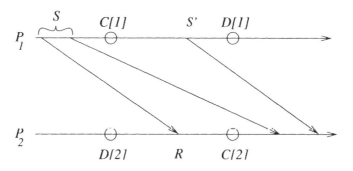

Figure 13.2: The set of cuts satisfying the predicate is not a sublattice.

13.3 A Centralized Algorithm

The method of detection of the GCP is divided among application processes and the checker process as in the centralized algorithm for WCP.

13.3.1 Application Processes

The application processes monitor local predicates. These processes also maintain information about the send and receive channel history for all channels incident to them. The application processes send a message to the checker process whenever the local predicate becomes true for the first time since the last program message was sent or received. This message is called a local snapshot and is of the form:

$$(vector, incsend, increcv)$$

where *vector* is the current vector and *incsend* and *increcv* are the list of messages sent to and received from other application processes since the last message for predicate detection was sent. An algorithm for this process is given in Figure 13.3.

13.3.2 Checker Process

The checker process for GCP shown in Figure 13.4 is similar to that of WCP except that now it also needs to worry about channels. Therefore, in addition to WCP data structures, it maintains three data structures for each channel:

```
var
      incsend, increcv: list of messages initially ∅;
      v: vectorClock;
      newinterval: boolean initially true;

To send m:
      newinterval := true;
      incsend := append(incsend, m);

Upon receive(m):
      newinterval := true;
      increcv := append(increcv, m);

Upon (local_pred = true ∧ newinterval):
      newinterval := false;
      send(v, incsend, increcv) to the checker process;
      incsend := ∅; increcv := ∅;
```

Figure 13.3: Application process algorithm for P_i

- $S[1..n, 1..n]$: sequence of messages—The pending-send list. This list is an ordered list of messages. The list contains all those messages that have been sent on the channel but not yet received according to the current cut.

- $R[1..n, 1..n]$: sequence of messages—The pending-receive list. The list contains each message that has been received from the channel, but not yet sent according to the current cut. Since the current cut is not necessarily consistent, states along the cut may be causally related, and hence it is possible for one state on the cut to be after a message has been received, and yet have another state on the cut from before that message was sent. If all states are part of a consistent cut, then every R list is empty.

- $CP[1..n, 1..n]$: $\{F_s, F_r, T\}$—The channel predicate state flags. When a channel predicate is evaluated, its value is written into CP. The value of a channel predicate cannot change unless there is activity along the channel. Hence, the checker can avoid unnecessarily recomputing channel predicates by recording which

```
var
    S, R: array[1..n, 1..n] of list of messages initially null;
    CP: array [1..n, 1..n] of {F_s, F_r, T};
    cut: array[1..n] of struct
        v: array[1..n] of integer;
        color: {red, green};
        incsend, increcv : list of messages
    endstruct initially (∀i : cut[i].color = red);
    detect: boolean initially false;

while (∃i : (cut[i].color = red)) do
    if (q[i] = null) and P_i terminated then return;
    else cut[i].v := receive(q[i]);// advance the cut
    paintState(i);
    update-channels(i);
endwhile;

detect := true;
```

Figure 13.4: GCP detection algorithm—checker process

predicates have remained true or false since the last time the predicate was evaluated.

The checker process searches for the candidate cut as in WCP. The data structures for the processes and channels are updated to reflect the new cut. This is done by the procedures *paintState* and *update_channels* respectively. The procedure *paintState* is the same as for WCP. We describe the procedure *update_channels*. This procedure is shown in Fig. 13.5. The parameter i is the index of the process from which a local snapshot was most recently received. The checker updates the value of the CP-state flags according to the activity in $cut[i].incsend$ and $cut[i].increcv$. As an optimization, the checker can take advantage of linearity when updating the channel-state vector. If a channel predicate is false along the current cut, and that predicate is currently send-monotonic, then it will remain false when more messages are sent. There will be no need to evaluate the predicate until at least one message receive occurs on the channel. There is a similar optimization for states when the predicate is receive-monotonic.

The incremental send and receive histories from the snapshot are used to update the data structures $S[\ldots]$ and $R[\ldots]$ as follows. Let P_j be the destination for some message in the incremental send history. If this message appears in $R[i, j]$, then delete it from $R[i, j]$. Since this message has already been received, it is not in the channel according to the current cut. If the message does not appear in $R[i, j]$, then the message is appended to $S[i, j]$. An analogous procedure is followed for each message in $cut[i].increcv$.

It should be noted that for many important channel predicates, the time to evaluate the channel predicate is constant. For example, the predicates "The channel is empty," "The channel has k or more messages," and "The minimum time stamp of messages in the channel is at least k" can all be evaluated in constant time if appropriate data structures are used to represent the messages in the S list.

$update\_channels(i)$

for all message $m \in incsend$ **do**
    $P_j := destination(m)$;
    if $(m \in R[i, j])$ **then** $R[i, j] := R[i, j] - \{m\}$;
    else $S[i, j] := S[i, j] \cup \{m\}$;
    $CP[i, j] := chanp_{ij}(S[i, j])$;
    if $(CP[i, j] = F_s)$ **then** $cut[j].color := red$;
    else if $(CP[i, j] = F_r)$ **then** $cut[i].color := red$;
endfor

for all message $m \in increcv$ **do**
    $P_j := source(m)$;
    if $(m \in S[j, i])$ **then** $S[j, i] := S[j, i] - \{m\}$;
    else $R[j, i] := R[j, i] \cup \{m\}$;
    $CP[j, i] = chanp_{ji}(S[j, i])$;
    if $(CP[j, i] = F_s)$ **then** $cut[i].color := red$;
    else if $(CP[j, i] = F_r)$ **then** $cut[j].color := red$;
endfor

Figure 13.5: Procedure $update\_channels$

13.3.3   Overhead Analysis

We analyze the time, the space, and the message complexity of the algorithm.

Time Complexity: $O(mn^2)$ time is spent in the *paintState* function. The function *update_channels* performs two operations: subtracting and appending of message sequences. If the sequences are ordered, both of these operations require linear time in the size of the sequences. Because each process sends and receives at most m messages, the sum of the sizes of these sequences is $O(m)$. Therefore, the time spent in a single invocation of *update_channels* is $O(m)$. Since there are mn states, the total time spent in this function is $O(m^2n)$. The value of a channel predicate can change only when a message is sent or received on the channel. Thus there are at most two evaluations of the predicate per message. There are at most mn messages. If each predicate evaluation takes time proportional to the size of the channel, then each predicate evaluation is $O(m)$. Therefore, the total amount of time required to evaluate channel predicates is $O(m^2n)$.

Based on this evaluation, the time complexity of the checker process is $O(n^2m + m^2n)$. However, it should be observed that, in practice, the time complexity is much closer to $O(n^2m)$. First, the time required for *update_channels* is typically much smaller than $O(m^2n)$. In fact for FIFO channels, the total computation for *update_channels* is $O(mn)$. Second, evaluating a channel predicate is often a constant time operation, as discussed earlier. In these cases, the total time spent by the checker process evaluating channel predicates is also $O(mn)$.

Space Complexity: The main space requirement of the checker process is the buffer for the local snapshots. Each local snapshot consists of a *vector* and incremental send and receive histories. The *vector* requires $O(n)$ space. Typically, evaluating a channel predicate does not require the entire contents of the messages. We assume that the relevant information from each message can be encoded in a constant number of bits. Hence, the total space required for all incremental send and receive histories is $O(mn)$. Therefore, the total amount of space required by the checker process is $O(mn^2)$.

Message Complexity: Every process sends $O(m)$ local snapshots to the checker process. Using the same assumptions as made for space complexity, it follows that $O(mn)$ bits are sent by each process.

13.4 Problems

13.1. Show that the following predicate is linear:"There are at most k messages in transit that are destined to P_1." Observe that in this predicate we have used a more general notion of channel—one that may have more than one sender.

13.2. Design a centralized direct dependency-based algorithm for GCP.

13.3. Derive an algorithm for detecting distributed termination-based on the distributed algorithm for GCP in the previous problem.

*13.4. **(due to [GCKM97])** Design a distributed token-based algorithm for detecting GCP.

13.5. Design a distributed direct dependency-based algorithm for GCP.

13.6. Show how you will optimize the algorithm for detecting channel predicates when

   (a) Channel predicates are independent of message content, i.e., they are based only on the number of messages in the channel. Termination and buffer overflow are problems with channel predicates that are content independent.

   (b) Channel predicates are independent of message ordering. An example of such a predicate is "There exists a marker in the channel."

   (c) Channel predicates always evaluate either to T or to F_s. An example of such a predicate is "There are at most k request messages in the channel."

   (d) Channel predicates always evaluate either to T or to F_r. An example of such a predicate is "There are at least k request messages in the channel."

13.5 Bibliographic Remarks

The algorithm for detecting generalized conjunctive predicates is taken from Garg, Chase, Mitchell, and Kilgore [GCKM97]. Mitchell and Garg have shown that many distributed detection algorithms for specialized predicates, such as termination, can be derived from a general channel predicate detection algorithm [MG95a].

Chapter 14

Termination Detection

What we call the beginning is often the end. And to make an end is to make a beginning. The end is where we start from. — *T.S. Eliot*

14.1   Introduction

Consider a computation on a distributed system that is started by a special process called environment. This process starts up the computation by sending messages to some of the processes. Each process in the system is either passive or active. It is assumed that a passive process can become active only on receiving a message (an active process can become passive at any time). Furthermore, a message can be sent by a process only if it is in the active state. Such a computation is called a diffusing computation. Algorithms for many problems such as computing the breadth-first search-spanning tree in an asynchronous network or determining the shortest paths from a processor in a network can be structured as diffusing computations (see Problems 14.3 and 14.4).

From properties of a diffusing computation, it follows that if all processes are passive in the system and there are no messages in transit, then the computation has terminated. Our problem is to design a protocol by which the environment process can determine whether the computation has terminated. Our solution is based on an algorithm by Dijkstra and Scholten.

This chapter is organized as follows. Section 14.2 describes a variant of Dijkstra and Scholten's algorithm, and Section 14.3 gives an optimization of the variant. With the optimization, the algorithm has the same message complexity as Dijkstra and Scholten's algorithm.

The notation used in this chapter is summarized in Figure 14.1.

D	Deficit of a process
O	Set of outgoing channels
T	Tree
E	Set of edges of the tree

Figure 14.1: Notation

14.2   Dijkstra and Scholten's Algorithm

We say that a process is in a green state if it is passive and all of its outgoing channels are empty; otherwise, it is in a red state. How can a process determine whether its outgoing channel is empty? This can be done if the receiver of the channel signals the sender of the channel the number of messages received along that channel. If the sender keeps a variable $D[i]$ (for deficit) for each outgoing channel i, which records the number of messages sent minus the number of messages that have been acknowledged via signals, it can determine that the channel i is empty by checking whether $D[i] = 0$. Observe that $D[i] \geq 0$ is always true. Therefore, if O is the set of all outgoing channels, it follows that

$$\forall i \in O : D[i] = 0$$

is equivalent to

$$\sum_{i \in O} D[i] = 0.$$

Thus it is sufficient for a process to maintain just one variable D that represents the total deficit for the process.

It is clear that if all processes are in the green state then the computation has terminated. To check this condition, we will maintain a set T with the invariant:

(I0) All red processes are part of the set T.

Observe that green processes may also be part of T—the invariant is that there is no red process outside T. When the set T becomes empty, termination is true.

When the diffusing computation starts, the environment is the only red process initially (with nonempty outgoing channels); the invariant is made true by keeping environment in the set T. To maintain the invariant that all red processes are in T, we use the following rule. If P_j turns P_k red (by sending a message), and P_k is not in T, then we add P_k to T.

We now induce a directed graph (T, E) on the set T by defining the set of edges E as follows. We add an edge from P_j to P_k, if P_j was responsible for addition of P_k to the set T. We say that P_j is the parent of P_k. From now on we use the terms *node* and *process* interchangeably. Because every node (other than the environment) has exactly one parent and an edge is drawn from P_j to P_k only when P_k is not part of T, the edges E form a spanning tree on T rooted at the environment. Our algorithm will maintain this as invariant:

(I1) The edges E form a spanning tree of nodes in T rooted at the environment.

Up to now, our algorithm only increases the size of T. Because detection of termination requires the set to be empty, we clearly need a mechanism to remove nodes from T. Our rule for removal is simple: a node is removed from T only if it is a green leaf node. When a node is removed from T, the incoming edge to that node is also removed from E. Thus the invariants (I0) and (I1) are maintained by this rule. To implement this rule, a node needs to keep track of the number of its children in T. This can be implemented by keeping a variable at each node *numchild* initialized to 0 that denotes the number of children it has in T. Whenever a new edge is formed, the child reports this to the parent, who can increment the count. When a leaf leaves T, it reports this to the parent, who decrements the count. If the node has no parent (it must be the environment) and it leaves the set T, then termination is detected. By assuming that a green leaf node eventually reports to its parent, we conclude that once the computation terminates, it is eventually detected. Conversely, if termination is detected, then the computation has indeed terminated on account of the invariant (I0).

Observe that the property that a node is green is not stable and hence a node, say P_k, that is green may become active once again on receiving a message. However, because a message can only be sent by an active process we know that some active process (which is already a part of the spanning tree) will be now responsible for the node P_k. Thus the tree T changes with time but maintains the invariant that all active nodes are part of the tree.

14.3 An Optimization

The algorithm given above can be optimized by combining messages from the reporting process and the messages for detecting whether a node is green. To detect whether an outgoing channel is empty we assumed a mechanism by which the receiver tells the sender the number of messages it has received. One implementation could be based on control messages called signal. For every message received, a node is eventually required to send a signal message to the sender. To avoid the use of report messages, we require that a node not send the signal message for the message that made it active until it is ready to report to leave T. When it is ready to report, the signal message for the message that made it active is sent. With this constraint we get an additional property that a node will not turn green unless all its children in the tree have reported. Thus we have also eliminated the need for maintaining *numchild*: only a leaf node in the tree can be green. A node is ready to report when it has turned green, that is, it is passive and $D = 0$. The algorithm obtained after the optimization is shown in Figure 14.2

14.4 Problems

14.1. What is the message complexity of Dijkstra and Scholten's algorithm?

14.2. Assume that all processes in the system are organized as a logical ring. Design an algorithm in which a token circulates in the ring carrying appropriate information to detect termination.

14.3. Give an algorithm based on diffusing computation to determine the breadth-first search tree from a given processor.

14.4. Consider a network of processors connected by bidirectional links with different but fixed delays. Our interest is in determining the shortest path from all processors to a fixed processor, say P_0. Design a diffusing computation in which each processor maintains

---

var
> $state : \{passive, active\}$ initially $passive$ except for environment;
> D: integer initially 0;
> $parent$: process id initially $null$;

Upon receiving a message from P_j:
> **if** $(parent = null)$ **then**
> > $parent := P_j$;
> > $state := active$;
>
> **else** send signal to P_j;

Upon receiving a signal:
> $D := D - 1$;

To send a message (**enabled if** $(state = active)$):
> $D := D + 1$;

on $(state = passive) \land (D = 0) \land (parent \neq null)$:
> send signal to $parent$;
> $parent := null$;

environment detects termination when $(D = 0)$.

Figure 14.2: Termination detection algorithm

two variables: *cost* and *parent*. The *cost* represents the cost of the shortest path from that processor to P_0, and the *parent* points to the neighbor that is the next node in the path to P_0. Assume that each node knows the delay on links to its neighbors.

14.5. Assume that each process uses a simple acknowledgment scheme. Whenever a message is received it is acknowledged. Further assume that each process maintains a variable D that records the total deficit for that process. Define a process P_i to satisfy the local predicates l_i if it is passive and $D = 0$. Show that detecting termination is equivalent to WCP detection with this setup. What is the message complexity of centralized WCP algorithm if used in this manner?

14.6. Consider the WCP detection problem. Assume that a monitor process responsible for WCP detection runs with every application process. The application process sends its state interval index and the dependence list whenever the local predicate becomes true. Show that a termination detection algorithm can be used to solve the WCP detection problem.

14.7. Extend Dijkstra and Scholten's algorithm for the case when there can be multiple initiators of the diffusing computation.

14.8. Because termination is equivalent to conjunction of local predicates and channel predicates we can employ the algorithms in Chapter 13 for detecting termination. Compare the message complexity of those algorithms for detecting termination with the algorithm in this chapter.

*14.9. Observe that the termination detection algorithm by Dijkstra and Scholten requires as many *control* messages as the basic application messages. Show that for every termination detection algorithm, there exists a basic computation that exchanges M messages for which the detection algorithm requires M control messages.

14.5 Bibliographic Remarks

The algorithm discussed in this chapter is a slight variant of the algorithm by Dijkstra and Scholten [DS80]. There are many other termination detection algorithms (for example, Mattern [Mat87]).

Chapter 15

Control of a Distributed Computation

Who controls the past controls the future, who controls the present controls the past ... — George Orwell

15.1 Introduction

In this chapter, we study the natural step after observation—control. We propose the notion of a *supervisory process*. A supervisory process not only observes the underlying user process but also controls it by delaying (or disabling) some events or changing the order of messages in the user process. There are many reasons why we need the ability to control a distributed computation via supervisory processes.

First, a supervisory process is essential for fault tolerance. The current programming methodology views programming task as a simple execution of instructions. This execution may result in a fault that could have been avoided if critical events were verified for their suitability before execution. This is in contrast to human beings, who mix introspection with actual execution of a task. For example, if a human is using a recipe to cook some item and comes across an instruction asking him to put his hand on fire, his common sense will dictate to him that he must not do so. Thus a human being rarely follows an instruction blindly. He observes and controls the instruction he executes. Similarly, every process has associated with it a *meta-process* that observes and controls the underlying process. Thus a supervisor can be viewed as the meta-process that deals with events executed by the process itself. It may check integrity of data structures before or during any execution of critical events.

A supervisory process can also be viewed as an auxiliary process that monitors and adapts a program to varying external behavior. Supervisors have long been used for this purpose in control theory. A feedback supervisor can be used for tuning the parameters of the plant that may affect its behavior or even switch from one policy to the other. For example, assume that two procedures achieve the same result, but one procedure performs better than the other if the network is highly loaded and vice versa if it is lightly loaded. The underlying process may nondeterministically call both procedures, and the supervisor may enable the procedure that is more suitable for conditions at that point in time.

Last but not least, the notion of supervision is also important in debugging and testing of a distributed program. Debugging or testing a distributed program is, in essence, a search for anomalous behavior and the identification of its cause. For this, the programmer needs to observe the program under some controlled environment. Why controlled environment? The programmer may suspect that the bug arises when the execution satisfies certain constraints (for example, when message m_1 is delivered before message m_2). Thus the programmer is interested only in those executions that satisfy these constraints.

How does a supervisor exercise control? There are four possibilities:

1. *Off-line versus on-line control:* We say that a supervisor exercises on-line control if it does not know about the future of the computation. Not knowing the future, the controller has only limited ability to meet the desired specifications. In the off-line control model, we assume that the supervisor knows about the future. At first this model seems unrealistic, but it has many applications. Consider distributed debugging. Assume that a computation was run in which the final results were unexpected. The programmer may want to run the same computation, but now under the supervisor, so that the computation goes through some controlled execution. Of course, another possibility is to work in an intermediate model in which only partial information is available about the future.

2. *Delaying events versus changing order:* Here we address the issue of the power of the supervisor. A mild form of the supervision

exists when the supervisor is only allowed to introduce delay between events. Thus the only difference between an uncontrolled and controlled computation is that fewer executions are possible under control. The crucial problem here is the introduction of deadlocks. The controller must ensure that no new deadlocks are introduced in the system by the delaying of events.

A more powerful controller can decide to change the order of events. For example, the controller may change the order of messages received to meet the desired specification. Observe that both off-line and on-line scenarios are possible. Under off-line control, the controller may know that in the last run the message m_1 was received before m_2. Therefore, in the next run it may deliver m_2 before m_1, possibly by delaying the receive of m_1. This change of message ordering may be used for generating a different test case or during recovery from a software fault. Under on-line control, the controller may not know the future but still be able to exercise some control. The simplest example of such control is imposition of the first in first out (FIFO) ordering on messages. By including sequence numbers, it is easy to control the message ordering so that the FIFO order is maintained.

In this chapter, we will discuss off-line control where the supervisor can only delay events. By delaying events, a supervisor can ensure that bad global states are avoided in an execution.

This chapter is organized as follows. Section 15.2 shows that the problem of off-line control is NP-complete in general. Section 15.3 gives an efficient algorithm for controlling mutex predicates, and Section 15.4 gives an efficient algorithm for controlling disjunctive predicates.

The notation used in this chapter is summarized in Figure 15.1.

15.2 Hardness of the Control Problem

The problem of off-line control by delaying events can be posed as follows. We are given a deposet S representing the computation. We are also given a boolean predicate B. The goal of the controller is to determine whether there exists a way of delaying events in S such that B is always true in the controlled execution. The task of delaying events can also be viewed as imposing an additional precedence relationship $\overset{c}{\leadsto}$ between events. Of course, the new relation should not

N	The number of processes
$\{P_1, P_2, \ldots, P_N\}$	Processes
S	Deposet
l_i	Local predicate on P_i
B	Global boolean predicate
G	Global state
I, J, K, L	State intervals
$\stackrel{c}{\rightsquigarrow}$	Control order

Figure 15.1: Notation

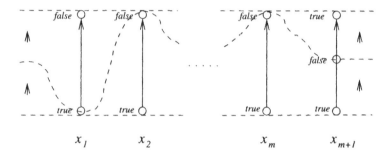

$$x_1 \qquad x_2 \qquad\qquad x_m \qquad x_{m+1}$$

Figure 15.2: Transformation for NP-completeness proof of SGSD problem

interfere with the existing causality relationship. In other words, on adding edges from the $\stackrel{c}{\rightsquigarrow}$ relation to the graph corresponding to the computation, the graph should remain acyclic. We show that even if the computation is free from communication, and the boolean predicate is simply a boolean expression of local predicates, the problem of determining whether a control strategy exists is NP-complete. Formally, we consider the following problem.

Satisfying Global Sequence Detection (SGSD): Given a deposet S and a global predicate B, determine whether there exists a global sequence in S that satisfies B.

Lemma 15.1 *SGSD is NP-complete.*

Proof: The problem is in NP because it takes polynomial time to check that a candidate global sequence is valid and that it satisfies B.

To show that it is NP-hard, we map the satisfiability problem to it (see Figure 15.2). If b is the boolean expression in satisfiability, then for each variable, $x_1, \ldots, x_m$, in b we assign a separate process with two states, one *true* and one *false* (Fig. 15.2). We define a process for an extra boolean variable x_{m+1} which starts *true*, goes through a *false* state, and ends *true* again. We define $B = b \vee x_{m+1}$ and then apply SGSD to find a satisfying global sequence. If it finds one, then the global state with $x_{m+1} = false$ will have a satisfying assignment for the variables of b.

Conversely, if b is satisfiable, then there must be a satisfying global sequence. Note that the initial global state satisfies B because x_{m+1} is true in the initial state. We then keep P_{m+1} in the initial state and advance any process that has $x_i, (1 \leq i \leq m)$ assigned false in the satisfying assignment. The resulting global state satisfies b. Now we advance P_{m+1} to the false state. The global predicate B continues to hold because b is true. After that, we advance P_{m+1} to its final true state. After this point B will continue to hold because x_{m+1} is true. Thus there exists a satisfying global sequence.

■

Considering that the problem of predicate detection for boolean expression is also NP-complete, this is not surprising. The important issue here is whether there exists a useful class of predicates that can be controlled efficiently. We discuss some of these classes next.

15.3 Mutual Exclusion

Given a system with N processes where N is at least 2, let l_i $(1 \leq i \leq N)$ denote the local condition that the process P_i is *not* in the critical section. We now define the global predicate B as

$$\forall i, j : i \neq j : l_i \vee l_j.$$

Clearly, if B is maintained in the global sequence, then the mutual exclusion will not be violated.

The sequence of local states of P_i can be divided into intervals that are *true* or *false* with respect to local predicate l_i. We define a *false interval I* as a maximal sequence of consecutive states in P_i for which l_i is false. $I.lo$ and $I.hi$ denote the beginning and ending states on I. To indicate that a false interval is on P_i, we use the notation I_i.

Given a run, we define its interval graph as follows. There is a vertex for each false interval. There is a directed edge from a false interval I to another false interval J iff

$$(initial(I.lo) \vee final(J.hi) \vee (I.lo.prev \to J.hi.next).$$

We denote this by $I \rightsquigarrow J$. The following lemma gives an implication of $I \rightsquigarrow J$ on global sequences.

Lemma 15.2 (Interval Lemma) *If $I \rightsquigarrow J$, then every global sequence enters $I.lo$ before it leaves $J.hi$.*

Proof: Let the interval I be on process P_i and the interval J be on P_j. If $initial(I.lo)$ or $final(J.hi)$, then this is trivially true. Otherwise, $I.lo.prev \to J.hi.next$. If $I.lo$ is not entered before $J.hi.next$, then there exists a global state G in the global sequence such that $G[j] = J.hi.next$ and $G[i] \leq I.lo.prev$. But this global state is inconsistent because $G[i] \to G[j]$.

■

The following result gives the condition under which a supervisor cannot avoid violation of mutual exclusion by delaying events, that is, there is no global sequence that avoids violation of mutual exclusion.

Theorem 15.3 *If the interval graph of a run has a cycle, then there is no global sequence of that run that maintains mutual exclusion.*

Proof: Consider a cycle formed by k intervals, $I_1, I_2, \ldots, I_k$. Consider any global sequence g. Without loss of generality assume that it enters the interval I_1 first. Since $I_k \rightsquigarrow I_1$, by the Interval Lemma this global sequence cannot leave $I_1.hi$ before it enters $I_k.lo$. In that global state, the mutual exclusion is violated.

■

The following lemma, whose proof is left as an exercise, is useful for proving the converse of the above theorem.

Lemma 15.4 (Sequence Lemma) *If $s \to t$, then no global sequence enters t before leaving s.*

Theorem 15.5 *If the interval graph of a run does not have a cycle, then there is a global sequence of that run that maintains mutual exclusion.*

Proof: If the interval graph does not have a cycle, then it is a directed acyclic graph. Let there be r incomparable pairs of vertices in the interval graph. We will prove the theorem by induction on r.

(Base case: $r = 0$) If r is 0, then the interval graph is a total order, say $I_1, I_2, \ldots, I_k$. We construct a new run as follows. We add an arrow from $I_i.hi$ to $I_{i+1}.lo$ for all $1 \leq i < k$ one at a time and show that acyclicity is preserved. If not, let a cycle be formed when an edge is added from $I_i.hi$ to $I_{i+1}.lo$. This implies that there is a path in the graph from $I_{i+1}.lo$ to $I_i.hi$. Let j be the first false interval from $I_1, \ldots, I_i$ that is seen in that path . We know that j exists because the path ends at I_i. Consider the path from $I_{i+1}.lo$ to a state in I_j. By definition of j this path does not use any of the arrows added so far. Therefore, $I_{i+1}.lo \rightarrow I_j.hi$. But this implies $I_{i+1} \rightsquigarrow I_j$ for some $1 \leq j \leq i$. This is not possible by our assumption on the interval graph. This implies that no cycle is formed when arrows are added. We now claim that the run, so constructed, cannot violate mutual exclusion. Since $I_i.hi \rightarrow I_{i+1}.lo$ for all i, it follows from the Sequence Lemma that I_{i+1} is entered only after I_i. Thus all accesses to the critical section are in a sequence.

(Induction case: $r > 0$) Now consider the case when there is at least one incomparable pair of vertices. Let these intervals be I_i and I_j. We construct another run as follows. We add an arrow from $I_i.hi$ to $I_j.lo$. The resulting graph can have a cycle only if $I_j.lo \rightarrow I_i.hi$. But this implies $I_j \rightsquigarrow I_i$, which is not possible. The resulting run has an interval graph in which there are strictly less than r incomparable intervals. By induction hypothesis, the new run has a global sequence which maintains mutual exclusion. This sequence is also valid in the original run.

■

The above proof can be used to construct an algorithm for controlling a computation to maintain mutual exclusion.

15.4 Disjunctive Predicates

A disjunctive predicate can be written as $l_1 \vee l_2 \vee \ldots \vee l_n$ where each l_i is a local predicate. This can be viewed as avoiding a bad combination of states. One example is avoidance of deadlock in the classic dining philosophers problem. We can avoid deadlock by ensuring that at least one of the philosophers does not have any fork at all times. As another example, consider availability of servers for critical tasks. We may impose a requirement on the system that at least one server is available at all times for critical tasks. One use of control in these applications would be rollback of the system under a fault and then its reexecution under control.

Our problem can be stated formally as follows:

Given a global predicate, $B = l_1 \vee \ldots \vee l_n$, and a deposet S for the underlying system, construct a global sequence that satisfies B whenever possible.

Our approach to constructing the satisfying control strategy will be to construct a satisfying controlled deposet of S with $\overset{c}{\leadsto}$. A control strategy can be implemented from the controlled deposet by forcing the causal order of each tuple in $\overset{c}{\leadsto}$ by sending and receiving (with blocking) a control message on the concerned processes at the appropriate states.

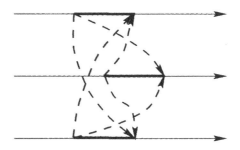

Figure 15.3: Overlapping intervals

We use interval graph as before—each interval is a vertex, and there is an edge from interval I to J if $I \leadsto J$. We first give the condition under which no control strategy exists. To that end, it is convenient to define *pure* run.

Definition 15.6 (pure run) *A run is pure with respect to a disjunctive predicate if its interval graph does not have a completely connected subgraph of size n.*

We now have

Theorem 15.7 *Consider a disjunctive predicate $B = l_1 \vee l_2 \vee \ldots \vee l_n$ where each l_i is a local predicate. If a run is not pure (with respect to B), then there is no control strategy to maintain B.*

Proof: First observe that all n vertices in the subgraph must be on distinct processes. This is because it cannot happen that two intervals

I and J on the same process satisfy $I \rightsquigarrow J$ and $J \rightsquigarrow I$. Now from the Interval Lemma, we get that none of the intervals can be left before all other intervals are entered. This implies that for any global sequence, there is a global state in which n processes are respectively in their intervals. In that global state B is false.

■

For an example of a run in which this happens, see Figure 15.3. The dashed line in the figure denotes happened before order.

We now prove the converse.

Theorem 15.8 *If a run is pure with respect to B, then there is a control strategy to maintain B.*

Proof: We use induction on the total number of intervals in the run. If a run does not have any interval on a process, then it trivially maintains B. Thus the claim is trivially true when the total number of intervals is less than n. Now consider any pure run. Our proof strategy will be as follows. We will split the pure run into two pure runs, each with a smaller number of intervals.

We consider the first interval at each process. If some process does not have any interval, then we are done, because all global sequences in that run will maintain B. Because the run is pure, there exist at least two processes, P_i and P_j, such that first intervals I and J on them satisfy $\neg(I \rightsquigarrow J)$. Consider the least global state G that contains $J.hi.next$. Note that $J.hi.next$ exists because $\neg(I \rightsquigarrow J)$ and the least global state containing $J.hi.next$ exists because the predicate "the global state contains the given local state" is linear. The global state G divides the run into two runs $pre(G)$ and $post(G)$. We show that each one of them is pure.

First consider the run $pre(G)$. We claim that $pre(G)$ does not contain any interval from P_i, which will imply that $pre(G)$ is pure. Since $\neg(I \rightsquigarrow J)$, we know that $I.lo.prev$ exists and $\neg(I.lo.prev \rightarrow J.hi.next)$. This implies that $G[i] \leq I.lo.prev$. But I is the first interval in the run at P_i. This means that $pre(G)$ has no interval on P_i and therefore is pure.

Now consider the interval graph of $post(G)$. If for any i, $G[i]$ does not belong to any interval, then there are no new edges added in the interval graph of $post(G)$ from any interval on P_i to any other interval. If for some i, $G[i]$ belongs to an interval, then by definition of

$\rightsquigarrow$, a directed edge is added from that interval to all other intervals in
$post(G)$. We need to show that this does not result in a completely
connected subgraph of size n. It is sufficient to show this for first
intervals on each process in $post(G)$. These intervals do not form a
clique in the interval graph of the original run. This implies that there
exist two intervals, K and L, such that $\neg(K \rightsquigarrow L)$ in the interval
graph of the original run. If this continues to be the case for the interval graph of $post(G)$, then we are done. Else, $(K \rightsquigarrow L)$ in $post(G)$.
This can happen only if $G[k]$ lies in the interval K. This implies that
$K.lo.prev \rightarrow J.hi.next$. Consider the first interval on P_j after J. If
there is no such interval, then $post(G)$ is pure and we are done. Otherwise, call that interval J'. We claim that $\neg(J' \rightsquigarrow L)$ in $post(G)$. By
the definition of G, it is clear that $initial(J'.lo)$ is not true in $post(G)$.
It is sufficient to show $\neg(J'.lo.prev \rightarrow L.hi.next)$. Since $K.lo.prev \rightarrow$
$J.hi.next$ and $J.hi.next \preceq J'.lo.prev$, $J'.lo.prev \rightarrow L.hi.next$ would
imply $K.lo.prev \rightarrow L.hi.next$, which is false because $\neg(K \rightsquigarrow L)$ in the
original computation. Therefore, $\neg(J' \rightsquigarrow L)$ is true in $post(G)$. This
implies that $post(G)$ is also pure.

By induction hypothesis there is a global sequence in both $pre(G)$
and $post(G)$ that maintains B. The concatenation of these two global
sequences gives us the desired global sequence.

■

15.5   Relationship Between Observation and Control

In Chapter 11, we discussed detection of predicates under various modalities. A global predicate B is definitely true for a deposet S iff for all
paths from the initial state to the final state in the lattice $C(S)$, B is
true on some state. Furthermore, $controllable : B \equiv \neg definitely : \neg B$.
From Theorems 15.7 and 15.8, it follows that for a predicate B of the
form $l_1 \vee l_2 \vee \ldots \vee l_n$, where each l_i is a local predicate, $controllable : B$
can be determined efficiently (in polynomial time). From the duality
of $controllable$ and $definitely$, we get that $definitely : B$ for predicates
B of the form $l_1 \wedge l_2 \wedge \ldots \wedge l_n$ can also be detected efficiently.

15.6 Problems

15.1. Give an algorithm that takes as input a deposet S and a disjunctive predicate B and outputs the control order $\stackrel{c}{\leadsto}$ such that when $\stackrel{c}{\leadsto}$ is imposed on S, B is always true. It should output "no" whenever S is not controllable with respect to B.

15.2. Let there be two types of accesses to the critical section: read and write. The desired predicate B is that no two processes access the critical section concurrently with one of them as write. Thus two concurrent reads are okay, but we disallow two writes or one read and one write. Give an algorithm to detect whether a given run can be controlled to maintain B and to output a control strategy if possible.

15.3. Give an efficient algorithm to determine whether the interval graph of a computation on N processes has a clique of size N. (Hint: You have to exploit properties of the interval graph to get an efficient algorithm.)

15.4. (**due to [MG00]**)We call a predicate B, a p-region predicate if given a local state s of process p, the set of global states containing s that satisfy B is a convex sublattice of the lattice of all consistent cuts. A predicate is called a region predicate if it is a conjunction of p-region predicates with possibly different p's. Show that the predicate "There are at most k messages in transit from p to q" is a region predicate. Give an algorithm to maintain region predicates.

*15.5. (**due to [MG00]**) Assume that a deposet S is controllable with respect to a disjunctive predicate B. Give an algorithm that outputs $\stackrel{c}{\leadsto}$ relation with the *smallest* size such that when $\stackrel{c}{\leadsto}$ is imposed on S, B is always true.

*15.6. Let there be k different locks. Let B, the desired predicate, be that no two processes access the same lock concurrently. Prove that the problem of maintaining B is NP-complete.

15.7. (**due to [TG94]**) Give an algorithm for *on-line* control of a distributed application to ensure that a global assertion of the form

$$\sum_{j=1}^{N} x_1^j x_2^j \dots x_{N_j}^j \geq K$$

where each x_i^j is a variable local to a process and K is a constant. Assume that the assertion is true initially and every change of a variable is enabled by the controller only when it does not violate the assertion.

*15.8. **(due to [SG02])** Give an efficient algorithm to detect *controllable* : B for a linear predicate B.

15.7 Bibliographic Remarks

The discussion on various modes of control is taken from Garg [Gar97]. The NP-completeness of the satisfying global sequence detection problem was first shown in Tarafdar and Garg [TG98b]. The algorithm for controlling strategy for disjunctive predicates is a variant of the algorithm in Garg and Waldecker [GW96]. Also see [TG99, MG00] for related discussion. The discussion of controlling strategy for mutual exclusion for a single lock or multiple locks (see the Problem set) is taken from Tarafdar and Garg [TG99].

Chapter 16

Causal Message Ordering

Let all things be done decently and in order. — I Corinthians 14:40, The Bible

16.1 Introduction

Distributed programs are difficult to design and test because of their nondeterministic nature, that is, a distributed program may exhibit multiple behaviors on the same external input. This nondeterminism is caused by reordering of messages in different executions. It is sometimes desirable to control this nondeterminism by restricting the possible message ordering in a system.

Figure 16.1: A FIFO computation that is not causally ordered

A *fully asynchronous* computation does not have any restriction on the message ordering. It permits maximum concurrency, but algo-

195

rithms based on fully asynchronous communication can be difficult to design because they are required to work for all ordering of the messages. Therefore, many systems restrict message delivery to a FIFO order. This results in simplicity in design of distributed algorithms based on the FIFO assumption. For example, we used the FIFO assumption in Lamport's algorithm for mutual exclusion and Chandy and Lamport's algorithm for a global snapshot.

A FIFO-ordered computation is implemented generally by using sequence numbers for messages. However, observe that by using FIFO ordering, a program loses some of its concurrency. When a message is received out of order, its processing must be delayed.

A stronger requirement than FIFO is that of *causal ordering*. Intuitively, causal ordering requires that a single message should not be overtaken by a sequence of messages. For example, the computation in Figure 16.1 satisfies FIFO ordering of messages but does not satisfy causal ordering. A sequence of messages from P_1 to P_2 and from P_2 to P_3 overtakes a message from P_1 to P_3 in this example. Causal ordering of messages is useful in many contexts. In Chapter 6, we considered the problem of mutual exclusion. Assume that we use a centralized coordinator for granting requests to the access of the critical section. The fairness property requires that the requests be honored in the order they are made (and not in the order they are received). It is easy to see that if the underlying system guaranteed a causal ordering of messages, then the order in which requests are received cannot violate the order in which they are made. For another example of the usefulness of causal ordering, see Problem 16.5.

The relationship among various message orderings can be formally specified based on the happened before relation. For convenience, we denote the receive event corresponding to the send event s_i by r_i and vice versa. The message is represented as (s_i, r_i). Thus $s_i \rightsquigarrow r_i$ for any i.

Now, FIFO and causally ordered computations can be defined as follows.

FIFO : Any two messages from a process P_i to P_j are received in the same order as they were sent. Formally, let s_1 and s_2 be any two send events and r_1 and r_2 be corresponding receive events. Then,

$$s_1 \prec s_2 \quad \Rightarrow \quad \neg(r_2 \prec r_1). \qquad \text{(FIFO)}$$

Causally Ordered : Let any two send events s_1 and s_2 in a distributed computation be related such that the first send happened before the second send. Then, the second message cannot be received before the first message by any process. Formally,

$$s_1 \to s_2 \quad \Rightarrow \quad \neg(r_2 \prec r_1). \tag{CO}$$

This chapter is organized as follows. Section 16.2 gives an algorithm to ensure causal ordering of messages. Section 16.3 gives a proof of its correctness.

The notation used in this chapter is summarized in Figure 16.2.

N	The number of processes
i, j, k	Process numbers
s, t	Local states
$s.p$	Process id of the state s
m	Matrix clock

Figure 16.2: Notation

16.2 Algorithm

We now describe an algorithm to ensure causal ordering of messages. We assume that a process never sends any message to itself. Each process maintains a matrix m of integers. The entry $s.m[j, k]$ records the number of messages sent by process P_j to process P_k as known by process $P_{s.p}$ in the state s. The algorithm for process P_i is given in Figure 16.3. Whenever a message is sent from P_i to P_j, the matrix m is piggybacked with the message. The entry $m[i, j]$ is incremented to reflect the fact that one more message has been sent from P_i to P_j. Whenever messages are received by the communication system at P_i, they are first checked for eligibility before delivery to P_i. If a message is not eligible it is simply buffered until it becomes eligible. In the following discussion, we identify a message with the state it is sent from. A message u is eligible to be received at state s, when the number of messages sent from any process P_k to P_i, as indicated by the matrix $u.m$ in the message, is less than or equal to the number recorded in the matrix $s.m$. Formally, this condition is

$$\forall k : s.m[k, i] \geq u.m[k, i]$$

If for some k, $u.m[k, i] > s.m[k, i]$, then there is a message that was sent in the casual history of the message u and has not arrived by the state s. Therefore, P_i must wait for that message to be delivered before it can accept the message u.

P_i::
  var
      m:array$[1..N,\ 1..N]$ of integer initially $\forall j, k : m[j, k] = 0$;

$(s, send, t)$ to P_j:
    $t.m := s.m$;
    $t.m[i, j] := t.m[i, j] + 1$;

$(s, recv(u), t)$: **enabled if** $\forall k : s.m[k, i] \geq u.m[k, i]$
    $t.m := max(s.m, u.m)$;
    $t.m[u.p, i] := t.m[u.p, i] + 1$;

Figure 16.3: An algorithm for causal ordering of messages at P_i

16.3   Proof of Correctness

Before we show the correctness of the algorithm, we give the interpretation of the matrix m. Let $S[i, j]$ denote the set of send events from process P_i to process P_j. Note that $S[i, j]$ is a totally ordered set. We show that $s.m[k, l]$ is equal to the number of send events from P_k to P_l that happened before s.

Lemma 16.1

$$s.m[k, l] = \#\{u \in S[k, l] \mid u \to s\}.$$

Proof: Left as an exercise in induction.

■

Theorem 16.2 (Safety) $s_1 \to s_2 \Rightarrow \neg(r_2 \prec r_1)$.

Proof: If $r_1.p \neq r_2.p$, then the result holds trivially. Otherwise, assume that $r_1.p = r_2.p$. Let $i = r_1.p$. We will use induction on n, the total number of messages delivered in process P_i. If no message has been delivered so far, process P_i clearly satisfies the safety property. We will assume that process P_i satisfies the safety property for the first $n - 1$ messages, and show that the nth message delivered maintains the property. We will show that $(s_1 \rightarrow s_2) \wedge (r_2 \prec r_1)$ leads to a contradiction. Assume that r_2 corresponds to the nth message, and the message r_1 is not yet delivered.

Let w be the state in which the nth message is received. Because $s_1 \rightarrow s_2$, it follows that (from Problem 16.3)

$$s_1.m[s_1.p, i] < s_2.m[s_1.p, i].$$

At the state w, the process P_i has received at most $s_1.m[s_1.p, i]$ messages from $s_1.p$. This is because $s_1.m[s_1.p, i]$ messages have been sent before s_1. We have assumed that s_1 has not been received. Furthermore, no message sent after s_1 has been received so far because that would violate induction hypothesis. Therefore, from the program text $w.m[s_1.p, i] \leq s_1.m[s_1.p, i]$. This implies that $w.m[s_1.p, i] < s_2.m[s_1.p, i]$. From the receiving condition, we know that the receive of s_2 is not enabled at this point. But earlier we had assumed, that r_2 is received at w, a contradiction.

■

The above theorem tells us that our algorithm will deliver messages only in causal ordering. However, this does not guarantee that any message will be delivered. In fact, an algorithm that does not deliver any message will trivially satisfy the Safety Theorem. We also need to show that every message sent is eventually delivered.

Theorem 16.3 (Liveness) *Assuming that every message sent is eventually buffered at the destination, every message is also delivered.*

Proof: Let $channel(G, s)$ be the set of all messages sent to the process $P_{s.p}$ in the channel in the consistent cut G (which includes the state s). Let $M = min(channel(G, s))$ represent the set of messages minimal in $channel(G, s)$ with respect to $\rightarrow$. Let $g \in M$. We show that g is deliverable.

We show the contrapositive, that is, if g is not deliverable at s, then $g \notin M$. The fact that the message g is not deliverable at s implies that

$$\exists k : s.m[k, s.p] < g.m[k, s.p].$$

Let $g.m[k, s.p] = y$. This means that there are y messages sent from k to $s.p$ that happened before g (from Lemma 16.1). If all these messages have been received before state s, then $s.m[k, s.p] = g.m[k, s.p]$, a contradiction. Otherwise, there exists a message whose send happened before g and is not delivered before state s. Thus $g \notin M$.

■

16.4 Problems

16.1. Prove Lemma 16.1.

16.2. Let $e, f \in \mathcal{E}$. Then, show that $e \to f \Rightarrow e.m \leq f.m$.

16.3. Let s_1 be the send event of a message from P_i to P_j and s_2 be any other send event. Then, $s_1 \to s_2 \Rightarrow s_1.m[i, j] < s_2.m[i, j]$.

16.4. Prove or disprove: For any send event s, and any event w,

$$s \to w \text{ iff } s.m[s.p, w.p] < w.m[s.p, w.p].$$

16.5. Assume that you have replicated data for fault tolerance. Any file (or a record) may be replicated at more than one site. To avoid updating two copies of the data, assume that a token-based scheme is used. Any site possessing the token can update the file and broadcast the update to all sites which have that file. Show that if the communication is guaranteed to be causally ordered, then the above scheme will ensure that all updates at all sites happen in the same order.

16.6. Let M be the set of messages in a distributed computation. Given a message x, we use $x.s$ to denote the send event and $x.r$ to denote the receive event. We say that a computation is *causally* ordered if

$$\forall x, y \in M : (x.s \to y.s) \Rightarrow \neg(y.r \to x.r).$$

We say that a computation is *mysteriously* ordered if

$$\forall x, y \in M : (x.s \to y.r) \Rightarrow \neg(y.s \to x.r).$$

(a) Prove or disprove that every causally ordered computation is also mysteriously ordered.
(b) Prove or disprove that every mysteriously ordered computation is also causally ordered.

16.7. Show the relationship between conditions (C1), (C2), and (C3) on message delivery of a system.

$$(C1) \qquad s_1 \rightarrow s_2 \Rightarrow \neg(r_2 \rightarrow r_1)$$

$$(C2) \qquad s_1 \prec s_2 \Rightarrow \neg(r_2 \rightarrow r_1)$$

$$(C3) \qquad s_1 \rightarrow s_2 \rightarrow \neg(r_2 \prec r_1)$$

where s_1 and s_2 are sends of any two messages and r_1 and r_2 are corresponding receives. Note that a computation satisfies a delivery condition if and only if the condition is true for all pairs of messages.

16.8. Let $R_1 = (S_1, S_2, \ldots, S_N, \rightsquigarrow_1)$ and $R_2 = (T_1, T_2, \ldots, T_N, \rightsquigarrow_2)$ be two distributed computations. We define $R_1.R_2$ as the pasting of two runs together, that is,

$$R_1.R_2 = (S_1.T_1, S_2.T_2, \ldots, S_N.T_N, \rightsquigarrow_1 \cup \rightsquigarrow_2).$$

Show that if R_1 and R_2 are causal, then so is $R_1.R_2$.

16.9. How will the algorithm for causal ordering change if messages can be multicast instead of point to point?

16.10. Assume that all messages are broadcast messages. How can you simplify the algorithm for guaranteeing causal ordering of messages under this condition?

16.11. Consider a system of $N + 1$ processes $\{P_0, P_1, \ldots, P_N\}$ in which processes P_1 through P_N can only send messages to P_0 or receive messages from P_0. Show that if all channels in the system are FIFO, then any computation on this system is causally ordered.

16.12. In this chapter, we have used the happened before model for modeling dependency of one message to the other. Thus all messages within a process are totally ordered. For some applications, messages sent from a process may be independent. Give an algorithm to ensure causal ordering of messages when the send events from a single process do not form a total order (See Chapter 2).

16.13. Suppose that the system is composed of nonoverlapping groups such that any communication outside the group is always through the group leader, that is, only group leaders are permitted to send or receive messages from outside the group. How will you exploit this structure to reduce the overhead in causal ordering of messages?

*16.14. **(due to [MG97])** A forbidden predicate is a conjunction of causality relationships between sends and receives of messages. A message ordering is acceptable only if it does not satisfy the given forbidden predicate. For example, the following forbidden predicate specifies violation of causal ordering:

$$\exists x, y : (x.s \rightarrow y.s) \wedge (y.r \rightarrow x.r)$$

where $x.s$ denotes send of the message x and $x.r$ denotes receive of the message x. By associating colors and processes with messages, we can define many useful message orderings. Show how a controller can take a specification as a forbidden predicate and decide whether that specification is implementable or not.

*16.15. The matrix used in the algorithm for causal ordering can be viewed as N vectors, one for each process. Give an algorithm that sends a variable number of vectors with each message. In the best case it sends only one vector, and in the worst case it sends all N vectors. (Hint: Show that it is sufficient to include vectors of only those send events that are maximal in the causal history of a message.)

16.5   Bibliographic Remarks

Causal ordering was first proposed by Birman and Joseph [BJ87]. The algorithm for causal ordering described in this chapter is essentially the same as in Raynal, Schiper, and Toueg [RST91]. However, our proof of correctness is different.

Chapter 17

Synchronous and Total Order

Freedom cannot exist without the concept of order. — Prince Metternich

17.1 Introduction

Synchronous ordering is a stronger requirement than causal ordering. A computation satisfies synchronous ordering of messages if it is equivalent to a computation in which all messages are logically instantaneous. Figure 17.1 gives an example of a synchronously ordered computation and Figure 17.2 an example of a computation that does not satisfy synchronous ordering.

Algorithms for synchronous systems are easier to design than those for causally ordered systems. The model of synchronous message passing lets us reason about a distributed program under the assumption that messages are instantaneous or "points" rather then "intervals" (i.e., we can always draw the time diagrams for the distributed programs with the message arrows being vertical). If we assume messages as points instead of intervals, we can order the messages as a partial order and therefore, we can have vector clocks with respect to messages. One of the applications for synchronous ordering of messages is that it enables us to reason about distributed objects as if they were centralized. Assume that a process invokes an operation on a remote object by sending a message. If synchronous ordering of messages is assumed,

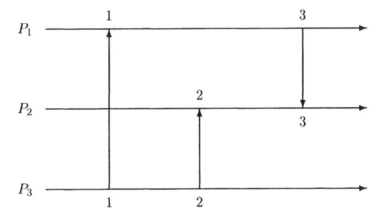

Figure 17.1: A computation that is synchronously ordered

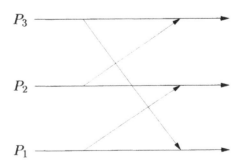

Figure 17.2: A computation that is not synchronously ordered

then all operations on the objects can be ordered based on when the messages are sent because messages can be considered instantaneous.

For example, consider a system with three distributed sites A, B, C, each with a set of processes and a set of objects. Let the sites A and B have objects queue q_1 and queue q_2, respectively. Let there be two processes P_1 at site B and P_2 at site C, specified as follows. Process P_1 inserts c in q_1 followed by d in q_2, whereas P_2 inserts a in q_2 followed by b in q_1. Thus the execution traces of P_1 and P_2 are

$$P_1 = insert(q_1, c); insert(q_2, d).$$

$$P_2 = insert(q_2, a); insert(q_1, b).$$

In a shared memory system, it can be verified that the system cannot reach a global state in which q_1 has b followed by c and q_2 has d followed by a denoted as:

q_1	b	c
q_2	d	a

The reason is that if b appears before c in q_1, then we know that the operation $insert(q_1, b)$ must have been done before the operation $insert(q_1, c)$. Because of process order, this implies that $insert(q_2, a)$ must have been done before $insert(q_2, d)$.

If we assume that a process invokes an operation by simply sending a message, then under asynchronous message passing we can indeed end up in the inconsistent state as shown in figure 17.3. In this case, at site A, c is inserted after b in queue q_1 and at site B, a is inserted after d.

If we consider each message as a point and draw all possible time diagrams with vertical messages, it will result only in one of the consistent states (see Figure 17.4). If we observe the time diagram as shown in Figure 17.3, we notice that, it cannot be redrawn with all messages vertical. Thus it is not a synchronously ordered computation.

It should be observed that as we restrict message ordering we lose concurrency but make it easier to solve problems.

Total ordering of messages is useful when messages may be multicast. One of the applications of total ordering of messages is in implementing an object that is replicated across multiple sites. If different processes invoke different operations on the object, the sequence of operations applied at each site must be identical. Implementing this

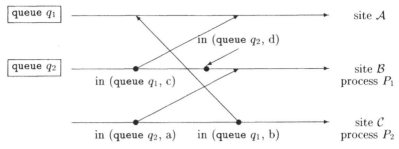

Figure 17.3: Inconsistent memory state

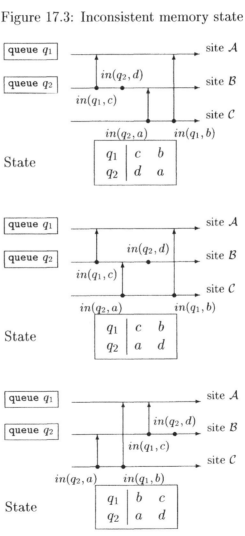

Figure 17.4: Time diagrams under synchronous message passing

constraint in a distributed system is significantly easier if there is a total ordering of messages.

This chapter is organized as follows. Section 17.2 defines synchronous ordering and describes its relationship with causal ordering of messages. It also gives a characterization of synchronously ordered computations using crowns. Section 17.3 gives a distributed algorithm to implement synchronous ordering of messages. Section 17.4 gives algorithms to implement total ordering of messages.

The notation used in this chapter is summarized in Figure 17.5.

e, f	Events
s_1, s_2	Send events
r_1, r_2	Receive events
$\mathcal{E}$	Events for application messages
T	Timestamp of the event

Figure 17.5: Notation

17.2   Synchronous Ordering

A computation is synchronous if its time diagram can be drawn such that all message arrows are vertical, that is, all external events can be assigned a timestamp such that time increases within a single process and for any message its send and receive are assigned the same timestamp. Formally, let $\mathcal{E}$ be the set of all external events. Then,

Definition 17.1 (SYNC) *A computation is synchronous iff there exists a mapping* T *from* $\mathcal{E}$ *to the set of natural numbers such that for all* $s, r, e, f \in \mathcal{E}$:

$$s \rightsquigarrow r \Rightarrow \mathrm{T}(s) = \mathrm{T}(r)$$

and

$$e \prec f \Rightarrow \mathrm{T}(e) < \mathrm{T}(f).$$

It is easy to see that, for any two external events e and f

$$(e \to f) \wedge \neg(e \rightsquigarrow f) \quad \Rightarrow \quad \mathrm{T}(e) < \mathrm{T}(f). \tag{17.1}$$

17.2.1   Relationship Among Message Orderings

The following theorem describes the hierarchy of various message orderings.

Theorem 17.2 *The hierarchy associated with the various message orderings is*

$$Synchronous \subseteq Causally \ Ordered \subseteq FIFO \subseteq Asynchronous.$$

Proof:

FIFO $\subseteq$ Asynchronous : Obvious.

Causally Ordered $\subseteq$ FIFO : This is true because

$$s_1 \prec s_2 \quad \Rightarrow \quad s_1 \to s_2.$$

Synchronous $\subseteq$ Causally Ordered : We show that if a computation is synchronous then it is also causally ordered. Because the communication is synchronous, there exists a function T satisfying SYNC.

For any set of send events s_1, s_2 and receive events r_1, r_2 such that $s_1 \rightsquigarrow r_1$, $s_2 \rightsquigarrow r_2$ and $s_1 \to s_2$:

$$\text{T}(s_1) = \text{T}(r_1), \quad \text{T}(s_2) = \text{T}(r_2), \quad \text{and} \quad \text{T}(s_1) < \text{T}(s_2).$$

It follows that $\text{T}(r_1) < \text{T}(r_2)$. Therefore, (17.1) implies

$$\neg(r_2 \to r_1).$$

■

17.2.2   Crowns in a Distributed Computation

A computation can also be characterized as synchronous based on the absence of a structure called "crown". We now present the definition of a crown and prove that a computation is synchronous if and only if it does not contain any crown.

Definition 17.3 (Crown) *A crown (of size $k \geq 2$) is a sequence $\langle (s_i, r_i), i \in \{0, 1 \ldots, k-1\} : s_i \rightsquigarrow r_i \rangle$ of pairs of corresponding send and receive events such that (see Fig. 17.6)*

$$s_0 \to r_1, s_1 \to r_2, \cdots, s_{k-2} \to r_{k-1}, s_{k-1} \to r_0.$$

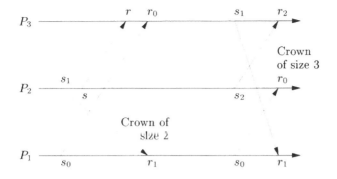

Figure 17.6: Crowns of size 2 and 3

Theorem 17.4 *A computation is synchronous iff there is no crown in it.*

Proof:

Synchronous $\Rightarrow$ ¬Crown :

Since the computation is synchronous, there exists a function T satisfying SYNC, and for any two events e and f such that $(e \rightarrow f) \wedge \neg(e \rightsquigarrow f)$, $T(e) < T(f)$.

Suppose, if possible, the computation has a crown of size k, $s_0 \rightarrow r_1, \cdots, s_{k-1} \rightarrow r_0$. Then,

$$\forall i \in \{0, 1, \ldots, k-1\} \qquad T(s_i) < T(r_{(i+1) \bmod k}) \qquad (*)$$
$$\forall i \in \{1, 2, \ldots, k-1\} \qquad T(s_i) = T(r_i). \qquad (**)$$

Therefore, from equations $(*)$ and $(**)$, $T(s_0) < T(r_0)$, which is a contradiction because SYNC implies that $T(s_0) = T(r_0)$.

¬Crown $\Rightarrow$ Synchronous :

Given a computation, we form a directed graph $G(V, E)$, as follows. The vertex set V consists of all messages in the computation, that is, $v_i = \{s_i, r_i\}$. There is an edge from v_i to v_j if there is an event $e \in v_i$ and an event $f \in v_j$ such that $e \rightarrow f$. Thus $(v_i, v_j) \in E$ iff $(s_i \rightarrow s_j) \vee (s_i \rightarrow r_j) \vee (r_i \rightarrow s_j) \vee (r_i \rightarrow r_j)$. It is easy to see that each of the four disjuncts implies $s_i \rightarrow r_j$. Hence, $(v_i, v_j) \in E$ iff $s_i \rightarrow r_j$.

Since the computation does not have any crown, it follows that the graph G is acyclic and can be topologically sorted. Therefore, there exists a function $T : \mathcal{E} \rightarrow \mathcal{N}$ satisfying SYNC.

■

17.3   Algorithm

The algorithm implements the desired ordering using control messages. Note that control messages are not required to satisfy synchronous ordering. Thus $\mathcal{E}$ includes the send and receive events only of application messages. It does not include send and receive of control messages sent by the algorithm to ensure synchronous ordering.

The algorithm shown in Figure 17.7 is for the process P_i. All processes have the same algorithm. Observe that the protocol to implement synchronous message ordering cannot be completely symmetric. If two processes desire to send messages to each other, then there is no symmetric synchronous computation that allows this—one of them must succeed before the other. To introduce asymmetry, we use process numbers to totally order all processes. Each send event, s, is either from a bigger process (denoted by $big(s)$) or from a smaller process (denoted by $small(s)$). We assume that processes do not send messages to themselves.

In our algorithm, a process can be in two states—*active* or *passive*. Every process is initially active. We first consider the algorithm for a send event corresponding to $big(s)$. A process is allowed to send a message to a smaller process only when it is active. After sending the message it turns passive until it receives an *ack* message from the receiver of the message. While passive, it cannot send any other message nor can it accept any other message. Thus the following condition is satisfied.

$$\forall e \in \mathcal{E} : (s \prec e) \land big(s) \Rightarrow (r \rightarrow e)$$

It follows that

$$\forall e \in \mathcal{E} : (s \rightarrow e) \land big(s) \Rightarrow (r \rightarrow e) \tag{17.2}$$

Note that the protocol for a message from a bigger process requires only one control message (ack).

To send a message to a bigger process, say P_j, P_i first needs permission from P_j. It can request the permission at any time. P_j can grant permission only when it is active. Furthermore, after granting the permission, P_j turns passive until it receives the message for which it has granted the permission. Thus the protocol for a message from a smaller process requires two control messages (*request* and *permission*). Because the process that grants the permission turns passive until it receives the message, we get that

$$\forall e \in \mathcal{E} : (e \prec r) \land small(s) \Rightarrow (e \rightarrow s)$$

It follows that

$$\forall e \in \mathcal{E} : (e \rightarrow r) \land small(s) \Rightarrow (e \rightarrow s) \tag{17.3}$$

By taking the contrapositive and using asymmetry of $\rightarrow$, we also get

$$\forall e \in \mathcal{E} : (s \rightarrow e) \land small(s) \Rightarrow \neg(e \rightarrow r) \tag{17.4}$$

17.3.1 Proof of Correctness

The correctness of the above algorithm is proved in the usual two steps: safety and liveness.

Theorem 17.5 (Safety) *Any distributed computation that satisfies Equations 17.2 and 17.3 is synchronous.*

Proof: To prove that the computation is synchronous, we will show that it does not have any crown. We first show that if the computation has any crown of size greater than two, then it also has a crown of size two.

Pick any message s_i in the crown. If s_i is big, then from $(s_i \rightarrow r_{i+1})$ and $big(s_i)$ and Equation 17.2, we get that $r_i \rightarrow r_{i+1}$. Combining this with $(s_{i-1} \rightarrow r_i)$, we get $(s_{i-1} \rightarrow r_{i+1})$. Thus a smaller crown can be obtained by dropping the message i.

Now consider the case when s_i is small. Then, from $(s_{i-1} \rightarrow r_i)$ and $small(s_i)$, and Equation 17.3, we get that $s_{i-1} \rightarrow s_i$. Combining this with $(s_i \rightarrow r_{i+1})$, we get $(s_{i-1} \rightarrow r_{i+1})$. Thus a smaller crown can be obtained by dropping the message i.

We now show that there cannot exist any crown of size two. Assume, if possible, that there exist two messages such that $(s_1 \rightarrow r_2) \land (s_2 \rightarrow r_1)$. First consider the case when one of them is big. Without loss of generality, let $big(s_1)$ be true. This implies $(r_1 \rightarrow r_2)$ from Equation 17.2 by using r_2 for e. Now if $big(s_2)$ holds, we get that $(r_2 \rightarrow r_1)$, and if $small(s_2)$ holds, then we get $\neg(r_1 \rightarrow r_2)$ (by applying Equation 17.4). Both cases contradict $(r_1 \rightarrow r_2)$.

Now consider the case when $small(s_1)$ and $small(s_2)$ are true. From Equation 17.3, we get $s_2 \rightarrow s_1$ as well as $s_1 \rightarrow s_2$. Thus this case is also not possible. Hence, we conclude that no crown is possible.

$P_i ::$
var
    $state : \{active, passive\}$ initially $active;$

To send m to P_j, $(j < i)$
    enabled if $(state = active)$:
    send m to P_j
    $state := passive;$

Upon receive m from P_j, $(j > i)$
    enabled if $(state = active)$:
        send ack to $P_j;$

Upon receive ack:
    $state := active;$

To send a message $(message\_id, m)$ to P_j, $(j > i)$
    send $request(message\_id)$ to $P_j;$

Upon receive $request(message\_id)$ from P_j, $(j < i)$
    enabled if $(state = active)$:
    send $permission(message\_id)$ to P_j
    $state := passive;$

Upon receive $permission(message\_id)$ from P_j, $(j > i)$
    enabled if $(state = active)$:
    send m to $P_j;$

Upon receive m from P_j, $(j < i)$
    $state := active;$

Figure 17.7: The algorithm at P_i for synchronous ordering of messages

∎

Theorem 17.6 (Liveness) *In a distributed computation (that implements the algorithm), every process P_k that wants to send a message will eventually be able to send it and every message will eventually be delivered.*

Proof: The smallest process P_1 is always *active*. It sends a reply as soon as it gets a message. Now, to apply induction, given that k smallest processes will eventually be in the *active* state, we show that the $(k+1)^{th}$ process if *passive* will eventually turn *active*. P_{k+1} can be passive only if it has sent a message or a permission to a smaller process. In either case, because all smaller processes are active, it will get a reply and thus become active.

∎

17.4 Total Order for Multicast Messages

So far we have assumed that messages were point-to-point. In many applications, where a message may be sent to multiple processes, it is desirable that all messages are delivered in the same order at all processes. For example, consider a server that is replicated at multiple sites for fault tolerance. If a client makes a request to the server, then all copies of the server should handle requests in the same order. The total ordering of messages can formally be specified as:

For all messages x and y and all processes P and Q, if x is received at P before y, then y is not received before x at Q. (**Total Order**)

We require that y not be received before x, rather than that x be received before y, to address the case where x is not sent to Q. Observe that we do not require that a message be broadcast to all processes.

In this section we discuss algorithms that will provide the total ordering of messages. Observe that the property of total order of messages does not imply causal or even FIFO property of messages. Consider the case when P sends messages m_1 followed by m_2. If all processes receive m_2 before m_1, then the total order is satisfied even though FIFO is not. The algorithms described in this section will satisfy causal order in addition to the total order. We will call this ordering of messages *causal total order*.

The algorithms for ensuring total order are very similar to mutual exclusion algorithms. After all, mutual exclusion algorithms ensure that all accesses to the critical section form a total order. If we ensure that messages are received in the "critical section" order, then we are done. We will discuss a centralized algorithm and a distributed algorithm for causal total ordering of messages.

17.4.1 Centralized Algorithm

We first modify the centralized algorithm for mutual exclusion to guarantee causal total ordering of messages. We assume that channels between the coordinator process and other processes satisfy the FIFO property. A process that wants to multicast a message simply sends it to the coordinator with its vector clock. This step corresponds to requesting the lock in the mutual exclusion algorithm. Furthermore, in that algorithm, the coordinator maintains a request queue and whenever a request by a process becomes eligible, it sends the lock to that process. In the algorithm for causal total ordering of messages, the coordinator will simply multicast the message corresponding to the request instead of sending the lock. Since all multicast messages originate from the coordinator, and the channels are FIFO, the total order property holds. Since the requests are served in the causal order, the algorithm also satisfies causal ordering of messages.

We can avoid the use of vector clocks if we need only the total order. In that case, all requests are considered eligible.

In the above algorithm, the coordinator has to perform more work than the other nodes. One way to perform load balancing over time is by suitably rotating the responsibility of the coordinator among processes. This can be achieved using the notion of a token. The token assigns sequence numbers to broadcasts, and messages are delivered only in the sequence order.

17.4.2 Lamport's Algorithm for Total Order

We modify Lamport's algorithm for mutual exclusion to derive an algorithm for total ordering of messages. As in that algorithm, we assume FIFO ordering of messages. We also assume that a message is broadcast to all processes. To simulate multicast, a process can simply ignore a message that is not meant for it. Each process maintains a logical clock (used for timestamps) and a queue (used for storing undelivered messages). The algorithm is given by the following rules.

- To send a broadcast message, a process sends a timestamped message to all other processes including itself. This step corresponds to requesting the critical section in the mutual exclusion algorithm.

- On receiving a broadcast message, the message and its timestamp are stored in the queue and an acknowledgment is returned.

- A process can remove the message from the request queue with the smallest timestamp, t, if it has received a message from every other process with timestamp greater than t. This step corresponds to executing the critical section for the mutual exclusion algorithm.

- When a process removes its own message from its queue, it informs all other processes that this message is deliverable. Other processes can deliver the message on receiving this notification. This step corresponds to releasing of the critical section in the mutual exclsuion algorithm.

In this algorithm, the total order of messages delivered is given by the logical clock of send events of the broadcast messages.

17.4.3   Skeen's Algorithm

The distributed algorithm of Skeen is given by the following rules. It also assumes that processes have access to Lamport's logical clock.

- To send a multicast message, a process sends a timestamped message to all the destination processes.

- On receiving a message, a process marks it as *undeliverable* and sends the value of the logical clock as the proposed timestamp to the initiator.

- When the initiator has received all the proposed timestamps, it takes the maximum of all proposals and assigns that timestamp as the final timestamp to that message. This value is sent to all the destinations.

- Upon receiving the final timestamp of a message, it is marked as deliverable.

- A deliverable message is delivered to the site if it has the smallest timestamp in the message queue.

In this algorithm, the total order of message delivery is given by the final timestamps of the messages.

We leave the formal description and proof of correctness of these algorithms as exercises.

17.5   Application: Replicated State Machines

Assume that we are interested in providing a fault-tolerant service in a distributed system. The service is expected to process *requests* and provide *outputs*. We would also like the service to tolerate up to t faults where each fault corresponds to a crash of a processor. We can build such a service using $t + 1$ processors in a distributed system as follows. We structure our service as a *deterministic* state machine. This means that if each nonfaulty processor starts in the same initial state and executes the requests in the same order, then each will produce the same output. Thus by combining outputs of the collection we can get a t fault-tolerant service. The key requirement for implementation is that all state machines process all requests in the same order. The total ordering of messages (for example, Lamport's algorithm) satisfies this property.

17.6   Problems

17.1. Design an algorithm for synchronous ordering for point-to-point messages that does not use a static priority scheme. (Hint: Impose an acyclic directed graph on processes. The edge from P_i to P_j means that P_i is bigger than P_j for the purpose of sending messages. Give a rule by which the direction of edges is reversed, such that acyclicity of the graph is maintained.)

17.2. Extend the algorithm for synchronous ordering to the case when a process may send a message to itself. The message, whenever enabled, is considered to take zero time.

17.3. Consider the partial order generated by the messages in a synchronously ordered computation on N processes. Show that the width of the partial order is at most $N/2$.

17.4. Prove the correctness of Lamport's algorithm for providing causal total ordering of messages.

17.5. Prove the correctness of Skeen's algorithm for providing total ordering of messages.

*17.6. Let $G = (V, E)$ be communication topology of a system that uses synchronous ordering of messages. Let d be the size of a vertex cover of G. Show that there exists an on-line algorithm to timestamp messages with at most d dimensions, such that order between messages in the system can be determined using timestamps.

*17.7. Show that every message in a synchronously ordered computation on N processes can be timestamped with a $\lfloor N/2 \rfloor$ dimensional vector such that the order relationship between messages can be determined using the vector timestamps.

17.7 Bibliographic Remarks

The algorithm for implementing synchronous ordering is taken from [MG95b]. For discussion on total ordering of messages, see [BJ87]. The distributed algorithm for causal total ordering of messages is implicit in the replicated state machine construction in [Lam78]. Skeen's algorithm is taken from [Ske82].

Chapter 18

Computation of a Global Function

> *Learning without thoughts is labor lost, thoughts without learning is perilous — Confucius*

18.1 Introduction

As we have seen earlier, one of the fundamental difficulties of distributed computing is that no processor has access to the global state. This difficulty can be alleviated by developing mechanisms to compute functions of the global state. We call such functions *global functions*. More concretely, assume that we have x_i located at process P_i. Our aim is to compute a function $f(x_1, x_2, \ldots, x_N)$ that clearly depends on states of all processes.

First, we present an algorithm for convergecast and broadcast on a network, assuming that there is a predefined spanning tree. The convergecast requires information from all nodes of the tree to be collected at the root of the tree. Once all the information is present at the root node, it can compute the global function and then broadcast the value to all nodes in the tree. Both the convergecast and the broadcast require a spanning tree on the network. We also give an algorithm to build the spanning tree.

Next we present an algorithm to compute a global function that does not use a spanning tree. In this algorithm, a processor informs its neighbors of any new information it receives as soon as possible. Although this algorithm is expensive in terms of messages, it has many

219

desirable properties. First, at the end of their algorithm all processors know the value of the function f. Moreover, the algorithm is completely symmetric. It does not assume that the underlying topology of the communication network is known, except that all processors know about their neighbors. The algorithm is presented first for a special case, when the global function to be computed is the routing table for each processor. This algorithm is then generalized so that it can be used for any global function.

We assume in this chapter that all links are bidirectional unless otherwise stated.

This chapter is organized as follows. Section 18.2 gives algorithms for convergecast, broadcast, and construction of a spanning tree. Section 18.3 gives an algorithm to compute the global function.

The notation used in this chapter is summarized in Figure 18.1.

N	The number of processes
m	The number of channels
D	The diameter of the network
P, Q	Processes
$V(P)$	Neighbors of P
c	Channel

Figure 18.1: Notation

18.2 Convergecast and Broadcast

The algorithms for convergecast and broadcast are very simple if we assume a rooted, spanning tree. For convergecast, the algorithm is shown in Figure 18.2. Each node in the spanning tree is responsible to report to its *parent* the information of its subtree. The variable *parent*, for a node x, is the identity of the neighbor of x, which is the parent in the rooted, spanning tree. For the root, this value is *null*. The variable *numchildren* keeps track of the total number of its children, and *numreports* keeps track of the number of its children who have reported. When the root node hears from all its children, it has all the information to compute the global function.

The broadcast algorithm shown in Figure 18.3 is dual of the convergecast algorithm. The algorithm is initiated by the root process by

```
var
     parent: process id;// initialized based on the spanning tree
     numchildren: integer; // initialized based on the spanning tree
     numreports: integer initially 0;

on receiving a report from P_j
     numreports := numreports + 1;
     if (numreports = numchildren) then
          if (parent = null) then // root node
               compute global function;
          else send report to parent;
     endif;
```

Figure 18.2: A convergecast algorithm

```
P_root ::
 send m to all children;

P_i :: i ≠ root
 on receiving a message m from parent
      send m to all children;
```

Figure 18.3: A broadcast algorithm

sending the broadcast message to all its children. In this algorithm messages traverse down the tree.

Thus the only task remaining is to build a rooted, spanning tree. We assume that there is a distinguished processor *root*. This algorithm, called the *flooding algorithm*, can also be used to broadcast a message m, when there is no predefined spanning tree. The algorithm for flooding a message is simple. Whenever a processor P_i receives a message m (from P_j) for the first time, it sends that message to all its neighbors except P_j. To P_j it sends a *parent* message, indicating that P_j is the parent of P_i. If P_i receives m from some other process, then it simply replies with a *reject* message. Every node keeps a count of the number

```
var
    parent: process id initially null;
    numchildren: integer initially 0;
    childrenlist: list initially null;
    numneighbors: integer initially the number of neighbors;
    numreports: integer initially 0;
    notdone: boolean initially true except for the root;

Upon receiving a message m from Pj
    if notdone then
        parent = Pj;
        notdone := false;
        send m to all neighbors except Pj;
        send (parent) to Pj;
    else
        send (reject) to Pj;

Upon receiving a (parent) message
    numchildren := numchildren + 1;
    append(childrenlist, Pj);
    numreports := numreports + 1;
    if (numreports = numneighbors − 1) then halt;

Upon receiving a (reject) message
    numreports := numreports + 1;
    if (numreports = numneighbors − 1) then halt;
```

Figure 18.4: A spanning tree construction algorithm

of *parent* messages and *reject* messages that it receives in the variable *numreports*. When this value reaches $numneighbors - 1$, P_i knows that it has heard from all processes that it had sent m (all neighbors except the *parent*). At this point, P_i can be sure that it knows all its children and can halt.

The algorithm shown in Figure 18.4 is initiated by the root processor by sending message m to all its neighbors. The proof of correctness is left as an exercise.

What if there is no distinguished processor? We assume that each process has unique *id*, but initially every process knows only its own *id*. In this case, each node can start the spanning tree construction assuming that it is the distinguished processor. Thus many instances of spanning tree construction may be active concurrently. To distinguish these instances, all messages in the spanning tree started by P_i, contain the *id* for P_i. By ensuring that only the instance started by the process with the largest *id* succeeds, we can build a spanning tree even when there is no distinguished processor. The design of the algorithm is left as an exercise (see Problem 18.4). Note that this algorithm also solves the problem of leader election in a general graph.

18.3   Global Functions

Before we present a general algorithm for computing a global function, we describe an algorithm that computes routing tables in a distributed system. This will not only make the general algorithm easier to understand, but also illustrate the application of the general algorithm. The problem of computing a routing table is as follows. Each process P in the system can send messages directly only to a subset of processes. These processes, called neighbors of P, have direct *channels* to P. Let c be any channel adjacent to P. The problem of computing a routing table is to assign for each channel c a list of processes, $route(c)$ such that $Q \in route(c)$ iff the shortest path from P to Q goes through c.

The algorithm to compute the routing table in a distributed system works in phases. Each process goes through initialization and then through a series of phases $phase_1, phase_2, \ldots, phase_n$. In each phase a process will possibly learn some new information. If a process does not receive any new information in any phase, then it terminates.

Let D be the diameter of the graph of the communication network topology. We assume that D is known. We use d to denote the number of the current phase and c to denote any channel incident on any process P. All channels are assumed to be bidirectional.

The variables used by the algorithm are:

d: phase number.
info: global information known by P
    { identities of the nodes for which P knows a shortest route }
new: new information obtained since the beginning of this phase.
$sent(c)$: message sent on channel c at the current phase.
$received(c)$: message received through channel c.
$route(c)$: set of processes for which channel c must be used by P.

The program for any process is in Figure 18.5.

```
var
      d: integer initially 0;
      info: set of information initially { identity of the node };
      sent(c): information initially info for all c

while d < D do
      d := d + 1;
      send⟨sent(c)⟩ on all channels c;
      new := ϕ;
      for every channel c do
            receive ⟨ received(c)⟩ on c;
            for y ∈ received(c) − info − new do
                  route(c) := route(c) ∪ {y};
            new := new ∪ (received(c) − info);
      endfor
      info := info ∪ new;
      sent(c) := new − received(c);
endwhile;
```

Figure 18.5: An algorithm to compute the routing tables

Each process in the above algorithm first sends out some information on all channels incident to it. Then it receives information along those channels. On the basis of that information, it updates its routing tables and the information that it will send out in the next phase.

It is easily seen that the above algorithm will generate correct routing tables (see Problem 18.5).

We now generalize this algorithm for computing any global function. Furthermore, we will not assume that D is known. We use the variable *open* to denote the set of channels open at any phase. The algorithm is in Figure 18.6.

---

var

       d: integer initially 0;

       info, *new*: set of information initially { initial data };

       $sent(c)$: information initially *info* for all c

       open: set of channels initially *all*;

       $received(c)$: information initially $\forall c : received(c) = \phi$

while $open \neq \phi$ **do**

    $d := d + 1$;

    for $c \in open$ **do**

        $sent(c) := new - received(c)$;

        send $\langle sent(c) \rangle$ on c;

    endfor

    $new := \phi$;

    for $c \in open$ **do**

        receive $\langle received(c) \rangle$ on c;

        if $(received(c) = sent(c))$ **then** $open := open - \{c\}$;

        $new := new \cup (received(c) - info)$;

        compute problem specific information;

    endfor;

    $info := info \cup new$;

Figure 18.6: An algorithm to compute a general global function

The algorithm works using the notion of phases. Such algorithms are much easier to verify than those that do not work in phases. The easiest method to verify these algorithms is to view them as sets of equations relating variables at phase d and $d - 1$. The message sent on channel c in phase d is viewed as the state of the variable $sent_d(c)$. Using $\bar{c}$ to denote the channel at the other process, we also get that $received_d(c) = sent_d(\bar{c})$. Then, most claims can be verified using induction. On rewriting the algorithm, we obtain:

$$\begin{aligned}
\forall c \in open_{d-1} : sent_d(c) &:= new_{d-1} - received_{d-1}(c) \\
\forall c \in open_{d-1} : received_d(c) &:= sent_d(\bar{c}) \\
new_d &:= \bigcup_c received_d(c) - info_{d-1} \\
open_d &:= open_{d-1} - \{\, c \mid sent_d(c) = received_d(c) \,\} \\
info_d &:= info_{d-1} \cup new_d
\end{aligned}$$

Let $V^i(P)$ denote the information at nodes that are at distance i from P. When $i = -1$, $V^{-1}(P)$ will simply be $\emptyset$. Furthermore, let

$$T^i(P) = \bigcup_{j \leq i} V^j(P).$$

The variable $T^i(P)$ denotes the information at nodes that are at distance less than or equal to i from P. The initial values for variables in the algorithm are:

$info_0 = V^0(P)$;
$new_0 = V^0(P)$;
$open_0 = all$;
$\forall c : received_0(c) = \emptyset$.

Before we present the properties of the algorithm, we need the following lemma.

Lemma 18.1 *Let P and Q be two adjacent processes.*

$$T^{d-1}(P) = T^{d-1}(Q)$$

if and only if

$$V^{d-1}(P) - V^{d-2}(Q) = V^{d-1}(Q) - V^{d-2}(P).$$

Proof: ($\Leftarrow$)
$\quad T^{d-1}(P)$
$= \{$nodes at distances at most $d - 3$, and at $d - 1$ and $d - 2$ from $P\}$
$\quad T^{d-3}(P) \cup V^{d-1}(P) \cup V^{d-2}(P)$
$= \{$because $T^{d-3}(P) \subseteq T^{d-2}(Q) \wedge T^{d-2}(Q) \subseteq T^{d-1}(P)\}$
$\quad T^{d-2}(Q) \cup V^{d-1}(P) \cup V^{d-2}(P)$
$= \{$because $V^{d-2}(Q) \subseteq T^{d-2}(Q)\}$

$$T^{d-2}(Q) \cup \left(V^{d-1}(P) - V^{d-2}(Q)\right) \cup V^{d-2}(P)$$
$$= \{\text{given}\}$$
$$T^{d-2}(Q) \cup \left(V^{d-1}(Q) - V^{d-2}(P)\right) \cup V^{d-2}(P)$$
$$= \{\text{because } V^{d-2}(P) \subseteq T^{d-1}(Q) \}$$
$$T^{d-2}(Q) \cup V^{d-1}(Q)$$
$$= \{\text{definition of } T \}$$
$$T^{d-1}(Q)$$

$(\Rightarrow)$

Given $T^{d-1}(P) = T^{d-1}(Q)$, we have to show that

$$V^{d-1}(P) - V^{d-2}(Q) = V^{d-1}(Q) - V^{d-2}(P).$$

By symmetry, it is sufficient to show

$$V^{d-1}(P) - V^{d-2}(Q) \subseteq V^{d-1}(Q) - V^{d-2}(P).$$

Let $x \in V^{d-1}(P) - V^{d-2}(Q)$. This implies that x is at a distance of $d-1$ from P and not at a distance $d-2$ from Q. Its distance from Q cannot be smaller than $d-2$, otherwise its distance from P is strictly smaller than $d-1$. Since $T^{d-1}(P) = T^{d-1}(Q)$, it follows that x is exactly $d-1$ distance away from Q. Thus, $x \in V^{d-1}(Q) - V^{d-2}(P)$.

∎

Now, we have the following theorem.

Theorem 18.2 *For all $d \geq 1$, the following holds.*

$$
\begin{aligned}
sent_d(c) &= V^{d-1}(P) - V^{d-2}(Q) \\
received_d(c) &= V^{d-1}(Q) - V^{d-2}(P) \\
new_d &= V^d(P) \\
open_d &= \{(P,Q) \mid T^{d-1}(P) \neq T^{d-1}(Q)\} \\
info_d &= T^d(P)
\end{aligned}
$$

Proof: The proof is by induction on d. For $d = 1$, we get

$$
\begin{aligned}
sent_1(c) &= V^0(P) \\
received_1(c) &= V^0(Q) \\
new_1 &= V^1(P) \\
open_1 &= \{(P,Q) \mid T^{1-1}(P) \neq T^{1-1}(Q)\} = all \\
info_1 &= T^1(P)
\end{aligned}
$$

These equations are easily verified by substituting the values at phase 1 in the program.

Now, we verify the general case when $d > 1$.

- $sent_d(c)$
  $= new_{d-1} - received_{d-1}(c)$ (from the program)
  $= V^{d-1}(P) - (V^{d-2}(Q) - V^{d-3}(P))$ (from induction)
  $= V^{d-1}(P) - V^{d-2}(Q)$ ($V^i(P)$ and $V^j(P)$ are disjoint for $i \neq j$)

- $received_d(c)$
  $= sent_d(\bar{c})$ (from the program)
  $= V^{d-1}(Q) - V^{d-2}(P)$;   (expression for $sent$)

- new_d
  $= \bigcup_c received_d(c) - info_{d-1}$ (from the program)
  $= \bigcup_c V^{d-1}(Q) - V^{d-2}(P) - T^{d-1}(P)$ (from induction
  hypothesis)
  $= V^d(P)$ (simplification)

- $open_d$
  $= open_{d-1} - \{ c \mid sent_d(c) = received_d(c) \}$ (from the program)
  $= \{ (P, Q) \mid T^{d-2}(P) \neq T^{d-2}(Q) \}$
        $- \{ c \mid V^{d-1}(P) - V^{d-2}(Q) = V^{d-1}(Q) - V^{d-2}(P) \}$ (induction)
  $= \{ (P, Q) \mid T^{d-1}(P) \neq T^{d-1}(Q) \}$ (simplification, Lemma 18.1)

- $info_d$
  $= info_{d-1} \cup new_d$ (from program)
  $= T^{d-1}(P) \cup V^d(P)$ (induction hypothesis)
  $= T^d(P)$.

                                                  ■

The following lemma gives the message complexity of the above algorithm.

Lemma 18.3 *Let N be the total number of processes, m be the total number of channels, D be the diameter of the communication graph and τ be the maximum transmission delay on a channel. Then:*

1. *The number of messages is at most $2(D + 1)m$.*

2. *Assuming that the initial information is of size $\log N$, the total number of bits communicated is at most $O(mN \log N)$.*

3. *The running time of the algorithm is at most* $(2D+1)\tau$.

Proof:

1. During each phase a process sends and receives one message along each open channel. There are $D+1$ phases in the algorithm.

2. Information about any node is transmitted on a channel at most twice.

3. A node will be awakened in at most $D\tau$ time. Each phase takes at most τ time, and there are $D+1$ phases.

■

18.4 Problems

18.1. Analyze the time and message complexity of the convergecast, the broadcast and the spanning tree construction algorithms.

18.2. Show that the spanning tree algorithm in Figure 18.4 constructs a breadth-first search tree in a synchronous network (where every message takes one unit time and computation takes zero time). Also show that this is not true for an asynchronous network.

18.3. Give an algorithm that constructs a depth-first search spanning tree assuming that there is a distinguished processor *root*.

18.4. Give an algorithm that constructs a depth-first search spanning tree assuming that there is no distinguished processor. You may assume that each processor has a unique processor id.

18.5. Show that the algorithm in Figure 18.5 adds a process Q to *route*(c) for process P iff a shortest path from P to Q goes through c.

18.6. Consider a completely connected network of processors. What is the message complexity of algorithm in Figure 18.6 to compute a global function?

18.7. Modify the algorithm compute a global function to incorporate the notion of open input and open output channels. Give conditions when a process P need not send further messages along a channel c. What is the message complexity of this algorithm?

18.8. How will you use the algorithm to compute a global function to compute (a) the diameter of a graph, (b) the centers of a graph, (c) the eccentricity of a graph?

*18.9. **(due to [GHS83])** Assume that each channel has a fixed delay called its *weight* that is known to both the nodes adjacent to that channel. Give a distributed algorithm to build a *minimum-weight* spanning tree in a network with $O(m + N \log N)$ message complexity and $O(N \log N)$ time complexity where m is the total number of edges in the communication graph.

18.5   Bibliographic Remarks

The algorithms for broadcast, convergecast, and flooding appear to be folklore. The discussion of the algorithm for computation of a global function is taken from Bermond, Konig, and Raynal [BKR87]. The distributed algorithm for a minimum spanning tree in the problem set is due to Gallaghar, Humblet, and Spira [GHS83].

Chapter 19

Repeated Global Computation

Repetition is the only form of permanence that Nature can achieve.
— *George Santayana*

19.1 Introduction

We introduce in this chapter a mechanism that can be used to compute a global function repeatedly. Examples of applications that require repeated computation of a global function are deadlock detection, clock synchronization, distributed branch and bound, parallel alpha-and-beta search, global snapshot computation, and N+1-section search. Examples of information necessary to compute the global function are local *wait-for* graphs for the deadlock detection problem and the value of local bounds for distributed branch-and-bound search.

A distributed data gathering problem requires that one process receive enough data from everybody, directly or indirectly, to be able to compute a function of the global state. Let a time step of the algorithm be the time it takes for a process to send a message, that is, a process cannot send two messages in one time step. The desirable properties of any algorithm that achieves data gathering in a distributed system are:

1. Light Load: No process should receive more than k messages in one time step of the algorithm, where k is a parameter dependent on the application and on the physical characteristics of the network. A small value of k guarantees that no process is swamped by a large number of messages.

2. High Concurrency: Given the above constraint and the fact that there must be some communication, directly or indirectly, from every process to the coordinator process, it can be deduced that any algorithm takes at least $log_k(N)$ time steps. Our second requirement is that the algorithm must not take more than $O(\log(N))$ steps.

3. Equal Load: For the purposes of load balancing and fairness each process should send and receive the same number and the same size of messages over time. In addition, they should perform the same set of operations in the algorithm. This requirement assumes special importance for algorithms that run for a long time or when the processes belong to different organizations. The condition of equitable load is different from the symmetry requirement because processes in our algorithms can have different roles at a specific phase of the algorithm. However, in most practical applications, it is sufficient to ensure that all processes share the workload and responsibilities equally over time, rather than at every instant.

This chapter is organized as follows. Section 19.2 gives an algorithm that satisfies all the above properties. Section 19.3 discusses implementation and complexity issues of the algorithm. Finally, Section 19.4 gives an application of the algorithm for distributed branch-and-bound search.

The notation used in this chapter is summarized in Figure 19.1.

P	Set of processes
N	Total number of processes
x, y	Process ids
t	Time step
n	$\log(N + 1)$

Figure 19.1: Notation

19.2   An Equitable, Revolving Hierarchy

In this section, we present an algorithm that satisfies all three desired properties of a distributed data gathering scheme.

Let there be N processes, numbered uniquely from the set $P = \{1, \ldots, N\}$, that are organized in the form of a k-ary tree. This tree also

Time	Message 1	Message 2	Idle
0	$1,3 \rightarrow 2$	$5,7 \rightarrow 6$	4
1	$2,6 \rightarrow 4$	$1,3 \rightarrow 5$	7
2	$4,5 \rightarrow 7$	$2,6 \rightarrow 1$	3
3	$7,1 \rightarrow 3$	$4,5 \rightarrow 2$	6

Figure 19.2: A message sequence for repeated computation of a function

has N positions. Let $pos(x,t)$ be the position of the process x at time
t. For simplicity, let $pos(x,0) = x$ for all $x \in P$. The reconfiguration of
hierarchy consists of the remapping of processes to different positions.
This reconfiguration is defined using a function $next : P \rightarrow P$ that gives
the new position of the process that was earlier in position x, that is, if
for some y and t, $pos(y,t) = x$, then $pos(y,t+1) = next(x)$. Because
two processes cannot be assigned the same position, $next$ is a 1-1 and
onto function on the set P. Such functions are called permutations.
Any permutation can be written as the product of disjoint cycles. For
any permutation f defined on the set P, the orbit of any element $x \in P$
is defined to be:

$$orbit(x) = \{f^i(x) \mid i \geq 0\}$$

Thus $orbit(x)$ contains all elements in the cycle that contains x. f is
called primitive if there exists a $x \in P$ such that $orbit(x) = P$. We
require $next$ to be primitive so that any process occupies all positions
in N time units.

As an illustration of a revolving hierarchy, consider the case when
$N = 7$ and $k = 2$. Figure 19.2 shows a sequence of message transmissions that exhibit all the desired properties. At time $t = 1$, process
4 is able to obtain information from all other processes, because the
messages received by it from processes 2 and 6 include the (possibly
partially processed) messages sent by processes 1, 3, 5, and 7 in the
previous time step. Thus it can compute a global function at the end
of this time step. Similarly, at $t = 2$, process 7 can compute a global
function.

The sequence of messages given in Figure 19.2 is obtained by the
revolving hierarchy illustrated in Figure 19.3. To recognize this, consider an initial assignment of process i to node i of tree T_1, using an
in-order labeling. The in-order labeling of a tree is simply the order
in which nodes are traversed using the in-order traversal of the tree.

At $t = 0$, the leaves of this tree send a message to their parents. At $t = 1$, we want to continue the propagation of these messages to the root of T_1, and simultaneously initiate messages needed for the next global computation. This can be achieved by defining another tree T_2 of N nodes such that the internal nodes of T_1 form one subtree of T_2, say the left subtree, and the leaf processes are remapped onto the root and the other subtree of T_2. The messages sent at $t = 1$ are precisely those sent by the leaf nodes of T_2 to their parents. Subsequent message sequences are obtained in a similar fashion by forming a new tree at each time step, as illustrated in Figure 19.3. The trees $T_1, T_2, \ldots$ are called *gather trees* because each such tree determines the sequence of messages used to collect all information required to compute one global function. Thus, a throughput of one global result per unit time is achieved after an initial startup delay of $\lceil \log N \rceil - 1$ steps. Note that this is possible because of the use of a message in $\lceil \log N \rceil - 1$ gather trees. Also, all messages may not be of equal size, because a message sent by a process may include a portion of the messages that it received in the previous time step. The actual content of messages is application dependent and will be examined in Section 19.4. In this section, we shall concentrate on the sequence of messages generated and on the properties that they satisfy.

The sequence of logical trees $T_1, T_2, \ldots$ represents the time evolution of the assignment of N processes to positions in a revolving tree. At every step, the processes are remapped onto the nodes of this tree according to a permutation function, $next(x)$, applied to the current position x, $1 \le x \le N$. For the example in Fig. 19.3, with an in-order labeling of the nodes, this permutation is:

$$\left(\begin{array}{ccccccc} 1 & 2 & 3 & 4 & 5 & 6 & 7 \\ 5 & 1 & 7 & 2 & 6 & 3 & 4 \end{array} \right) \tag{19.1}$$

Thus process 1, which is in position 1 in T_1, goes to position 5 in T_2 and position 6 in T_3.

To generate a revolving hierarchy, $next(x)$ must satisfy the following two constraints:

1) *Gather Tree Constraint*: The interior nodes of T_i should form a subtree of T_{i+1}, that is, interior nodes at level j in T_i should be mapped to level $j+1$ in T_{i+1}, and the parent-child relationships among these nodes should be preserved. This restriction ensures that the message sequences required for the root process at each snapshot to

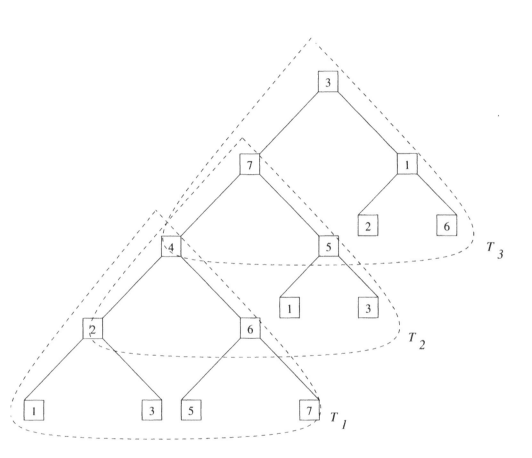

Figure 19.3: Overlapping trees that determine message sequences

obtain global information are not disturbed during the reorganization needed to initiate messages for the next computation.

The following permutation function on in-order labels satisfies the gather tree constraint:

$$next(x) = x/2, \text{ for } even(x)$$

2) *Fairness Constraint*: The permutation should be primitive. This ensures that a process visits each position in the logical tree exactly once in N steps. Thus, if different positions require different workloads, then each process will end up doing an equal amount of work after N time units.

We now present a permutation that satisfies gather tree and fairness constraints. Let $lead0(x)$ be the number of leading zeros in the n bit binary representation of x. For $x = 1, 2, \ldots, N = 2^n - 1$, consider the $next(x)$ function shown in Figure 19.4.

```
function next(x)::
    // Type I move
    if (even(x)) then
        x' := x/2;

    // Type II move
    if (odd(x) ∧ (x < 2^{n-1})) then
        x' := x * 2^{lead0(x)} + 1;

    // Type III move
    if (odd(x) ∧ (x > 2^{n-1})) then
        x' := (x + 1) ;
        if (x' = N + 1)  then  x' := x'/2;
    endif;

    return(x');
```

Figure 19.4: The function *next*

The *next* function is applied to determine the next position of a process in an in-order-labeled complete binary tree. Let N nodes be divided into four disjoint groups:

Name	Members
$RInt$	$even(x) \wedge (x \geq 2^{n-1})$
$LInt$	$even(x) \wedge (x < 2^{n-1})$
$LLeaf$	$odd(x) \wedge (x < 2^{n-1})$
$RLeaf$	$odd(x) \wedge (x > 2^{n-1})$

Type I moves are required by the gather tree constraint. Thus if x is even, it moves down the tree until it becomes a left leaf. Type II and Type III moves just visit the right subtree using in-order traversal. For a Type II move, $x * 2^{lead0(x)}$ gives the last node visited in the right subtree. The next node to be visited is obtained by adding 1 to the previous node visited. Note that as $x \in LLeaf$ for a Type II move, $lead0(x) \geq 1$, hence x' is odd. Also the msb of x' is 1, because x is multiplied by $2^{lead0(x)}$. Thus a Type II move maps a left leaf node to a right leaf node. A Type III move just visits the next node in the in-order traversal, unless $x = N$, in which case x' is made to be the root to start the cycle all over again.

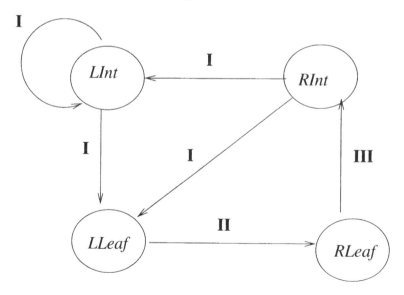

Figure 19.5: Node groups and transitions

We are now ready for our first main result.

Theorem 19.1 *The function next(.) is a primitive permutation that satisfies the gather tree constraint.*

Proof: We first show that *next* is a permutation. Let $x, y \in \{1, \ldots, N\}$ be such that $x \neq y$. A Type I move is 1-1 because for any even x_1, x_2, $(x_1/2 = x_2/2)$ implies that $(x_1 = x_2)$. A Type II move is 1-1, because for any odd x_1, x_2, if $lead0(x_1) \neq lead0(x_2)$, then $x_1 * 2^{lead0(x_1)} \neq x_2 * 2^{lead0(x_2)}$ as they have a different number of trailing zeros. Otherwise, $x_1' = x_2'$ clearly implies that $x_1 = x_2$. Type III is also 1-1. Also, no element other than N maps to $(N + 1)/2$ because the only other possibility, $x = (N+1)/2 - 1 = 2^{n-1} - 1$, does not belong to the domain of type III moves. Thus, if the same type of move is applicable for both x and y, then $next(x) \neq next(y)$ because each type of move (type I, type II, and type III) is 1-1. Furthermore, the ranges of different types of move are disjoint; for an illustration see Figure 19.5. Hence, if different types of moves are applied to x and y, then also $next(x) \neq next(y)$. Therefore, *next* is 1-1. Furthermore, the domain and the range of *next* have finite and equal cardinality, therefore it is also onto. Thus it is a permutation.

We now need to show that the permutation *next* is primitive. Any cycle starting from a node x in RLeaf first visits vertex $x + 1$ (or $(x + 1)/2)$) in *RInt*, followed by a sequence of vertices in *LInt* followed by a vertex in *LLeaf*, which is followed again by the next vertex in *RLeaf*. Thus the vertices in *RLeaf* are visited in sequence. Because every cycle must visit *RLeaf* and all the nodes in *RLeaf* are visited in a sequence, there can only be one cycle in the permutation. Thus *next* is primitive.

Finally, *next* also satisfies the gather tree constraint because of Type I moves.

∎

Significance: If $next(x)$ is used to determine the remapping of the processes to nodes for the next time step, then:
(i) A global function can be computed in $\lceil \log N \rceil - 1$ steps after its initiation; and
(ii) A throughput of one global function computation per time step can be obtained.

Note that the gather trees are only tools to determine the sequence of message transmissions. The goal is to find, at any time t, whether a given process needs to send a message, and if so, which process should be the recipient of that message.

Let $parent(x)$ yield the parent of node x and $msg(x, t)$ be the process number to which process x sends a message at time t. If x does

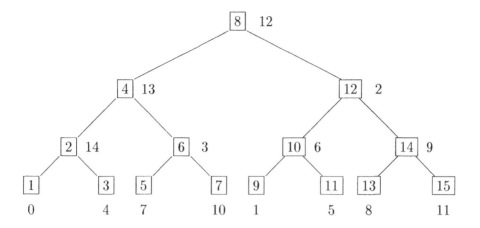

Figure 19.6: Node labels generated by *next*. Original in-order labels are shown inside the nodes.

not send a message at time t, then $msg(x,t) = nil$. For an in-order labeling, a node has an odd label *iff* it is a leaf node. Since only leaf nodes send messages, we obtain:

$$msg(x,t) = \begin{cases} next^{-t} \left(parent \left(next^{t}(x) \right) \right) & \text{if } odd(next^{t}(x)) \\ nil & otherwise \end{cases}$$

For an in-order labeling, the parent of a leaf node has the same binary representation as that node except that the two least significant bits are 10. For example, node 1010 is the parent of nodes 1001 and 1011. Thus, the parent can be readily evaluated.

19.3   Implementation Issues

We can simplify the computation of $next^{t}(x)$ and $next^{-t}(x)$ by renumbering the tree nodes in the sequence traversed by a process. This is shown in Figure 19.6, where the tree nodes are relabeled 0 through $N-1$. Let the processes be numbered $0,\ldots,N-1$ also and let process i be mapped onto node i at $t=0$. This relabeling causes the $next(.)$ and $parent(.)$ functions to be transformed into $new\_next(.)$ and $new\_parent(.)$, respectively. Moreover, $new\_next^{t}(x)$ is simply equal to

$x + t$. Therefore,

$$msg(x, t) = \begin{cases} new\_parent(x + t) - t & \text{if } x + t \text{ is a leaf}; \\ nil & otherwise \end{cases} \qquad (19.2)$$

For $N = 31$, we obtain:

$$
\begin{array}{llcccccccc}
leaf\ node, i & : & 0 & 15 & 7 & 22 & 3 & 10 & 18 & 25 \\
new\_parent(i) & : & 30 & 30 & 14 & 14 & 6 & 6 & 21 & 21
\end{array}
$$

$$(19.3)$$

$$
\begin{array}{llcccccccc}
leaf\ node, i & : & 1 & 4 & 8 & 11 & 16 & 19 & 23 & 26 \\
new\_parent(i) & : & 2 & 2 & 9 & 9 & 17 & 17 & 24 & 24
\end{array}
$$

We only need to store the new_parent function for the leaf nodes to determine whom to send a message at any time t. Thus the destination can be calculated in constant time, by looking up a table of size $O(N)$. Alternatively, one can generate the new_parent function and trade-off storage for computation time.

Let us define a *communication distance set*, CDS, as:

$$CDS = \{i \mid i = new\_parent(j) - j; \ j \text{ a leaf node}\}. \qquad (19.4)$$

Lemma 19.2 *Process x will send a message (at some time) to process y iff $y - x \in CDS$.*

Proof: ($\Rightarrow$) $y - x \in CDS$ means that there exists a leaf node j_1 such that $y - x = new\_parent(j_1) - j_1$.
Let $t_1 = j_1 - x$. Then $y - x = new\_parent(x + t_1) - (x + t_1)$
or $y = new\_parent(x + t_1) - t_1$. Since $(x + t_1) = j_1$ is a leaf, from Equation 19.2 we infer that x sends a message to y at time t_1.

($\Leftarrow$)   Let x send a message to y at time t_2. From Equation 19.2, we have
$y = new\_parent(x + t_2) - t_2$ and that $x + t_2$ is a leaf node. Substituting $j_2 = x + t_2$, we get
$y = new\_parent(j_2) - (j_2 - x)$, or $y - x = new\_parent(j_2) - j_2 \in CDS$ because j_2 is a leaf node.

■

Using the above lemma one can define a communication graph corresponding to a given *next* function with a node for each process and a directed edge (a, b) between two nodes only if a sends a message to b at some time. Each node of this graph has the same in-degree and out-degree, given by the size of the set CDS.

The *next* function is not the only permutation that satisfies the gather tree and fairness constraints. Type I moves are mandated by the gather tree constraint, but there are several choices for Type II and Type III moves. The following two criteria are proposed for choosing among several candidates for the *next* function:

a) If the derived *new_parent* function is simpler to generate, it is preferred.

b) A *next* function whose corresponding CDS set has a smaller size is preferred.

The following theorem shows that the *next* function has CDS of size $2(log_2(N + 1) - 1)$. Its proof is left as an exercise (see Problem 19.6).

Theorem 19.3 *For $N = 2^n - 1$, the CDS for the* next(x) *labeling is of size $2(n - 1)$, and its members are given by*

$$CDS = \bigcup_{i=1 \ to \ n-1} \{2^i - 1, \ -2^{i-1}\}. \tag{19.5}$$

19.4 Application: Branch-and-Bound Algorithm

A distributed branch-and-bound problem requires multiple processors to cooperate in search of a minimum solution. Each processor reduces its search space by using the known bound on the required solution. In our description of the algorithm, we assume that the *search (known-bound)* procedure searches for a solution for some number of steps and returns the value of its current minimum solution. The crucial problem, then, is the computation of the global bound and its dissemination to all processes. We use the result of Problem 19.4, which permits us to use the same permutation for the gather tree and the broadcast tree. This permutation is implemented by means of *tosend* and *torec* functions, which return the receiver and the sender of the message in the current step. The function *tosend* returns -1 if no message needs to be sent in the current time step. In the algorithm given in Figure 19.7, we have assumed that at most one message can be received in one time step.

```
P_i::
  var
      knownbound, mymin, hismin: real;
      step, numsteps, dest: integer;

  Initialization;
  knownbound := ∞;
  for step := 0 to numsteps do
      mymin := search(knownbound);
      dest = tosend(i, step);
      if (dest ≠ −1) then
          send(dest, mymin);
      else begin
          receive(torec(i, step), hismin);
          knownbound := min(mymin, hismin);
      end;
  endfor;
```

Figure 19.7: Distributed branch-and-bound algorithm

In this algorithm, each process process receives a global minimum bound every $2\log(N)$ steps, and sends/receives an equal number of messages.

19.5   Problems

19.1. Give a message schedule table (or a method to generate it) that can be used to repeatedly compute a global function in a network of 15 processes.

19.2. Can the following permutation be used to derive a message sequence table for repeated computation of a global function? If it can be used, then give the message sequence table for two time steps; otherwise, give a reason why the permutation cannot be used. Assume that in-order labeling is used to denote positions of processes in a tree.

(a)

$$\begin{pmatrix} 1 & 2 & 3 & 4 & 5 & 6 & 7 \\ 7 & 1 & 5 & 2 & 6 & 3 & 4 \end{pmatrix}$$

(b)

$$\begin{pmatrix} 1 & 2 & 3 & 4 & 5 & 6 & 7 \\ 7 & 1 & 5 & 2 & 4 & 3 & 6 \end{pmatrix}$$

19.3. A list representation for message patterns can be defined as follows. The list positions are numbered from 0 to $2^{n-1} - 1$. At any step, a process in an even-numbered position i sends a message to the process in the position $i + 1$. Consider the mapping of the list positions by $n\_snext2(x)$ described below. List position 0 is labeled as 0 by $n\_snext2(x)$ to form a convenient starting point. The position x' to be labeled next is determined from the current list position, x, as follows:

if $b_0 = 1$ **then** $x' := \mathrm{RS0}(x)$;
else if $(b_0 = 0) \wedge (b_{n-1} = 1)$ **then** $x' := x + 1$;
else $x' := $ first available position in $REven$
         (from left to right).

The labels generated by $n\_snext2(x)$ for $N = 16$ are:

list position	0	1	2	3	4	5	6	7
label	0	15	7	14	3	6	10	13
list position	8	9	10	11	12	13	14	15
label	1	2	4	5	8	9	11	12

(19.6)

The corresponding CDS is { 1, 3, 7, 15 }. Show that this mapping satisfies gather tree and fairness constraints and has CDS of size $\log N$.

19.4. In several applications, such as the distributed branch-and-bound algorithm, the result of a global computation also needs to be transmitted to all the processes. Show that by using the permutation given by $bcnext$ such broadcasts can be performed by attaching a copy of the result to the *same* set of message sequences that are used to gather information for future global computations. The permutation is given using the list representation as in Problem 19.3. The operations $RS0, RS1, LS0$ and $LS1$ yield the numbers obtained by a right (left) shift of the bits with a 0/1 in the most (least) significant bit position.

---

function bcnext(x)::
   // Type S1 move
   if $(b_0 = 1)$ **then** $x' := RS0(x)$;

   // Type S2 move
   if ($(b_0 = 0) \wedge (b_1 = 0)$) **then** $x' := RS1(x)$;

   // Type S3 move
   if $((b_0 = 0) \wedge (b_1 = 1))$ **then**
      $x' := LS1^a((LS0^b(x) + 2) \; mod \; 2^{n-1})$;
   //. a and b are the number of leading 0's and 1's in the argument

   return(x');

Figure 19.8: The function *bcnext*

19.5. Assume that we are given N equations in N variables. We are required to find a solution of this set of equations. Formally, we have to determine x_i such that, $x_i = f_i(x_1, x_2, \ldots, x_N)$ for all $1 \leq i \leq N$. This problem arises in many contexts, such as computation of stationary probability distributions for discrete Markov chains. We assume that equations are on different processors and every processor computes one coordinate of the x vector. Give a distributed algorithm to compute the solution via repeated iterations.

*19.6. Prove Theorem 19.3.

19.6   Bibliographic Remarks

The algorithm for repeated computation of a global function is from Garg and Ghosh [GG94].

Chapter 20

Synchronizers

Don't walk behind me; I may not lead. Don't walk in front of me; I may not follow. Just walk beside me and be my friend. — Albert Camus

20.1 Introduction

The design of distributed algorithms is easier if we assume that the underlying network is synchronous rather than asynchronous. A prime example is that of computing a breadth-first search (BFS) tree in a network. Section 20.6 gives a simple algorithm to determine the breadth-first search tree in a graph, assuming a synchronous network. The corresponding problem on an asynchronous graph is more difficult. This motivates methods by which a synchronous network can be simulated by an asynchronous network. We show that, in the absence of failures, this is indeed possible using a mechanism called a synchronizer.

A synchronous network can be abstracted with the notion of a *pulse*. A pulse is a counter at each process with the property that any message sent in pulse i is received at pulse i. A synchronizer is simply a mechanism that indicates to a process when it can generate a pulse. In this chapter we will study synchronizers and their complexity.

To define properties of synchronizers formally, we associate a pulse number with each state s on the process. It is initialized to 0 for all processes. A process can go from pulse i to $i + 1$ only if it knows that it has received all the messages sent during pulse i.

Given the notion of a pulse, the execution of a synchronous algorithm can be modeled as a sequence of pulses. In each pulse, a process first performs internal computation based on the messages received in the previous round, if any. After the computation, it sends messages to its neighbors as required by the application. Finally, it receives messages from neighbors that were sent in this round. It can execute the next pulse only when indicated by the synchronizer.

There are two aspects of the complexity of a synchronizer—the message complexity and the time complexity. The message complexity indicates the additional number of messages required by the synchronizer to simulate a synchronous algorithm on top of an asynchronous network. The time complexity is the number of time units required to simulate one pulse where a time unit is defined as the time required for an asynchronous message.

Some synchronizers have a nontrivial initialization cost. Let M_{init} be the number of messages and T_{init} be the time required for initialization of the synchronizer. Let M_{pulse} and T_{pulse} be the number of messages and time required to simulate one pulse of a synchronous algorithm. If a synchronous algorithm requires T_{synch} rounds and M_{synch} messages, then the complexity of the asynchronous protocol based on the synchronizer is given by:

$$M_{asynch} = M_{init} + M_{synch} + M_{pulse} * T_{synch}$$

$$T_{asynch} = T_{init} + T_{pulse} * T_{synch}$$

We model the topology of the underlying network as an undirected, connected graph. We assume that processes never fail. It is not possible to simulate a synchronous algorithm on an asynchronous network when processes can fail. In Chapter 26, we show algorithms that can achieve consensus despite process failures in synchronous systems, and in Chapter 25 we show that consensus is impossible in asynchronous systems when even a single process may fail. We also assume that all channels are reliable. Again, Chapter 24 shows that the consensus problem is impossible to solve when channels are unreliable.

The notation used in this chapter is summarized in Figure 20.1.

This chapter is organized as follows. Section 20.2 describes a simple synchronizer that requires exactly one message along each link in each direction per pulse. Section 20.3 describes a synchronizer called α that is optimal with respect to the time required for simulating a pulse but inefficient with respect to the message complexity. Section 20.4 describes a synchronizer called β that is efficient with respect to the

N	The number of nodes in the network
E	The number of edges in the network
D	Diameter of the network

Figure 20.1: Notation

message complexity but inefficient with respect to the time required for simulating a pulse. Section 20.5 presents a parameterized synchronizer that allows one to explicitly trade off the time complexity for the message complexity. Section 20.6 presents an application of synchronizers for designing a distributed algorithm for building the breadth-first search tree in an asynchronous network. Finally, Section 20.7 discusses limitations of simulating synchronous algorithms on asynchronous networks.

20.2 A Simple Synchronizer

A simple synchronizer can be built using the following rule: Every process sends exactly one message to all neighbors in each pulse. With this rule, a process can simply wait for exactly one message from each of its neighbors. To implement this rule, even if the synchronous algorithm did not require P_i to send any message to its neighbor P_j in a particular round, it must still send a "null" message to P_j. Furthermore, if the synchronous algorithm required P_i to send multiple messages, then these messages must be packed as a single message and sent to P_j.

The simple synchronizer generates the next pulse for process p at pulse i when it has received exactly one message sent during pulse i from each of its neighbors. The algorithm is shown in Figure 20.2.

The algorithm in 20.2 ensures that a process in pulse i receives only the messages sent in pulse i. If a process is in round i and it gets a message with pulse number $i+1$, then it buffers that message and waits for the message with pulse number i. Note that in an asynchronous network with the simple synchronizer, a process at pulse i can only receive messages sent during pulses i or pulse $i+1$. Thus instead of including the pulse number i with each message, it is sufficient to include a bit, $i \bmod 2$.

There is no special requirement for initialization of this synchronizer. When any process starts pulse 1, within D time units all other

P_j::
var
        $pulse$: integer initially 0;

round i :
        $pulse := pulse + 1$;
        simulate the round i of the synchronous algorithm;
        send messages to all neighbors with $pulse$;
        wait for exactly one message from each neighbors with $(pulse = i)$;

Figure 20.2: The implementation of a simple synchronizer at P_j

processes will also start pulse 1. Therefore, the complexity of initializing the simple synchronizer is

$$M_{init} = 0; \quad T_{init} = D.$$

Because each pulse requires a message along every link in both directions, we get the complexity of simulating a pulse as

$$M_{pulse} = 2E; \quad T_{pulse} = 1.$$

20.3 Synchronizer α

The synchronizer α is very similar to the simple synchronizer. We cover this synchronizer because it is a special case of a more general synchronizer γ that will be covered later. All the synchronizers discussed from now on are based around the concept of *safety* of a process. Process P is safe for pulse i if it knows that all messages sent from P in pulse i have been received.

The α synchronizer generates the next pulse at process P if all its neighbors are safe. This is because if all neighbors of P are safe then all messages sent to process P have been received.

To implement the α synchronizer, it is sufficient for every process to inform all its neighbors whenever it is safe for a pulse. How can a process determine whether it is safe? This is a simple matter if all messages are required to be acknowledged.

The complexity of synchronizer α is given below:

$$T_{init} = D; \qquad M_{init} = D$$

$$T_{pulse} = O(1); \qquad M_{pulse} = O(E)$$

20.4 Synchronizer β

Although the synchronizers discussed so far appear to be efficient, they have high message complexity when the topology of the underlying network is dense. For large networks, where every node may be connected to a large number of nodes, it may be impractical to send a message to all neighbors in every pulse. The message complexity can be reduced at the expense of time complexity as illustrated by the β synchronizer.

The β synchronizer assumes the existence of a rooted, spanning tree in the network. A node in the tree sends a message *subtree-safe* when all nodes in its subtree are safe. When the root of the tree is safe and all its children are safe, then we can conclude that all nodes in the tree are safe. Now a simple broadcast of this fact via a *pulse* message can start the next pulse at all nodes. The broadcast can be done using the rooted spanning tree. Thus this algorithm simply uses the *convergecast* and *broadcast* algorithms discussed in Chapter 18.

The initialization phase of this synchronizer requires a spanning tree to be built. This can be done using $O(N \log N + E)$ messages and $O(N)$ time. For each pulse, we require messages only along the spanning tree. Thus the message complexity for each pulse is $O(N)$. Each pulse also takes time proportional to the height of the spanning tree, which in the worst case is $O(N)$. In summary, the complexity of the β synchronizer is

$$T_{init} = O(N); \qquad M_{init} = O(N \log N + E)$$

$$T_{pulse} = O(N); \qquad M_{pulse} = O(N).$$

20.5 Synchronizer γ

We have seen that the α synchronizer takes $O(1)$ time unit but has high message complexity $O(E)$ and the β synchronizer has low message complexity $O(N)$ but requires $O(N)$ time per pulse. We now describe the γ synchronizer that is a generalization of both α and β synchronizers.

It takes a parameter k such that when k is $N - 1$, it reduces to the α synchronizer and when k is 2 it reduces to the β synchronizer.

The γ synchronizer is based on *clustering*. In the initialization phase, the network is divided into clusters. Within each cluster the algorithm is similar to the β synchronizer and between clusters it is similar to the α synchronizer. Thus each cluster has a cluster spanning tree. The root of the cluster spanning tree is called the cluster leader. We say that two clusters are neighboring if there is an edge connecting them. For any two neighboring clusters, we designate one of the edges as the *preferred* edge.

The algorithm works as follows. There are two phases in each pulse. In both the phases, the messages first travel upward in the cluster tree and then travel downward. The goal of the first phase is to determine when the cluster is safe and inform all cluster nodes when it is so. In this phase, *subtree safe* messages first propagate up the cluster tree. When the root of the cluster gets messages from all its children and it is safe itself, it propagates the *cluster safe* message down the cluster tree. This phase corresponds to the β synchronizer running on the cluster. We also require that the nodes that are incident on preferred edges also send out *our cluster safe (ocs)* over preferred edges.

The goal of the second phase is to determine whether all neighboring clusters are safe. In this sense, it is like an α synchronizer. It uses additional two message types: *neighboring cluster safe (ncs)* and *pulse*. When a leaf in the cluster tree receives the *our cluster safe* message from all preferred edges incident to it, it sends *ncs* to its parent. Now consider an internal node in the cluster tree that has received *ncs* messages from all its children and has received *ocs* on all preferred edges incident to it. If it is not the cluster leader, then it propagates the *ncs* message upward; otherwise, it broadcasts the *pulse* message in its group.

For any clustering scheme c, let E_c denote the number of tree edges and preferred edges and H_c denote the maximum height of a tree in c. The complexity of the γ synchronizer is given by

$$M_{pulse} = O(E_c)$$

$$T_{pulse} = O(H_c)$$

The following theorem shows that any graph can be decomposed into clusters so that there is an appropriate trade-off between the cluster height and the number of tree and preferred edges.

Theorem 20.1 *For each k in the range $2 \leq k < N$, there exists a clustering c such that $E_c \leq kN$ and $H_c \leq \log N / \log k$.*

Proof: We give an explicit construction of the clustering. In this scheme, we add clusters one at a time. Assume that we have already constructed r clusters and there are still some nodes left that are not part of any cluster. We add the next cluster as follows.

Each cluster C consists of multiple layers. For the first layer, any node that is not part of the clusters so far is chosen. Assume that i layers ($i \geq 1$) of the cluster C have already been formed. Let S be the set of neighbors of the node in layer i that are not part of any cluster yet. If the size of S is at least $(k - 1)$ times the size of C, then S is added as the next layer of the cluster C; otherwise, C's construction is finished.

Let us compute H_c and E_c for this clustering scheme. Since each cluster with level i has at least k^{i-1} nodes, it follows that H_c is at most $\log N / \log k$. E_c has two components—tree edges and preferred edges. The tree edges are clearly at most N. To count the preferred edges, we charge a preferred edge between two clusters to the first cluster that is created in our construction process. Note that for a cluster C, its construction is finished only when there are at most $(k - 1)|C|$ neighboring nodes. Thus, for the cluster C, there can be at most $(k - 1)|C|$ preferred edges charged to it. Adding up the contribution from all clusters, we get that the total number of preferred edges is at most $(k - 1)N$.

■

20.6 Application: BFS Tree Algorithm

Assume that we are given a distinguished node v and our job is to build a breadth-first search tree rooted at v. A synchronous algorithm for this task is quite simple. We build the tree level by level. The node v is initially at level 0. A node at level i is required to send messages to its neighbor at pulse i. A process that receives one or more of these messages, and does not have a level number assigned yet, chooses the source of one of these messages as its parent and assigns itself level number $i + 1$. It is clear that if the graph is connected, then every node will have its level number assigned in at most D pulses assuming that any message sent at pulse i is received at pulse $i + 1$.

To simulate the synchronous algorithm on an asynchronous network, all we need is to use one of the synchronizers discussed in this chapter.

20.7   Limitations of Synchronizers

On the basis of discussion on synchronizers, it may appear to the reader that any synchronous algorithm can be simulated on an asynchronous network with little increase in time complexity. In particular, the simple synchronizer and synchronizer α take $O(1)$ time to simulate a pulse. But the reader should note that the simulation is valid if the correctness of the synchronous algorithm depends only on the order of messages received and sent by each process, that is, it does not use any *external* timing information for correctness.

To illustrate this point, let us consider the *k-session problem*. This problem requires each process to perform k special events called *flash* events. The constraint is based on the notion of a *session*. A session is simply an interval of time during the execution. The correctness property for the protocol is that in any timed execution there are k *disjoint* sessions, such that each process has performed its *flash* event exactly once in each session.

A synchronous protocol can solve this problem in exactly k time units. In each time unit, every process performs its *flash* event. However, in an asynchronous system the time required is at least $(k-1)D$ as shown by the following result.

Theorem 20.2 *Any algorithm that solves the k-session problem in an asynchronous network has a time complexity of at least $(k-1)D$.*

Proof: Let $flash_{i,r}$ be the rth flash event by process i. We first claim that, for all r such that $1 \leq r < k$:

$$\forall i, j : flash_{i,r} \rightarrow flash_{j,r+1}.$$

If not, we know that there exists an asynchronous execution (a global sequence of events) in which event $flash_{j,r+1}$ is executed before $flash_{i,r}$, which violates disjointness of the sessions. Choose i and j to be the most distant processes in the network. Then, it follows that there are at least D time units between $flash_{i,r}$ and $flash_{j,r+1}$ for all r. This implies that the total time complexity of the algorithm is at least $(k-1)D$ time units.

■

This result shows that simulation of a synchronous algorithm may increase the time complexity by a factor of D. The synchronizers cannot be used for the k-session problem because the correctness of the protocol is based on the timing information.

20.8 Problems

20.1. Give the pseudo-code for α, β, and γ synchronizers.

20.2. What is the message complexity of the asynchronous algorithm to construct a breadth-first search tree when it is obtained by combining the synchronous algorithm with (1) the α synchronizer, (2) the β synchronizer, and (3) the $\gamma(k)$ synchronizer?

20.3. Show how synchronizers can be used in a distributed algorithm to solve a set of simultaneous equations by an iterative method.

*20.4. (**due to [Awe85]**) Give a distributed algorithm to carry out the clustering used by the γ synchronizer.

*20.5. (**due to [Lub85]**) Let $G = (V, E)$ be an undirected graph corresponding to the topology of a network. A set $V' \subseteq V$ is said to be *independent* if there is no edge between any two vertices in V'. An independent set is *maximal* if there is no independent set that strictly contains V'. Give a distributed synchronous randomized algorithm that terminates in $O(\log |V|)$ rounds. Also, give an algorithm that works on asynchronous networks.

20.9 Bibliographic Remarks

The concept of synchronizers, and the synchronizers α, β, and γ were introduced by Awerbuch [Awe85]. The k-session problem and the lower bound on the time complexity of any asynchronous algorithm that solves the k-session problem is due to Arjomandi, Fischer, and Lynch [AFL83]. The reader is referred to the book by Raynal and Helary [RH90] for more details on synchronizers.

Chapter 21

Slicers

*He who can properly define and divide is to be considered a god. —
Plato*

21.1 Introduction

The analysis of executions of distributed programs is useful in various
applications such as design, testing, debugging, and fault tolerance of
distributed systems. In this chapter, we introduce the notion of a slice
of a distributed computation. A slice of a distributed computation,
with respect to a global predicate, is the smallest computation that
captures all those consistent cuts of the original computation that satisfy the global predicate. A slice can significantly reduce the size of
the computation to be analyzed, thereby making the understanding of
program behavior easier.

As an illustration, consider the computation shown in Figure 21.1(a).
The computation consists of three processes P_1, P_2, and P_3 hosting integer variables x_1, x_2, and x_3, respectively. An event, represented by a
solid circle is labeled with the value of the variable immediately after
the event is executed.

Suppose we want to determine whether the property (or the pred-
icate) $(x_1 * x_2 + x_3 < 5) \wedge (x_1 \geq 1) \wedge (x_3 \leq 3)$ ever holds in the
computation. In other words, does there exist a global state of the
computation that satisfies the predicate? The predicate could represent the violation of an invariant. Without computation slicing, we are
forced to examine all global states of the computation, twenty-eight

in total, to ascertain whether some global state satisfies the predicate. Alternatively, we can compute a slice of the computation automatically with respect to the predicate $(x_1 \geq 1) \wedge (x_3 \leq 3)$ as shown in Figure 21.1(b).

We can now restrict our search to the global states of the slice, which are only six in number, namely:
$\{a, e, f, u, v\}$, $\{a, e, f, u, v, b\}$, $\{a, e, f, u, v, w\}$, $\{a, e, f, u, v, b, w\}$, $\{a, e, f, u, v, w, g\}$, and $\{a, e, f, u, v, b, w, g\}$.

The slice has much fewer global states than the computation itself—exponentially smaller in many cases—resulting in substantial savings.

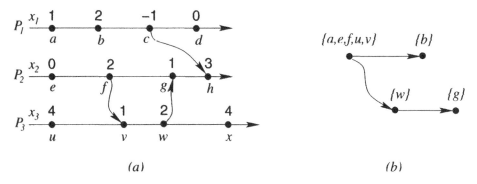

(a)   (b)

Figure 21.1: (a) A computation and (b) its slice with respect to $(x_1 \geq 1) \wedge (x_3 \leq 3)$.

In this chapter, we focus on *lean* slices. A slice of a computation with respect to a predicate is lean if and only if every consistent cut of the slice satisfies the predicate. We show that a slice of a computation with respect to a predicate is lean iff the set of consistent cuts that satisfy the predicate form a sublattice, that is, the predicate is *regular* (see Chapter 11).

This chapter is organized as follows. Section 21.2 gives a complete characterization of the set of consistent cuts of a computation. This characterization is based on Birkhoff's representation theorem for finite distributive lattices. Section 21.3 gives a formal definition of a slice and a lean slice. It shows that the notion of the "smallest" computation is well-defined and that the slice of a computation exists for all predicates. It also shows that the slice is lean iff the predicate is regular. Section 21.4 gives an efficient algorithm to compute a computation slice for a regular predicate. Finally, in Section 21.5 we discuss some applications of slicing.

The notation used in this chapter is summarized in Figure 21.2.

e, f, g	Events
$\sqcup$	Join of two elements in a poset
$\sqcap$	Meet of two elements in a poset
G, H	Consistent cuts
$C(E)$	Lattice of consistent cuts of $(E, \rightarrow)$
$C_B(E)$	Set of consistent cuts that satisfy B
L	a lattice
$J(L)$	Set of join-irreducible elements of L
B	A global predicate
$(I_B, F, \rightarrow_B)$	Computation slice of $(E, \rightarrow)$ with respect to B

Figure 21.2: Notation

21.2 Characterization of an Execution Lattice

In this chapter, we have used the event-based model for distributed computations. From Chapter 10, we know that

Theorem 21.1 *The set of consistent cuts of any distributed computation $(E, \rightarrow)$ forms a distributive lattice under the relation $\subseteq$.*

We denote the set of consistent cuts of any distributed computation $(E, \rightarrow)$ by $C(E)$ ($\rightarrow$ is implicit). We exploit the property that the lattice is distributive to derive the notion of a computation slice.

We first show that Theorem 21.1 is a complete characterization of $C(E)$ under the relation $\subseteq$. In other words, there is no additional structure property satisfied by this set. To prove this, given any finite distributive lattice L, it is sufficient to construct a distributed computation (a poset P) such that the set of consistent cuts (set of down-sets) is exactly L. To this end, first define *join-irreducible* elements as follows.

Definition 21.2 (Join-Irreducible Elements) *An element $x \in L$ is join-irreducible if*

1. $x \neq 0$, and

2. $\forall a, b \in L : x = a \sqcup b \Rightarrow (x = a) \vee (x = b)$.

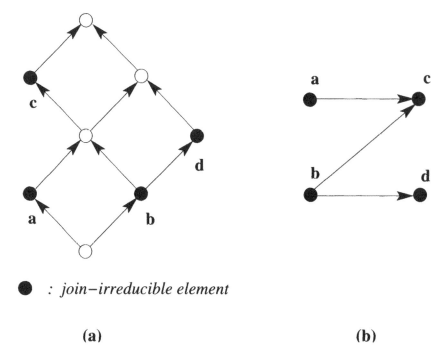

● : *join−irreducible element*

(a)   **(b)**

Figure 21.3: (a) An example of a distributive lattice (b) its partial order representation.

Pictorially, in a finite lattice, an element is join-irreducible iff it has exactly one lower cover, that is, there is exactly one edge coming into the element. Figure 21.3(a) shows a distributive lattice with its join-irreducible elements. Intuitively, the set of join-irreducible elements of a distributive lattice are analogous to basis elements of a linear vector space in the sense that the lattice can be generated using join-irreducible elements in the same way as the vector space can be generated by linear combination of basis elements. Let $J(L)$ denote the set of join-irreducible elements in L. Now we can state Birkhoff's theorem for finite distributive lattices.

Theorem 21.3 (Birkhoff's Representation Theorem) *Let L be a finite distributive lattice. Then the map $f : L \to C(J(L))$ defined by*

$$f(a) = \{x \in J(L) \mid x \leq a\}$$

is an isomorphism of L onto $C(J(L))$. Dually, let P be a finite poset.

Then the map $g : P \rightarrow J(C(P))$ defined by

$$g(a) = \{x \in P \mid x \leq a\}$$

is an isomorphism of P onto $J(C(P))$.

The above theorem implies one-to-one correspondence between a finite poset and a finite distributive lattice. Given a finite poset, we get the finite distributive lattice by considering its set of down-sets. Given a finite distributive lattice, we can recover the poset by focusing on its join-irreducible elements. Informally, any element of a lattice can be written as a join of a subset of join-irreducible elements of the lattice. For example, Figure 21.3(b) gives the poset corresponding to the lattice in Figure 21.3(a).

From the above discussion it is clear that given any finite distributed computation, the structure *finite distributive lattice* completely characterizes its execution graph. We will see implications of this observation in later sections.

Birkhoff's theorem is also useful in a computational sense because the set of join-irreducible elements of a lattice is generally exponentially smaller than the size of the lattice itself. In fact, for a finite distributive lattice, the number of join-irreducible elements is exactly equal to the size of the longest chain in the lattice (see Problem 21.3). In our case, the length of the longest chain is bounded by the number of events $|E|$. Hence, if some computation on L can instead be done on $J(L)$, then we get a significant computational advantage. This will be shown in Section 21.5.

21.3 Slicing a Distributed Computation

In this section, we define the notion of a slice of a distributed computation with respect to a global predicate. It is convenient to first define a *lean* slice (for regular predicates) and then use that definition to define a slice for general predicates. Informally, a slice consists of a partial order defined on subsets of events such that the set of down-sets (or consistent cuts) of the slice contains the set of those consistent cuts of the original computation that satisfy the given predicate. Of all the partial orders that satisfy the above condition, we are interested in the partial order with the smallest number of consistent cuts. That partial order is called a slice. If the slice contains precisely those consistent cuts that satisfy the predicate, then it is called a lean slice.

As mentioned before, an element of a slice is a subset of events in general. This can be interpreted as the subset of events corresponding to an element must be executed *atomically*. In other words, an external observer cannot see the intermediate states. This is similar to the concept of transactions in databases where operations in a transaction *appear* to have been executed atomically. The slicing of a computation serves two purposes. First, it tells us which subsets of events have to be executed atomically. Second, it tells us the order in which they must be executed.

We now define a lean slice formally.

Definition 21.4 (Lean Slice) *Given any distributed computation* $(E, \rightarrow)$ *and a global predicate* B, *we call a tuple* $(I_B, F, \rightarrow_B)$ *(where* $I_B \subseteq E, F \subseteq 2^E$, *and* $\rightarrow_B$ *is a partial order on* F) *a lean slice if*

1. I_B *is the least consistent cut of* E *that satisfies* B.

2. F *is a partition of some subset of* E, *and*

3. $\forall\, G \in C(E) : B(G) \equiv (G = I_B \cup H)$ *for some* $H \in C(F, \rightarrow_B)$.

The first requirement on a lean slice is that I_B is the least cut that satisfies B. To get other consistent cuts in E that satisfy B, we simply take a consistent cut of the lean slice $(F, \rightarrow_B)$ and add all those events to I_B. Thus the third requirement states that a lean slice captures all the consistent cuts that satisfy the predicate B.

As an example of a lean slice, consider the computation in Figure 21.4(a). The lattice corresponding to the computation is shown in Figure 21.4(b). The label of each element in the lattice is a triple denoting the index of the maximal event on each process for the corresponding consistent cut. For example, the label for the consistent cut G is $(2, 1, 1)$. For the predicate "all channels are empty," the sublattice is shown in Figure 21.4(c) along with its join-irreducible elements. The lean slice of the computation with respect to the predicate is shown in Figure 21.4(d). It can be verified that the set of consistent cuts of the lean slice are exactly those that satisfy the given predicate in the original computation. Furthermore, the length of the longest chain of the sublattice is 4, which is exactly equal to the number of its join-irreducible elements. In this example, $I_B = \emptyset$, which may not be the case in general. Finally, in the lean slice, events e_1 and f_1 and events f_2 and g_2 must be executed atomically.

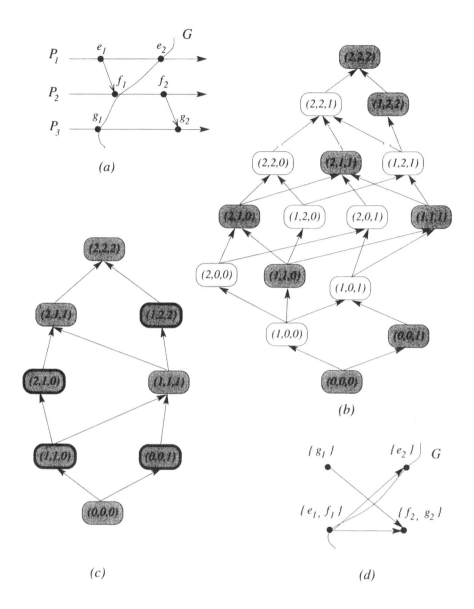

predicate: all channels are empty

⬜ : consistent cut   ▨ : consistent cut that satisfies the predicate

▨ : join−irreducible element of the sublattice induced by the predicate

Figure 21.4: (a) A computation, (b) its lattice, (c) a sublattice, and (d) the corresponding slice.

We first show that a lean slice exists iff the predicate B is a regular predicate.

Theorem 21.5 *A computation $(E, \rightarrow)$ has a nonempty lean slice with respect to a predicate B iff B is a regular predicate and $C_B(E)$ is nonempty.*

Proof: Assume that B is a regular predicate and $C_B(E)$ is nonempty. Therefore, the set of consistent cuts in $C_B(E)$ form a lattice. Let $\mathcal{J}$ denote the set of join-irreducible elements of $C_B(E)$, that is, $\mathcal{J} = J(C_B(E))$. We set $I_B = $ "the least consistent in $C_B(E)$" and $F = \mathcal{J}$. Any sublattice of a finite distributive lattice is also a finite distributive lattice. Thus, using Birkhoff's representation theorem for finite distributive lattices, $C_B(E)$ is isomorphic to $C(\mathcal{J})$.

Now, assume that a computation $(E, \rightarrow)$ has a nonempty lean slice, say $(I_B, F, \rightarrow_B)$, with respect to the predicate B. Clearly, $C_B(E)$ is nonempty. Furthermore, since $C_B(E)$ is isomorphic $C(F)$ and $C(F)$ is a finite distributive lattice, $C_B(E)$ is a lattice. Thus B is a regular predicate.

■

What if the predicate B is not regular? In this case, the set of consistent cuts that satisfy B, $C_B(E)$, is not a sublattice. We define a slice by weakening our requirement that all consistent cuts of the slice satisfy B. Instead, we require that the set of consistent cuts of the slice *contain* all consistent cuts that satisfy B. The following result shows that we can use the smallest computation that contains $C_B(E)$.

Theorem 21.6 *For every predicate B there exists a unique smallest sublattice that contains $C_B(E)$.*

Proof: Let $L(E, B)$ be the set of all sublattices of $C(E)$ that contain $C_B(E)$. The set $L(E, B)$ is nonempty because $C(E) \in L(E, B)$. Furthermore, the set $L(E, B)$ is closed under arbitrary intersection because the intersection of sublattices is also a sublattice and the intersection also contains $C_B(E)$. This implies that there is a unique smallest sublattice that contains $C_B(E)$, namely, the intersection of all sublattices in $L(E, B)$.

■

We are now ready to present a definition for a *slice* of any arbitrary predicate.

Definition 21.7 (Slice) *Given any distributed computation $(E, \rightarrow)$ and a global predicate B, we call a tuple $(I_B, F, \rightarrow_B)$ (where $I_B \subseteq E, F \subseteq 2^E$, and $\rightarrow_B$ is a partial order on F) a slice if*

1. *I_B is the least consistent cut of E that satisfies B.*

2. *F is a partition of some subset of E, and*

3. *$\forall\, G \in C(E) : B(G) \Rightarrow (G = I_B \cup H)$ for some $H \in C(F, \rightarrow_B)$.*

4. *Of all tuples that satisfy the first three properties, $(I_B, F, \rightarrow_B)$ has the smallest number of consistent cuts.*

We will focus only on regular predicates in this chapter. For regular predicates, slices are always lean. Problems 21.11 and 21.7 gives some methods for computing slices of nonregular predicates.

21.4 Algorithm for Slicing Regular Predicates

In this section we give an efficient algorithm to construct the slice of a distributed program given a regular predicate. Note that the size of the lattice and the size of the sublattice satisfying predicate B may be exponential in the number of processes; therefore, a naive algorithm that enumerates all the consistent cuts satisfying B may be prohibitively expensive.

The efficient algorithm is specified formally in Figure 21.5. It takes as input a distributed computation specified as the happen before diagram on the set of events and a regular predicate B. There are two possible outcomes. There may not be any consistent cut in E that satisfies B. The algorithm will detect this condition and output it in Step 1. Otherwise, the algorithm outputs a computation slice in Step 4. We now describe each step in greater detail.

21.4.1 Step 1: Computing the Least Cut

This step determines whether the predicate B is true on any consistent cut in E. Since B is a regular predicate, it is also linear. Therefore, we can apply the algorithm for detecting linear predicates. In fact, the algorithm returns the least consistent cut, say V, in E that satisfies B, if it exists.

The complexity of the algorithm depends on the complexity of determining an event to advance a given consistent cut G. In this chapter,

Input: A Computation $(E, \rightarrow)$ and a regular predicate B

Output: A computation slice $(I_B, F, \rightarrow_B)$ such that (1) Every consistent cut of F is also a consistent cut of E (2) All consistent cuts of F satisfy B (3) All consistent cuts of E that satisfy B are also consistent cuts of F.

- Step 1. Let V be the least consistent cut in E that satisfies B. Since B is a regular predicate it is linear and hence V can be determined, if it exists. If no such cut exists, output "B not possible".

- Step 2. Let W be the greatest consistent cut in E that satisfies B.

- Step 3. For each event $e \in W - V$, compute the least consistent cut in E that satisfies B and includes e. Call that cut $J(e)$.

- Step 4. Let R be an equivalence relation defined on events in $W - V$ as follows:

$$(e, f) \in R \equiv J(e) = J(f)$$

Let the equivalence classes induced by R be C_i, $1 \leq i \leq m$. For a class C, let $J(C)$ be $J(e)$ for some event e in C. Output $(V, F, \rightarrow_B)$, where

$$F := \{C_i \mid 1 \leq i \leq m\}$$

$$\rightarrow_B := \{(C_i, C_j) \mid J(C_i) \subseteq J(C_j) \wedge J(C_i) \neq J(C_j)\}$$

Figure 21.5: An algorithm to construct the slice

we will assume that the complexity of determining the required event is $O(N)$, and therefore, the complexity of this step is $O(N|E|)$. In this step, we have exploited the closure of B under meets.

21.4.2 Step 2: Computing the Greatest Cut

This step is dual of Step 1. Since B is a regular predicate, it is also closed under joins. Thus, if there is any consistent cut that satisfies B, then there exists the greatest consistent cut, say W, that satisfies B. To determine this cut, one could apply the algorithm for detecting linear predicates backwards on the computation.

Observe that if the least cut exists in Step 1, then we are guaranteed that the set of cuts satisfying B is nonempty. This, in turn, guarantees that the greatest cut satisfying B exists.

The computational complexity of this algorithm is the same as Step 1—$O(N|E|)$. In this step, we have exploited the closure of B under joins.

21.4.3 Step 3: Computing Join-Irreducible Elements

In this step, we determine the join-irreducible elements for the sublattice. For all events $e \in W - V$, we define a new predicate

$$B_e(X) \equiv B(X) \wedge (e \in X)$$

The following lemma shows that B_e is also a regular predicate.

Lemma 21.8 *Given any regular predicate B, B_e as defined above is also a regular predicate.*

Proof: Define a predicate I_e that is true on a cut X iff e is included in X. Given consistent cuts X_1 and X_2 that satisfy I_e, it is clear that $X_1 \cup X_2$ and $X_1 \cap X_2$ also satisfy I_e. Since the set of consistent cuts form a lattice, $X_1 \cup X_2$ and $X_1 \cap X_2$ are also consistent. Therefore, I_e is a regular predicate. This implies that B_e is a conjunction of two regular predicates and is therefore a regular predicate.

■

We define $J(e)$ as the least consistent cut that satisfies B_e. Since $e \in W$, we know that W satisfies B_e. Thus the set of cuts satisfying

B_e is nonempty. Since B_e is a regular predicate, we conclude that $J(e)$ is well-defined.

We now show that $J(e)$ is a join-irreducible element of the lattice $(C_B(E), \subseteq)$.

Lemma 21.9 $J(e)$ *is a join-irreducible element of* $(C_B(E), \subseteq)$.

Proof: Let $X, Y \in C_B(E)$ be such that $J(e) - X \sqcup Y$. Since $c \in J(e)$, we get $e \in X \lor e \in Y$. Assume the former without loss of generality. Since $e \in X$ and X satisfies B, we get that X is a consistent cut that includes e and satisfies B. However, $J(e)$ is the least consistent cut with these properties. Therefore, $J(e) \subseteq X$. But we also have $X \subseteq J(e)$. Therefore, $X = J(e)$.

■

A naive implementation of this step will have $O(N|E|^2)$ complexity because the algorithm to compute $J(e)$ will be invoked exactly $|E|$ times. However, the next lemma enables to reduce the complexity of this step.

Lemma 21.10 *Let e and f be events of $(E, \to)$ and B be a regular predicate. Then,*

$$e \to f \;\Rightarrow\; J(e) \le J(f)$$

Proof: Since e happened before f and $J(f)$ is a consistent cut, $e \in J(f)$. Since both $J(e)$ and $J(f)$ satisfy B, and $J(e)$ is the least consistent that contains e and satisfies B, $J(e) \le J(f)$.

■

Lemma 21.10 allows us to compute $J(e)$ for all events $e \in W - V$ on some process P in a single scan of the computation. Thus the complexity of this step can be reduced to $O(N^2 |E|)$.

21.4.4 Step 4: Forming Equivalence Classes

In this step we enumerate all the elements of the computation slice. We first define a relation R on events in $W - V$ as follows:

$$(e, f) \in R \;\equiv\; J(e) = J(f)$$

It can be easily verified that the relation R is an equivalence relation and will partition the set of events in $W - V$ into equivalence classes, say C_i, $1 \leq i \leq m$, where m is the number of equivalence classes. Intuitively, each equivalence class constitutes an element of the slice and all events in an equivalence class must be executed atomically. Note that $m \leq |W - V|$. For a class C, let $J(C)$ be $J(e)$ for some event e in C. The slice $(I_B, F, \rightarrow_B)$ is given by

$$I_B := V$$

$$F := \{C_i \mid 1 \leq i \leq m\}$$

$$\rightarrow_B := \{(C_i, C_j) \mid J(C_i) \subseteq J(C_j) \wedge J(C_i) \neq J(C_j)\}$$

It can be proved that

$$J(C_i) = V \cup \left(\bigcup_{C_j \rightrightarrows_B C_i} C_j \right)$$

It is clear from the construction and Lemma 21.9 that F contains only the join-irreducible elements. To justify this step, we will show that F contains all the join-irreducible elements of $(C_B(E), \subseteq)$. To that end, it is sufficient to show the following.

Lemma 21.11 *Every cut X in $C_B(E)$ can be written as a join of elements of F.*

Proof: Since X satisfies B, it satisfies $V \subseteq X \subseteq W$. This implies that X can be written as $V \cup Y$, where $Y \subseteq W - V$. Let

$$Z = \bigcup_{e \in Y} J(e)$$

It is clear that Z is a join of elements in F. We will show that $X = Z$. Since $J(e)$ contains e and at least V, it is clear that $X \subseteq Z$. We show that $Z \subseteq X$. To prove that, it is sufficient to show that

$$\forall e \in Y : J(e) \subseteq X$$

This follows from the fact that $e \in X$, X satisfies B, and $J(e)$ is the least cut that satisfies these properties.

■

We can compute equivalence classes as follows. We construct a graph with vertices as events in $W - V$. Moreover, we add an edge from event e to event f iff $J(e) \leq J(f)$. In the graph so constructed, each strongly connected component corresponds to an equivalence class. The complexity of determining strongly connected components in a directed graph is linear in the number of vertices and edges. Since the graph has at most $O(E)$ vertices and $O(NE)$ edges, the complexity of this step is $O(NE)$.

We are now ready for the main result of this chapter.

Theorem 21.12 *Given any computation $(E, \rightarrow)$ and a regular predicate B, the algorithm outputs the computation slice, if it exists, in $O(N^2 |E|)$ time.*

Proof: We will show that all consistent cuts of F satisfy B and every cut of E that satisfies B is also a cut of F. The first part follows from the definition of F and that the predicate B is a regular predicate. The second part follows from Lemma 21.11. The complexities of Step 1, Step 2, Step 3, and Step 4 are $O(N |E|)$, $O(N |E|)$, $O(N^2 |E|)$, and $O(N |E|)$, respectively, giving us an overall complexity of $O(N^2 |E|)$.

∎

21.5 Application: Predicate Detection and Control

To see an application of slicing for predicate detection, consider any global predicate B that is expressed as a conjunction of a regular predicate B_1 and another global predicate B_2. Given that the predicate B_2 does not have any structure that can be exploited for efficient detection, the predicate detection algorithm is forced to traverse the execution lattice. However, with the results of this chapter we can proceed as follows. Instead of searching the original lattice, we can search the reduced lattice—the one in which all cuts satisfy B_1.

Computation slicing is also useful for predicate control. A predicate can be controlled in a computation if and only if there exists a path in the lattice from the initial to the final consistent cut such that every consistent cut in the path satisfies the predicate. A regular predicate B can therefore be controlled in a computation $(E, \rightarrow)$ iff the length of the longest chain in $C_B(E)$ is $|E|$. Equivalently, $|J(C_B(E))| = |F| = |E|$, where $(F, \rightarrow_B)$ is the slice of $(E, \rightarrow)$ with respect to B.

21.6   Problems

21.1. Show that $x \in L$ is join-irreducible iff
  (i) $x \neq 0$
  (ii) $\forall a, b : (a < x) \wedge (b < x) \Rightarrow ((a \sqcup b) < x)$

21.2. The dual notion of join-irreducible elements is *meet-irreducible* elements. Let $M(L)$ denote the ordered set of meet-irreducible elements of L. Show that the ordered set $J(L)$ is isomorphic to the set $M(L)$.

21.3. Prove that the length of a finite distributive lattice L equals the size of $J(L)$.

21.4. Show that the slice of any computation $(E, \rightarrow)$, with respect to a global predicate that is a conjunction of local predicates, can be constructed in $O(|E|)$. (Hint: Add edges such that a false event cannot be in the frontier of a consistent cut.)

21.5. Give an algorithm to compute the slice of any computation with respect to the channel predicate: "There are at most k messages in the channel from P_i to P_j."

21.6. Generalize the notion of a consistent cut for any directed graph (not just partial order).

  (a) Show that the set of consistent cuts form a distributive lattice.

  (b) Define two directed graphs on the same set of vertices to be *cut-equivalent* if the their sets of consistent cuts are identical. Define two directed graphs on the same set of vertices to be *path-equivalent* if for any pair of vertices, directed path in one graph implies existence of a directed path in the other. Show that two graphs are cut-equivalent iff they are path-equivalent.

21.7. Give an algorithm to compute the slice of a linear predicate.

21.8. The *slice* of a directed graph with respect to a predicate is the smallest directed graph (with minimum number of consistent cuts) that contains all consistent cuts of the original graph that satisfy the predicate. Show that the smallest directed graph is well-defined for every predicate.

21.9. Assume that the given regular predicate B depends only on n processes out of a total of N processes. How can you optimize the algorithm for computing the slice for B with this assumption?

21.10. **(due to [SG02])** Give an efficient algorithm to detect *invariant* : B for a linear predicate B.

*21.11. **(due to [MG01c])** Assume that you are given slices for a computation with respect to regular predicates B_1, and B_2. Give efficient algorithms for computing the slice with respect to $B_1 \wedge B_2$, $B_1 \vee B_2$, and $\neg B_1$.

*21.12. **(due to [SG01])** Given a computation $(E, \rightarrow)$ and a consistent cut G, *possibly* : B is true on G if *possibly* : B is true in the sublattice that starts in the cut G and ends in the cut E. Truthness of *invariant* : B and *controllable* : B is similarly defined. Show that if B is a regular predicate, then *possibly* : B, *invariant* : B and *controllable* : B are also regular. Show that this is not true for *definitely* : B. Given a slice for B, how will you compute slices for *possibly* : B, *invariant* : B and *controllable* : B?

21.7 Bibliographic Remarks

The notion of a slice of a program was first proposed by Mark Weiser [Wei82]. The notion of a slice of a computation was proposed in Garg and Mittal [GM01] and later generalized in Mittal and Garg [MG01c].

Chapter 22

Distributed Shared Memory

Many a man fails to become a thinker only because his memory is too good. — Nietzche

22.1   Introduction

In this chapter we discuss an abstraction that allows a distributed application programmer to hide the details of sending messages between processes in the network. The entire system can be viewed as a collection of objects without any regard to the actual locations of the objects. Processes in the network do not send messages to each other; they communicate and synchronize simply through these shared objects. A process can access an object by simply invoking a *method* on it. When the object is remote, this method invocation results in a *remote method invocation.*

In the object-oriented view described above, one must deal with concurrency. What happens when multiple processes invoke a method concurrently? Let us define a concurrent object as one that allows multiple processes to execute its operations concurrently. For example, a concurrent queue in a shared memory system may allow multiple processes to invoke *enqueue* and *dequeue* operations. Or, in a client-server system, a server may handle concurrent remote procedure calls from multiple clients. The natural question, then, is to define which behavior of the object under concurrent operations is consistent (or

271

correct). Consider the case when a process P first enqueues x and then dequeues while process Q concurrently enqueues y. Is the queue's behavior acceptable if process P gets y as the result of dequeue? The objective of this chapter is to clarify such questions.

The notion of consistency is also required when objects are *replicated*. There are two reasons for replicating objects— fault tolerance and efficiency. If an object has multiple copies, then even when a node that contains one of the copies of the object goes down, the system may still be able to function correctly by using other copies. Second, accessing a remote object may incur a large overhead because of communication delays. Suppose that we knew that most accesses of the object are for *read-only*. In this case, it may be better to replicate that object. A process can read the value from the replica that is closest to it in the system. Of course, when we perform a *write* on this object, we have to worry about consistency of data. This again requires us to define data consistency. Observe that any system that uses *caches*, such as multi-processor systems, has to grapple with similar issues.

The notation used in this chapter is summarized in the Figure 22.1.

P, Q, R	Processes
H	Concurrent history
S	Sequential history
$<_H$	Occurred before order
e, f, g	Operations
x, y	Objects
u, v	Values of objects

Figure 22.1: Notation

This chapter is organized as follows. In Section 22.2, we define our system model formally. Section 22.3 describes *sequential consistency* and algorithms to guarantee sequential consistency in a system with replicated objects. Section 22.4 describes a stronger consistency condition called *linearizability* that has the attractive property that it can be implemented on a per-object basis, that is, if implementation of every object in the system is linearizable, then the entire collection is also linearizable. Finally, in Section 22.5 we describe some consistency conditions that are weaker than sequential consistency.

22.2 System Model

Objects and Processes

A *concurrent system* consists of a finite set of *sequential processes* that communicate through *concurrent objects*. Each object has a name and a type. The type defines the set of possible values for objects of this type and the set of primitive operations that provide the only means to manipulate objects of this type. Execution of an operation takes some time; this is modeled by two events, namely an *invocation* event and a *response* event. Let *op(arg)* be an operation on object x issued at P; *arg* and *res* denote *op*'s input and output parameters, respectively. Invocation and response events $inv(op(arg))$ *on* x *at* P and $resp(op(res))$ *from* x *at* P will be abbreviated as *inv(op)* and *resp(op)* when parameters, object name and process identity are not necessary. For any operation e, we use $proc(e)$ to denote the process and $object(e)$ to denote the set of objects associated with the operation. In this chapter, we assume that all operations are applied by a single process on a single object. In the problem set, we explore generalizations to operations that span multiple objects.

Histories

A *history* is an execution of a concurrent system modeled by a poset $(H, <_H)$, where H is the set of operations and $<_H$ is an irreflexive transitive relation that captures the "occurred before" relation between operations. Sometimes we simply use H to denote the history when $<_H$ is clear from the context. Formally, for any two operations e and f:

$$e <_H f \quad \text{if} \quad resp(e) \text{ occurred before } inv(f) \text{ in real-time.}$$

Observe that this relation includes the following relations.

Process Order: $(proc(e) = proc(f)) \wedge (resp(e) \text{ occurred before } inv(f))$.

Object Order: $(object(e) \cap object(f) \neq \emptyset) \wedge (resp(e) \text{ occurred before } inv(f))$.

For example, a message passing system can be modeled as a set of processes and channels. A channel is a shared object between two processes such that one process can invoke the send operation on the channel and the other process can invoke the receive operation. The send operation adds the message to a set of messages and the receive operation deletes and returns one of the messages from the set (if nonempty). In this case $(H, <_H)$ corresponds to our model of a distributed computation based on the happened before relation in Chapter 2.

A process subhistory $H|P$ (H at P) of a history H is the subposet of all events e in H such that $proc(e) = P$. An object's subhistory is defined in a similar way for an object x; denoted by $H|x$ (H at x). Two histories H and H' are *equivalent* if they are composed of exactly the same set of invocation and response events.

A history $(H, <_H)$ is a *sequential* history if $<_H$ is a total order. Such a history would happen if there was only one sequential process in the system. A sequential history is *legal* if it meets the sequential specification of all the objects. For example, if we are considering a read-write register x as a shared object, then a sequential history is legal if for every read operation that returns its value as v, there exists a write on that object with value v, and there does not exist another write operation on that object with a different value between the write and the read operation.

Our goal is to determine whether a given *concurrent* history is correct.

22.3 Sequential Consistency

Definition 22.1 (Sequentially Consistent) *A history* $(H, <_H)$ *is sequentially consistent if there exists a sequential history* S *equivalent to* H *such that* S *is legal and it satisfies process order.*

Thus a history is sequentially consistent if its execution is equivalent to a legal sequential execution and each process's behavior is identical in the concurrent and sequential execution. In the following histories, P, Q, and R are processes operating on shared registers x, y, and z. We assume that all registers have 0 initially. The response of a read operation is denoted by $ok(v)$, where v is the value returned, and the response of a write operation is denoted by $ok()$.

1. $H_1 = P\ write(x, 1),\ Q\ read(x),\ Q\ ok(0),\ P\ ok()$.
   Note that H_1 is a concurrent history. Q invokes the $read(x)$ operation before the $write(x, 1)$ operation is finished. Thus $write(x, 1)$ and $read(x)$ are concurrent operations in H_1.

H_1 is sequentially consistent because it is equivalent to the following legal sequential history.
Q $read(x)$, Q $ok(0)$, P $write(x, 1)$, P $ok()$.

2. $H_2 = P$ $write(x, 1)$, P $ok()$, Q $read(x)$, Q $ok(0)$
Somewhat surprisingly, H_2 is also sequentially consistent. Even though P got the response of its write before Q, it is okay for Q to have read an old value. Note that H_2 is a sequential history but not legal. However, it is equivalent to the following legal sequential history.
Q $read(x)$, Q $ok(0)$, P $write(x, 1)$, P $ok()$.

3. $H_3 = P$ $write(x, 1)$, Q $read(x)$, P $ok()$, Q $ok(0)$, P $read(x)$, P $ok(0)$
H_3 is not sequentially consistent. Any sequential history equivalent to H_3 must preserve process order. Thus the *read* operation by P must come after the *write* operation. This implies that the *read* cannot return 0.

Given a history, is it easy to check whether it is sequentially consistent? We now show that even for simple read-write registers, checking sequential consistency is NP-complete.

Theorem 22.2 *Given a concurrent history H on a read-write register, it is NP-complete to determine whether it is sequentially consistent.*

Proof: The problem is clearly in NP because the sequential history S serves as a witness for sequential consistency. The NP-hardness follows using a reduction from a 3-SAT problem. The details of the reduction are left as an exercise (see Problem 22.11).

∎

Since sequential consistency is NP-complete, it is natural to impose additional constraints on the system. Two of the constraints commonly used are:

- *Write-write (WW) constraint*: We assume that the system totally orders all write operations on all objects.

- *Object-ordered (OO) constraint*: We assume that the system totally orders all pairs of conflicting operations ((read, write) and (write, write)) on every object.

We now have the polynomial time algorithms to determine sequential consistency for read-write objects. In the following discussion we use $r(x, v)$ to denote a read operation on x that returns the value v and use subscripts such as $r_i(x, u)$ and $r_j(x, v)$ to denote different read operations. Similarly, we use $w_i(x, v)$ to denote a write operation of v on object x. We say that an operation $r_i(x)$ is a read *from* a write operation $w_j(x, v)$ if $r_i(x)$ returns the value written by the $w_j(x, v)$, namely v.

We first extend the definition of legality to any history (not just sequential history). A history $(H, <_H)$ is *legal* if for every read operation $r_i(x, v)$

- There exists a write $w_j(x, v)$

- There does not exist another write operation on the object x with different value between $w_j(x)$ and the read $r_i(x)$, that is, there does not exist $w_k(x, u)$ such that

$$(w_j(x, v) <_H w_k(x, u)) \quad \wedge \quad (w_k(x, u) <_H r_i(x, v)).$$

Theorem 22.3 *Let H be a history under WW-constraint. If H is legal then it is sequentially consistent.*

Proof: Assume that H is legal. Consider the acyclic graph corresponding to H. This graph is acyclic and legal. We will add edges to this graph one at a time, preserving acyclicity and legality until all operations on a single object are ordered.

We proceed as follows. Given any read operation $r_i(x, v)$ from write $w_j(x, v)$, and any write operation $w_k(x, u)$ such that $w_j(x, v)$ is ordered before $w_k(x, u)$, we put an edge from $r_i(x, v)$ to $w_k(x, u)$. This cannot create a cycle, because legality of H implies that there is no path from $w_k(x, u)$ to $r_i(x, v)$. Moreover, we preserve legality of the graph as shown next.

Legality can only be violated if addition of an edge results in creation of a path from some write operation, say w_a, to some read operation, say r_b. Assume, if possible, that by adding the edge from r_i to w_k, a new path from w_a to r_b is formed. Thus there was a path before from w_a to r_i and a path from w_k to r_b. Since writes are totally ordered, we have:

Case 1: $w_a \leq w_k$. But this implies that there is a path from w_a to r_b that does not use the edge (r_i, w_k). This path goes from w_a to

w_k and then from w_k to r_b.

Case 2: $w_k < w_a$. But this implies that there was a path from w_k to r_i in the original graph. This path goes from w_k to w_a and then from w_a to r_i. However, the existence of this path violates our assumption of legality of H.

Thus by adding this edge we have preserved acyclicity and legality. We continue to do so until every read operation on any object x is ordered with respect to all write operations. Now consider S any linear extension of the resulting graph. It is easy to see that S preserves process order as well as legality.

∎

Theorem 22.4 *Let H be a history under OO-constraint. If H is legal, then it is sequentially consistent.*

Proof: Assume that H is legal. Consider any linear order S compatible with H. It is easy to verify that S is also legal.

∎

The above results indicate that so long as we can enforce legality of reads under WW or OO-constraint, we are guaranteed to have a sequentially consistent execution. We now restrict our attention to WW-constraint. Under WW-constraint, we can assume that all writes are totally ordered by the system. The total order at any point of time is called the *ww-list*. It is necessary and sufficient to ensure that every read is from the most recent write. Thus, if a read operation on x reads from w_j then there does not exist a write that was after w_j and happened before r_i. The necessity of reading from the most recent write is obvious because of legality. It is sufficient, because writes that occur after this read cannot make it illegal, that is, no later write can have a path to this read. This is because an edge from operation s to t implies that s occurred before t in real time.

22.3.1 Local Read Algorithm

In this section we give an algorithm for maintaining replicated objects that guarantees that the system execution is sequentially consistent. We will assume that there is complete replication—every processor keeps a copy of all objects. This algorithm is efficient for *reads*, but not for *writes*.

The algorithm shown in Figure 22.2 uses a totally ordered broadcast (see Chapter 17). To perform a read, a process can simply read its local copy. However, to perform a write, the process must broadcast the new value to all other processes using a totally ordered broadcast. When a process receives its own totally ordered broadcast, then it can signal the end of the write operation.

```
P::
  Upon read(x):
      generate Ok(v) where v is the value of P's copy of x;

  Upon write(x, v):
      totally-ordered-broadcast (x, v);

  Upon receive of totally-ordered-broadcast(x, v) from Q:
      set local copy of x to v;
      if P = Q then generate Ok() for write(x, v);
```

Figure 22.2: Sequential consistency: local read algorithm

This algorithm follows WW-constraint because all writes are ordered. The equivalent sequential history can be constructed as follows. All writes are first arranged in the order of the totally ordered broadcast. Now all reads are inserted between appropriate writes depending on the value read. It can be easily verified that this sequential history is legal and that it preserves process order.

22.3.2 Local Write Algorithm

We now describe an algorithm for sequential consistency that is more efficient for writes. The algorithm shown in Figure 22.3 also uses totally ordered broadcasts. However, it generates a response for write as soon as it has invoked the totally ordered broadcast operation and does not wait for the totally ordered broadcast to be finished as required by the local read algorithm.

The read operation by P requires it to wait for all pending writes that are issued by P. The number of pending writes is maintained in the variable *num*. It is incremented for every invocation of write and decremented when the corresponding totally ordered broadcast is finished.

```
P::
  Upon read(x):
      if (num = 0) then
            generate Ok(v) where v is the value of P's copy of x;

  Upon write(x, v):
      num := num + 1;
      totally-ordered-broadcast(x, v);
      generate Ok() for write;

  Upon receive of totally-ordered-broadcast (x, v) from Q:
      set local copy of x to v;
      if (P = Q) then
          num := num - 1;
          if (num = 0) then
                generate OK(v) where v is the value of P's copy of x;
```

Figure 22.3: Sequential consistency: local write algorithm

Theorem 22.5 *The algorithm in Figure 22.3 ensures sequential consistency.*

Proof: We first observe that because writes are done using a totally ordered broadcast, every history totally orders all writes in the system. From Theorem 22.3, it is sufficient to show that all reads in any history H are legal.

Let $r_i(x, v)$ read from $w_j(x, v)$. We need to show that there does not exist any $w_k(x, u)$ in H such that $w_j(x, v) <_H w_k(x, u)$ and $w_k(x, u) <_H r_i(x, v)$. There are two cases.

Case 1: The write $w_k(x, u)$ and the read $r_i(x, v)$ are on the same processor, say P. By the algorithm for *read*, the *num* should be 0 before the value v is returned. This means that $P's$ copy of x with value v would have been updated by $w_k(x, u)$. (Since $w_j(x, v) <_H w_k(x, u)$, we know that update to v was before update to u). Thus it could not have returned v, a contradiction.

Case 2: The write $w_k(x, u)$ and $r_i(x, v)$ are on different processors, say Q and P, respectively. Since $w_k(x, u) <_H r_i(x, v)$, there exists an operation O on P preceding $r_i(x, v)$ such that $w_k(x, u) <_H O$. Suppose O is a write. This implies that $r_i(x)$ must wait for O to finish before returning the value. From the totally ordered broadcast property it follows that $w_k(x, u)$ has also taken effect before $r_i(x, v)$. Thus $r_i(x)$ could not have returned v. Now suppose that O is a read. Since $w_k(x, u) <_H O$, either O is a read on object x in which case r_i again could not have returned v; or, O is on a object y from a write $w_l(y)$ such that $w_k(x) <_H w_l(y)$. But this again implies from the totally ordered broadcast property that the processor P has updated $x's$ value with $w_k(x, u)$. Hence, $r_i(x)$ could not have returned v.

∎

22.4 Linearizability

Linearizability is a stronger consistency condition than sequential consistency. Intuitively, an execution of a concurrent system is linearizable if it could appear to an external observer as a sequence composed of the operations invoked by processes that respect object specifications and real-time precedence ordering on operations. So, linearizability provides the illusion that each operation on shared objects issued by concurrent processes takes effect instantaneously at some point between the beginning and the end of its execution. Formally,

Definition 22.6 (Linearizable) *A history $(H, <_H)$ is linearizable if there exists a sequential history $(S, <)$ equivalent to H such that S is legal and it preserves $<_H$.*

Since $<_H$ includes process order, it follows that a linearizable history is always sequentially consistent.

Let us reexamine some histories that we saw earlier.

1. $H_1 = P \ write(x, 1), \ Q \ read(x), \ Q \ ok(0), \ P \ ok()$
   H_1 is linearizable because the following legal sequential history,
   $Q \ read(x), \ Q \ ok(0), \ P \ write(x, 1), \ P \ ok()$
   preserves $<_H$.

2. $H_2 = P\ write(x,1),\ P\ ok(),\ Q\ read(x),\ Q\ ok(0)$

   H_2 is sequentially consistent but not linearizable. The legal sequential history used for showing sequential consistency does not preserve $<_H$.

A key advantage of linearizability is that it is a local property.

Theorem 22.7 $\forall$ *objects* $x : H|x$ *is linearizable iff* H *is linearizable.*

Proof: The backward direction is obvious. For the proof in the forward direction, assume that $(S_x, <_x)$ is a linearization of $H|x$, that is, $(S_x, <_x)$ is a sequential history that is equivalent to $H|x$. As before, we will construct an acyclic graph that orders all operations on any object and also preserves occurred before order $<_H$. Any sort of this graph will then serve as a linearization of H. The graph is constructed as follows. The vertices are all the operations. The edges are all the edges given by union of $<_x$'s and $<_H$. This graph totally orders all operations on any object. Moreover, it preserves $<_H$. The only thing that remains to be shown is that it is acyclic. Since $<_x$'s are acyclic, it follows that any cycle, if it exists, must involve at least two objects.

We will show that cycle in this graph implies a cycle in $<_H$. If any two consecutive edges in the cycle are due to just $<_x$ or just $<_H$, then they can be combined. Note that $e <_x f <_y g$ for distinct objects x and y is not possible because all operations are unary ($e <_x f <_y g$ implies that f operates on both x and y). Now consider, any sequence of edges such that $e <_H f <_x g <_H h$.

   $e <_H f$ implies $res(e)$ precedes $inv(f)$ { definition of $<_H$ }

   $f <_x g$ implies $inv(f)$ precedes $res(g)$ { $<_x$ is a total order }

   $g <_H h$ implies $res(g)$ precedes $inv(h)$ { definition of $<_H$ }.

   These can be combined to give that $res(e)$ precedes $inv(h)$. Therefore, $e <_H h$. Thus any cycle in the graph can be reduced to a cycle in $<_H$, a contradiction because $<_H$ is irreflexive.

■

Linearizability can be implemented by using a totally ordered broadcast for each operation. The invocation of the object corresponds to performing the totally ordered broadcast. When the totally ordered broadcast is delivered at a processor, then the actual operation is performed on the local copy and a response is generated for the operation. We leave the proof of correctness as an exercise (see Problem 22.3).

22.5   Other Consistency Conditions

Although we have focused on sequential consistency and linearizability, there are many consistency conditions that are weaker than sequential consistency. A weaker consistency condition allows more efficient implementation at the expense of increased work by the programmer, who has to ensure that the application works correctly despite weaker consistency condition.

Consider a program consisting of two processes P and Q with two variables x and y. Assume that the initial values of x and y are both 0. P writes 1 in x and then reads the value of y; Q writes 1 in y and then reads the value of x. Strong consistency conditions like sequential consistency or linearizability prohibit the results of both reads from being 0. However, if we assume that the minimum possible time to read plus the minimum possible time to write is less than the communication latency, then both reads must return 0. The latency is the information delivery time and each processor cannot possibly know of the events that have transpired at the other processor. So, no matter what the protocol is, if it implements sequential consistency, it must be slow.

Causal consistency is weaker than sequential consistency. Causal consistency allows for implementation of read and write operations in a distributed environment that do not always incur communication delay, that is, causal consistency allows for cheap read/write operations.

With sequential consistency, all processes agree on the same legal sequential history S. The agreement defined by causal consistency is weaker. Given a history H, it is not required that two processes P and Q agree on the same ordering for the write operations, which are not ordered in H. The reads are, however, required to be legal. Each process considers only those operations that can affect it, that is, its own operations and only write operations from other processes. Formally, for read-write objects causal consistency can be defined as follows.

Definition 22.8 (Causally Consistent) *A history* $(H, <_H)$ *is causally consistent if for each process* P_i, *there is a legal sequential history* $(S_i, <_{S_i})$ *where* S_i *is the set of all operations of* P_i *and all write operations in* H, *and* $<_{S_i}$ *respects the following order:*

Process Order: *If* P_i *performs operation* e *before* f, *then* e *is ordered before* f *in* S_i.

> Object Order: *If any process P performs a write on an object x with value v and another process Q reads that value v, then the write by P is ordered before read by Q in S_i.*

Intuitively, causal consistency requires that causally related writes are seen by all processes in the same order. The concurrent writes may be seen in different order by different processes.

It can be proved that sequential consistency implies causal consistency but the reverse does not hold. As an example consider history H_1 in which P_1 does $w_1(x, 1)$, $r_1(x, 2)$ and P_2 does $w_2(x, 2)$, $r_2(x, 1)$.

The history is causally consistent because the following serializations exist:
$$S_1 = w_1(x, 1), w_2(x, 2), r_1(x, 2)$$
$$S_2 = w_2(x, 2), w_1(x, 1), r_2(x, 1)$$

Thus we only require that there is a legal sequential history for every process and not one for the entire system. P_1 orders w_1 before w_2 in S_1 and P_2 orders w_2 before w_1 but that is considered causally consistent because w_1 and w_2 are concurrent writes. It can be easily proved that history H_1 is not sequentially consistent.

The following history is not even causally consistent. Assume that the initial value of x is 0. The history at process P is
$$H|P = P\ read(x), P\ ok(4), P\ write(x, 3), P\ ok().$$
The history at process Q is
$$H|Q = Q\ read(x), Q\ ok(3), Q\ write(x, 4), Q\ ok().$$

Since, Q reads the value 3 and then writes the value of x, the write by Q should be ordered after the write by P. P's read is ordered before its write; therefore, it cannot return 4 in a causally consistent history. We have left the implementation of causal consistency as an exercise (see Problem 22.6).

The table in Figure 22.4 summarizes the requirements of all consistency conditions considered in this chapter. The second column tells us whether the equivalent legal history required for the consistency condition is global or not. The third column tells us the requirement on the legal history in terms of the order preserved. For example, linearizability requires that there be a single equivalent legal history that preserves the occured before order.

Consistency	Legal History	Order Preserved
Linearizability	Global	Occurred before order
Normality (Problem 22.8)	Global	Process, object order
Sequential	Global	Process order
Causal	Per process	Process, object order
FIFO (Problem 22.7)	Per process	Process order

Figure 22.4: Summary of consistency conditions

22.6 Problems

22.1. Consider a concurrent stack. Which of the following histories are linearizable? Which of the them are sequentially consistent? Justify your answer.

a) $P\ push(x), P\ ok(), Q\ push(y), Q\ ok(), P\ pop(), P\ ok(x)$

b) $P\ push(x), Q\ push(y), P\ ok(), Q\ ok(), Q\ pop(), Q\ ok(x)$

22.2. Show that the local read and the local write algorithms for sequential consistency may generate a history that is not linearizable.

22.3. Show that if all operations are performed using a totally ordered broadcast, then the history is linearizable.

22.4. Assume that a server keeps all the objects in a system. All other processors in the system maintain a cache of a subset of objects accessed by that processor. Give an algorithm that guarantees sequential consistency of reads and writes of the objects.

22.5. Assume that you have an implementation of a concurrent system that guarantees causal consistency. Show that if you ensure that the system does not have any concurrent writes, then the system also ensures sequential consistency.

22.6. Give an algorithm to ensure causal consistency in a distributed system for read-write objects. (Hint: Use the causal ordering of messages.)

22.7. FIFO consistency requires that the writes done by the same process must be seen in the same order. Writes done by different processes may be seen in different order. Show a history that is FIFO consistent but not causally consistent.

22.8. Given a poset $(H, <_H)$ denoting a system execution, we define a relation $\rightarrow_H$ as the transitive closure of union of process and object order. We call $(H, <_H)$ *normal* if there exists an equivalent sequential history that preserves $\rightarrow_H$. Show that when all operations are unary, a history is linearizable iff it is normal.

22.9. Consider the following history of six events in which operations span multiple objects. Assume that A and B are initialized to 0.

$$
\begin{array}{llllll}
ev_1 = & inv(write(1)) & on & A & at & P_1 \\
ev_2 = & inv(sum()) & on & A, B & at & P_2 \\
ev_3 = & resp(write()) & from & A & at & P_1 \\
ev_4 = & inv(write(2)) & on & B & at & P_3 \\
ev_5 = & resp(write()) & from & B & at & P_3 \\
ev_6 = & resp(sum(2)) & from & A, B & at & P_2
\end{array}
$$

Show that the above history is not linearizable but normal.

*22.10. Assume that every message delay is in the range $[d - u, d]$ for $0 < u < d$. Show that in any system that ensures sequential consistency of read-write objects, the sum of delays for a read operation and a write operation is at least d.

*22.11. **(due to [Tay83])** Show that the problem of determining whether $(H, <_H)$ is sequentially consistent for read-write registers is NP-complete.

*22.12. **(due to [MG98])** Generalize the definition of sequential consistency and linearizability for the model in which operations span multiple objects. Give distributed algorithms to ensure sequential consistency and linearizability in this model.

22.7 Bibliographic Remarks

Sequential consistency was first proposed by Lamport in [Lam79]. The notion of linearizability for read/write registers was also introduced by Lamport in [Lam86] under the name of atomicity. The concept was generalized to arbitrary data types and termed as linearizability by Herlihy and Wing in [HW90]. The NP-completeness of checking sequential consistency is shown in Taylor [Tay83]. The discussion of the write-write constraint and the object-ordered constraint is taken from [MRZ95]. The algorithms for sequential consistency are taken from Attiya and Welch [AW94]. For extension of these consistency conditions to multi-object operations see Garg and Raynal [GR99] and Mittal and Garg [MG98]. Causal consistency was introduced by Hutto and Ahamad [HA90].

Chapter 23

Self-Stabilization

Prudent, cautious self-control is wisdom's root — *Robert Burns*

23.1 Introduction

The algorithms for resource allocation problems that we have discussed so far do not work in the presence of faults. In this chapter we discuss a class of algorithms, called *self-stabilizing* algorithms, that can tolerate many kinds of faults.

We assume that the system states can be divided into legal and illegal states. The definition of the legal state is dependent on the application. Usually, system and algorithm designers are very careful about transitions from the legal states, but illegal states of the system are ignored. When a fault occurs, the system moves to an illegal state and if the system is not designed properly, it may continue to execute in illegal states. A system is called self-stabilizing if regardless of the initial state, the system is guaranteed to reach a legal state after a finite number of moves.

This chapter is organized as follows. Section 23.2 presents Dijkstra's self-stabilizing algorithm for mutual exclusion on a ring. This algorithm requires each machine on the ring to have at least as many states as the number of machines. Section 23.3 presents another mutual exclusion algorithm also due to Dijkstra, which requires only three states per machine.

The notation used in this chapter is summarized in Figure 23.1.

287

N	Number of processes
S	State of a process
K	Total number of states per machine
L	State of the left neighbor
R	State of the right neighbor
B	State of the bottom machine
T	State of the top machine

Figure 23.1: Notation

23.2   Mutual Exclusion with K-State Machines

We will model the mutual exclusion problem as follows. A machine can enter the critical section only if it has a *privilege*. Therefore, in the case of mutual exclusion, legal states are those global states in which exactly one machine has a privilege. The goal of the self-stabilizing algorithm is to determine who has the privilege and how the privileges move in the network.

> Bottom:
>   **if** $(L = S)$ **then** $S := S + 1 \; mod \; K$;
>
> For other machines:
>   **if** $(L \neq S)$ **then** $S := L$;

Figure 23.2: K-state self-stabilizing algorithm

We assume that there are N machines numbered $0 \ldots N - 1$. The state of any machine is determined by its *label* from the set $\{0 \ldots K-1\}$. We use L, S, and R to denote the labels of the left neighbor, itself, and the right neighbor for any machine. Machine 0, also called the *bottom* machine, is treated differently from all other machines. The program is given in Figure 23.2, and a sample execution of the algorithm is shown in Figure 23.3. The bottom machine has a privilege if its label has the same value as its left neighbor, i.e., $(L = S)$. In Figure 23.3, the bottom machine and its left neighbor have labels 2 and therefore the bottom machine has a privilege. Once a machine possessing a privilege executes its critical section, it should execute the transition given by

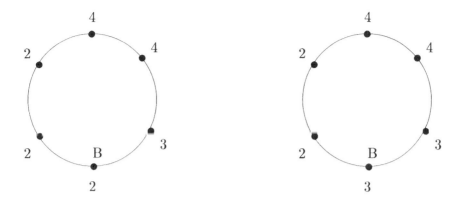

Figure 23.3: A move by the bottom machine in the K-state algorithm

the program. In Figure 23.3, on exiting from the critical section, the bottom machine executes the statement $S := S+1 \bmod K$ and acquires the label 3.

A normal machine has a privilege only when $L \neq S$. On exiting the critical section it executes $S := L$ and thus loses its privilege. In Figure 23.4, P_5 moves and makes it label as 4.

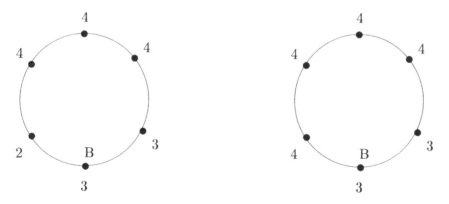

Figure 23.4: A move by a normal machine in the K-state algorithm

23.2.1 Proof of Correctness

In the above algorithm, the system is in a legal state if exactly one machine has the privilege. It is easy to verify that $(x_0, x_1, \ldots, x_{N-1})$ is legal if and only if either all $x_i's$ are equal or there exists $m < N - 1$ such that all $x_i's$ with $i \leq m$ are equal to some value and all other $x_i's$

are equal to some other value. In the first case, the bottom machine has the privilege. In the second case the machine P_{m+1} has the privilege. It is easy to verify that

Lemma 23.1 *If the system is in a legal state, then it will stay legal.*

Now we consider any unbounded sequence of moves. The proof of the following lemma is left as an exercise.

Lemma 23.2 *A sequence of moves in which the bottom machine does not move is at most $O(N^2)$.*

The following lemma exploits the fact that $K \geq N$.

Lemma 23.3 *Given any configuration of the ring, either*
(1) no other machine has the same label as the bottom, or
(2) there exists a label that is different from all machines.
Furthermore, within a finite number of moves, (1) will be true.

Proof: We show that if (1) does not hold, then (2) is true. If there exists a machine that has the same label as that of bottom, then there are now $K - 1$ labels left to be distributed among $N - 2$ machines. Since $K \geq N$, we get that there is some label which is not used.

To show the second part, first note that if some label is missing from the network, then it can only be generated by the bottom machine. Moreover, the bottom machine simply cycles among all labels. Since, from Lemma 23.2, the bottom machine moves after some finite number of moves by normal machines, we get that the bottom machine will eventually get the missing label.

■

We now show that system reaches a legal state in $O(N^2)$ moves.

Theorem 23.4 *If the system is in illegal state, then within $O(N^2)$ moves, it reaches a legal state.*

Proof: It is easy to see that once the bottom machine gets the unique label, the system stabilizes in $O(N^2)$ moves.

The bottom machine can move at most N times before it acquires the missing label. Machine 1 therefore can move at most $N + 1$ times before the bottom acquires the label. Similarly, machine i can move at most $N + i$ times before the bottom gets the label.

By adding up all the moves, we get
$$N + (N + 1) + \ldots + (N + N - 1) = O(N^2) \text{ moves.}$$

■

23.3   Mutual Exclusion with Three-State Machines

Bottom:
    if $(B + 1 = R)$ **then** $B := B + 2$;

Normal:
    if $(L = S + 1)$ **or** $(R = S + 1)$ **then** $S := S + 1$;

Top:
    if $(L = B)$ **and** $(T \neq B + 1)$ **then** $T := B + 1$;

Figure 23.5: Three-state self-stabilizing algorithm

The above algorithm requires that the number of states per machine K to be at least N. Therefore the algorithm is not independent of the number of machines. We now show another algorithm due to Dijkstra that requires only three states per machine independent of the total number of machines in the system. Assume that there is a ring of at least three machines. The program consists of three types of machines. In this configuration, we view machines as a sequence starting with a *bottom* machine, followed by one or more *normal* machines, and ending with a *top* machine. The state of any machine ranges over $\{0, 1, 2\}$. In the algorithm shown in Figure 23.5, all additions are performed modulo 3. A sample execution is shown in Figure 23.6.

23.3.1   Proof of Correctness

To prove correctness of the algorithm, it is useful to view the state of the system as a string starting with B, then states of the normal machines S's, and ending with T. Between any two consecutive states, there are only two possibilities—either they are the same or they differ by 1. In case they differ by 1, we put an arrow between the state such that arrow points to the direction in which the number decreases by 1 modulo 3. Thus 2 points to 1, 1 points to 0, and 0 points to 2.

Our proof uses the following three different metrics based on the

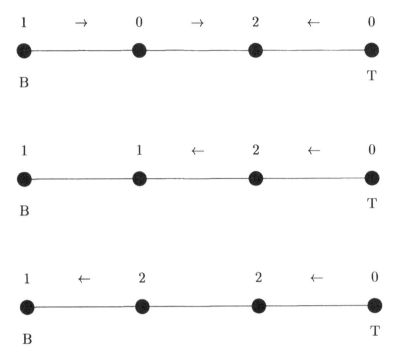

Figure 23.6: A sample execution of the Three-state self-stabilizing algorithm

arrows present in the string.

x = the number of arrows

y = the number of left-pointing arrows +
twice the number of right-pointing arrows

z = $\sum\limits_{\substack{\text{left-pointing} \\ \text{arrows}}}$ distance from bottom + $\sum\limits_{\substack{\text{right-pointing} \\ \text{arrows}}}$ distance from top

The three-state machine algorithm can be rewritten as:

For bottom:

(0) $B \leftarrow R$ to $B \rightarrow R$ $\Delta x = 0$ $\Delta y = +1$ $\Delta z = N - 1$

For a normal machine:

(1) $L \rightarrow S$ R to L $S \rightarrow R$ $\Delta x = 0$ $\Delta y = 0$ $\Delta z = -1$

(2) L $S \leftarrow R$ to $L \leftarrow S$ R $\Delta x = 0$ $\Delta y = 0$ $\Delta z = -1$

(3) $L \rightarrow S \leftarrow R$ to L S R $\Delta x = -2$ $\Delta y = -3$ $\Delta z = -N + 1$

(4) $L \rightarrow S \rightarrow R$ to L $S \leftarrow R$ $\Delta x = -1$ $\Delta y = -3$ $\Delta z \leq N - 2$

(5) $L \leftarrow S \leftarrow R$ to $L \rightarrow S$ R $\Delta x = -1$ $\Delta y = 0$ $\Delta z \leq N - 2$

For top:

(6) $L \rightarrow T$ to $L \leftarrow T$ $\Delta x = 0$ $\Delta y = -1$ $\Delta z = N - 1$

(7) L T to $L \leftarrow T$ $\Delta x = +1$ $\Delta y = +1$ $\Delta z = N - 1$

It is easy to see that if a string has a single arrow then the system is in a legal state. Furthermore, the arrow remains the only one. It moves left to right using moves (1) and (2). It gets reflected by the bottom using the move (0) and by the top using the move (6). The move (6) is possible because if there is a single arrow, the precondition $(L = B)$ and $(T \neq B + 1)$ holds.

Moreover, if the system does not have any arrows, then move (7) is the only eligible move and it will create a single arrow. It also follows that at least one move is always possible in the system. Our goal is to bound the number of moves before the string gets into a legal state.

Let m_i denote the number of moves corresponding to the transformation (i), where $i \in [0 \dots 7]$, made by the system before it stabilizes.

Lemma 23.5 *Between two successive moves of top at least one move of bottom takes place.*

Proof: The top machine moves only when $T \neq B + 1$. When it moves, it makes T equal to $B + 1$. Now the top machine can move only when B changes.

■

Lemma 23.6 *A sequence of moves in which bottom does not move is finite.*

Proof: From Lemma 23.5, it is sufficient to consider the moves of the normal machines. Moves (3),(4), and (5) decrease the number of arrows, and no moves of the normal machines increase the number of arrows; therefore, it is sufficient to show that a sequence of moves (1) and (2) is finite. However, this follows from the structure and the finiteness of the string. The move (1) takes the arrow from left to right, and therefore the arrow must eventually hit the top machine. A similar argument applies to move (2).

■

Lemma 23.7 *If the string has not reached a legal state, then y decreases by at least 1 per move of bottom.*

Proof: Between successive moves of bottom, falsification of "leftmost arrow exists and points to the right" happens in (3), (4), or (6). If this happens in move (6), then the string is legal and we are done. If the falsification happens in (3) or (4), then y decreases by 3. But y can increase by at most 2 on account of moves (0) and (7) between two successive moves of bottom, Therefore, we get that y decreases by at least 1 per move of bottom.

■

Theorem 23.8 *Within $O(N^2)$ moves, there is one arrow in the string.*

Proof: From Lemma 23.7, if the algorithm has not yet reached a legal state, then y decreases by at least 1 per move of bottom. As the initial value of y is at most $2N$,

$$m_0 \leq 2N.$$

Also, from Lemma 23.5, between two successive moves of top at least one move of bottom takes place. Therefore,

$$m_6 + m_7 \leq 2N.$$

We now bound the number of moves made by normal machines. Note that the transformations (3), (4), and (5) decrease x whereas the transformations (0), (1), and (2) do not change x at all. Furthermore, a move by top increases x by at most 1 and the total number of such moves is upper-bounded by $2N$. Since the maximum initial value of x is N,

$$m_3 + m_4 + m_5 \leq 3N.$$

Finally, since the transformations (1) and (2) decrease z, the other transformations—which are at most $7N$ in total—increase it by at most N and the maximum initial value of z is N^2,

$$m_1 + m_2 \leq 8N^2$$

giving us an upper bound of $O(N^2)$ on the total number of moves required for the system to stabilize.

∎

The following example establishes that it is, in fact, a tight upper bound. Consider the string consisting of $(N-1)/2$ right-pointing arrows followed by $(N-1)/2$ spaces, for some odd $N > 3$. By repeatedly using transformation (1) $(N-1)^2/4$ times, we obtain the string consisting of $(N-1)/2$ spaces followed by $(N-1)/2$ right-pointing arrows; each arrow moves to the right by $(N-1)/2$ places, with the system staying in an illegal state throughout.

23.4 Problems

23.1. Show that a system with four machines may not stabilize if it uses the K-state machine algorithm with $K = 2$.

23.2. Prove Lemma 23.2.

23.3. Show that the K-state machine algorithm converges to a legal state in at most $O(N^2)$ moves by providing a norm function on the configuration of the ring that is at most $O(N^2)$, decreases by at least 1 for each move, and is always nonnegative.

23.4. In our K-state machine algorithm we have assumed that a machine can *read* the value of the state of its left machine and *write* its own state in one atomic action. Give a self-stabilizing algorithm in which a processor can only *read* a remote value or *write* a local value in one step, but not both.

*23.5. [**due to [Dij74]**] Show that the four-state machine algorithm in Figure 23.7 is self-stabilizing. The state of each machine is represented by two booleans xS and upS. For the bottom machine $upS = true$ and for the top machine $upS = false$ always hold.

Bottom:
    if $(xS = xR)$ and $\neg upR$ then $xS := \neg xS$;

Normal:
    if $xS \neq xL$ then $xS := \neg xS; upS := true$;
    if $xS = xR$ and upS and $\neg upR$ then $upS := false$;

Top:
    if $(xS \neq xL)$ then $xS := \neg xS$;

Figure 23.7: Four-state self-stabilizing algorithm

23.6. A self-stabilizing algorithm is *uniform* if all processes are equal and do not have any process identifiers. Show that there is no self-stabilizing algorithm for mutual exclusion in a ring with a nonprime number of processes.

*23.7. Assume that each process P_i has a pointer that is either null or points to one of its neighbors. Give a self-stabilizing, distributed algorithm on a network of processes that guarantees that the system reaches a configuration where (1) if P_i points to P_j then P_j points to P_i, and (2) there are no two neighboring processes such that both have null pointers.

23.5 Bibliographic Remarks

The idea of self-stabilizing algorithms first appeared in Dijkstra [Dij74], where three self-stabilizing algorithms were presented for mutual exclusion in a ring. The proof for the Three-state algorithm is taken from Mittal and Garg [MG01b].

Chapter 24

Knowledge and Common Knowledge

Imagination is more important than knowledge. — *Albert Einstein*

24.1 Introduction

Many problems in a distributed system arise from the lack of global knowledge. By sending and receiving messages, processes increase the knowledge they have about the system. However, there is a limit to the level of knowledge that can be attained. In this chapter, we use the notion of knowledge to prove some fundamental results about distributed systems. In particular, we show that agreement is impossible to achieve in an asynchronous system in the absence of reliable communication.

The notion of knowledge is also useful in proving lower bounds on the message complexity of distributed algorithms. In particular, knowledge about remote processes can be gained in an asynchronous distributed system only by message transfers. For example, consider the mutual exclusion problem. It is clear that if process P_i enters the critical section and later process P_j enters the critical section, then there must be some knowledge gained by process P_j before it can begin eating. This gain of knowledge can happen only through a message transfer. Observe that our assumption of asynchrony is crucial in requiring the message transfer. In a synchronous system with a global clock, the knowledge can indeed be gained simply by passage of time. Thus for a mutual exclusion algorithm, one may have time-division multiplexing in which processes enter the critical section on their pre-assigned slots. Thus mutual exclusion can be achieved without any message transfers.

This chapter is organized as follows. In Section 24.2 we discuss the notion of knowledge and common knowledge in a distributed system. In this section, we use knowledge as the primitive concept. Section 24.3 shows an application of these concepts to the agreement problem. Finally, Section 24.4 gives a definition of knowledge based on the notion of isomorphism of program execution, from the perspective of a subset of processes. Using these definitions, one can derive properties satisfied by knowledge.

The notation used in this chapter is summarized in Figure 24.1.

p	A process
G	A group of processes
b	A predicate
$K_i(b)$	Process i in the group knows b
$S(b)$	Someone in the group knows b
$E(b)$	Everyone in the group knows b
$C(b)$	b is common knowledge in the group
X	Set of all system computations
$[P]$	Isomorphism relation on X
$x \models b$	b is true at computation x

Figure 24.1: Notation

24.2   Knowledge and Common Knowledge

Let G be a group of processes in a system. We use $K_i(b)$ to denote that the process i in the group G knows the predicate b. We will assume that a process can know only true predicates, that is,

$$K_i(b) \Rightarrow b$$

The converse may not be true. A predicate b may be true, but it may not be known to process i. For example, let b be that there is a deadlock in the system. It is quite possible that b is true but process i does not know about it.

Now, it is easy to define the meaning of "someone in the group knows b," denoted by $S(b)$, as follows:

$$S(b) \stackrel{\text{def}}{=} \bigvee_{i \in G} K_i(b)$$

Similarly, we define "everyone in the group knows b," denoted by $E(b)$, as:

$$E(b) \stackrel{\text{def}}{=} \bigwedge_{i \in G} K_i(b)$$

It is important to realize that $S(b)$ and $E(b)$ are also predicates—in any system state they evaluate to true or false. Thus it makes perfect sense to use $E(b)$ or $S(b)$ for a predicate. In particular, $E(E(b))$ means that everyone in the group knows that everyone in the group knows b.

This observation allows us to define $E^k(b)$, for $k \geq 0$, inductively as follows:

$$E^0(b) = b$$

$$E^{k+1}(b) = E(E^k(b))$$

It is important to realize that although

$$\forall k : E^{k+1}(b) \Rightarrow E^k(b)$$

the converse does not hold in general. To appreciate this fact, consider the following scenario. Assume that there are $n \geq 1$ children who have gone out to play. These children were told before they went for play, that they should not get dirty. However, children being children, $k \geq 1$ of the children have dirty foreheads. Now assume that the children stand in a circle such that every child can see everyone else but cannot see his or her own forehead. Now consider the following predicate b:

$$b \stackrel{\text{def}}{=} \text{there is at least one child with a dirty forehead}$$

In this case $E^{k-1}(b)$ is true but $E^k(b)$ is not. For concreteness, let n be 10 and k be 2. It is clear that since k is 2, b is true. Furthermore, since every child can see at least one other child with a dirty forehead, $E(b)$ is also true. Is $E^2(b)$ true? Consider a child, say child i with a dirty forehead. That child can see exactly one other child, say child j, with a dirty forehead. So from child i's perspective, there may be just one child, namely child j, who has a dirty forehead. However, in that case child j would not know that b is true. Thus $K_i(E(b))$ does not hold; therefore, $E^2(b)$ is also false.

The next higher level of knowledge called *common knowledge* and denoted by $C(b)$ is defined as

$$C(b) \overset{\text{def}}{=} \forall k : E^k(b).$$

It is clear that for any k,

$$C(b) \Rightarrow E^k(b).$$

In the example of the children with a dirty forehead, assume that one of the parents walks to the children and announces "At least one of you has a dirty forehead." Every child hears the announcement. Not only that, they also know that everybody else heard the announcement. Furthermore, every child knows that every other child also knows this. We could go on like that. In short, by announcing b, the level of knowledge has become $C(b)$.

Now, assume that the parent repeatedly asks the question: "Can anyone prove that his or her own forehead is dirty?" Assuming that all children can make all logical conclusions and they reply simultaneously, it can be easily shown using induction that all children reply *no* to the first $k - 1$ questions and all the children with a dirty forehead reply *yes* to the kth question (See Problem 24.1).

To understand the role of common knowledge, consider the scenario when $k \geq 2$. At first, it may seem that the statement made by the parent "At least one of you has a dirty forehead." does not add any knowledge because every child can see at least one other child with a dirty forehead and thus already knew b. But this is not true. To appreciate this the reader should also consider a variant in which the parent repeatedly asks the question: "Can anyone prove that his or her own forehead is dirty?" without first announcing b. In this case, the children will never answer *yes*. By announcing b, the parent gives common knowledge of b and therefore $E^k(b)$. $E^k(b)$ is required for the children to answer *yes* in the kth round.

24.3   Application: Two-Generals Problem

We now prove a fundamental theorem about common knowledge—it cannot be gained in a distributed system with unreliable messages. We explain the significance of the theorem in the context of the coordinating general problem under unreliable communication. Assume that there are two generals who need to coordinate an attack on the enemy army. The armies of the generals are camped on the hills surrounding a valley, which has the enemy army. Both the generals would like to attack the enemy army simultaneously because each general's army is outnumbered by the enemy army. They had no agreed plan before hand, and on some night they would like to coordinate with each other so that both attack the enemy the next day. The generals are assumed to behave correctly, but the communication between them is unreliable. Any messenger sent from one general to the other may be caught by the enemy. The question is whether there exists a protocol that allows the generals to agree on a single bit denoting *attack* or *retreat*.

It is clear that in the presence of unreliable messages no protocol can guarantee *agreement* for *all* runs. None of the messages sent by any general may reach the other side. The real question is whether there is some protocol that can guarantee agreement for *some* run (for example, when some messages reach their destination). Unfortunately, we have the following:

Theorem 24.1 *Let there be two processors P and Q that communicate with unreliable messages. There is no protocol that allows common knowledge to be gained in any of its run.*

Proof: If not, let r be a run with the smallest number of messages that achieves common knowledge. Let m be the last message in the run. Assume without loss of generality that the last message was sent from the processor P to processor Q. Since messages are unreliable, processor P does not know whether Q received the message. Thus if P can assert $C(b)$ after m messages, then it can also do so after $m - 1$ messages. But $C(b)$ at P also implies $C(b)$ at Q. Thus $C(b)$ is true after $m - 1$ messages violating minimality of the run r.

■

In contrast, the lower levels of knowledge are attainable. Indeed, to go from $S(b)$ to $E(b)$, it is sufficient for the processor with the knowledge of b to send messages to all other processors indicating the truthness of b. In the run in which all messages reach their destination $E(b)$ will hold. The reader should also verify that $E^2(b)$ will not hold for any run after the protocol. The reader is asked to design a protocol that guarantees $E^2(b)$ from $S(P)$ in one of its runs in Problem 24.2.

24.4   Defining Knowledge Based on Isomorphism

In Section 24.2, we assumed that a process can know only true predicates, that is,

$$K_i(b) \Rightarrow b.$$

How do we justify such assumptions? Furthermore, one may ask questions about other properties of knowledge. For example, is it true that if a process knows b, then it knows that it knows b? This is a form of introspection. Answers to such questions can be postulated based on one's *belief* about knowledge. Alternatively, and preferably, we can give a definition of knowledge from which answers to these questions can be derived systematically. We give one such definition in this section.

Our definition is based on the interleaving model of a distributed computation. In Problem 24.5, we explore another definition based on consistent cuts of a computation. Let X be the set of all sequences of events possible in a system. This set is clearly prefix-closed, that is, if a sequence of events is possible in the system, then all its prefixes are also possible sequences in the system. Given any predicate b, we denote that b is true after execution of x by $x \models b$.

Given a sequence x and a process p, we can restrict our attention to the subsequence of events that are executed at any process p. We denote this subsequence by x_p. We say that two sequences x and y are *isomorphic* with respect to $P \subseteq G$, denoted by $x[P]y$ if

$$x[P]y \stackrel{\text{def}}{=} \forall p \in P : x_p = y_p.$$

In other words, none of the processes in P can perceive any difference in the execution x or y. Note that $[P]$ defines an equivalence relation of X.

Now, we can define knowledge as follows. P knows b at x if b is true for all executions y that are isomorphic with respect to processes in P. Formally,

Definition 24.2 (Knowledge) *Let $P \subseteq G$ be a subset of processes. Let $K_P(b)$ denote the predicate that P knows the predicate b. Then,*

$$x \models K_P(b) \stackrel{\text{def}}{=} \forall y \in X : x[P]y \Rightarrow y \models b.$$

At this point, we have a complete mathematical definition of knowledge that we can use to justify our earlier rules regarding knowledge such as introspection. In fact, we have the following.

Theorem 24.3

1. $K_P(b) \Rightarrow b$.

2. $K_P(b) \Rightarrow K_P(K_P(b))$.

3. $K_P(b \Rightarrow b') \Rightarrow (K_P(b) \Rightarrow K_P(b'))$.

Proof:

1. $K_P(b) \Rightarrow b$.

   For any x,
   $$x \models K_P(b)$$
   $= \{ \text{ definition } \}$
   $$\forall y \in X : x[P]y \Rightarrow y \models b.$$
   $= \{ x[P]x \text{ trivially true } \}$
   $$x \models b.$$

2. $K_P(b) \Rightarrow K_P(K_P(b))$.

   For any x,
   $$x \models K_P(b)$$
   $= \{ \text{ definition } \}$
   $$\forall y \in X : x[P]y \Rightarrow y \models b.$$
   $\Rightarrow \{ [P] \text{ is an equivalence relation on } X \}$
   $$\forall y \in X : x[P]y \Rightarrow \forall z : y[P]z : z \models b.$$
   $= \{ \text{ definition of } K \}$
   $$\forall y \in X : x[P]y \Rightarrow y \models K_P(b)$$
   $= \{ \text{ definition of } K \}$
   $$K_P(K_P(b)).$$

3. $K_P(b \Rightarrow b') \Rightarrow (K_P(b) \Rightarrow K_P(b'))$.
   Left as en exercise (see Problem 24.4).

   ∎

24.5 Problems

24.1. Show using induction on k that when the parent repeatedly asks the question all children reply *no* to the first $k - 1$ questions and all the children with a dirty forehead reply *yes* to the kth question.

24.2. Design a protocol that guarantee $E^2(b)$ from $S(P)$ in one of its runs.

24.3. Consider a game in which two people are asked to guess each other's number. They are told that they have consecutive natural numbers. For example, the person with number 50 can deduce that the other person has either 51 or 49. Now they are repeatedly asked in turn "Can you tell the other person's number?". Will any of them ever be able to answer in the affirmative? If yes, how? If no, why not?

24.4. Show that $K_P(b \Rightarrow b') \Rightarrow (K_P(b) \Rightarrow K_P(b'))$.

24.5. Let X to be the set of all consistent global states in the system. Define a binary relation $[P]$ on this set as

$$x[P]y \stackrel{\text{def}}{=} \forall p \in P : x[p] = y[p]$$

where $x[p]$ denotes the state of process p in the global state x. Define the predicate $K_P(b)$ based on this definition of $[P]$. What properties are satisfied by knowledge in this set-up?

*24.6. Let X be the set of all possible global sequences. The relation $[P]$ is an equivalence relation on X. Show the relationship between this model and the system S5 of modal logic. Give a sound and complete deduction system (set of axioms and inference rules) for this model.

*24.7. Consider a distributed system in which every message takes either d units of time or $d + \epsilon$ units of time where $\epsilon > 0$. Assume that initially at time t_0, predicate b is not common knowledge. Is there a protocol that achieves $C(b)$ in finite time?

*24.8. **(due to [CM85])** Show that for any k, there exists a computation with k messages such that detection termination of that computation requires at least k overhead messages.

24.6   Bibliographic Remarks

The discussion of knowledge and common knowledge is taken from [HM84]. The "two-generals problem" first appeared in [Gra78]. The definition of knowledge based on the isomorphism relation between system computations is due to Chandy and Misra [CM85]. For background on modal logic, the reader is referred to the book by Chellas [Che80].

Chapter 25

Consensus Under Asynchrony

Every noble work is at first impossible. — Thomas Carlyle

25.1 Introduction

Consensus is a fundamental problem in distributed computing. Consider a distributed database in which a transaction spans multiple sites. In this application it is important that either all sites agree to commit or all sites agree to abort the transaction. In absence of failures this is a simple task. We can use either a centralized scheme or a quorum-based scheme. What if processes can fail? It may appear that if links are reliable, the system can tolerate failure of a single process. In this chapter, we show the surprising result that even in the presence of one unannounced process death, the consensus problem is impossible to solve. This result, called the FLP (Fischer, Lynch and Patterson) result, is named after the people who first discovered it.

The FLP result for consensus shows a fundamental limitation of asynchronous computing. The problem itself is very basic—processes need to agree on a single bit. Most problems we have discussed such as leader election, mutual exclusion, and computation of global functions are harder than the consensus problem because any solution to these problems can be used to solve the consensus problem. The impossibility of consensus implies that all these problems are also impossible to solve in the presence of process failures.

The FLP result is remarkable in another sense. It assumes only a mild form of failures in the environment. First, it assumes only process failures and not link failures. Any message sent takes a finite but unbounded amount of time. Furthermore, it assumes that a process fails only by crashing and thus ceasing all its activities. Thus it does not consider failures in which the process omits certain steps of the protocol or colludes with other processes to foil the protocol. Since the impossibility result holds under weak models of failures, it is also true for stronger failure models.

This chapter is organized as follows. Section 25.2 specifies the requirements of the problem and the assumptions on the environment formally. Section 25.3 gives an informal proof of the result. This proof allows the reader to grasp the intuition behind the impossibility result. Because of the importance of the FLP result, we also prove it formally in Section 25.4.

The notation used in this chapter is summarized in Figure 25.1.

G, H, J, K	Global states of the system
X, Y, Z	Initial global states
$G[i]$	State of process i in the global state G
$G \leq H$	H reachable from G
$\mathcal{G}, \mathcal{H}$	Set of global states
s	Sequence of events
$s(G)$	Global state resulting from application of s to G.
$proc(s)$	Set of processes on which events in s are defined.

Figure 25.1: Notation

25.2   Requirements and Assumptions

The consensus problem is as follows. We assume that there are $N, (N \geq 2)$ processes in the system, and the value of N is known to all processes. Each process starts with an initial value of $\{0,1\}$. This is modeled as one bit input register x. A nonfaulty process decides by entering a decision state. We require that *some* process eventually make a decision. Making a decision is modeled by output registers. Each process also has an output register y that indicates the value decided or committed by the process. The value of 0 in y indicates that the process has decided on the value 0. The same holds for the value 1. The value $\perp$ indicates that the process has not agreed on any value. Initially, we require all processes to have $\perp$ in their register y. We require that once a process has decided it does not change its value, that is, output registers are write-once. We also assume that each process has unbounded storage.

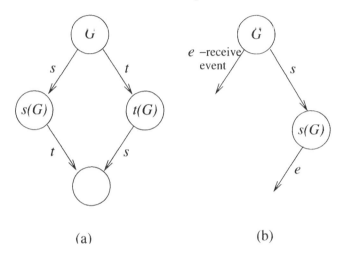

(a)   (b)

Figure 25.2: (a) Commutativity of disjoint events (b) Asynchrony of messages

Before we list formal requirements of the consensus problem, we discuss our assumptions on the environment.

- **Initial Independence**: First, we assume that initial global states satisfy the following independence property: For any two distinct initial global states X and Y that differ in the ith component, there exists an initial global state Z that is identical to X in all components other than the ith component and identical to Y in the ith component. Let $init(X)$ denote that X is an initial global state. Then, the initial independence assumption can be formalized as:

$$init(X) \wedge init(Y) \wedge (X[i] \neq Y[i])$$

  implies that

$$\exists Z : init(Z) \wedge (\forall j : j \neq i : Z[j] = X[j]) \wedge (Z[i] = Y[i])$$

  In other words, we allow processes to choose their input in an independent manner.

- **Commute Property of Disjoint Events:** Let G be any global state such that two events e and f are enabled in it. If e and f are on different processes, then they commute. To formalize this property, let $enabled(G, e)$ mean that e is enabled in the global state G and let $s(G)$ denote the global state resulting from application of a sequence of events s to G. Then,

$$enabled(G, e) \wedge enabled(G, f) \wedge (proc(e) \neq proc(f)) \Rightarrow ef(G) = fe(G)$$

Equivalently, for any two sequences of events s and t

$$enabled(G, s) \wedge enabled(G, t) \wedge (proc(s) \cap proc(t) = \phi) \Rightarrow st(G) = ts(G)$$

This is shown in Figure 25.2(a). The global state reached after executing st at G is identical to the one reached after executing ts at G.

- **Asynchrony of Events:** The asynchronous message system is modeled as a buffer with two operations. The operation $send(p, m)$ by process p places (p, m) in the buffer. The operation $receive()$ from p by any process q deletes (p, m) and returns m or returns *null*. The system may return *null* to model the fact that the asynchronous messages may take an unbounded amount of time. The condition we impose on the message system is that if the $receive()$ event is performed an unbounded number of times, then every message is eventually delivered.

  The asynchrony assumption states that any *receive* event may be arbitrarily delayed. Let $receive(e)$ denote that e is a receive event. Then, the assumption can be stated as

$$receive(e) \wedge enabled(G, e) \wedge enabled(G, s) \wedge e \notin s \Rightarrow enabled(G, se) \tag{25.1}$$

  In Figure 25.2(b), e is an enabled event after executing $s(G)$ because $e \notin s$.

  Note that the above assumption does not state that $se(G) = es(G)$. The event e commutes with s only when $proc(e) \notin proc(s)$.

Our model of a faulty process is as follows. We only consider infinite runs. A faulty process is one that takes only a finite number of steps in that run. A run is *admissible* if at most one process is faulty. Since the message system is reliable, all messages sent to nonfaulty processes are eventually delivered. A run is *deciding* if some process reaches a decision state.

The requirements of the protocol can be summarized as:

- **Agreement**: Two processes cannot commit on different values.

- **Nontriviality**: Both values 0 and 1 should be possible outcomes. This requirement eliminates protocols that return fixed value 0 or 1 independent of initial input.

- **Termination**: The system reaches agreement in finite time.

25.3 An Informal Proof of the Impossibility Result

In this section we show the FLP result—there is no protocol that satisfies agreement, nontriviality, and termination in an asynchronous system in presence of one fault. The main idea behind the proof consists of showing that there exists an admissible run that remains forever indecisive. Specifically, we show that (1) there is an initial global state in which the system is indecisive, and (2) there exists a method to keep the system indecisive.

To formalize the notion of *indecision*, we use the notion of valences of a global state. Let $G.V$ be the set of decision values of global state reachable from G. Since the protocol is correct, $G.V$ is nonempty. We say that G is bivalent if $|G.V| = 2$ and univalent if $|G.V| = 1$. In the latter case, we call G 0-valent if $G.V = \{0\}$ and 1-valent if $G.V = \{1\}$. The bivalent state captures the notion of indecision.

The next lemma states that for every protocol, there exists an initial global state in which the system is undecided.

Lemma 25.1 *Every consensus protocol has a bivalent initial global state.*

Proof: Assume if possible that the protocol does not have any bivalent initial global state. By the nontriviality requirement, the protocol must have both 0-valent and 1-valent global states. Let us call two global states *adjacent* if they differ in the local state of exactly one process. Since any two initial global states can be connected by a chain of initial global states each adjacent to the next, there exist adjacent 0-valent and 1-valent global states. Assume that they differ in the state of p. We now apply to both of these global states a sequence in which p takes no steps. Since they differ only in the state of p, the system must reach the same decision value which is a contradiction.

■

Our next step is to show that we can keep the system in an indecisive state.

Lemma 25.2 *Let G be a bivalent global state of a protocol. Let event e on process p be applicable to G, and $\mathcal{G}$ be the set of global states reachable from G without applying e. Let $\mathcal{H} = e(\mathcal{G})$. Then $\mathcal{H}$ contains a bivalent global state.*

Proof: Assume if possible that $\mathcal{H}$ contains no bivalent global states. We show a contradiction.

Claim 1: $\mathcal{H}$ contains both 0-valent and 1-valent states.
Let E_i ($i \in \{0..1\}$) be an i-valent global state reachable from G. If $E_i \in \mathcal{G}$, then define $F_i = e(E_i)$. Otherwise, e was applied in reaching E_i. In this case, there exists $F_i \in \mathcal{H}$ from which E_i is reachable. Thus $\mathcal{H}$ contains both 0-valent and 1-valent states. *[end of Claim 1]*

We call two global states neighbors if one results from the other in a single step.

Claim 2: There exist neighbors G_0, G_1 such that $H_0 = e(G_0)$ is 0-valent, and $H_1 = e(G_1)$ is 1-valent.
Let t be the smallest sequence of events applied to G without applying e such that $et(G)$ has different valency from $e(G)$. Such a sequence exists because of *claim 1*. To see this, assume that $e(G)$ is 0-valent. From *claim 1*, there exists a global state in $\mathcal{H}$ which is 1-valent. Let t be a minimal sequence that leads to a 1-valent state. The case when $e(G)$ is 1-valent is similar. The last two global states reached in this sequence gives us the required neighbors. *[end of Claim 2]*
    Without loss of generality let $G_1 = f(G_0)$, where f is an event on process q. We now do a case analysis.
    case 1: p different from q (see Figure 25.3(a))
This implies that f is applicable to H_0, resulting in H_1. This is a contradiction because H_0 is 0-valent and H_1 is 1-valent.

case 2: $p = q$ (see Figure 25.3(b))

Consider any finite deciding run from G_0 in which p takes no steps. Let s be the corresponding sequence. Let $K = s(G_0)$. From the Commuting Lemma, s is also applicable to H_i and it leads to i-valent global states $E_i = s(H_i)$. Again, by the commute property, $e(K) = E_0$ and $e(f(K)) = E_1$. Hence K is bivalent, which is a contradiction.

∎

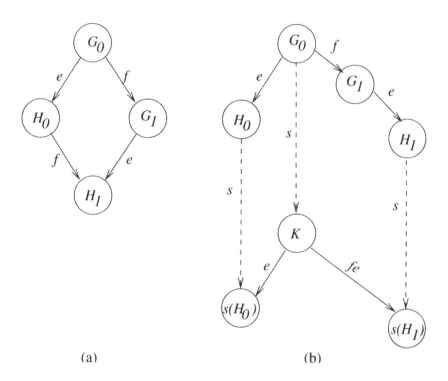

(a)   (b)

Figure 25.3: (a) Case 1: $proc(e) \neq proc(f)$ (b) Case 2: $proc(e) = proc(f)$

The intuition behind the proof is as follows. Any protocol that goes from a bivalent global state to a univalent state must have a critical step in which the decision is taken. This critical step cannot be based on the order of events done by different processes because execution of events at different processes commutes. This observation corresponds to case 1 in the above proof. This implies that the critical step must be taken by one process. But this method also does not work because other processes cannot distinguish between the situation when this process is slow and the situation when the process has crashed. This observation corresponds to case 2 in the above proof.

We are now ready for the main result.

Theorem 25.3 *No consensus protocol satisfies agreement, nontriviality, and termination despite one fault.*

Proof: We construct an admissible nondeciding run as follows. The run is started from any bivalent initial global state G_0 and consists of a sequence of stages. We ensure that every stage begins from a bivalent global state G. We maintain a queue of processes and maintain the message buffer as a FIFO queue. In each stage the process p at the head of the queue receives the earliest message m (if any). Let e be the event corresponding to p receiving the message m. From Lemma 25.2, we know that there is a bivalent global state H reachable from G by a sequence in which e is the last event applied. We then move the process to the back of the queue and repeat this set of steps forever. This method guarantees that every process executes infinitely often and every message sent is eventually received. Thus, the protocol stays in bivalent global states forever.

■

25.4   A Formal Proof of the Impossibility Result

Because of the importance of the impossibility result, we cover this proof once again, but in a more rigorous fashion. This proof makes the assumptions required for the impossibility result explicit. It also avoids proof by contradiction, thereby providing an insight into the structure of computation trees for asynchronous systems.

To specify the requirements of the consensus problem formally, we define a predicate *match* for a global state H and a value $v \in \{0, 1\}$ as follows.

$$match(H, v) = \exists i : H[i].y = v$$

We require that the output register y be write-once.

$$G[i].y = v \Rightarrow \forall H : G \leq H : H[i].y = v$$

From the write-once nature of the y register, and the definition of *match*, we deduce that *match* is a stable property.

$$\forall G, v : match(G, v) \Rightarrow \langle \forall H : G \leq H : match(H, v) \rangle$$

The predicate $match(H)$ denotes the condition that one of the values is matched, i.e.,

$$match(H) = match(H, 0) \vee match(H, 1)$$

25.4.1 Requirements

The binary consensus protocol requires:

- **Agreement**: Two processes cannot commit on different values.

$$\forall G : \neg match(G, 0) \vee \neg match(G, 1)$$

- **Nontriviality**: Both values 0 and 1 should be possible outcomes.

$$\exists G0 : match(G0, 0) \wedge \exists G1 : match(G1, 1)$$

- **Termination**: The system reaches agreement in finite time. To formalize this requirement, we first define *runs*. A run is a sequence of global states. An *admissible* run is one in which at most one process crashes and all messages sent to nonfaulty processes are eventually reached. We define $future(G)$ as the set of possible admissible sequences of events from G. Now termination can be stated as:

$$\forall G : init(G) : \langle \forall \sigma \in future(G) : (\exists H \in \sigma : match(H)) \rangle$$

25.4.2 Classification of Global States

In this section we classify global states of any protocol depending on the *match* predicate. Informally, a 0-valent state is one in which the protocol will eventually decide 0. Similarly, a 1-valent state will eventually result in a decision of 1. If a state is *undecided*, then there exists an admissible execution that will result in neither 0 nor 1 being committed. A *bivalent* state is neither a 0-valent state nor a 1-valent state. Note that every undecided state is a bivalent state, but not vice versa. Formally,

Definition 25.4

$$0\text{-}valent(G) \stackrel{\text{def}}{=} \forall \sigma \in future(G) : \exists H \in \sigma : match(H, 0).$$
$$1\text{-}valent(G) \stackrel{\text{def}}{=} \forall \sigma \in future(G) : \exists H \in \sigma : match(H, 1).$$
$$bivalent(G) \stackrel{\text{def}}{=} \neg 0\text{-}valent(G) \wedge \neg 1\text{-}valent(G)$$
$$undecided(G) \stackrel{\text{def}}{=} \exists \sigma \in future(G) : \forall H \in \sigma : \neg match(H).$$

The following lemma shows that a 1-valent state G can never reach a state H in which $match(H, 0)$ is true. It uses *agreement* and stability of *match*.

Lemma 25.5
$$\forall G, H : G \leq H : match(H, 0) \Rightarrow \neg 1\text{-}valent(G)$$

Proof:

$$G \leq H$$
$\equiv \{$ definition of $\leq \}$
$$\exists \sigma \in future(G) : H \in \sigma.$$

To show $\neg 1$-valent(G), we prove, for this σ,

$$\forall K \in \sigma : \neg match(K, 1).$$

We do a case analysis.
Case 1: $H \leq K$.
$$match(H, 0)$$
$\Rightarrow \{$ $H \leq K$ and stability of *match* $\}$
$$match(K, 0)$$
$\Rightarrow \{$ agreement $\}$
$$\neg match(K, 1).$$

Case 2: $K \leq H$.
$$match(H, 0)$$
$\Rightarrow \{$agreement$\}$
$$\neg match(H, 1)$$
$\Rightarrow \{$ stability of *match*, $K \leq H$ $\}$
$$\neg match(K, 1).$$

∎

Similarly, the following results can be established.

Lemma 25.6
a) $(G \leq H) \wedge match(H, 1) \Rightarrow \neg 0\text{-}valent(G)$.
b) $(G \leq H) \wedge 0\text{-}valent(G) \Rightarrow 0\text{-}valent(H)$.
c) $(G \leq H) \wedge 1\text{-}valent(G) \Rightarrow 1\text{-}valent(H)$.
d) $0\text{-}valent(G) \Rightarrow \neg 1\text{-}valent(G)$.

25.4.3 Impossibility Result

Lemma 25.7 *Assume nontriviality and initial independence.*

$$\exists X : init(X) \wedge bivalent(X)$$

Proof:

  nontriviality
$\Rightarrow \{$ $G0$ and $G1$ are reachable global states $\}$
  $\exists X0 : init(X0) \wedge X0 \leq G0 : match(G0, 0)$
    $\wedge \exists X1 : init(X1) \wedge X1 \leq G1 : match(G1, 1)$.

  $X0 \leq G0 \wedge match(G0, 0)$
$\Rightarrow \{$ Lemma 25.5 $\}$
  $\neg 1\text{-}valent(X0)$
$\Rightarrow \{$ definition of *bivalent* $\}$
  $bivalent(X0) \vee 0\text{-}valent(X0)$

Similarly, $bivalent(X1) \vee 1\text{-}valent(X1)$. If either $X0$ or $X1$ is bivalent we are done. Therefore, we consider the case $0\text{-}valent(X0) \wedge 1\text{-}valent(X1)$. We do a case analysis on k equal to the number of components in which $X0$ and $X1$ differ.

Case 1: $(k = 1)$.
Let $X0$ and $X1$ differ in only one component—i.
  Consider an admissible sequence of moves σ from $X0$ in which process i does not move.
    $0\text{-}valent(X0)$
$\Rightarrow \{$ σ admissible, definition of 0-valent$\}$
  $\exists s : match(s(X0), 0) \wedge i \notin procs(s)$
$\Rightarrow \{$ $\forall j : j \neq i : X0[j] = X1[j]$ and $X0[i].y = X1[i].y = \bot$ $\}$
  $match(s(X1), 0)$
$\Rightarrow \{$ Lemma 25.5, $X1 \leq s(X1)$ $\}$
  $\neg 1\text{-}valent(X1)$

Case 2: $(k > 1)$.

Let i be first component in which $X0$ and $X1$ differ. From initial independence, there exists an initial state Z such that Z and $X1$ differ in $k - 1$ components.

and Z and $X0$ differ in 1 component. We now do a case analysis on Z.

Case 2.1: $bivalent(Z)$

We are done because Z is also an initial state.

Case 2.2: 0-valent(Z).

We have two initial states Z and $X1$ such that 0-valent(Z) and 1-valent$(X1)$ that differ in $k - 1$ components. Hence, the induction is applicable.

Case 2.3: 1-valent(Z).

We have two initial states $X0$ and Z such that 0-valent$(X0)$ and 1-valent(Z). Furthermore, $X0$ and Z differ in exactly one component. Therefore, the base case is applicable.

■

In the following lemma, we exploit the asynchronous nature of computation. We show

Lemma 25.8

For all receive events e,

$$enabled(G, e) \land match(t(G), 1) \Rightarrow \exists s : \neg 0\text{-}valent(se(G))$$

Proof: We do a case analysis.

Case 1: $e \in t$

$\quad match(t(G), 1))$

$\Rightarrow$ { let t be rewritten as seu }

$\quad \exists s, u : match(seu(G), 1)$

$\Rightarrow$ { Lemma 25.5 }

$\quad \exists s : \neg 0\text{-valent}(se(G))$

Case 2: $e \notin t$

$\quad match(t(G), 1))$

$\Rightarrow$ { $enabled(G, e)$, Assumption of asynchrony 25.1}

$\quad match(t(G), 1) \land enabled(G, te)$

$\Rightarrow$ { stability of $match$ }

$$match(te(G), 1)$$
$\Rightarrow$ { Lemma 25.5 }
$$\exists s : \neg 0\text{-}valent(se(G))$$

∎

Tho following lemma givcs a forbiddcn structurc in thc statc transition graph of any protocol.

Lemma 25.9

$$\forall G, e, f : \neg 0\text{-}valent(e(G)) \lor \neg 1\text{-}valent(fe(G)) \lor undecided(G)$$

Proof:

   Case 1: $proc(e) \neq proc(f)$
   $0\text{-}valent(e(G))$
$\Rightarrow$ { 0-valency is stable }
   $0\text{-}valent(ef(G))$
$\Rightarrow$ { $fe(G) = ef(G)$ from the commute property}
   $0\text{-}valent(fe(G))$
$\Rightarrow$

   $\neg 1\text{-}valent(fe(G))$.

   Case 2: $proc(e) = proc(f)$.
   true
$\Rightarrow$ { definition of admissible }
   $\exists \sigma \in future(G) : i \notin procs(\sigma)$.

We have the following three subcases.
Case 2.1: $\forall H \in \sigma : H \geq G : \neg match(H)$.
$\Rightarrow$ { definition }
   $undecided(G)$.

Case 2.2: $\exists H \in \sigma : H \geq G : match(H, 0)$
$\Rightarrow$ { definition of σ }
   $\exists s : match(s(G), 0) \land proc(e) \notin proc(s)$
$\Rightarrow$ { fe disjoint from s }
   $\exists s : match(sfe(G), 0)$
$\Rightarrow$ { Lemma 25.5 }
   $\neg 1\text{-}valent(fe(G))$

Case 2.3: $\exists H \in \sigma : H \geq G : match(H, 1)$
$\Rightarrow$ { definition of σ }
$\quad \exists s : match(s(G), 1) \wedge i \notin proc(s)$
$\Rightarrow$ { e disjoint from s }
$\quad \exists s : match(se(G), 1)$
$\Rightarrow$ { Lemma 25.5 }
$\quad \neg 0\text{-valent}(e(G))$

∎

Lemma 25.10 _For any state G and any receive event e,_

$$bivalent(G) \wedge enabled(G, e) \Rightarrow undecided(G) \vee \exists s : bivalent(se(G))$$

Proof:

If $e(G)$ is bivalent, we are done with s as an empty sequence. If not, let $0\text{-valent}(e(G))$ without any loss of generality.

$\quad\quad bivalent(G)$
$\Rightarrow$
$\quad\quad \neg 0\text{-valent}(G)$
$\Rightarrow$
$\quad\quad \exists \sigma \in future(G) : \langle \forall H \in \sigma : \neg match(H, 0) \rangle.$

Case 1: $\forall H \in \sigma : \neg match(H, 1)$.
$\Rightarrow$
$\quad\quad \forall H \in \sigma : \neg match(H, 0) \wedge \neg match(H, 1).$
$\equiv$ { definition of undecided }
$\quad\quad undecided(G)$

Case 2: $\exists H \in \sigma : match(H, 1)$.
$\Rightarrow$
$\quad\quad \exists t : match(t(G), 1)$
$\Rightarrow$ { $enabled(G, e)$, Lemma 25.8 }
$\quad\quad \exists s : \neg 0\text{-valent}(se(G)$
$\equiv$ { definition }
$\quad\quad \exists s : 1\text{-valent}(se(G)) \vee bivalent(se(G)).$
If $bivalent(se(G))$, then we are done. Therefore, we have $bivalent(G)$, $0\text{-valent}(e(G))$, and $1\text{-valent}(se(G))$. We now claim that

$$\exists C, f : 0\text{-valent}(e(C)) \wedge 1\text{-valent}(fe(C))$$

We use induction on the length of $k = length(s)$.

Base Case: $(k = 1)$
s has only one event. Define $C = G$ and $f = s$.

Induction Case: $(k > 1)$
Let $s = dt$. Consider $d(C)$. It cannot be 0 valent because $dt e(C)$ is 1-valent

<u>Case 1</u>: $d(G)$ is bivalent

If $de(G)$ is 1-valent, let $f = d$.
If $de(G)$ is 0-valent, we have $bivalent(d(G)), 0\text{-valent}(e(d(G)))$, and $1\text{-valent}(te(d(G)))$.
If $de(G)$ is bivalent, we have the required result.

<u>Case 2:</u> $d(G)$ is 1-valent

This implies $de(G)$ is 1-valent. Let $f = d$.
$\qquad$ Thus we have
$\qquad\qquad \exists C, f : 0\text{-valent}(e(C)) \wedge 1\text{-valent}(fe(C))$
$\Rightarrow \{\text{from Lemma 25.9 }\}$
$\qquad\ undecided(C)$

$\blacksquare$

We can now state the impossibility result.

Theorem 25.11 *Any protocol that satisfies nontriviality and agreement has an initial state G such that $undecided(G)$ holds.*

Proof: From Lemma 25.7, there exists an initial global state G such that $bivalent(G)$ holds. We construct an admissible sequence from G in which no decision is reached. We run processes in a round robin fashion. Each process receives the first message from its buffer. Let e be the event that is enabled next according to this sequence. From Lemma 25.10, either G is undecided or there exists a sequence s such that on executing se, the system stays in a bivalent state. By indefinitely repeating this process, we get the desired result.

$\blacksquare$

25.5   Terminating Reliable Broadcast

Impossibility of consensus in the presence of a failure implies that many other interesting problems are impossible to solve in asynchronous systems as well. Consider, for example, the problem of the terminating reliable broadcast specified as follows. Assume that there are N processes in the system $P_0, \ldots, P_{N-1}$ and that P_0 wishes to broadcast a single message to all processes (including itself). The terminating reliable broadcast requires that a correct process always delivers a message even if the sender is faulty and crashes during the protocol. The message in that case may be "sender faulty." The requirements of the problem are:

- *Termination*: Every correct process eventually delivers some message.

- *Validity*: If the sender is correct and broadcasts a message m, then all correct processes eventually deliver m.

- *Agreement*: If a correct process delivers a message m, then all correct processes deliver m.

- *Integrity*: Every correct process delivers at most one message, and if it delivers m different from "sender faulty," then the sender must have broadcast m.

We now show that the Terminating Reliable Broadcast (TRB) is impossible to solve in asynchronous system. We show this by providing an algorithm for consensus given an algorithm for TRB. The algorithm for consensus is simple. Process P_0 is required to broadcast its input bit using the TRB protocol. If a correct process receives a message different from "sender faulty" it decides on the bit received. Otherwise, it decides on 0. It is easy to verify that this algorithm satisfies the termination, agreement, and nontriviality requirements of the consensus problem.

25.6   Problems

25.1. Why does the following algorithm not work for consensus under FLP assumptions? Give a scenario under which the algorithm fails. It is common knowledge that there are 6 processes in the system numbered P_0 to P_5. The algorithm is as follows: Every process sends its input bit to all processes (including itself) and waits for five messages. Every process decides on the majority of the five bits received.

25.2. Show that all the following problems are impossible to solve in an asynchronous system in the presence of a single failure.

(a) **Leader Election**: Show that the special case when the leader can only be from the set $\{P_0, P_1\}$ is equivalent to consensus.

(b) **Computation of a global function**: Show a deterministic nontrivial global function such as *min*, *max* and addition can be used to solve consensus.

25.3. Atomic Broadcast requires the following properties.

- *Validity*: If the sender is correct and broadcasts a message m, then all correct processes eventually deliver m.

- *Agreement*: If a correct process delivers a message m, then all correct processes deliver m.

- *Integrity*: For any message m, q receives m from p at most once and only if p sent m to q.

- *Order*: All correct processes receive all broadcast messages in the same order.

Show that Atomic Broadcast is impossible to solve in asynchronous systems.

*25.4. (**due to [FLP85]**) Show that if it is known that processes will not die *during* the protocol, then consensus can be reached (despite some initially dead processes).

*25.5. Give a randomized algorithm that achieves consensus in an asynchronous distributed system in the presence of f crash failures under the assumption that $N \geq 2f + 1$.

25.7 Bibliographic Remarks

The impossibility of achieving consensus in asynchronous system is due to Fischer, Lynch, and Paterson [FLP85].

Chapter 26

Consensus Under Synchrony

Honest disagreement is often a good sign of progress. — *Mahatma Gandhi*

26.1 Introduction

We have seen that consensus is impossible to solve in asynchronous systems even in the presence of a single crash. In this chapter, we show that the main difficulty in solving consensus lies in the asynchrony assumption. Thus there exist protocols to solve consensus when the system is synchronous. A system is synchronous if there is an upper bound on the message delay and on the duration of actions performed by processes. We show that under suitable conditions not only crash failures but also malevolent faults in which faulty processes can send arbitrary messages can be tolerated by consensus algorithms.

In general, we can classify the faults in a distributed system as follows.

- **Crash**: In the crash model, a fault corresponds to a processor halting. When the processor halts, it does not performs any other action and stays halted forever. The processor does not perform any wrong operation such as sending a corrupted message. As we have seen earlier, crashes may not be detectable by other processors in asynchronous systems, but they are detectable in synchronous systems.

- **Crash+Link**: In this model, either a processor can crash or a link may go down. If a link goes down, then it stays down. When we consider link failures, it is sometimes important to distinguish between two cases—one in which the network is *partitioned* and the second in which the underlying communication graph stays connected. When the network gets partitioned, some pairs of nodes can never communicate with each other.

- **Omission**: In this model, a processor fails either by sending only a proper subset of messages that it is required to send by the algorithm or by receiving only a proper subset of messages that have been sent to it. The fault of the first kind is called a *send omission* and that of the second kind is called a *receive omission*.

- **Byzantine Failure**: In this model, a processor fails by exhibiting arbitrary behavior. This is an extreme form of a failure. A system that can tolerate a Byzantine fault can tolerate any other fault.

In this chapter, we will consider only the crash and Byzantine failures. We assume that links are reliable for crash failures. A processor that is not faulty is called a *correct* processor. This chapter is organized as follows. In Section 26.2 we present an algorithm to solve consensus under the crash model, and in Section 26.3 we present an algorithm to solve consensus under Byzantine failures. The notation used in this chapter is summarized in Figure 26.1.

N	The number of processes
f	The maximum number of allowable faults
v_i	Value input to process P_i
$v_\perp$	Default value
y	Value decided

Figure 26.1: Notation

26.2　Consensus Under Crash Failures

In this chapter, we will mainly be concerned with *algorithms* for synchronous systems. It is generally advantageous to prove impossibility results with as weak a specification of the problem as possible because the same proof will hold for a stronger specification. However, when designing algorithms it is better for the algorithm to satisfy a strong specification because the same algorithm will work for all weaker specifications.

We first generalize the set of values on which consensus is required. Instead of a single bit, the set of values can be any totally ordered set. We will assume that each process P_i has as its input a value v_i from this set. The goal of the protocol is to set the value y at each process such that the following constraints are met. The value y can be set at most once and is called the value *decided* by the process. Thus the requirements of the protocol are:

- **Agreement**: Two nonfaulty processes cannot decide on different values.

- **Validity**: If all processes propose the same value, then the decided value should be that proposed value. It is easy to verify that this condition implies the nontriviality condition discussed in Chapter 25.

- **Termination**: The system reaches agreement in finite time.

26.2.1   An Algorithm for Consensus

An algorithm for achieving consensus in the presence of crash failures is quite simple. In the algorithm we use the parameter f to denote the maximum number of processors that can fail. The algorithm shown in Figure 26.2 works based on rounds. Each process maintains V, which contains the set of values it knows that have been proposed by processors in the system. Initially, a process P_i knows only the value it proposed. The algorithm takes $f + 1$ rounds for completion; thus the algorithm assumes that the value of f is known. In each round, a process sends to all other processes values from V that it has not sent before. So, initially the process sends its own value and in later rounds it sends only those values that it learns for the first time in the previous round. In each round, the processor P_i also receives the values sent by P_j. In this step, we have used the synchrony assumption. P_i waits for a message from P_j for some fixed predetermined time after which it assumes that P_j has crashed. After $f + 1$ rounds each process decides on the minimum value in its set V.

P_i::
  var
      V: set of values initially $\{v_i\}$;

  for $k := 1$ to $f + 1$ **do**
      send $\{v \in V \mid P_i$ has not already sent $v\}$ to all;
      receive S_j from all processes $P_j, j \neq i$;
      $V := V \cup S_j$;
  endfor;

  $y := min(V)$;

Figure 26.2: Algorithm at P_i for consensus under crash failures

The above algorithm satisfies termination because each correct process terminates in exactly $f + 1$ rounds. It satisfies validity because the decided value is chosen from the set V, which contains only the proposed values. We show the agreement property in the following theorem.

Theorem 26.1 *All correct processors decide on the same value.*

Proof: Let V_i denote the set of values at P_i after the round $f + 1$. We show that if any value x is in the set V_i for some correct processor P_i, then it is also in the set V_j for any other correct processor P_j.

First assume that the value x was added to V_i in a round $k < f+1$. Since P_i and P_j are correct processes P_j will receive that value in round $k + 1$ and will therefore be present in V_j after round $f + 1$.

Now assume that the value x was added to V_i in the last round (round number $f + 1$). This implies that there exists a chain of $f + 1$ distinct processors that transferred the value from one of the processors that had x as its input value to P_i. If all the processors in the chain are faulty, then we contradict the assumption that there are at most f faulty processors. If any processor in the chain is nonfaulty, then it would have succeeded in sending x to all the processors in that round. Hence x was also added to V_j by at most $f + 1$ rounds.

■

The above algorithm requires $O((f+1)N^2)$ messages because each round requires every process to send a message to all other processes. If each value requires b bits, then the total number of communication bits is $O(bN^3)$ bits because each processor may relay up to N values to all other processors. See Problem 26.2 for ways to reduce the message and communication complexity.

26.2.2 An Early Stopping Algorithm

The above algorithm requires $f + 1$ rounds even if the actual number of failures is small. In particular, the above algorithm requires $f+1$ rounds even when there are no failures. We now describe an algorithm that has an *early stopping* property, that is, the number of rounds depends on the actual number of faults and not the maximum allowable faults of the algorithm.

We change our algorithm for consensus with crash failures as follows. We require every (correct) processor to send a message even if it has no new value to report in a round. Every processor P_i also keeps a set of faulty processors that it knows at the end of round k in a set $faulty(i, k)$. Let $V(k)$ be the values known at the end of round k. At the end of round k the processor decides on the value $min(V(k))$ if $k = f + 1$ or if the size of $faulty(i, k)$ is strictly smaller than k. If $k < f + 1$, then the processor sends its decided value to all other processors for one more round.

The algorithm is shown in Figure 26.3.

Note that $faulty(i, k)$ satisfies the following assertion. For any P_j, if there exists a round $k' \leq k$ in which P_j has not sent a message to P_i but may have sent a message to some other processor, then j is in $faulty(i, k)$.

The validity and termination are obvious. We prove the agreement property.

Theorem 26.2 *All correct processors decide on the same value.*

Proof: Let process p decide in round r and q decide in round r'. We will show that any value that is in p's set when p decides is also in q's set when q decides. By symmetry, we get that both have identical sets when they decide.

Case 1: $r < r'$
Any value in p's set is also in q's set because both p and q are correct

var
    V: set of values initially $\{v_i\}$
    decided: boolean initially *false*;
    faulty: set of indices initially $\{\}$;

Phase I:
for $k := 1$ to $f + 1$ **do**
    send $\{v \in V \mid P_i$ has not already sent $v\}$ to all
    receive S_j from all processes $P_j, j \neq i$
    $V := V \cup S_j$;
    if $(k = f + 1)$ **then**
        $y := min(V)$;
        halt;
    endif;

    faulty := *faulty* $\cup \{j \mid P_i$ did not receive any value from P_j and
        P_j has not informed P_i that it has decided$\}$
    if $(|faulty| < k)$ **then**
        decided := *true*;
        goto phase II;
    endif;
endfor;

Phase II:
send $\{v \in V \mid P_i$ has not already sent $v\}$ and "I have decided" to all
$y := min(V)$;
halt;

Figure 26.3: Early stopping algorithm for crash failures

processors. Whenever p learned the value, it must have sent to q.

Case 2: $r \geq r'$.
Let u be a value in p's set V, when it decided. If p learned it in a round $k < r'$, then q also knows that value because both p and q are correct processors. If p learned it in round $k \geq r'$, then there is a chain of k distinct processes that transferred the value to p. Consider the first r' processors in this chain. Since process q decides in round r', it could not view all of them as faulty (otherwise its faulty set would be at least r'). This implies that q must have received the value u from the processor it does not consider faulty from that chain.

■

26.3 Consensus Under Byzantine Faults

Byzantine faults allow for malicious behavior by the processes. The consensus problem in this model can be understood in the context of the Byzantine General Agreement problem, which is defined as follows. There were N Byzantine generals who were called out to repel the attack by a Turkish Sultan. These generals camped near the Turkish army. Each of the N Byzantine generals had a preference for whether to *attack* the Turkish army or to *retreat*. The Byzantine armies were strong enough that the loyal generals of the armies knew that if their action was coordinated (either attack or retreat) then they would be able to resist the Sultan's army. The problem was that some of the generals were treacherous and would try to foil any protocol that loyal generals might devise for the coordination of the attack. They might, for example, send conflicing messages to different generals, and might even collude to mislead loyal generals. The Byzantine General Agreement (BGA for short) problem requires us to design a protocol by which the loyal generals can coordinate their actions. It is assumed that generals can communicate with each other using reliable messangers.

The BGA problem can easily be seen as the consensus problem in a distributed system under Byzantine faults. We call a protocol f-resilient if it can tolerate f Byzantine faulty processors. It has been shown that

Theorem 26.3 *Let $N \geq 1$. There is no f-resilient protocol for BGA if $N \leq 3f$.*

In this section we give an algorithm that takes $f + 1$ rounds, each round of 2 phases, to solve the BGA problem. This algorithm uses constant-size messages but requires that $N > 4f$. Each processor has a preference for each round, which is initially its input value.

The algorithm is shown in Figure 26.4. The algorithm is based on the idea of rotating coordinator (or king). Processor P_i is assumed to be the coordinator or the king for round k. In the first phase of a round, each processor exchanges its value with all other processors. Based on its V vector, it determines its estimate in the variable *myvalue*. In the second phase, the processor receives the value from the coordinator. If it receives no value (because the coordinator has failed), then it assumes $v_\perp$ (a default value) for the king value. Now, it decides whether to use its own value or the *kingvalue*. This decision is based on the multiplicity of *myvalue* in the vector V. If V has more than $N/2 + f$ copies of *myvalue*, then *myvalue* is chosen for $V[i]$; otherwise, *kingvalue* is used.

We first show that agreement persists, that is, if all correct processors prefer a value v at the beginning of a round, then they continue to do so at the end of a round. This property holds because

$N > 4f$
$\equiv N - N/2 > 2f$
$\equiv N - f > N/2 + f.$

Since the number of correct processors is at least $N - f$, each correct processor will receive more than $N/2 + f$ copies of v and hence choose that at the end of the phase 2.

Now we can prove our main result.

Theorem 26.4 *The algorithm in Figure 26.4 solves the agreement problem.*

Proof: The validity property follows from the persistence of agreement. If all processors start with the same value v, then v is the value decided. Termination is obvious because the algorithm takes exactly $f + 1$ rounds. We now show the agreement property. Since there are $f + 1$ rounds and at most f faulty processors, at least one of the rounds has a correct king. Each correct processor decides either on the value sent by the king in that round or its own value. It chooses its own value w only if its multiplicity in V is at least $N/2 + f + 1$. Therefore, the king of that round must have at least $N/2 + 1$ multiplicity of w in its vector. Thus the value chosen by the king is also w. Hence, each processor decides on the same value at the end of a round in which

```
Pᵢ::
var
 V: array[1..N] of values
          initially (V[i] = x) ∧ ∀j : j ≠ i : V[j] = v⊥

 for k := 1 to f + 1 do

     first phase :
          send V[i] to all other processors;
          set V[j], (j ≠ i) to the value received from Pⱼ;
          myvalue := majority value in the vector V (v⊥ if no majority);

     second phase:
          if (k = i) then
               send myvalue to all other processors;
          receive kingvalue from Pₖ;
          if V vector has more than N/2 + f copies of myvalue then
               V[i] := myvalue;
          else V[i] := kingvalue;

 endfor;

 y := V[i];
```

Figure 26.4: An algorithm for Byzantine General Agreement at P_i

the king is nonfaulty. From persistence of agreement, the agreement property at the end of the algorithm follows.

■

26.4 Problems

26.1. Show by an example that if the consensus algorithm decided the final value after f rounds instead of $f + 1$ rounds, then it might violate agreement property.

26.2. Observe that processors use only the minimum value in the set V to decide on the agreement problem. Use this observation to reduce the space and the communication complexity for consensus under the crash model.

26.3. Give an example of an execution of a system with six processes, two of which are faulty in which the Byzantine General Agreement algorithm does not work correctly.

26.4. Give an algorithm that solves BGA problem whenever $N \geq 3f+1$.

*26.5. [**due to [DS83]**] In the Byzantine failure model a faulty process could forward incorrect information about messages received from other processes. A less malevolent model is called *Byzantine failure with mutual authentication*. In this model, we assume that a message can be signed digitally for authentication. There exist many cryptographic algorithms for digital signatures. Give an algorithm for Byzantine General Agreement assuming authentication that is f-resilient for $f < N$, requires only $f + 1$ rounds, and uses a polynomial number of messages.

*26.6. Show that the number of rounds required to solve consensus under the crash model is at least $f+1$ in the worst case when $f \leq N-2$.

26.5 Bibliographic Remarks

The theory for consensus problem and its generalizations is quite well-developed. We have covered only the very basic ideas from the literature. The reader will find many results in the book by Lynch [Lyn96]. The consensus problem with Byzantine faults was first introduced and solved by Lamport, Shostak and Pease [LSP82, PSL80]. The lower bound on the number of bounds needed for solving the problem under Byzantine faults was given by Fischer and Lynch [FL82] and under crash failures by Dolev and Strong [DS83].

Chapter 27

Failure Detectors

In order to attain the impossible, one must attempt the absurd. —
Miguel de Cervantes Saavedra

27.1 Introduction

A useful module in any distributed program is that of a failure detector.
By incorporating a failure detector in a distributed program all the
details of time-outs are localized to only one module. In the absence of
a failure detector module, the wait of any message must be relinquished
after a time-out to prevent a process from waiting for a message from
a process that is crashed. When a failure detector module is available,
a blocking receive such as

$$wait \text{ for message } m \text{ from } P_i$$

is changed to

$$(wait \text{ for message } m \text{ from } P_i) \text{ or } (P_i \text{ is suspected}).$$

With this modification the program becomes nonblocking despite
process failures.

There is another motivation to study failure detectors. We show
that, given sufficiently powerful failure detectors, the consensus problem can be solved efficiently in asynchronous systems.

This chapter is organized as follows. Section 27.2 gives the properties satisfied by various failure detectors. Section 27.3 gives the relationship among these failure detectors. Section 27.4 gives an algorithm

to solve the consensus using one of the failure detectors described in this chapter.

The notation used in this chapter is summarized in Figure 27.1.

S	Set of states
s, t	States
Π	Set of all processes
i, j	Process indices
Π_c	Set of correct processes
C	Set of states on correct processes
C_j	States on a correct process P_j

Figure 27.1: Notation

27.2 Completeness and Accuracy Properties

We assume that a processor crashes by ceasing all its activity and that once a process has failed (or crashed) it stays failed throughout the run. The predicate *failed*(i) holds if process P_i has failed in the given run. A process that has not failed is called a *correct* process. We denote the set of all processes and the set of correct processes by Π and Π_c, respectively.

We note here that, by definition of asynchronous processing, it is impossible to distinguish a failed process from a correct process in a finite amount of time. This implies that one needs to look at infinite runs to even define a failed process. Thus, given an infinite run, we define a failed process as one that takes only a finite number of steps in that run.

We use the following notation. The set $C \subseteq S$ denotes the set of states on processes that have not failed, and the set C_j denotes the states on any correct process P_j. The predicate *suspects*(s, i) holds if the process P_i is suspected in the state s (by the process that contains s).

A failure detector is responsible for maintaining the value of the predicate *suspects* at all correct processes.

We would like our failure detectors to satisfy certain suspicion completeness and suspicion accuracy properties. Intuitively, the completeness properties require suspicion of failed processes. The *weak completeness* property requires that every failed process is eventually permanently suspected by some correct process. Let the predicate $permsusp(s, i)$ (process i is permanently suspected in state s) be defined as

$$permsusp(s, i) \equiv \forall t \geq s : suspects(t, i)$$

Based on the above definition, a detector is defined to be weak complete if for any run,

$$\forall i : \langle failed(i) \Rightarrow \exists s \in C : permsusp(s, i) \rangle$$

The *strong completeness* property requires the failed process to be eventually suspected by *all* correct processes. Formally,

$$\forall i, j : \langle failed(i) \wedge \neg failed(j) \Rightarrow \exists s \in C_j : permsusp(s, i) \rangle$$

We now turn our attention to accuracy properties. A detector satisfies *strong* accuracy if no process is suspected before it crashes. A detector satisfies *weak* accuracy if some correct process is never suspected. Formally,

$$\exists i \in \Pi_c, \forall s \in C : \neg suspects(s, i)$$

Even weak accuracy in conjunction with weak completeness is impossible to obtain in an asynchronous system. Therefore, we consider even weaker versions of accuracy properties.

A detector satisfies *eventual strong accuracy* if eventually all correct process are never suspected by any correct process. Formally,

$$\forall i \in \Pi_c, \forall j \in \Pi_c, \exists s \in C_j, \forall t \geq s : \neg suspects(t, i)$$

A detector satisfies *eventual weak accuracy* if eventually some correct process is never suspected by any correct process. Formally,

$$\exists i \in \Pi_c, \forall j \in \Pi_c, \exists s \in C_j, \forall t \geq s : \neg suspects(t, i)$$

By choosing a completeness property and an accuracy property, we can build various classes of failure detectors. In the table shown in Figure 27.2, we list all the failure detectors that guarantee strong completeness properties.

The failure detectors that satisfy weak completeness properties can similarly be defined. We will use only one of them — a failure detector is called eventually weak (denoted by $\Diamond \mathcal{W}$) if it satisfies weak completeness and eventual weak accuracy.

Name	Symbol	Accuracy Property
Perfect	P	Strong
Strong	S	Weak
Eventually perfect	$\Diamond\,\mathcal{P}$	Eventually strong
Eventually strong	$\Diamond\,\mathcal{S}$	Eventually weak

Figure 27.2: Failure detectors with strong completeness property

27.3 Relationship Among Various Failure Detectors

We say that a failure detector X' is *weaker than* the failure detector X if there exists a transformation in an asynchronous system that uses information provided by the failure detector X to implement X'. For example, consider the *eventually strong* detector denoted by $\Diamond\,\mathcal{S}$, which provides strong completeness and eventual weak accuracy. Because strong completeness implies weak completeness, it is obvious that $\Diamond\,\mathcal{W}$ is a weaker detector than $\Diamond\,\mathcal{S}$. More surprising is the fact that $\Diamond\,\mathcal{S}$ is also weaker than $\Diamond\,\mathcal{W}$. Let *EW.suspects* and *ES.suspects* be the set of processes suspected by the $\Diamond\,\mathcal{W}$ and $\Diamond\,\mathcal{S}$ detectors, respectively. The algorithm to implement the $\Diamond\,\mathcal{S}$ detector using the $\Diamond\,\mathcal{W}$ is given in Figure 27.3. The detector is based on two activities. Each process sends its suspicion list to all other processes infinitely often. On receiving such a message from P_i, a process queries its $\Diamond\,\mathcal{W}$ detector and adds the suspicion list of P_i and removes P_i from the suspicion list if present.

P_j::
var
      ES.suspects: set of processes initially *EW.suspects*;

(I1) send *EW.suspects* to all processes infinitely often;

(I2) On receiving $m.suspects$ from P_i;
      $ES.suspects := ES.suspects \cup m.suspects - \{i\}$;

Figure 27.3: Implementation of a $\Diamond\,\mathcal{S}$ detector using a $\Diamond\,\mathcal{W}$ detector

The following theorem proves the correctness of the transformation.

Theorem 27.1 *ES.suspects satisfies strong completeness and eventual weak accuracy.*

Proof: Consider a failed process P_i. By the property of $\diamond\, \mathcal{W}$, there exists a correct process P_j that eventually permanently suspects P_i. In other words, $i \in EW.suspects$ of P_j. Since P_j sends this list to all other processes infinitely often, it will be part of $ES.suspects$ of all correct processes. Furthermore, the only time a process P_i is removed from the suspicion list is when a message is received from P_i. Therefore, P_i will eventually be in the suspicion list of all correct processes permanently. This proves strong completeness of $ES.suspects$.

We now show the property of eventual weak accuracy. By the property of $\diamond\, \mathcal{W}$ there exists some correct process, say P_i, that is not suspected by any other correct process. This implies that eventually P_i will not be part of any $EW.suspects$. Thus it will never be part of $m.suspects$ for any process. Furthermore, a message will eventually be received by every other process, thus removing it from $ES.suspects$. Hence, eventually P_i will not be part of any of the $ES.suspects$ list.

$\blacksquare$

From the above result it follows that $\diamond\, \mathcal{S}$ and $\diamond\, \mathcal{W}$ are equivalent.

27.4   Algorithm for Consensus Using $\diamond\, \mathcal{S}$

We now show an application of the $\diamond\, \mathcal{S}$ failure detector. We show that, given a module that implements $\diamond\, \mathcal{S}$ (or equivalently, $\diamond\, \mathcal{W}$ detector), one can solve the problem of consensus in an asynchronous environment. The protocol to solve the consensus problem uses a rotating coordinator paradigm. It assumes that the majority of processes, that is, at least $\lceil (n + 1)/2 \rceil$ processes are alive. The algorithm shown in Figure 27.4 works in asynchronous rounds. Each process knows that the process number ($r \bmod n$) is the coordinator for the round number r. A round r consists of four phases. In phase 1, each process sends its estimate to the coordinator of this round. In phase 2, the coordinator gathers values from a majority of processes and broadcasts a new estimate. During phase 3, each process waits for an estimate value from the coordinator. If it receives a value from the coordinator, it sends back a positive acknowledgment. Otherwise, if it suspects the coordinators, the process sends a negative acknowledgment. During phase 4, the coordinator waits for a majority of acknowledgments. If it receives a majority of positive acknowledgments then it decides on its estimated value and broadcasts this to all processes. On receiving a decision value, the process decides on that value and stops.

Before we show the correctness of the protocol formally, let us see the two main ideas in the algorithm. First, the rotating coordinator paradigm guarantees termination when eventual weak accuracy is present. This is because eventually a correct process, say P_i, will not be suspected by any other process (actually, we only require that the majority of the processes not suspect it). This process will eventually become a coordinator and receive the required number of positive acknowledgments. Its estimate will then be decided. The second idea is that of "locking" in a value. Once a value is locked in, no process can ever decide on a different value. This is achieved in phase 2 by the way a coordinator computes an estimate for the current round. Each process P_i is required to send in phase 2, along with its estimate, a timestamp that is the last round number in which P_i updated its estimate. The coordinator chooses a value corresponding to the largest timestamp. We will show later that this has the advantage that once a decision has been made all the estimates with a greater timestamp will have the same value.

27.4.1   Proof of Correctness

We show that the above protocol satisfies all the requirements of the consensus problem.

Theorem 27.2 *The rotating coordinator protocol solves the consensus problem.*

Proof: *(Agreement)* We show that no two processes decide differently. Let r be the smallest round in which the coordinator received a majority of positive acks. Let est_c be the estimate of the coordinator at the end of that round. We claim that for all rounds $r' \geq r$, the coordinator does not send any different estimate. This claim is shown by using induction on $r' - r$. The claim is trivially true when $r' - r = 0$. Assume that is it true for all rounds such that $r' - r < k$. Now consider the case when the coordinator sends an estimate in the round $r + k$. The estimate that the coordinator sends has the largest timestamp of all the estimates received. It follows that this timestamp is at least r since

```
p::
  var
      v := input bit;
      r := 0; // round number
      t := 0;// timestamp

  while undecided do
      r := r + 1;
      c := (r mod n) + 1;// coordinator

      //phase 1:
      send (p, r, v, t) to c;

      // phase 2:
      c waits for first n/2 + 1 estimates;
      c chooses the estimate w with the largest timestamp;
      c proposes that value as (c, r, w);

      // phase 3:
      p waits for a message or failure suspicion of c;
      if proposal (c, r, w) is received then
          v := w; t := r;
          send (r, ACK) to c;
      else
          send (r, NACK) to c;

      // phase 4:
      c waits for n/2 + 1 ACK/NACK messages;
      if there are n/2 + 1 ACK messages then
          c sends (decide, w) to all including itself;
  endwhile;


  Upon receiving (decide, w)
      p sends (decide, w) to all;
      p decides on w and halts.
```

Figure 27.4: Consensus using $\diamond \mathcal{S}$ detector

the coordinator receives a majority of timestamps and at least one of these processes updated its estimate on the round r. Assume that the estimate chosen by the coordinator in r' is from the process q. We have already shown that the timestamp of the estimate sent by q is at least r. It also follows from the program that the timestamp is at most $k-1$. It follows from the induction hypothesis that the coordinator of that round must have sent the same estimate as that in round r. Thus the coordinator of round r' will also come up with the same estimate.

(Termination) We show that every correct process eventually decides some value. None of the steps in the algorithm is blocking when there are failures of less than a majority of processes. By the eventual weak accuracy of the failure detectors we will reach a round number in which a correct process will receive a high enough number of positive acknowledgments. It will then broadcast its decision, which will be received by all correct processes.

(Validity) It is easy to see that a value that is decided is proposed by some process.

■

27.5   Problems

27.1. Show that strong completeness in conjunction with any of the four accuracy properties discussed in this chapter is equivalent to weak completeness and the same accuracy property. (Hint: Use the transformation similar to that from $\Diamond \mathcal{W}$ to $\Diamond \mathcal{S}$)

27.2. Show that any failure detector that gives eventual guarantees cannot solve the consensus problem in presence of $n/2$ faults. (Hint: Consider a run in which exactly $n/2$ processes have 0 as input and $n/2$ processes have 1 as input.)

27.3. Consider a failure detector $\mathcal{S}$ that satisfies strong completeness and weak accuracy. $\mathcal{S}$ never suspects some correct process. Show that $\mathcal{S}$ can be used to solve consensus in a system with up to $n - 1$ failures.

*27.4. Show that $\Diamond \mathcal{W}$ is the weakest failure detector that can be used to solve the consensus problem.

27.6 Bibliographic Remarks

The notion of failure detectors and the algorithm for consensus using failure detectors are taken from [CT96].

Chapter 28

Solvable Problems in Asynchronous Systems

The real problem is what to do with the problem-solvers after the problems are solved. — Gay Talese

28.1 Introduction

In this chapter we discuss problems that can be solved in asynchronous distributed systems despite process failures. We first introduce a failure detector that is implementable in asynchronous systems. All failure detectors we have discussed so far can solve the consensus problem in asynchronous systems. It follows from the FLP result that these failure detectors are not implementable in asynchronous systems. The failure detector introduced in this chapter, called the Infinitely Often Accurate detector (IO detector for short), can be implemented efficiently in asynchronous systems. Although the IO detector cannot be used to solve the consensus problem, it can be used to solve other problems in asynchronous systems. We show one such application in this chapter.

Next, we consider a weaker version of the consensus problem. The consensus problem requires all processes to agree on a single value. The k-set consensus problem requires that the number of different values that are decided by all processes be at most k. When k is 1, we get the original consensus problem. We show that the k-set consensus problem is solvable in an asynchronous environment so long as the number of failures f is less than k.

347

Finally, we give an algorithm for the Reliable Broadcast problem, which is a weaker version of the Terminating Reliable Broadcast problem considered in Chapter 25.

This chapter is organized as follows. Section 28.2 describes IO detectors. We give an implementation of IO detectors and also show its application to the problem of maintaining a leader in an asynchronous system. Section 28.3 gives an algorithm for the k-set consensus problem, and Section 28.4 gives an algorithm for the Reliable Broadcast problem.

The notation used in this chapter is summarized in Figure 28.1.

C	Set of states on correct processes
i, j	Process numbers
s, t	Local states
G, H	Global states
f	The number of failed processes

Figure 28.1: Notation

28.2 Failure Detection

An IO detector satisfies even weaker accuracy than eventual weak accuracy. Intuitively, eventual weak accuracy requires that the detector eventually never suspects at least one correct process. It is precisely this requirement that makes it possible to solve the consensus problem by using, for example, the rotating coordinator technique. On the other hand, this is also the requirement that is impossible to implement in an asynchronous system (while requiring that the failed processes are suspected). An IO detector only requires that a correct process is not permanently suspected. By assuming that messages do not get lost, this requirement can be met by an algorithm that will be presented later. We formalize the exact properties guaranteed by that algorithm and show its usefulness in asynchronous systems. We also show that some other natural "time-out" implementations of failure detectors do not satisfy the properties of IO detector.

Although the IO detector cannot be used to solve the consensus problem, we show that it is useful for other applications. In particular, we give its application to a fault-tolerant server maintenance problem.

This problem requires the presence of at least one server during the computation. Our solution works despite up to $N - 1$ failures in a system of N processes. For this application, we require an additional accuracy property from the IO detectors. If the underlying run is partially synchronous with respect to a process in the sense that eventually messages sent by that process reach destination in bounded delay, then we require the IO detector to satisfy the eventual weak accuracy property. We show that this property is also satisfied by our algorithm for IO detectors.

28.2.1 Infinitely Often Accurate Detectors

We first introduce an accuracy property called infinitely often accuracy. A detector is infinitely often accurate if no correct process permanently suspects a correct process. Formally,

Definition 28.1 *A detector is infinitely often accurate if*

$$\forall i : \langle \neg failed(i) \Rightarrow \forall s \in C : \neg permsusp(s, i) \rangle$$

An IO detector is a failure that satisfies weak completeness and infinitely often accuracy. By combining the two properties, we get the following pleasant property of an IO detector.

$$\forall i : failed(i) \equiv \exists s \in C : permsusp(s, i)$$

Intuitively, this says that a failure of a process is equivalent to permanent suspicion by some correct process. How does this detector compare to $\Diamond \, \mathcal{W}$? For comparison, we use the notion of reduction between detectors. We first show that the IO detector can be implemented using a $\Diamond \, \mathcal{W}$ detector. Let *IO.suspects* and *EW.suspects* be the set of processes suspected by the IO detector and the $\Diamond \, \mathcal{W}$ detector, respectively. The algorithm to implement IO detector using $\Diamond \, \mathcal{W}$ is given in Figure 28.2. The detector is based on two activities. Each process sends an "alive" message to all other processes infinitely often. On receiving such a message from P_i, a process queries the $\Diamond \, \mathcal{W}$ suspector and removes the suspicion of P_i.

We now have the following lemma.

Lemma 28.2 *The algorithm in Figure 28.2 implements an IO detector.*

P_j::
  var
      $IO.suspects$: set of processes initially $EW.suspects$;

  (I1) send "alive" to all processes infinitely often;

  (I2) Upon receiving "alive" from P_i;
      $IO.suspects := EW.suspects - \{i\}$;

Figure 28.2: Implementation of an IO detector using a $\diamond W$ detector

Proof: We first show the weak completeness property. Consider any process P_i that has failed. This implies that eventually P_i will be in $EW.suspects$ for some correct process, say P_j, by the property of the $\diamond W$ detector. Furthermore, eventually no correct process will receive an "alive" message from P_i. This implies that P_i will be permanently in $IO.suspects$ of P_j.

We now show the infinitely often accuracy property. Consider any process P_i that has not failed. This implies that any correct process will receive "alive" message from P_i infinitely often. Therefore, P_i will be not be in $IO.suspects$ infinitely often.

■

Note that the above proof has not even used the eventual weak accuracy property of the $\diamond W$ detector.

We now introduce another useful property of failure detectors that is also implementable in an asynchronous environment. The property says that if we happen to be lucky in some asynchronous computation in the sense that eventually all messages sent by at least one process reach under some bound, then the failure detector will eventually be accurate with respect to that process. We call this property *conditional eventual weak accuracy*. We first introduce the notion of a *partially synchronous* run.

Definition 28.3 *A run is partially synchronous if there exists a state s in a correct process P_i and a bound δ such that all messages sent by P_i after s take at most δ units of time.*

In the above definition we do not require the knowledge of P_i, s, or δ. This lets us define:

Definition 28.4 *A failure detector satisfies conditional eventual weak accuracy if for all partially synchronous runs it satisfies eventual weak accuracy.*

It is easy to verify that the algorithm in Figure 28.2 also satisfies *conditional eventual weak accuracy.* The algorithm only removes suspicion from the set *EW.suspects.* Since $\diamond\ W$ satisfies eventual weak accuracy, it follows that the IO detector built from $\diamond\ W$ also satisfies this property.

We now consider the converse question. Is there an asynchronous algorithm that implements $\diamond\ W$ using an IO detector? We answer this question in the negative by giving an implementation of an IO detector. A possible implementation is shown in Figure 28.3. The algorithm maintains a time-out period for each process. The variable $watch[i]$ is the timer for the process P_i. When the timer expires, the process is suspected. On the other hand when a message is received while a process is under a suspicion, the time-out period for that process is increased.

Theorem 28.5 *The algorithm in Figure 28.3 guarantees IO detection with conditional eventual weak accuracy.*

Proof: First we show the weak completeness property. If a process P_i has failed, then it will stop sending messages. All the messages sent by it will eventually be received. After that point, all other processes will not hear from this process and start suspecting P_i using rule (A2). Because they will never hear from it again, it will then be permanently in *IO.suspects.*

The property of infinitely often accuracy follows from the proof of Lemma 28.2.

Finally, we show that the algorithm satisfies conditional eventual weak accuracy. Consider any partially synchronous run. Let P_i be the correct process in that run for which messages obey the synchrony condition after some state s. Since messages sent after that state are received in less than δ units of time, there can only be a bounded number of false suspicions of P_i by any process (because the time-out period is increased by 1 after every false suspicion). Thus, eventually, P_i is never suspected by any process.

∎

```
Pⱼ::
  var
        IO.suspects : set of processes initially ∅;
        timeout: array[1..N] of integer initially t;
        watch: timer initially set to timeout;


(A1) send "alive" to all processes after every t units;

(A2) Upon receiving "alive" from Pᵢ;
     if i ∈ IO.suspects then
         IO.suspects := IO.suspects − {i};
         timeout[i] := timcout[i] + 1;
     endif;
     Set watch[i] timer for timeout;

(A3) Upon expiry of watch[i]
         IO.suspects := IO.suspects ∪ {i};
```

Figure 28.3: Implementation of an IO detector

Observe that one needs to be careful in designing algorithms for failure detectors. Some natural approaches do not satisfy the IO property. For example, consider the following approach:

> The crash detection manager is responsible to multicast polling messages periodically to all other processes under surveillance. The other processes are expected to reply to these polling requests with "I am alive" messages immediately. If the answer is missing for three times consecutively, the crash manager assumes that this process has crashed.

As another example, consider the algorithm in Figure 28.4 which is similar to the *rup* command in UNIX.

Note that it is tempting to implement failure detectors using the algorithm in Figure 28.4 because it only requires the failure detector to listen for incoming messages during the time-out interval. This algorithm, however, does not satisfy IO accuracy. It may show some

P_j::
  var
  $RUP.suspects$: set of processes initially $\emptyset$;

  (B1) infinitely often broadcast a query message to all processes;

  (B2) Upon expiry of $timeout[i]$ time units
        if (P_i did not respond to the query) **then**
              $RUP.suspects := RUP.suspects \cup \{i\}$;
        else $RUP.suspects := RUP.suspects - \{i\}$;

  (B3) Upon receiving a query from P_i
        send "I am alive" to P_i

Figure 28.4: A detector that does not satisfy IO accuracy

process P_i to be suspected at all times even when P_i is alive and just slow. Even if the time-out period is changed on receiving a message from P_i, the algorithm still does not satisfy the IO property. For example, assume that we add the following rule to that algorithm:

  (B4) On receiving "I am alive" message from P_i
  $timeout[i] := timeout[i] + 1$;

The above rule increases the waiting period for time-out for P_i but does not remove suspicion. This rule is not sufficient because the message from P_i may always take $timeout[i] + 1$ units of time no matter what the value of $timeout[i]$ is.

28.2.2 Application: Maintaining a Leader

Because IO detectors are implementable, it is clear that they cannot be used for solving binary consensus problem. What good are they then? We now discuss a practical problem that can be solved using IO detectors. Consider a service that is required in a distributed system consisting of N processes. We require that at least one process always acts as the provider of that service. We abstract this requirement using the concept of a token. Any process that has a token considers itself to be the provider of the service. Because the process holding the token may fail, we clearly need a mechanism to regenerate the token to avoid interruption of the service. To avoid triviality, we only consider those runs in which at least one process never fails. The following predicates and functions are used for specifying the requirements.

- $hastoken(G)$: This predicate is true if the global state G has a token. It may have multiple tokens.

- $failed(G)$: This function returns the set of failed processes in the global state G.

- $G[i].token$: This predicate is true if P_i has the token in the global state G.

We will present our solution in stages. We first consider the requirements of this problem as follows.

1. *Availability:* There exists a global state such that all later global states have at least one token. Formally,

$$\exists G, \forall H \succeq G : hastoken(H)$$

2. *Efficiency:* For every global state G in which two different processes have tokens, there exists a later global state in which the token from at least one of the process is removed. Formally,

$$\forall G, i, j : \langle (i \neq j) \wedge G[i].token \wedge G[j].token$$

implies
$$\exists H \succeq G : \neg H[i].token \vee \neg H[j].token \rangle$$

3. *No duplicates under synchrony:* If after any global state G all messages sent by a correct process P_i arrive in less than a predetermined bounded delay, then there exists a later global state H such that no process P_j with $j > i$ has a token after H. If this condition is true for the smallest correct process, then we are guaranteed that there are no duplicate tokens eventually. Formally,

$$\forall G : boundedafter(G, i) \Rightarrow \exists H, \forall H' \succeq H, \forall j > i : \neg H'[j].token$$

4. *No loss under failure-free operation:* Let G be any global state in which there is a token. If H is any global state later than G in which no additional process has failed, then H has at least one token. Formally, for all G,

$$hastoken(G) \Rightarrow \forall H \succeq G : (failed(G) \neq failed(H)) \vee hastoken(H)$$

The algorithm that satisfies above requirements is shown in Figure 28.5. We assume that initially P_1 has the token.

```
Pi:
 var
 token: boolean; initially false for all i ≠ 1 and true for i = 1.
 // false represents absence of the token

 suspected: array[1..N] of boolean; // set by the failure detector

 Upon change from unsuspicion to suspicion of any process
     if ∀j < i : suspected[j] then
     // is there any smaller process that is unsuspected
         token := true; // generate the token

 Upon change from suspicion to unsuspicion of Pk
 if (k < i) then
     token := false;
```

Figure 28.5: An algorithm for the alive token problem

We now show that the above algorithm satisfies all our requirements.

Theorem 28.6 *The algorithm in Figure 28.5 satisfies all four required properties.*

Proof:

- *Availability:* Consider the global state G. By our assumption, at least one process is alive in the run. Let P_k be the smallest such process. By strong completeness of the IO failure detector, eventually P_k will suspect all smaller processes. In that global state, P_k will generate the token.

- *Efficiency*: Consider the global state G in which two processes P_i and P_j ($i < j$) have tokens. For any continuation of run after G in which P_i or P_j fails we have a global state state H in which $\neg H[i].token \lor \neg H[j].token$. Otherwise, by the IO accuracy property of the IO detector, P_j will remove the suspicion of P_i eventually. In that global state H, $\neg H[j].token$ holds.

- *No duplicates under synchrony*: Consider any global state G such that $boundedafter(G, i)$ holds. This implies that the IO detector for any process P_j will eventually never suspect P_i. Therefore, P_j will never get the token.

- *No loss under failure-free operation*: This property is true because the token is removed in the algorithm only when there is a failure.

∎

If all the failure suspicions are accurate, then the above algorithm will keep at most one token. Furthermore, if in addition to synchrony (or accuracy of failure detectors) there are no failures after a certain point, then the system will keep exactly one token in the system.

In the above solution if the partial synchrony condition was satisfied with respect to the smallest correct process, then the system works in the desirable manner. There is exactly one token eventually. However, if the partial synchrony is satisfied with respect to some other process, then this condition is not met. We now present a solution that meets this condition even when the partial synchrony is satisfied by some other process.

Intuitively, the idea behind the algorithm is as follows. In addition to the suspicion list maintained by the failure detector, each process maintains a timestamp for each process called *ticket time*. The ticket time of a process P_i is the logical time when it learned that it was suspected by some process while P_i had the token. When P_j suspects a process P_i, a message is sent to P_i regarding this suspicion. If P_i is alive it will receive this message. If P_i has the token then it will realize that some process considers it slow and will record the logical time of this event. This is the ticket time of this process. It will then send out a message to all processes informing them of the suspicion along with its ticket time.

Process P_i has the token if all processes that are currently not suspected by P_i have ticket times that are greater than that of P_i. If a process with the token is suspected, its ticket time will become greater than all the ticket times that it has. This way the token is moved from a slow process to the next process that is alive. The formal description of the algorithm is given in Figure 28.6. The algorithm assumes that all channels are FIFO.

P_i:

var

      ticket: array$[1..N]$ of (integer,integer) initially $\forall i : ticket[i] = (0, i)$
      suspected: array$[1..N]$ of boolean; // set by the failure detector

(R1) Upon change from unsuspicion to suspicion of any process P_k
      send "suspected" to P_k

(R2) Upon receiving "suspected"
    if $token(i)$ **then**
        $ticket[i] := Lamport's\_logical\_clock$;
        send "slow", i, $ticket[i]$ to all processes;

(R3) Upon receiving "slow",k, t
      $ticket[k] := t$;

$token(i) \equiv (\forall j \neq i : suspected[j] \vee (ticket[j] > ticket[i])) \wedge \neg suspected[i]$

Figure 28.6: An algorithm that eventually guarantees a single token

Lemma 28.7
1. $\forall G, i, j : G[i].ticket[j] \leq G[j].ticket[j]$.
2. $\forall G, i : \exists j : G[i].token(j)$.

Proof: 1. Process P_j updates its own ticket $ticket[j]$ before sending out the message. Process P_i receives this message only after it is sent. Furthermore all channels are FIFO; therefore, its value of $ticket[j]$ cannot be greater.

2. Since a process never suspects itself, the set of unsuspected processes at $G[i]$ is nonempty. The unsuspected process with the smallest ticket number will then have the token in P_i's view.

∎

Theorem 28.8 *The algorithm in Figure 28.6 satisfies all four required properties.*

Proof:

- *Availability:* Consider in any global state G the process with the smallest ticket number. Since a process never suspects itself and all other processes are either suspected or they have a greater ticket number, it follows that this process will eventually have the token.

- *Efficiency:* Consider the global state G in which two processes P_i and P_j have tokens. Since there is a total order on all tickets, and from Lemma 28.7, this can only happen when the process with the smaller ticket number, say P_i, is suspected by the other process, P_j. For any continuation of run after G in which P_i or P_j fails we have a global state state H in which $\neg H[i].token \vee \neg H[j].token$. Otherwise, by the IO accuracy property of the IO detector, P_j will remove the suspicion of P_i eventually. In that global state H, $\neg H[j].token$ holds.

- *Eventually exactly one token under partial synchrony:* Consider any global state G such that $boundedafter(G, i)$ holds. This implies that IO detector for any process P_j will eventually never suspect P_i. If there are multiple values of i such that $boundedafter(G, i)$ holds, then we choose the process with the smallest ticket number in G. This process is never suspected by anybody else after G and therefore no other process will ever have the token. Furthermore, this process will never lose the token because no process that is unsuspected can have a smaller ticket number.

∎

In a system in which no process fails, the above algorithm reduces to a token-based mutual exclusion algorithm. The process with the smallest ticket has the critical section. When it is ready to release the critical section, it sends out the "slow" message to all processes. By assuming that a process is suspected when it leaves the system and unsuspected when it joins the system, this algorithm can also be used when the number of processes in the system is dynamic.

Also observe that if suspicions are perfect, that is, a process is suspected only when it is failed, the algorithm ensures that there is at most one token. Thus the algorithm can also be seen as a fault-tolerant mutual exclusion algorithm.

28.3 *k*-Set Consensus Problem

We now present the *k*-set consensus problem, a weaker version of the consensus problem, which is solvable in asynchronous systems. The problem is defined as follows. Each process proposes a value as in the consensus problem. The protocol for *k*-set consensus requires processes to decide on values such that:

- *k*-**Agreement**: The set of decisions made by nonfaulty processes contains at most *k* values.

- **Validity**: Any value that is decided must be proposed by some process.

- **Termination**: Every nonfaulty process eventually decides on some value.

The algorithm for the *k*-set consensus shown in Figure 28.7 works correctly so long as $f < k$. Its correctness is left as an exercise.

```
P_i::
  var
  v: initial value;

  Send v to all processes;
  Upon receiving N − f proposals;
      decision := min(proposals);
```

Figure 28.7: An algorithm for solving the *k*-set consensus problem

28.4 Reliable Broadcast Problem

Just as consensus can be weakened so that it can be solved in asynchronous systems, the Terminating Reliable Broadcast problem can also be weakened. The *reliable broadcast* problem is defined as follows. Assume that there are N processes in the system $P_0, \ldots, P_{N-1}$ and that P_0 wishes to broadcast a single message to all processes. The requirements of the problem are:

- *Validity*: If the sender is correct and broadcasts a message m, then all correct processes eventually deliver m.

- *Agreement*: If a correct process delivers a message m, then all correct processes deliver m.

- *Integrity*: Every correct process delivers at most one message, and if it delivers m different from "sender faulty," then the sender must have broadcast m.

Thus we have removed the *termination* condition from the Terminating Reliable Broadcast problem. This problem can be solved easily by the algorithm in Figure 28.8. The algorithm works correctly in the presence of any number of failures.

```
P_0::
    send message m to all other processes;


P_i(i ∈ {1..N − 1})::
var
        notdone: boolean initially true;

On receiving a message m;
        if notdone then send message m to all processes;
        notdone := false;
```

Figure 28.8: An algorithm for reliable broadcast of message m

28.5 Problems

28.1. Assuming that at most f processes may fail, give a failure detector that never suspects more than f processes and yet provides strong completeness, infinitely often accuracy, and conditional eventual weak accuracy. (Hint: Maintain a queue of "slow" processes in addition to suspected processes.)

28.2. Give a failure detector that satisfies strong completeness and the following accuracy property: Every correct process has the correct suspicion list infinitely often.

28.3. Show that the algorithm in Figure 28.7 satisfies all the requirements of the k-set consensus problem.

28.4. Show that the algorithm in Figure 28.8 satisfies all the requirements of the reliable broadcast problem.

28.5. Give an algorithm for a reliable causal broadcast, i.e., if multiple messages are broadcasts (possibly by different processes) then causal ordering is preserved in the delivery. Your algorithm should tolerate any number of process failures.

28.6. The ϵ-*approximate agreement problem* is as follows. Assume that there are N processors, each processor with input value x_i from the domain of real numbers. The goal is for each processor to decide to another real value y_i such that (1) every nonfaulty processor is eventually assigned some value, (2) all decided values are within ϵ of each other, and (3) every decided value is within the range of the input values. Show that the ϵ-approximate problem is solvable in asynchronous systems for any number of failures. Assume that the input range is known.

*28.7. Show that the k-set consensus problem is impossible to solve in an asynchronous system when $f \geq k$.

28.6 Bibliographic Remarks

The discussion of the IO detector is taken from [GM98b]. The algorithm for IO detector is based on Dwork et al. [DLS88], which shows how consensus can be reached in partially synchronous systems. The notion of a *partially synchronous* run is similar to that used in

[DLP$^+$86a]. An application of IO detectors for predicate detection is discussed in Garg and Mitchell [GM98a]. The k-set consensus problem was first presented by Chaudhuri [Cha93]. The lower bound showing that k-set consensus cannot be solved in the presence of $f \geq k$ failures was proved independently by Borowsky and Gafni [BG93], Herlihy and Shavit [HS93], and Saks and Zaharoglou [SZ93]. The problem of approximate agreement (Problem 28.6) was first posed and solved by Dolev, Lynch, Pinter, Stark, and Weihl [DLP$^+$86b].

Chapter 29

Checkpointing for Recovery

Character is much easier kept than recovered. — Thomas Paine

29.1 Introduction

In this chapter, we study methods for fault tolerance using checkpointing. A checkpoint can be *local* to a process or *global* in the system. A global checkpoint is simply a global state that is stored on the stable storage so that in the event of a failure the entire system can be rolled back to the global checkpoint and restarted. To record a global state, one could employ methods presented in Chapter 10. These methods, called coordinated checkpointing, can be efficiently implemented. However, there are some disadvantages of using coordinated checkpoints. First, there is the overhead of computing a global snapshot. When a *coordinated* checkpoint is taken, processes are forced to take their local checkpoints whenever the algorithm for coordinated checkpoint requires it. It is better for this decision to be local because then a process is free to take its local checkpoint whenever it is idle. Second, in case of a failure, the entire system is required to roll back. In particular, even those processes that never communicated with the process that failed are also required to roll back. This results in wasted computation and slow recovery.

An alternative method is to let processes take their local checkpoints at their will. During a *failure-free* mode of computation, this will result in a lower overhead on computation than that for coordinated checkpointing. In case of a failure, a suitable set of local checkpoints is chosen to form a global checkpoint. Observe that processes that have not failed have their current states available, and those states can also serve as checkpoints. There are some disadvantages of uncoordinated checkpointing compared with coordinated checkpointing schemes. First, for coordinated checkpointing it is sufficient to keep just the most recent global snapshot in the stable storage. For uncoordinated checkpoints a more complex garbage collection scheme is required. Second, in the case of a failure the recovery method for coordinated checkpointing is simpler. There is no need to compute a consistent global checkpoint. Finally, but most importantly, simple uncoordinated checkpointing does not guarantee any progress. If local checkpoints are taken at inopportune times the only consistent global state may be the initial one. This problem is called the *domino effect*, and an example is shown in Figure 29.1. Assume that process P_1 crashes and therefore must roll back to $c_{1,1}$, its last checkpoint. Because a message was sent between $c_{1,1}$ and $c_{1,2}$ that is received before $c_{2,2}$, process P_2 is in an inconsistent state at $c_{2,2}$ with respect to $c_{1,1}$. Therefore, P_2 rolls back to $c_{2,1}$. But this forces P_3 to roll back. Continuing in this manner, we find that the only consistent global checkpoint is the initial one. Rolling back to the initial global checkpoint results in wasting the entire computation.

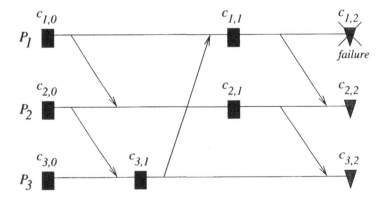

Figure 29.1: An example of the domino effect

A hybrid of the completely coordinated and the completely uncoordinated schemes is called *communication-induced checkpointing*. In this method, processes are free to take their local checkpoints whenever desired, but based on the communication pattern they may be forced to take additional local checkpoints. These methods guarantee that recovery will not suffer from the domino effect.

The characteristics of the application, the probability of failures, and technological factors may dictate which of the above choices of checkpointing is best for a given situation. In this chapter, we will study issues in uncoordinated checkpointing and communication-induced checkpointing.

This chapter is organized as follows. Section 29.2 describes a relation called the *zig-zag* relation that is weaker than the happened before relation and is useful in analysis of relationship between checkpoints. Section 29.3 describes construction of a graph called the *R-graph* that is also useful for analysis of dependency between checkpoints. Section 29.4 shows how slicing can be applied to compute the set of all consistent recoverable global states. Section 29.5 defines a condition called rollback dependency trackability of a computation. This condition allows easy on-line calculation of the maximum recoverable state. It also ensures that there are no useless checkpoints. Finally, Section 29.6 gives a rule called *fixed-dependency-after-send* that ensures that the computation satisfies rollback dependency trackability.

The notation used in this chapter is summarized in Figure 29.2.

c, d, e	Checkpoints
S	The set of all checkpoints
X	A set of checkpoints
$\xrightarrow{z}$	Zig-zag relation
$c.v$	Vector clock at c
$pred.c$	Predecessor of c
$succ.c$	Successor of c
B	Global boolean predicate
$\preceq$	Local precedes relation

Figure 29.2: Notation

29.2 Zig-Zag Relation

Consider any distributed computation with N processes $P_1, \ldots, P_N$. Each process P_i checkpoints its local state at some intermittent interval, giving rise to a sequence of local checkpoints denoted by S_i. We will assume that the initial state and the final state in any process are checkpointed. For any checkpoint c we denote by $pred.c$ the predecessor of the state c in the sequence S_i whenever it exists, that is, when c is not the initial checkpoint. Similarly, we use $succ.c$ for the successor of the checkpoint d.

Given a set of local checkpoints, X, we say that X is consistent iff $\forall c, d \in X : c \| d$. A set of local checkpoints is called global if it contains N checkpoints.

Let the set of all local checkpoints be S, i.e.,

$$S = \bigcup_i S_i.$$

We first tackle the problem of finding a global checkpoint that contains a given set of checkpoints $X \subseteq S$. A relation called *zig-zag precedes*, which is weaker (bigger) than $\rightarrow$, is useful in analysis of such problems.

Definition 29.1 *The relation zig-zag precedes, denoted by $\xrightarrow{z}$, is the smallest relation that satisfies:*
(Z1) $c \rightarrow d$ *implies* $c \xrightarrow{z} d$.
(Z2) $\exists e \in S : (c \rightarrow e) \wedge (pred.e \xrightarrow{z} d)$ *implies* $c \xrightarrow{z} d$.

The following property of the *zig-zag* relation is easy to show
(Z3) $(c \xrightarrow{z} e) \wedge (pred.e \xrightarrow{z} d)$ *implies* $(c \xrightarrow{z} d)$.

On the basis of the above relation, we say that a set of local checkpoints X is z-consistent iff $\forall c, d \in X : c \xcancel{\xrightarrow{z}} d$.

Observe that all initial local checkpoints c satisfy

$$\forall s \in S : s \xcancel{\xrightarrow{z}} c.$$

Similarly, if c is a final local checkpoint, then

$$\forall s \in S : c \xcancel{\xrightarrow{z}} s.$$

Alternatively, a zig-zag path between two checkpoints c and d is defined as follows. There is a zig-zag path from c to d iff
(a) Both c and d are in the same process and $c \prec d$.
(b) There is a sequence of messages $m_1, \ldots, m_t$ such that
    (i) m_1 is sent after the checkpoint c.
    (ii) If m_k is received by process r, then m_{k+1} is sent by process r

in the same or a later checkpoint interval. Note that the message m_{k+1} may be sent before m_k.

(iii) m_t is received before the checkpoint d.

In Figure 29.3, there is a zig-zag path from $c_{1,1}$ to $c_{3,1}$ even though there is no happened before path. This path corresponds to the messages m_3 and m_4 in the diagram. The message m_4 is sent in the same checkpoint interval in which m_3 is received. Also note that there is a zig-zag path from $c_{2,2}$ to itself because of messages m_5 and m_3. Such a path is called a *zig-zag cycle*.

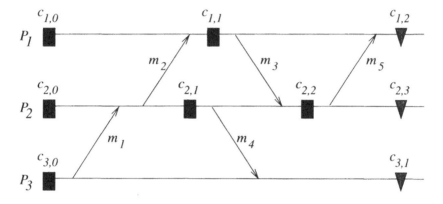

Figure 29.3: Examples of zig-zag paths

We leave it as an exercise for the reader to show that c *zig-zag precedes* d iff there is a zig-zag path from c to d.

Theorem 29.2 (Zig-Zag Theorem) *Given a set of local checkpoints X, there exists a consistent global checkpoint G containing X iff X is z-consistent.*

Proof: ($\Rightarrow$) We prove the contrapositive. Given c and d in X (possibly $c = d$), we show that $c \xrightarrow{z} d$ implies that there is no consistent global state G containing c and d. We prove a slightly stronger claim. We show that $c \xrightarrow{z} d$ implies that there is no consistent global state G containing c or any checkpoint preceding it and d.

The proof is based on induction on k, the minimum number of applications of rule $Z2$ to derive that $c \xrightarrow{z} d$. When $k = 0$, $c \rightarrow d$. Thus c or any checkpoint preceding c and d cannot be part of a consistent state by the definition of consistency. Now consider the case when $c \xrightarrow{z} d$ because $\exists e : (c \rightarrow e) \wedge (pred.e \xrightarrow{z} d)$. We show that any consistent set of states Y containing c and d cannot have any checkpoint from the process containing the checkpoint e. Y cannot contain e or any state following e because $c \to e$ would imply that c happened before that state. Furthermore, Y cannot contain any checkpoint previous to e because $pred.e \overset{z}{\to} d$ and the induction hypothesis ($pred.e \overset{z}{\to} d$ must have fewer applications of $Z2$ rule). Since any consistent set of checkpoints cannot contain any checkpoint from the process $c.p$ we conclude that there is no global checkpoint containing c and d.

($\Leftarrow$) It is sufficient to show that if X is not global then there exists Y strictly containing X that is z-consistent. By repeating the process the set can be made global. Furthermore, the set is always consistent because $x \overset{z}{\not\to} y$ implies $x \not\to y$. For any process, P_i, which does not have a checkpoint in X, we define

$$e = min\{f \in P_i \mid \forall x \in X : f \overset{z}{\not\to} x\}$$

where min is taken over the relation $\prec$. Note that the set over which min is taken is nonempty because the final checkpoint on process P_i cannot zig-zag precede any other checkpoint. We show that $Y = X \cup \{e\}$ is z-consistent. It is sufficient to show that $e \overset{z}{\not\to} e$ and $c \overset{z}{\not\to} e$ for any c in X. If e is an initial local checkpoint, then $e \overset{z}{\not\to} e$ and $c \overset{z}{\not\to} e$ for any c in X clearly hold. Otherwise, $pred.e$ exists. Since e is the minimum event for which $\forall x \in X : e \not\to x$ we get that there exists an event, say $d \in X$, such that $pred.e \overset{z}{\to} d$. Because $e \overset{z}{\to} e$ and $pred.e \overset{z}{\to} d$ imply that $e \overset{z}{\to} d$, we know that $e \overset{z}{\to} e$ is not possible. Similarly, $c \overset{z}{\to} e$ and $pred.e \overset{z}{\to} d$ imply $c \overset{z}{\to} d$, which is false because X is z-consistent.

■

The above result implies that if a checkpoint is part of a zig-zag cycle, then it cannot be part of any global checkpoint. Such checkpoints are called *useless* checkpoints.

29.3   R-Graphs

Given a computation, determining whether there is a zig-zag path from one local checkpoint to another is simplified by using the R-graph of the computation. An R-graph of a computation is constructed as follows. Each checkpoint is a node in the graph. There is an edge between two successive checkpoints between the graph. Furthermore, if $c.v < d.v$, then there is an edge from $succ.c$ to d where $c.v$ denotes the vector clock at checkpoint c. It is sufficient to put at most one edge outgoing from one checkpoint to any other process. For any checkpoint c and any process P_i, different from $c.p$, let d be the minimum state in P_i with $c.v < d.v$, if there is such a state. We put an edge from $succ.c$ to d.

Figure 29.4 shows the R-graph of the computation in Figure 29.3. An R-graph has the following property: There is a zig-zag path from c to d in the computation iff there is a path from $succ.c$ to d in the R-graph.

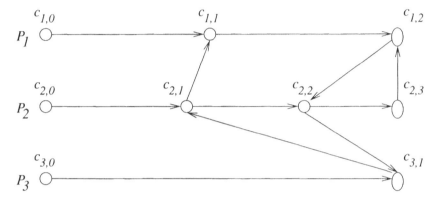

Figure 29.4: Example of an R-graph

29.4 Recoverable Global States: Using Slices

We now show that the analysis of checkpoints can also be carried out using slices. Let $(S, \rightarrow)$ be a partially ordered set with some of the states in S checkpointed. Define a global boolean predicate B to be true on a consistent global state G if all local states in G are checkpointed. Note that B captures precisely those consistent cuts that are recoverable. Because B is a conjunction of local predicates, it is a regular predicate. Therefore, we have

Theorem 29.3 *The set of all consistent recoverable global states form a distributive lattice.*

It follows that the maximum recoverable state and the minimum recoverable state are well-defined.

Furthermore, given a computation, we can compute its slice with respect to B. Since B is regular, the slice contains those cuts and only those cuts that satisfy B. Thus the slice captures all recoverable global states.

Given a set of checkpoints X, and the slice with respect to B, it is easy to determine whether X can be extended to a global checkpoint or not. We only need to verify that X is a consistent set in the slice. Recall that the slice of a conjunctive predicate requires that for every false event e there be an edge from $succ.e$ to e. For example, Figure 29.6 shows the slice of the computation in Figure 29.5. It is easy to see that a zig-zag path in the state diagram from x to y corresponds to a path in the event diagram from $succ(event(x))$ to $event(y)$.

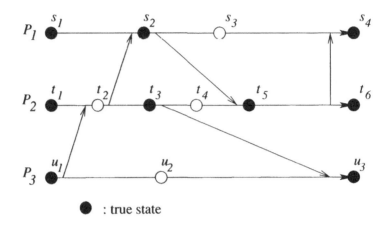

: true state

Figure 29.5: Example of a computation with local predicates

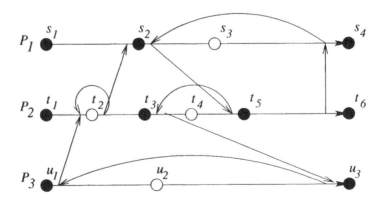

Figure 29.6: Slice of the computation

29.5   Rollback Dependency Trackability (RDT)

If a computation satisfies a condition called rollback dependency trackability, then for every zig-zag path there is also a causal path. In other words, rollback dependency is then trackable by tracking causality. Formally,

Definition 29.4 (RDT) *A computation with checkpoints satisfies rollback dependency trackability if for all checkpoints c, d: $c \to d \equiv c \overset{z}{\to} d$.*

Given a distributed computation as a sequence of vector clocks for each process, how can we check whether it satisfies RDT? We give two approaches below.

The first approach is based on the following result.

Lemma 29.5 *A computation satisfies RDT iff for any checkpoints c, d, a path from $succ.c$ to d implies $c.v < d.v$.*

Proof: A checkpoint computation satisfies RDT
$\equiv \{$ definition of RDT $\}$
  $\forall c, d : c \to d \equiv c \overset{z}{\to} d$
$\equiv \{$ causal path implies zig-zag path $\}$
  $\forall c, d : c \overset{z}{\to} d \Rightarrow c \to d$
$\equiv \{$ definition of R-graph $\}$
  $\forall c, d : succ.c$ has a path to $d \Rightarrow c \to d$
$\equiv \{$ definition of vector clock $\}$
  $\forall c, d : succ.c$ has a path to $d \Rightarrow c.v \to d.v$

■

Thus RDT condition can be checked by creating the R-graph of the computation.

The second method uses the zig-zag theorem. From that theorem it follows that a computation satisfies RDT iff for any two concurrent checkpoints (possibly same) there exists a consistent global state containing them. We use this observation to check for RDT based on weak conjunctive predicate detection. We first derive an equivalent condition for RDT that is easier to evaluate. Given any checkpoint c we denote by $conc(c, j)$ the set of checkpoints concurrent with c on process P_j. Since all the checkpoints within a process are totally ordered the minimum of $conc(c, j)$ is well defined whenever it is nonempty. Now we are ready to present the condition.

Lemma 29.6 *A computation is RDT iff for any checkpoint c and any process P_j*

   (C1) $conc(c, j)$ is nonempty, and
   (C2) $min.conc(c, j) \not\xrightarrow{z} c$.

Proof: ($\Rightarrow$) (C1) holds from the zig-zag consistency theorem and (C2) holds because $\rightarrow$ and $\xrightarrow{z}$ are equivalent for RDT computation.

   ($\Leftarrow$) Let c and d be any two checkpoints. It is sufficient to show that $d \xrightarrow{z} c$ implies $d \rightarrow c$. We show the contrapositive.

$\quad d \not\rightarrow c$

$\Rightarrow \{$ (C1), definition of min $\}$

$\quad min.conc(c, j) \preceq d$

$\Rightarrow \{$ (C2), definition of zig-zag relation$\}$

$\quad d \not\xrightarrow{z} c$.

                                                                  ■

Now we exploit the above lemma as follows. We first focus our attention on any process P_i. For any checkpoint c in that process let $L(c)$ be the least and the greatest consistent global states containing c. If there is no consistent cut containing c, then the computation is not RDT. Otherwise, it is sufficient to verify that $L(c)[j] = min.conc(c, j)$. This verification needs to be done for all checkpoints in c. $L(c)$ can be computed using the WCP algorithm. Because $c_1 \preceq c_2$ implies that $L(c_1) \leq L(c_2)$, by a single application of the WCP algorithm, the condition can be checked for all the checkpoints within a single process.

29.6 Communication-Induced Checkpointing

Because there are no cycles in happened before relation it follows that if a computation satisfies RDT then it does not have any zig-zag cycles. This implies that no checkpoint is useless in a computation that satisfies RDT. On the basis of conditions derived in Section 29.5, we now develop an algorithm for checkpointing to ensure RDT.

    The algorithm takes additional checkpoints before receiving some of the messages to ensure that the overall computation is RDT. The intuition behind the algorithm is that for every zig-zag path there should be a causal path. The difficulty arises when in a checkpoint interval a message is sent before another message is received. For example, in Figure 29.3 m_4 is sent before m_3 is received. When m_3 is received, a zig-zag path is formed from $c_{1,1}$ to $c_{3,1}$. The message m_3 had dependency on $c_{1,1}$, which was not sent as part of m_4. To avoid this situation we use the following rule:

Fixed-Dependency-After-Send (FDAS): A process takes additional checkpoints to guarantee that the transitive dependency vector remains unchanged after any send event (until the next checkpoint).

Thus a process takes a checkpoint before a receive of a message if it has sent a message in that checkpoint interval and the vector clock changes when the message is received.

A computation that uses FDAS is guaranteed to satisfy RDT because any zig-zag path from checkpoints c to d implies existence of a causal path from c to d. There are two main advantages for a computation to be RDT. First, it allows us to calculate efficiently the maximum recoverable global state containing a given set of checkpoints (see Problem 29.3). Second, every zig-zag path implies existence of a happened before path. Since there are no cycles in the happened before relation it follows that the RDT graph does not have any zig-zag cycles. Hence, using FDAS we can guarantee that there are no *useless* checkpoints in the computation.

29.7 Problems

29.1. Show that a computation is RDT iff for any checkpoint c
 (D1) $\forall j : conc(c, j)$ is nonempty, and
 (D2) $\forall j, k : min.conc(c, j) \not\to min.conc(c, k)$.

29.2. Show that the following rules are special cases of FDAS.

 (a) A process takes a checkpoint before every receive of a message.

 (b) A process takes a checkpoint after every send of a message.

 (c) A process takes a checkpoint before any receive after any send of a message.

29.3. Assume that a computation satisfies RDT. Given a set of checkpoints X from this computation show how you will determine whether there exists a global checkpoint containing X. If there exists one, then give an efficient algorithm to determine the least and the greatest global checkpoints containing X.

29.4. Assume that all processes maintain a variant of logical clocks defined as follows: The logical clock is incremented on any checkpointing event. The clock value is piggybacked on every message. On receiving a message, the logical clock is computed as the maximum of the local clock and the value received with the message. Processes are free to take their local checkpoints whenever desired. In addition, a process is forced to take a local checkpoint on receiving a message if

(1) it has sent out a message since its last checkpoint, and

(2) the value of its logical clock will change on receiving the message.

Show that the above algorithm guarantees that there are no *useless* checkpoints. Will this protocol force more checkpoints or fewer checkpoints than the FDAS protocol?

29.8 Bibliographic Remarks

The *zig-zag* relation was first defined by Netzer and Xu [NX95]. The definition we have used in this chapter is different but equivalent to their definition. The notion of the R-graph, RDT computation, and the rule Fixed-Dependency-After-Send was introduced by Wang [Wan97]. The protocol for preventing useless checkpoints in Problem 29.4 is a variant of the algorithm by Helary, Mostefaoui, Netzer, and Raynal [HMNR97].

Chapter 30

Message Logging for Recovery

Death—the last sleep? No, it is the final awakening. — Walter Scott

30.1   Introduction

In *checkpointing*-based methods for recovery, after a process fails, some or all of the processes roll back to their last checkpoints such that the resulting system state is consistent. For large systems, the cost of this synchronization is prohibitive. Furthermore, these protocols may not restore the maximum recoverable state.

If along with checkpoints, messages are logged to the stable storage, then the maximum recoverable state can always be restored. Theoretically, message logging alone is sufficient, but checkpointing speeds up the recovery. Messages can be logged either by the sender or by the receiver. In *pessimistic logging*, messages are logged either as soon as they are received or before the receiver sends a new message. When a process fails, its last checkpoint is restored and the logged messages that were received after the checkpointed state are replayed in the order they were received. Pessimism in logging ensures that no other process needs to be rolled back. Although this recovery mechanism is simple, it reduces the speed of the computation. Therefore, it is not a desirable scheme in an environment where failures are rare and message activity is high.

In *optimistic logging*, it is assumed that failures are rare. A process stores the received messages in volatile memory and logs it to stable storage at infrequent intervals. Since volatile memory is lost in a failure, some of the messages cannot be replayed after the failure. Thus some of the process states are *lost* in the failure. States in other processes that depend on these lost states become *orphan*. A recovery protocol must roll back these orphan states to *non-orphan* states. The following properties are desirable for an optimistic recovery protocol:

- *Asynchronous recovery*: A process should be able to restart immediately after a failure. It should not have to wait for messages from other processes.

- *Minimal amount of rollback*: In some algorithms, processes that causally depend on the lost computation might roll back more than once. In the worst case, they may roll back an exponential number of times. This is called the *domino* effect. A process should roll back at most once in response to each failure.

- *No assumptions about the ordering of messages*: If assumptions are made about the ordering of messages such as FIFO, then we lose the asynchronous character of the computation. A recovery protocol should make as weak assumptions as possible about the ordering of messages.

- *Handle concurrent failures*: It is possible that more than one processes fail concurrently in a distributed computation. A recovery protocol should handle this situation correctly and efficiently.

- *Recover maximum recoverable state*: No computation should be needlessly rolled back.

We present an optimistic recovery protocol that has all the above features. Our protocol is based on two mechanisms—a *fault-tolerant vector clock* and a *version end table* mechanism. The fault-tolerant vector clock is used to maintain causality information despite failures. The version end table mechanism is used to detect orphan states and obsolete messages. In this chapter, we present necessary and sufficient conditions for a message to be obsolete and for a state to be orphan in terms of the version end table data structure.

This chapter is organized as follows. In Section 30.2, we discuss our model of computation. In particular, we extend Lamport's "happened before" relation for ordering events in a failure-free system to a system where processes fail and roll back. Section 30.3 presents an algorithm to maintain fault-tolerant vector clocks. It also shows how to use them for detecting a 'happened before' relation between states that are neither lost nor orphan. Section 30.4 gives an algorithm for version end table maintenance by which orphan states are detected and rolled back. Section 30.5 presents and analyzes our protocol.

The notation used in this chapter is summarized in Figure 30.1.

i, j	Process numbers
k, l, v	Version number of a process
s, u, w, x, y	Local states
$P_{i,k}$	Version k of P_i
$s.ver$	Version number of the state s
t, t', t''	Timestamp
m	Message

Figure 30.1: Notation

30.2   Model

In our model, processes are assumed to be piecewise deterministic. This means that when a process receives a message, it performs some internal computation, sends some messages, and then blocks itself to receive a message. All these actions are completely deterministic, that is, actions performed after a message receive and before blocking for another message receive are completely determined by the contents of the message received and the state of the process at the time of message receive. A nondeterministic action can be modeled by treating it as a message receive.

The receiver of a message depends on the content of the message and therefore on the sender of the message. This dependency relation is transitive. The receiver becomes dependent only after the received message is delivered. From now on, unless otherwise stated, receive of a message will imply its delivery.

A process periodically takes its checkpoint. It also asynchronously logs to the stable storage all messages received in the order they are received. At the time of checkpointing, all unlogged messages are also logged.

A failed process *restarts* by creating a new version of itself. It restores its last checkpoint and replays the logged messages that were received after the restored state. Because some of the messages might not have been logged at the time of the failure, some of the old states, called *lost* states, cannot be recreated. Now, consider the states in other processes that depend on the lost states. These states, called *orphan* states, must be rolled back. Other processes have not failed, so before rolling back, they can log all the unlogged messages and save their states. Thus no information is lost in rollback. Note the distinction between restart and rollback. A failed process restarts, whereas an orphan process rolls back. Some information is lost in restart but not in rollback. A process creates a new version of itself on restart but not on rollback. A message sent by a lost or an orphan state is called an *obsolete* message. A process receiving an *obsolete* message must discard it. Otherwise, the receiver becomes an *orphan*.

In Figure 30.2, a distributed computation is shown. Process P_1 fails at state f_{10}, restores state s_{11}, takes some actions needed for recovery, and restarts from state r_{10}. States s_{12} and f_{10} are lost. Being dependent on s_{12}, state s_{22} of P_2 is an *orphan*. P_2 rolls back, restores state s_{21}, takes actions needed for recovery, and restarts from state r_{20}. Dashed lines show the lost computation. Solid lines show the useful computation at the current point.

30.2.1 Happened Before With Process Failures

Earlier, we saw the definition of the *happened before* relation between states in a failure-free computation. To take failures into account, we extend the *happened before* relation for states when processes may fail. For the states s and u, $s \rightarrow u$ is the transitive closure of the relation defined by the following three conditions:

- $s.p = u.p$ and s was executed immediately before u (for example, $s_{11} \rightarrow s_{12}$ in Figure 30.2), or

- $s.p = u.p$ and s is the state restored after a failure or a rollback and u is the state after $P_{u.p}$ has taken the actions needed for recovery (for example, $s_{11} \rightarrow r_{10}$ in Figure 30.2), or

- s is the sender of a message m and u is the receiver of m (for example, $s_{00} \rightarrow s_{11}$ in Figure 30.2).

In Figure 30.2, $s_{00} \to s_{22}$, but $s_{22} \not\to r_{20}$ (*not happened before*).

The protocol for recovery might cause some recovery messages to be sent among processes. From here onward "application message" will be referred to as "message" and "recovery message" will be referred to as "token." Tokens do not contribute to *happened before*; if s sends a token to u, then because of this token, s does not become dependent on u.

We say that s *knows* about $P_{i,l}$ through token or messages if,

1. $\exists u : u.p = s.p$ and u has received a token about $P_{i,l}$ and u was executed before s, or,

2. $\exists u : u \to s$ and $u \in P_{i,l}$.

30.2.2 Orphan States

A state is called *lost* if it cannot be restored from the stable storage after a process fails. To define a lost state more formally, let $restored(u)$ denote the state that is restored after a failure. Then,

$$lost(s) \equiv \exists u : restored(u) \wedge u.p = s.p \wedge u.ver = s.ver \wedge u \to s$$

Informally, a state s is lost if there exists a state u that was restored after a failure and s was executed after u in that version of the process.

States in other processes that are dependent on a lost state are called *orphan*. Formally,

$$orphan(s) \equiv \exists u : lost(u) \wedge u.p \neq s.p \wedge u \to s$$

A message sent by a lost or an orphan state is not useful in the computation, and it should be discarded. It is called *obsolete*. Formally,

$$obsolete(m) \equiv lost(m.sender) \vee orphan(m.sender)$$

If an obsolete message has been received, then the receiver should roll back.

30.3 Fault-Tolerant Vector Clock

Recall that a vector clock is a vector whose number of components equals the number of processes. Each entry is the timestamp of the

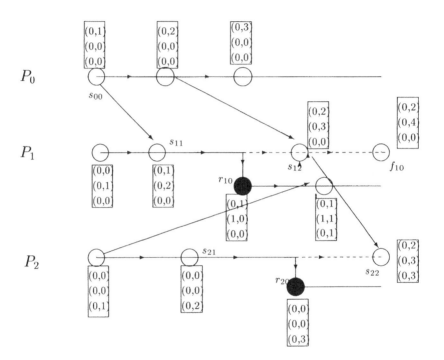

Figure 30.2: A distributed computation

corresponding process. To maintain causality despite failures, we extend each entry by a *version number*. The extended vector clock is referred to as the *Fault-Tolerant Vector Clock* (FTVC). We use the terms "clock" and FTVC interchangeably. Let us consider the FTVC of a process P_i. The version number in the ith entry of its FTVC (its own version number) is equal to the number of times it has rolled back. The version number in the jth entry is equal to the highest version number of P_j on which P_i depends. Let entry e correspond to a tuple(version v, timestamp ts). Then, $e_1 < e_2 \equiv (v_1 < v_2) \vee [(v_1 = v_2) \wedge (ts_1 < ts_2)]$.

A process P_i sends its FTVC along with every outgoing message. After sending a message, P_i increments its timestamp. On receiving a message, it updates its FTVC with the message's FTVC by taking the componentwise maximum of entries and incrementing its own timestamp. To take the maximum, the entry with the higher version number is chosen. If both entries have the same version number, then the entry with the higher timestamp value is chosen.

When a process restarts after a failure or rolls back because of failure of some other process, it increments its version number and sets its timestamp to zero. Note that this operation does not require access to previous timestamps that may be lost on a failure. It only requires its previous version number. As explained in Section 30.5, the version number is not lost in a failure. A formal description of the FTVC algorithm is given in Figure 30.3.

An example of FTVC is shown in Figure 30.2. The FTVC of each state is shown in a rectangular box near it.

30.3.1   Properties of FTVC

FTVC has properties similar to those of a vector clock. It can be used to detect causal dependencies between *useful* states, that is, the states that are neither lost nor orphan.

We define ordering between two FTVC values f and g as follows:

$$f < g \overset{\text{def}}{=} (\forall i : f[i] \leq g[i]) \wedge (\exists j : f[j] < g[j]).$$

Let $s.c$ denote the FTVC of $P_{s.p}$ in state s. The following lemma formalizes the meaning of a version number in an entry of FTVC.

Lemma 30.1 *Let $s \in P_i$. Then,*

1. $s.c[i].ver = |\{u \mid u \in P_i, u$ is a failure event $\}|$

P_i::
type $entry$ = (integer ver, integer ts); // version, timestamp
var $clock$: array $[1..N]$ of entry initially
    $\forall j : clock[j].ver = 0$;
    $\forall j : j \neq i : clock[j].ts = 0; clock[i].ts = 1;$

  To send message :
    send $(data, clock)$;
    $clock[i].ts := clock[i].ts + 1;$

  Upon receive of a message $(data, mclock)$:
    // P_i receives vector clock 'mclock' in incoming message
    $\forall j : clock[j] = max(clock[j], mclock[j]);$
    $clock[i].ts := clock[i].ts + 1;$

  Upon Restart (state s restored) :
    $clock = s.clock;$
    $clock[i].ver := clock[i].ver + 1;$
    $clock[i].ts = 0;$

  Upon Rollback(state s restored) :
    $clock = s.clock;$

Figure 30.3: Formal description of the fault-tolerant vector clock

2. $(j \neq i), s.c[j].ver = max_{u \in P_j}\{u.c[j].ver \mid u \rightarrow s\}$

Proof: On restarting after a failure, a process increments its version number. Furthermore, it increments its version number only then. Hence, the first part follows.

The relation $u \rightarrow s$ implies that there exists a message path between u and s. Now $c[j].ver$ can only be incremented by P_j. Since u is the maximum state in P_j, along each link of the path from u to s, and FTVC$[j].ver$ is updated by taking componentwise maximum,

$$\forall u : (u \rightarrow s) \Rightarrow s.c[j].ver \geq u.c[j].ver.$$

Or,

$$s.c[j].ver \geq max_{u \in P_j}\{u.c[j].ver \mid u \rightarrow s\}.$$

Since $s.c[j].ver$ is updated by taking a maximum only and it is never incremented otherwise, $s.c[j].ver \leq max_{u \in P_j}\{u.c[j].ver \mid u \rightarrow s\}$. Hence, the second part follows.

$\blacksquare$

The next lemma gives a necessary condition for the $\nrightarrow$ relation between two *useful* states.

Lemma 30.2 *Let s and u be useful states (neither lost nor orphan) and $s \neq u$. Then, $s \nrightarrow u \Rightarrow u.c[s.p] < s.c[s.p]$*

Proof: Let $s.p = u.p$. Since s and u are useful states, it follows that $u \rightarrow s$. After send and receive of a message or a rollback, $P_{s.p}$ increments the timestamp of its own component. On restart after a failure, $P_{s.p}$ increments its version number. Since for each state transition along the path from u to s, local FTVC is incremented, $u.c[s.p] < s.c[s.p]$.

Let $s.p \neq u.p$. As $s \nrightarrow u$, $P_{u.p}$ could not have seen $s.c[s.p]$, local clock of $P_{s.p}$. Hence, $u.c[s.p] < s.c[s.p]$.

$\blacksquare$

The next theorem shows that despite failures, FTVC keeps track of causality for the *useful* states.

Theorem 30.3 *Let s and u be useful states in a distributed computation. Then, $s \rightarrow u$ iff $s.c < u.c$.*

Proof: If $s = u$, then the theorem is trivially true. Let $s \to u$. There is a message path from s to u such that none of the intermediate states is either lost or orphan. Because of monotonicity of the FTVC along each link in the path, $\forall j : s.c[j] \leq u.c[j]$. Since $u \not\to s$, from Lemma 30.2, $s.c[u.p] < u.c[u.p]$. The converse follows from Lemma 30.2.

∎

Note that the FTVC does not detect the causality for either lost or orphan states. In Figure 30.2, $r_{20}.c < s_{22}.c$, even though $r_{20} \not\to s_{22}$. To detect causality for lost or orphan states, we use *version end table*, as explained in Section 30.4.

30.4   Version End Table

Orphan states and resulting obsolete messages are detected with the version end table mechanism. This method requires that, after recovering from a failure, a process notify other processes by broadcasting a *token*. The token contains the version number that failed and the timestamp of that version at the point of restoration. We do not make any assumption about the ordering of tokens among themselves or with respect to the messages. We assume that tokens are delivered reliably.

Every process maintains some information, called *vtable*, about other processes in its stable storage. In *vtable* of P_i, there is a record for every *known* version of processes that ended in a failure. If P_i has received a token about $P_{j,k}$, then it keeps that token's timestamp in the corresponding record in *vtable*. The routine $insert(vtable[j], token)$ inserts the *token* in that part of the *vtable* of P_i that keeps track of P_j.

A formal description of the version end table manipulation algorithm is given in Figure 30.4.

30.5   The Protocol

Our protocol for asynchronous recovery is shown in Figure 30.5. We describe the actions taken by a process, say P_i, on the occurrence of different events. We assume that each action taken by a process is atomic. This means that any failure during the execution of any action may be viewed as a failure before or after the execution of the entire action.

P_i::
  var
      $vtable$: array$[1..N]$ of set of entry initially empty;
      $token$: entry;
    Receive_token (v_1, t_1) from P_j :
      $insert(vtable[j], (v_1, t_1))$;
    Upon Restart
      $insert(vtable[i], (v, clock[i].ts))$;

Figure 30.4: A formal description of the version end table mechanism

Message Receive

On receiving a message, P_i first checks whether the message is obsolete. This is done as follows. Let e_j refer to the jth entry in the message's FTVC. Recall that each entry is of the form (v, t) where v is the version number and t is the timestamp. If there exists an entry e_j, such that e_j is (v, t) and (v, t') belongs to vtable$[j]$ of P_i and $t > t'$, then the message is obsolete. This is proved later.

If the message is obsolete, then it is discarded. Otherwise, P_i checks whether the message is deliverable. The message is not deliverable if its FTVC contains a version number k for any process P_j, such that P_i has not received all the tokens from P_j with the version number l less than k. In this case, the delivery of the message is postponed. Since we assume failures to be rare, this should not affect the speed of the computation.

If the message is delivered, then the vector clock and the version end table are updated. P_i updates its FTVC with the message's FTVC as explained in Section 30.3. The message and its FTVC are logged in the volatile storage. Asynchronously, the volatile log is flushed to the stable storage. The version end table is updated as explained in Section 30.4.

On Restart after a Failure

After a failure, P_i restores its last checkpoint from the stable storage (including the version end table). Then it replays all the logged messages received after the restored state, in the receipt order. To inform

P_i::

Receive_message (data, mclock) :
    // Check whether message is obsolete
    $\forall j$:**if** $((mclock[j].ver, t) \in vtable[j])$ **and** $(t < mclock[j].ts)$ **then**
        discard message ;
    if $\exists j, l$ s.t. $l < mclock[j].ver \wedge P_i$ has no token about $P_{j,l}$ **then**
        postpone the delivery of the message until that token arrives;

Restart (after failure) :
    restore last checkpoint;
    replay all the logged messages that follow the restored state;
    $insert(vtable[i], (v, clock[i].ts))$;
    $broadcast\_token(clock[i])$;

Receive_token (v,t) from P_j :
    synchronously log the token to the stable storage;
    if $((mes, v, t') \in vtable[j])$ **then**
        if $(t < t')$ **then** Rollback;
    // Regardless of rollback, following actions are taken
    update $vtable$;
    deliver messages that were held for this token;

Rollback (due to token (v, t) from P_j) :
    log all the unlogged messages to the stable storage;
    restore the maximum checkpoint such that
        either no record $(v, t') \in vtable[j]$ or $(t' < t)$ ..(I)
    discard the checkpoints that follow;
    replay the messages logged after this checkpoint
        until condition (I) holds;
    discard the logged messages that follow;

Figure 30.5: An optimistic protocol for asynchronous recovery

other processes about its failure, it broadcasts a token containing its current version number and timestamp. After that, it increments its own version number and resets its own timestamp to zero. Finally, it updates its version end table, takes a new checkpoint, and starts computing in a normal fashion. The new checkpoint is needed to avoid the loss of the current version number in another failure. Note that the recovery is unaffected by a failure during this checkpointing. The entire event must appear atomic despite a failure. If the failure occurs before the new checkpoint is finished, then it should appear that the restart never happened and the restart event can be executed again.

On Receiving a Token

We require all tokens to be logged synchronously, that is, the process is not allowed to compute further until the information about the token is in stable storage. This prevents the process from losing the information about the token if it fails after acting on it. Since we expect the number of failures to be small, this would incur only a small overhead.

The token enables a process to discover whether it has become an orphan. To check whether it has become an orphan it proceeds as follows. Assume that it received the token (v, t) from P_j. It checks whether its vector clock indicates that it depends on a state (v, t') such that $t < t'$. If so, then P_i is an orphan and it needs to roll back.

Regardless of the rollback, P_i enters the record (v, t) in version end table$[j]$. Finally, messages that were held for this token are delivered.

On Rollback

On a rollback due to token (v, t) from P_j, P_i first logs all the unlogged messages to the stable storage. Then it restores the maximum checkpoint s such that s does not depend on any state on P_j with version number v and timestamp greater than t. Then logged messages that were received after s are replayed as long as messages are not obsolete. It discards the checkpoints and logged messages that follow this state. Now the FTVC is updated by incrementing its timestamp. Note that it does not increment its version number. P_i then restarts computing as normal.

Remark

The following issues are relevant to all the optimistic protocols.

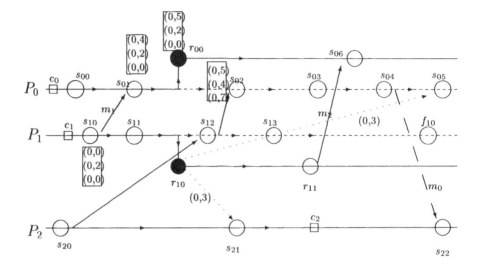

Figure 30.6: An example of recovery

1. On a failure, a process loses information about the messages that it received but did not log before the failure. These messages are lost forever, unless P_i also broadcasts its clock with the token and other processes resend all the messages that they sent to P_i (only those messages need to be retransmitted whose send states were concurrent with the token's state). This means that processes have to keep a send version end table. Observe that no retransmission of messages is required during rollback of a process that has not failed but has become orphan because of a failure of some other process. Before rolling back, it can log all the messages, and so no message is lost.

2. Some form of garbage collection is also required for reclaiming space. Before committing an output to the environment, a process must make sure that it will never roll back the current state or lose it in a failure.

30.5.1 An Example

In Figure 30.6, c_i is the checkpoint of process P_i. The value of the FTVC and the version end table is also shown for some of the states. The FTVC is shown in a box. The row i of the FTVC and the version end table corresponds to P_i. Some of the state transitions are not shown to avoid cluttering of the figure. The process P_1 fails in state f_{10}. It restores the checkpoint c_1 and replays the logged messages. Then it sends the token $(0, 3)$ (shown by dotted arrow) to other processes. It restarts in state r_{10}. P_0 receives the message m_2 in state s_{03}. m_2's FTVC contains an entry for version 1 of P_1. Because P_0's version end table does not contain the token about version 0 of P_1, it postpones the delivery of m_2. It receives the token in state s_{05}. It detects that it is an orphan and rolls back. It restores the checkpoint c_0, and replays the logged messages until the message that made it an orphan. It restarts in state r_{00}. Since message m_2 was held for this token, it is delivered now. On receiving message m_0, P_2 detects that it is obsolete and discards it.

Note that if state s_{03} of P_0 had delivered the message m_2, then message m_0's FTVC would have contained entry $(1, 1)$ for P_1. Then P_2 would not have been able to detect that m_0 is obsolete. So P_2 would have delivered m_0, resulting in an orphan state. Since P_2 had already received the token for version 0 of P_1, P_2 would never have rolled back the orphan state.

30.5.2   Proof of Correctness

The following lemma gives a necessary and sufficient condition for orphan detection. This condition is used in the *Receive_token* part of the algorithm.

Lemma 30.4 $orphan(s) \equiv \exists w : restored(w) \wedge (w.clock = (v, t) \wedge \exists (mes, v, t') \in s.vtable[w.p]$ such that $t < t'$.
Proof: $(\Leftarrow)$ Since $(mes, v, t') \in s.vtable[w.p]$, a message must have been received with (v, t') as clock entry for the process $P_{w.p}$. From properties of the FTVC, this implies that there exists a state u in $P_{w.p}$ with that vector clock that happened before s. Formally,

$$\exists u : u.p = w.p \wedge u.ver = w.ver \wedge u.clock[u.p] = (v, t) \wedge u \to s$$

Since $w.clock[w.p] = (v, t) \wedge (t < t')$, this implies that

$$\exists u : restored(w) \wedge u.p = w.p \wedge u.ver = w.ver \wedge w \to u \wedge u \to s$$

From the definition of $lost(u)$, this is equivalent to $\exists u : lost(u) \wedge u \to s$. Thus $orphan(s)$ is true.
$(\Rightarrow)$
By definition, $orphan(s) \equiv \exists y : lost(y) \wedge y \to s$. Among all such y's, let u be a maximum state for a given version of a given process.

Thus there exists u such that $lost(u) \wedge u \rightarrow s$, and
$\forall x : (x.p = u.p \wedge x.ver = u.ver \wedge x \neq u \wedge lost(x) \wedge x \rightarrow s) \Rightarrow x \rightarrow u$
$\dots (1)$

Let $u.clock[u.p] = (v, t)$. On any path from u to s, $u.p$th entry (v, t) of FTVC could not have been overwritten. From (1), it could not be overwritten by an entry from version v. For a higher version v', overwriting process would have waited for a token about version v and then that process would have rolled back.

■

The next lemma gives a sufficient condition to detect an obsolete message. It also states the circumstances in which this condition is necessary.

Lemma 30.5 *For any message m received in state s, if there exists an entry (v, t) in version end table of s for process P_j and $m.clock[j] = (v, t')$ such that $(t < t')$, then m is obsolete. Formally,*
$[(v, t) \in s.vtable[j] \wedge m.clock[j] = (v, t') \wedge t < t'] \Rightarrow obsolete(m).$
This condition is also necessary when there are no undelivered tokens.
Proof: Since $(v, t) \in s.vtable[j]$, $\exists w : w.p = j \wedge restored(w) \wedge w.clock[j] = (v, t)$. From the FTVC algorithm and $m.clock[j] = (v, t')$, we get that $\exists u \in P_j : u.clock[j] = (v, t')$. Since $(t < t')$ and a token (v, t) exists for P_j, it follows that u is a lost state.

Let x be the state from which the message m is sent, that is, $x = m.sender$. From $u.clock[j] = (v, t')$, $u \rightarrow x \vee u = x$. This implies that $lost(x) \vee orphan(x)$, that is, $obsolete(m)$.

Conversely, $obsolete(m)$ implies $lost(m.sender) \vee orphan(m.sender)$. This implies that $\exists u : restored(u) \wedge u \rightarrow m.sender$. Let $u.clock[u.p] = (v, t)$. $(u \rightarrow m.sender) \Rightarrow \{(m.sender).clock[u.p] = (v, t') \wedge (t' > t)\}$. This is because on the path from u to $m.sender$, (v, t') could not have been overwritten by an entry from higher version v' of $P_{u.p}$. Before overwriting, a process would have waited for a token about $P_{u.p,v}$ and then it would have rolled back. All tokens have been delivered, so trivially, $\exists s : (v, t) \in s.vtable[w.p]$.

■

The above test is optimal in the sense that, except for the conditions stated, a process $P_{s.p}$ will not be able to detect an obsolete message. It will accept it and as per the next lemma will become an orphan.

Lemma 30.6 *If a message m is obsolete and s accepts m then s is an orphan state.*

Proof: The message m is obsolete implies that $lost(m.sender)$ or $orphan(m.sender)$. Thus either $lost(m.sender)$ or there exists u such that $lost(u) \wedge u \rightarrow m.sender$. From, $m.sender \rightarrow s$, it follows that $orphan(s)$.

■

The next theorem shows that our protocol is correct.

Theorem 30.7 *This protocol correctly implements recovery, that is, either a process discards an obsolete message or the receiver of an obsolete message eventually rolls back to a nonorphan state.*

Proof: Let a failure of the version v of P_i cause a message m to become obsolete. If the receiver P_j has received a token about $P_{i,v}$ before receiving m, then by Lemma 30.5, it will recognize that m is obsolete and will discard m. Otherwise, it will accept m and by Lemma 30.6, will become an orphan. But P_j will eventually receive the token about $P_{i,v}$. Then by Lemma 30.4, it will recognize that it is orphan and will roll back to a nonorphan state.

■

30.5.3 Properties of the Protocol

Theorem 30.8 *This protocol has the following properties: asynchronous recovery, minimal rollback, handling concurrent failures, recovering maximum recoverable state.*

Proof:

Asynchronous Recovery: After a failure, a process restores itself and starts computing. It broadcasts a token about its failure, but it does not require any response.

Minimal Rollback: In response to the failure of a given version of a given process, other processes roll back at most once. This rollback occurs on receiving the corresponding token.

Handling Concurrent Failures: In response to multiple failures, a process rolls back in the order in which it receives information about different failures. Concurrent failures have the same effect as that of multiple nonconcurrent failures.

Recovering Maximum Recoverable State: Only orphan states are rolled back.

◾

30.5.4 Overhead Analysis

Except for application messages, the protocol causes no extra messages to be sent during failure-free run. It tags a FTVC to every application message. Let the maximum number of failures of any process be f. The protocol adds $\log f$ bits to each timestamp in the vector clock. Since we expect the number of failures to be small, $\log f$ should be small.

A token is broadcast only when a process fails. The size of a token is equal to just one entry of the vector clock.

Let the number of processes in the system be n. There are at most f versions of a process, and there is one entry for each version of a process in the version end table.

30.6 Problems

30.1. In many applications, the distributed program may output to the external environment such that the output message cannot be revoked (or the environment cannot be rolled back). This is called the *output commit* problem. What changes will you make to the algorithm to take care of such messages?

30.2. Give a scheme for garbage collection of obsolete local checkpoints and message logs.

30.3. A K-optimistic logging system is an optimistic recovery algorithm parameterized by K. Given any message m in a K-optimistic logging system, K is the maximum number of processes whose failures can revoke m. Give a distributed algorithm that implements a K-optimistic system.

*30.4. Consider implementation of an optimistic recovery algorithm for a *multithreaded* distributed program. Assume that all threads of a process fail together, but each thread can be rolled back individually. Assume that there are n processes each with t threads. Give an algorithm that uses timestamps of size $O(n)$ rather than $O(nt)$ but still guarantees that no state is needlessly rolled back.

30.7 Bibliographic Remarks

Strom and Yemini [SY85] initiated the area of optimistic message logging. Their scheme, however, suffers from the *exponential rollback* problem, where a single failure of a process can roll back another process an exponential number of times. Johnson and Zwaenepoel [JZ90] present a centralized protocol to optimistically recover the maximum recoverable state. Other distributed protocols for optimistic recovery can be found in [PK93, SJT95, SW89]. Peterson and Kearns [PK93] give a synchronous protocol based on the vector clock. Their protocol cannot handle multiple failures. Smith, Johnson, and Tygar [SJT95] present the first completely asynchronous, optimistic protocol. The main drawback of their algorithm is the size of its vector clock, resulting in high overhead during failure-free operations. The algorithm discussed in this chapter is taken from [DG96]. Problem 30.3 is due to Wang, Damani, and Garg [WDG97] and Problem 30.4 is due to Damani, Tarafdar, and Garg [DTG99].

Appendix A

Partial Order

Good order is the foundation of all good things. — Reflections on the Revolution in France, Edmund Burke.

A.1 Introduction

It is essential to understand the theory of partially ordered sets to study distributed systems. In this section, we give a concise introduction to this theory.

A partial order is simply a relation with certain properties. A *relation R* over any set X is a subset of $X \times X$. For example, let

$$X = \{a, b, c\}.$$

Then, one possible relation is

$$R = \{(a, c), (a, a), (b, c), (c, a)\}.$$

It is sometimes useful to visualize a relation as a graph on the vertex set X such that there is a directed edge from x to y iff $(x, y) \in R$. The graph corresponding to the relation R in the previous example is shown in Figure A.1

A relation is *reflexive* if for each $x \in X$, $(x, x) \in R$. In terms of a graph, this means that there is a self-loop on each node. If X is the set of natural numbers, then "x divides y" is a reflexive relation. R is *irreflexive* if for each $x \in X$, $(x, x) \notin R$. In terms of a graph, this means that there are no self-loops. An example on the set of natural

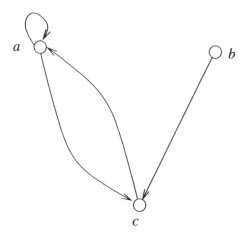

Figure A.1: The graph of a relation

numbers is the relation "x less than y." Note that a relation may be neither reflexive nor irreflexive.

A relation R is *symmetric* if $(x, y) \in R$ implies $(y, x) \in R$ for all $x, y \in X$. An example of a symmetric relation on the set of natural number is

$$R = \{(x, y) \mid x \bmod 5 = y \bmod 5\}.$$

A symmetric relation can be represented using an undirected graph. R is *antisymmetric* if for all x and y, $(x, y) \in R$ and $(y, x) \in R$ implies $x = y$. For example, the relation *less than or equal to* defined on the set of natural numbers is anti-symmetric. A relation R is *asymmetric* if for any x, y, $(x, y) \in R$ implies $(y, x) \notin R$. The relation *less than* is asymmetric. Note that an asymmetric relation is always irreflexive. A relation R is *transitive* if $(x, y) \in R$ and $(y, z) \in R$ implies $(x, z) \in R$ for all x, y and z. The relations *less than* and *equal to* on natural numbers are transitive.

A relation R is an *equivalence* relation if it is reflexive, symmetric, and transitive. When R is an equivalence relation, we use $x \cong y(R)$ (or simply $x \cong y$ when R is clear from the context) to denote that $(x, y) \in R$. Furthermore, for each $x \in X$, we use $[x](R)$, called the *equivalence class of x*, to denote the set of all $y \in X$ such that $y \cong x(R)$. It can be seen that the set of all such equivalence classes forms a *partition* of X. We use $|R|$, called the *index* of equivalence relation R, to denote the cardinality of equivalence classes under R. The relation on $\mathcal{N}$ defined as

$$\forall x, y \in \mathcal{N} : (x, y) \in R \Leftrightarrow [x \bmod 5 = y \bmod 5]$$

is an example of an equivalence relation. It partitions the set of natural numbers into five equivalence classes.

Given any binary relation R on a set X, we define its irreflexive transitive closure, denoted by R^+, as follows. For all $x, y \in X : (x, y) \in R^+$ iff there exists a sequence $x_0, x_1, ..., x_j, j \geq 1$ such that

$$\forall i : 0 \leq i < j : (x_i, x_{i+1}) \in R.$$

Thus $(x, y) \in R^+$ iff there is a nonempty path from x to y in the graph of the relation R. We define the reflexive transitive closure, denoted by R^*, as

$$R^* = R^+ \cup \{(x, x) \mid x \in X\}$$

. Thus $(x, y) \in R^*$ iff y is reachable from x by taking zero or more edges in the graph of the relation R.

A.2 Definition of Partial Orders

A relation R is a *reflexive partial order* if it is reflexive, antisymmetric, and transitive. The *divides* relation on the set of natural numbers is a reflexive partial order. A relation R is an *irreflexive partial order* if it is irreflexive and transitive. The *less than* relation on the set of natural numbers is an irreflexive partial order. When R is a reflexive partial order we use $x \leq y(R)$ (or simply $x \leq y$ when R is clear from the context) to denote that $(x, y) \in R$. A reflexive partially ordered set, *poset* for short, is denoted by $(X, \leq)$. When R is an irreflexive partial order we use $x < y(R)$ (or simply $x < y$ when R is clear from the context) to denote that $(x, y) \in R$. The set X together with the partial order is denoted by $(X, <)$. In this book, we use a partial order (poset) to mean an irreflexive partial order (poset) unless otherwise stated.

A relation is a *total order* if R is a partial order and for all distinct $x, y \in X$, either $(x, y) \in R$ or $(y, x) \in R$. The natural order on the set of integers is a total order, but the "divides" is only a partial order.

Finite posets are often depicted graphically using a *Hasse diagram*. To define Hasse diagrams, we first define a relation *covers* as follows. For any two elements x, y, y covers x if $x < y$ and $\forall z \in X : x \leq z < y$ implies $z = x$. In other words, there should not be any element z with

$x < z < y$. A Hasse diagram of a poset is a graph with the property that there is an edge from x to y iff y covers x. Furthermore, when drawing the figure in an Euclidean plane, x is drawn lower than y when y covers x. For example, consider the following poset $(X, \leq)$.

$$X \overset{\text{def}}{=} \{p, q, r, s\}; \quad \leq \overset{\text{def}}{=} \{(p, q), (q, r), (p, r), (p, s)\}.$$

Its Hasse diagram is shown in Figure A.2.

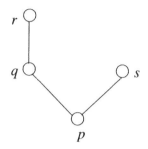

Figure A.2: Hasse diagram

Let $x, y \in X$ with $x \neq y$. If either $x < y$ or $y < x$, we say x and y are *comparable*. On the other hand, if neither $x < y$ nor $x > y$, then we say x and y are incomparable, and write $x\|y$. A poset $(X, <)$ is called a *chain* if every distinct pair of points from X is comparable. Similarly, we call a poset an *antichain* if every distinct pair of points from X is incomparable.

A chain C of a poset $(X, <)$ is a *maximum chain* if no other chain contains more points than C. We use a similar definition for *maximum antichain*. The *height* of the poset is the number of points in the maximum chain, and the *width* of the poset is the number of points in a maximum antichain.

A.3   Lattices

We now define two operators on subsets of the set $\check{X}$—*infimum* (or *inf*) and *supremum* (or *sup*). Let $Y \subseteq X$, where $(X, \leq)$ is a poset. For any $m \in X$, we say that $m = inf\, Y$ iff

1. $\forall y \in Y : m \leq y$.

2. $\forall m' \in X : (\forall y \in Y : m' \leq y) \Rightarrow m' \leq m$.

The condition (1) says that m is a lower bound of the set Y. The condition (2) says that if m' is another lower bound of Y, then it is less than m. For this reason, m is also called the *greatest lower bound* (*glb*) of the set Y. It is easy to check that the infimum of Y is unique whenever it exists. Observe that m is not required to be an element of Y.

The definition of *sup* is similar. We say that $s = sup\,Y$ iff

1. $\forall y \in Y : y \leq s$

2. $\forall s' \in X : (\forall y \in Y : y \leq s') \Rightarrow s \leq s'$

Again, s is also called the *least upper bound* (*lub*) of the set Y. We denote the *glb* of $\{a, b\}$ by $a \sqcap b$, and *lub* of $\{a, b\}$ by $a \sqcup b$. In the set of natural numbers ordered by the *divides* relation, the *glb* corresponds to finding the greatest common divisor (gcd) and the *lub* corresponds to finding the least common multiple of two natural numbers. The greatest lower bound or the least upper bound may not always exist. In Figure A.3, the set $\{e, f\}$ does not have any upper bound. In the third poset in Figure A.4, the set $\{b, c\}$ does not have any least upper bound (although both d and e are upper bounds).

$$X = \{a, b, c, d, e, f\}$$

$$R = \left\{ \begin{array}{l} (a, b), (a, c), (b, d), \\ (c, f), (c, e), (d, e) \\ (a, d), (a, e), (a, f), \\ (b, e) \end{array} \right\}$$

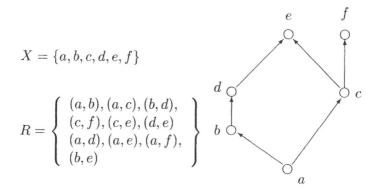

Figure A.3: A poset that is not a lattice.

We say that a poset $(X, \leq)$ is a *lattice* iff $\forall x, y \in X : x \sqcup y$ and $x \sqcap y$ exist. The first two posets in Figure A.4 are lattices, whereas the third one is not.

If $\forall x, y \in X : x \sqcup y$ exists, then we call it a *sup semilattice*. If $\forall x, y \in X : x \sqcap y$ exists then we call it an *inf semilattice*. A lattice is

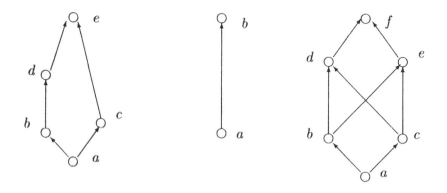

Figure A.4: Only the first two posets are lattices.

distributive if it satisfies the distributive law,

$$\forall x, y, z \in X : x \sqcap (y \sqcup z) = (x \sqcap y) \sqcup (x \sqcap z).$$

It is easy to verify that the above condition is equivalent to

$$\forall x, y, z \in X : x \sqcup (y \sqcap z) = (x \sqcup y) \sqcap (x \sqcup z).$$

Thus in a distributive lattice, $\sqcup$ and $\sqcap$ operators distribute over each other.

Any power-set lattice is distributive. The lattice of natural numbers with $\leq$ defined as the relation *divides* is also distributive. Some examples of nondistributive lattices (see Figure A.5) are:

1. *Diamond*

$$X = \{0, p, q, r, 1\}$$

$$\leq = \{(0, p), (0, q), (0, r), (p, 1), (q, 1), (r, 1), (0, 1)\}.$$

2. *Pentagon*

$$X = \{0, p, q, r, 1\},$$

$$\leq = \{(0, p), (0, q), (0, r), (p, 1), (q, 1), (r, 1), (0, 1), (p, q)\}.$$

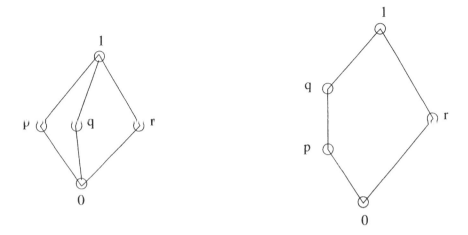

Figure A.5: Examples of nondistributive lattices

A.4   Properties of Functions on Posets

We now discuss properties of functions on posets. Let $(X, \prec_X)$ and $(Y, \prec_Y)$ be two posets.

Definition A.1 *A function $f : X \to Y$ is called monotone iff*

$$\forall x_1, x_2 \in X : x_1 \prec_X x_2 \Rightarrow f(x_1) \prec_Y f(x_2)$$

In other words, monotone functions preserve the ordering. An example of a monotone function on the set of integers is addition by any constant. This is because

$$x_1 \leq x_2 \Rightarrow x_1 + c \leq x_2 + c$$

for any integers x_1, x_2 and c.

A.5   Down-Sets and Up-Sets

Let $(X, <)$ be any poset. We call a subset $Y \subseteq X$ a down-set if

$$z \in Y \wedge y < z \Rightarrow y \in Y.$$

Similarly, we call $Y \subseteq X$ an up-set if

$$y \in Y \wedge y < z \Rightarrow z \in Y.$$

In the discussion of distributed systems, down-sets play an important role. We use $\mathcal{O}(X)$ to denote the set of all down-sets of X.

We now give a simple but important lemma.

Lemma A.2 *Let $(X, <)$ be any poset. Then, $(\mathcal{O}(X), \subseteq)$ is a distributive lattice.*

Proof: We need to show that if Y and Z are down-sets, then $Y \cup Z$ and $Y \cap Z$ are also down-sets. To prove that $Y \cup Z$ is a down-set, let $z \in Y \cup Z$ and $y < z$. There are two cases : $z \in Y$ or $z \in Z$. If $z \in Y$, then because Y is a down-set, $y \in Y$. Therefore, $y \in Y \cup Z$. The other case also leads to the same conclusion. Therefore, $Y \cup Z$ is a down-set.

We leave it for the reader to show that $Y \cap Z$ is also a down set. Distributivity of $(\mathcal{O}(X), \subseteq)$ follows from distributivity of $\cap$ over $\cup$.

■

A.6 Problems

A.1. Show that if P and Q are posets defined on set X, then so is $P \cap Q$.

A.2. Show that for all posets P on set X, there exists a total order Q on X such that $P \subseteq Q$.

A.3. Show that if C_1 and C_2 are down-sets for any poset $(E, <)$, then so is $C_1 \cap C_2$.

A.4. Consider the poset defined by the *divides* relations on the set of positive integers. Show that this poset is a lattice.

A.5. The *transitive closure* of a relation R on a finite set can also be defined as the smallest transitive relation on S that contains R. Show that the transitive closure is uniquely defined. We use "smaller" in the sense that R_1 is smaller than R_2 if $|R_1| < |R_2|$.

A.7 Bibliographic Remarks

The reader should consult Davey and Priestley [DP90] for a more comprehensive introduction to theory of posets and lattices.

Bibliography

[AA91]   D. Agrawal and A. E. Abbadi. An efficient and fault-tolerant solution for distributed mutual exclusion. *ACM Transactions on Computer Systems*, 9(1):1–20, February 1991.

[AFL83]   E. Arjomandi, M. J. Fischer, and N. A. Lynch. Efficiency of synchronous versus asynchronous distributed systems. *Journal of the ACM*, 30(3):449–456, July 1983.

[Ahu93]   M. Ahuja. An implementation of f-channels. *IEEE Transactions on Parallel and Distributed Systems*, 4(6):658–667, June 1993.

[Ang80]   D. Angluin. Local and global properties in networks of processors. In *Proceedings of the 12th ACM Symposium on Theory of Computing*, pages 82 – 93, 1980.

[AS90]   B. Awerbuch and M. Saks. A dining philosophers algorithm with polynomial response time. In IEEE, editor, *Proceedings: 31st Annual Symposium on Foundations of Computer Science: October 22–24, 1990, St. Louis, MO*, volume 1, pages 65–74, 1109 Spring Street, Suite 300, Silver Spring, MD 20910, USA, 1990. IEEE Computer Society Press.

[AW94]   H. Attiya and J. Welch. Sequential consistency versus linearizability. *ACM Transactions on Computer Systems*, 12(2):91–122, May 1994.

[AW98]   H. Attiya and J. Welch. *Distributed Computing— Fundamentals, Simulations and Advanced Topics*. McGraw Hill, Berkshire, SL6 2QL, England, 1998.

403

[Awe85]   B. Awerbuch. Complexity of network synchronization. *Journal of the ACM*, 32(4):804–823, October 1985.

[Bar96]   V. Barbosa. *An Introduction to Distributed Algorithms.* The MIT Press, Cambridge, MA, 1996.

[BG89]   V. Barbosa and E. Gafni. Concurrency in heavily loaded neighborhood-constrained systems. *ACM Transactions on Programming Languages and Systems*, 11(4):562–584, October 1989.

[BG93]   E. Borowsky and E. Gafni. Generalized FLP impossibility result for *t*-resilient asynchronous computations (extended abstract). In *Proceedings of the Twenty-Fifth Annual ACM Symposium on the Theory of Computing*, pages 91–100, San Diego, CA, 16–18 May 1993.

[BJ87]   K. P. Birman and T. A. Joseph. Reliable communication in the presence of failures. *ACM Transactions on Computer Systems*, 5(1):47–76, 1987.

[BKR87]   J. C. Bermond, J. C. Konig, and M. Raynal. General and efficient decentralized consensus protocols. In *2nd International Workshop on Distributed Algorithms*, pages 41–56. Springer-Verlag, Lecture Notes in Computer Science 312, 1987.

[Bou87]   L. Bouge. Repeated snapshots in distributed systems with synchronous communication and their implementation in CSP. *Theoretical Computer Science*, 49:145–169, 1987.

[BR95]   Ö. Babaoğlu and M. Raynal. Specification and verification of dynamic properties in distributed computations. *Journal of Parallel and Distributed Computing*, 28:173–185, 1995.

[Bur80]   J. Burns. A formal model for message passing systems. Technical Report TR–91, Indiana University, 1980. Department of Computer Science.

[CB91]   B. Charron-Bost. Concerning the size of logical clocks in distributed systems. *Information Processing Letters*, 39:11–16, July 1991.

[CBDGF95] B. Charron-Bost, C. Delporte-Gallet, and H. Fauconnier. Local and temporal predicates in distributed systems. *ACM Transactions on Programming Languages and Systems*, 17(1):157–179, January 1995.

[CDK94] G. Couloris, J. Dollimore, and T. Kindberg. *Distributed Systems: Concepts and Design*. Addison Wesley, Workingham, England, 1994.

[CG95] C. Chase and V. K. Garg. On techniques and their limitations for the global predicate detection problem. In *Proc. of the Workshop on Distributed Algorithms*, pages 303 – 317, Le Mont-Saint-Michel, France, September 1995.

[CG98] C. Chase and V. K. Garg. Efficient detection of global predicates in a distributed system. *Distributed Computing*, 11(4), 1998.

[Cha93] S. Chaudhuri. More *choices* allow more *faults*: Set consensus problems in totally asynchronous systems. *Information and Computation*, 105(1):132–158, July 1993.

[Che80] B. F. Chellas. *Modal Logic, an Introduction*. Cambridge University Press, Cambridge, UK, 1980.

[CJ97] R. Chow and T. Johnson. *Distributed Operating Systems and Algorithms*. Addison-Wesley Longman, Reading, MA, 1997.

[CK94] H. Chiou and W. Korfhage. Efficient global event predicate detection. In *14th Intl. Conference on Distributed Computing Systems*, Poznan, Poland, June 1994.

[CL85] K. M. Chandy and L. Lamport. Distributed snapshots: Determining global states of distributed systems. *ACM Transactions on Computer Systems*, 3(1):63–75, February 1985.

[CM84] K. M. Chandy and J. Misra. The drinking philosopher's problem. *ACM Transactions on Programming Languages and Systems*, 6(4):632–646, October 1984.

[CM85]   K. M. Chandy and J. Misra. How processes learn. In Ray Strong, editor, *Proceedings of the 4th Annual ACM Symposium on Principles of Distributed Computing*, pages 204–214, Minaki, ON, Canada, August 1985. ACM Press.

[CM89]   K. M. Chandy and J. Misra. *Parallel Program Design: A Foundation.* Addison-Wesley, Reading, MA, 1989.

[CM91]   R. Cooper and K. Marzullo. Consistent detection of global predicates. In *Proc. of the Workshop on Parallel and Distributed Debugging*, pages 163–173, Santa Cruz, CA, May 1991. ACM/ONR.

[CR79]   E. J. H. Chang and R. Roberts. An improved algorithm for decentralized extrema-finding in circular configurations of processes. *Communications of the ACM*, 22(5):281–283, 1979.

[CS92]   M. Choy and A. K. Singh. Efficient fault tolerant algorithms for resource allocation in distributed systems. In N. Alon, editor, *Proceedings of the 24th Annual ACM Symposium on the Theory of Computing*, pages 593–602, Victoria, BC, Canada, May 1992. ACM Press.

[CT96]   T. Deepak Chandra and S. Toueg. Unreliable failure detectors for reliable distributed systems. *JACM*, 43(2):225–267, March 1996.

[DG96]   O. P. Damani and V. K. Garg. How to recover efficiently and asynchronously when optimism fails. In *ICDCS '96; Proceedings of the 16th International Conference on Distributed Computing Systems; Hong Kong*, pages 108–115. IEEE, May 1996.

[Dij74]   E. W. Dijkstra. Self-stabilizing systems in spite of distributed control. *Communications of the ACM*, 17:643–644, 1974.

[Dij85]   E. W. Dijkstra. The distributed snapshot of K.M. Chandy and L. Lamport. In M. Broy, editor, *Control Flow and Data Flow: Concepts of Distributed Programming*, volume F14. NATO ASI Series, Springer-Verlag, New York, NY, 1985.

[DKR82]   D. Dolev, M. Klawe, and M. Rodeh. An $o(n \log n)$ uni-directional distributed algorithm for extrema finding in a circle. *Journal of Algorithms, 3:245–260*, 1982.

[DLP+86a] D. Dolev, N. A. Lynch, S. S. Pinter, E. W. Stark, and W. E. Weihl. Reaching approximate agreement in the presence of faults. *JACM*, 33(3):499–516, July 1986.

[DLP+86b] D. Dolev, N. A. Lynch, S. S. Pinter, E. W. Stark, and W. E. Weihl. Reaching approximate agreement in the presence of faults. *Journal of the ACM*, 33(3):499–516, July 1986.

[DLS88]   C. Dwork, N. Lynch, and L. Stockmeyer. Consensus in the presence of partial synchrony. *Journal of the ACM*, 35(2):288–323, April 1988.

[DP90]   B. A. Davey and H. A. Priestley. *Introduction to Lattices and Order*. Cambridge University Press, Cambridge, UK, 1990.

[DS80]   E. W. Dijkstra and C. S Scholten. Termination detection for diffusing computations. *Information Processing Letters*, 11(4):1–4, August 1980.

[DS83]   D. Dolev and H. R. Strong. Authenticated algorithms for Byzantine agreement. *SIAM Journal on Computing*, 12(4):656–666, 1983.

[DS90]   E. W. Dijkstra and C. S. Scholten. *Predicate Calculus and Program Semantics*. Springer-Verlag New York Inc., New York, NY, 1990.

[DTG99]   O. Damani, A. Tarafdar, and V. K. Garg. Optimistic recovery in multi-threaded distributed systems. In *Proceedings of the 18th IEEE Symposium on Reliable Distributed Systems (SRDS '99)*, pages 234–243, Washington - Brussels - Tokyo, October 1999. IEEE.

[DWG97]   O. P. Damani, Y.M. Wang, and V. K. Garg. Optimistic distributed simulation based on transitive dependancy tracking. In *Proc. ACM Workshop on Parallel and Distributed Simulation (PADS), Lockenhaus, Austria*, pages 90–97, June 1997.

[Fid89]   C. J. Fidge. Partial orders for parallel debugging. *Proceedings of the ACM SIGPLAN/SIGOPS Workshop on Parallel and Distributed Debugging, published in ACM SIGPLAN Notices*, 24(1):183–194, January 1989.

[FL82]   M. J. Fischer and N. A. Lynch. A lower bound on the time to assure interactive consistency. *Information Processing Letters*, 14(4):183–186, 1982.

[FLP85]   M. J. Fischer, N. Lynch, and M. Paterson. Impossibility of distributed consensus with one faulty process. *Journal of the ACM*, 32(2), April 1985.

[FRGT94]   E. Fromentin, M. Raynal, V. K. Garg, and A. I. Tomlinson. On the fly testing of regular patterns in distributed computations. In *Proc. of the 23rd Intl. Conf. on Parallel Processing*, volume 2, pages 73 – 76, St. Charles, IL, August 1994.

[Gar92]   V. K. Garg. Some optimal algorithms for decomposed partially ordered sets. *Information Processing Letters*, 44:39–43, November 1992.

[Gar96]   V. K. Garg. *Principles of Distributed Systems*. Kluwer Academic Publishers, Boston, MA, 1996.

[Gar97]   V. K. Garg. Observation and control for debugging distributed computations. In *Proc. Third International Workshop on Automated Debugging (AADEBUG'97)*, pages 1–12, May 1997. Keynote presentation.

[GC95]   V. K. Garg and C. Chase. Distributed algorithms for detecting conjunctive predicates. In *Proc. of the IEEE International Conference on Distributed Computing Systems*, pages 423–430, Vancouver, BC, Canada, June 1995.

[GCKM97]   V. K. Garg, C. Chase, R. Kilgore, and J. R. Mitchell. Efficient detection of channel predicates in distributed systems. *Journal of Parallel and Distributed Computing*, 45(2):134–147, September 1997.

[GG94]   V. K. Garg and J. Ghosh. Repeated computation of global functions in a distributed environment. *IEEE Transac-*

tions on Parallel and Distributed Systems, 5(8):823–834, August 1994.

[GHS83] R. G. Gallager, P. A. Humblet, and P. M. Spira. A distributed algorithm for minimum-weight spanning trees. *ACM Transactions on Programming Languages and Systems*, 5(1):66–77, January 1983.

[Gif79] D. K. Gifford. Weighted voting for replicated data. *Seventh SOSP*, OSR 13(5):150–162, December, 1979.

[GM97] V. K. Garg and J. R. Mitchell. Detecting conjunctions of global predicates. *Information Processing Letters*, 63(6):295–302, October 1997.

[GM98a] V. K. Garg and J. R. Mitchell. Detection of global predicates in a faulty environment. In *Proc. of the IEEE International Conference on Distributed Computing Systems*, pages 416–423, Amsterdam, May 1998.

[GM98b] V. K. Garg and J. R. Mitchell. Implementable failure detectors in asynchronous systems. In *Proc. 18th Conference on Foundations of Software Technology and Theoretical Computer Science*, number 1530 in Lecture Notes in Computer Science, Chennai, India, December 1998. Springer-Verlag.

[GM01] V. K. Garg and N. Mittal. On slicing a distributed computation. In *21st International Conference on Distributed Computing Systems (ICDCS' 01)*, pages 322–329, Washington - Brussels - Tokyo, April 2001. IEEE.

[GMB85] H. Garcia-Molina and D. Barbara. How to assign votes in a distributed system. *Journal of the Association for Computing Machinery*, 32(4):841–855, October 1985.

[Gos91] A. Goscinski. *Distributed Operating Systems, The Logical Design*. Addison-Wesley, Sydney, Australia, 1991. ISBN 0-201-41704-9.

[GR99] V. K. Garg and M. Raynal. Normality: A consistency condition for concurrent objects. *Parallel Processing Letters*, 9(1):123 – 134, March 1999.

[Gra78]   J. N. Gray. Notes on database operating systems. In G. Goos and J. Hartmanis, editors, *Operating Systems: An Advance Course*, volume 60 of *Lecture Notes in Computer Science*, pages 393–481. Springer-Verlag, 1978.

[GS01]   V. K. Garg and C. Skawratananond. String realizers of posets with applications to distributed computing. In *20th Annual ACM Symposium on Principles of Distributed Computing (PODC-00)*, pages 72 – 80. ACM, August 2001.

[GT93]   V. K. Garg and A. I. Tomlinson. Using induction to prove properties of distributed programs. In *Proc. of the 5th IEEE Symposium on Parallel and Distributed Processing*, pages 478–485, Dallas, TX, December 1993. IEEE.

[GT94]   V. K. Garg and A. I. Tomlinson. Causality versus time: How to specify and verify distributed programs. In *Proc. of the 6th IEEE Symposium on Parallel and Distributed Processing*, pages 249 – 256, Dallas, TX, October 1994.

[GTFR95]   V. K. Garg, A. I. Tomlinson, E. Fromentin, and M. Raynal. Expressing and detecting general control flow properties of distributed computations. In *Proc. of the 7th IEEE Symposium on Parallel and Distributed Processing*, pages 432 – 438, San Antonio, TX, October 1995.

[GW91]   V. K. Garg and B. Waldecker. Detection of unstable predicates. In *Proc. of the Workshop on Parallel and Distributed Debugging*, Santa Cruz, CA, May 1991. ACM/ONR.

[GW92]   V. K. Garg and B. Waldecker. Detection of unstable predicates in distributed programs. In *Proc. of 12th Conference on the Foundations of Software Technology & Theoretical Computer Science*, pages 253–264. Springer Verlag, December 1992. Lecture Notes in Computer Science 652.

[GW94]   V. K. Garg and B. Waldecker. Detection of weak unstable predicates in distributed programs. *IEEE Transactions on Parallel and Distributed Systems*, 5(3):299–307, March 1994.

[GW96]   V. K. Garg and B. Waldecker. Detection of strong un-
           stable predicates in distributed programs. *IEEE Trans-
           actions on Parallel and Distributed Systems*, 7(12):1323–
           1333, December 1996.

[HA90]   Phillip Hutto and Mustaque Ahamad. Slow memory :
           Weakening consistency to enhance concurrency in dis-
           tributed shared memories. *Proceedings of Tenth Inter-
           national Conference on Distributed Computing Systems*,
           May 1990.

[Hel89]   J. Helary. Observing global states of asynchronous dis-
           tributed applications. In *Workshop on Distributed Algo-
           rithms*, pages 124–135. Springer Verlag, LNCS 392, 1989.

[HM84]   J.Y. Halpern and Y. Moses. Knowledge and common
           knowledge in a distributed environment. In *Proc. of the
           ACM Symposium on Principles of Distributed Computing*,
           pages 50 – 61, 1984.

[HMNR97]   Jean-Michel Helary, Achour Mostefaoui, Robert H. B.
           Netzer, and Michel Raynal. Preventing useless check-
           points in distributed computations. In *Symposium on Re-
           liable Distributed Systems*, pages 183–190, 1997.

[HMRS98]   Michael Hurfin, Masaaki Mizuno, Michel Raynal, and
           Mukesh Singhal. Efficient distributed detection of con-
           junctions of local predicates. *IEEE Transactions on Soft-
           ware Engineering*, 24(8):664–677, August 1998.

[HPR93]   M. Hurfin, N. Plouzeau, and M. Raynal. Detecting atomic
           sequences of predicates in distributed computations. In
           *Proc. of the Workshop on Parallel and Distributed Debug-
           ging*, pages 32–42, San Diego, CA, May 1993. ACM/ONR.
           (Reprinted in SIGPLAN Notices, Dec. 1993).

[HS80]   D. S. Hirschberg and J. B. Sinclair. Decentralized
           extrema-finding in circular configurations of processors.
           Communications of the ACM, 23(11):627–628, 1980.

[HS93]   M. Herlihy and N. Shavit. The asynchronous computabil-
           ity theorem for t-resilient tasks (preliminary version). In
           Proceedings of the Twenty-Fifth Annual ACM Symposium

on the Theory of Computing, pages 111–120, San Diego, California, 16–18 May 1993.

[HW90]   M. P. Herlihy and J. M. Wing. Linerizability: A correctness condition for atomic objects. *TOPLAS*, 12(3):463–492, July 1990.

[JZ90]   D. B. Johnson and W. Zwaenepoel. Recovery in distributed systems using optimistic message logging and checkpointing. *Journal of Algorithms*, 11(3):462–491, September 1990.

[Lam78]   L. Lamport. Time, clocks, and the ordering of events in a distributed system. *Communications of the ACM*, 21(7):558–565, July 1978.

[Lam79]   L. Lamport. How to make a correct multiprocess program execute correctly on a multiprocessor. *IEEETC: IEEE Transactions on Computers*, 46, 1979.

[Lam86]   L. Lamport. On interprocess communication, part II: Algorithms. *Distributed Computing*, 1:86–101, 1986.

[Lov73]   L. Lovasz. Coverings and colorings of hypergraphs. In *4th Southeastern Conference on Combinatorics, Graph Theory, and Computing*, pages 3–12, 1973.

[LSP82]   L. Lamport, R. Shostak, and M. Pease. The Byzantine generals problem. *ACM Transactions on Programming Languages and Systems*, 4(3):382–401, July 1982.

[Lub85]   M. Luby. A simple parallel algorithm for the maximal independent set problem. In ACM, editor, *Proceedings of the seventeenth annual ACM Symposium on Theory of Computing, Providence, RI, May 6–8, 1985*, pages 1–10, New York, NY, USA, 1985. ACM Press.

[LY87]   T. H. Lai and T. H. Yang. On distributed snapshots. *Information Processing Letters*, pages 153–158, May 1987.

[Lyn96]   N. A. Lynch. *Distributed Algorithms*. Morgan Kaufmann series in data management systems. Morgan Kaufmann Publishers, Los Altos, CA, 1996. Prepared with LaTeX.

[Mae85]   M. Maekawa. A square root N algorithm for mutual exclusion in decentralized systems. *ACM Transactions on Computer Systems*, 3(2):145–159, May 1985.

[Mat87]   Friedemann Mattern. Algorithms for distributed termination detection. *Distributed Computing*, 2(3):161–175, 1987.

[Mat89]   F. Mattern. Virtual time and global states of distributed systems. In *Parallel and Distributed Algorithms: Proc. of the International Workshop on Parallel and Distributed Algorithms*, pages 215–226. Elsevier Science Publishers B.V. (North-Holland), 1989.

[Mat93]   F. Mattern. Efficient algorithms for distributed snapshots and global virtual time approximation. *Journal of Parallel and Distributed Computing*, pages 423–434, August 1993.

[MC88]   B. P. Miller and J. Choi. Breakpoints and halting in distributed programs. In *Proc. of the 8th International Conference on Distributed Computing Systems*, pages 316–323, San Jose, CA, July 1988. IEEE.

[MG95a]   J. R. Mitchell and V. K. Garg. Deriving distributed algorithms from a general predicate detector. In *The Nineteenth Intl. Computer Software and Applications Conference*, pages 268 – 273, Dallas, TX, 1995. IEEE Computer Society, Washington, DC.

[MG95b]   V. V. Murty and Vijay K. Garg. An algorithm to guarantee synchronous ordering of messages. In *Proceedings of Second International Symposium on Autonomous Decentralized Systems*, pages 208–214. IEEE Computer Society Press, 1995.

[MG97]   V. V. Murty and V. K. Garg. Characterization of message ordering specifications and protocols. In *Proc. of the International Conference on Distributed Computing Systems*, pages 492–499. IEEE, May 1997.

[MG98]   N. Mittal and V. K. Garg. Consistency conditions for multi-object distributed operations. In *Proc. of the 18th*

Int'l Conf. on Distributed Computing Systems (ICDCS-18), pages 582–589, May 1998.

[MG00]   N. Mittal and V. K. Garg. Debugging distributed programs using controlled re-execution. In *19th Annual ACM Symposium on Principles of Distributed Computing (PODC-00)*, pages 239 – 248. ACM, July 2000.

[MG01a]   N. Mittal and V. K. Garg. On detecting global predicates in distributed computations. In *21st International Conference on Distributed Computing Systems (ICDCS' 01)*, pages 3–10, Washington - Brussels - Tokyo, April 2001. IEEE.

[MG01b]   N. Mittal and V. K. Garg. A rigorous proof of $O(n^2)$ bound for Dijkstra's 3-state algorithm. Technical Report ECE PDSLAB 2001, University of Texas at Austin, Austin, TX, July 2001. Electrical and Computer Engineering Department.

[MG01c]   N. Mittal and V. K. Garg. Slicing a distributed computation: Techniques and theory. In *5th International Symposium on DIStributed Computing (DISC'01)*, October 2001.

[MRZ95]   M. Mizuno, M. Raynal, and J. Z. Zhou. Sequential consistency in distributed systems. In K. Birman, F. Mattern, and A. Schiper, editors, *Proc. of the Int'l Workshop on Theory and Practice in Distributed Systems*, number 938 in Lecture Notes in Computer Science, pages 224–241. Springer-Verlag, July 1995.

[Mul94]   S. Mullender. *Distributed Systems, edited book*. Addison-Wesley, Reading, MA, 1994.

[Nei92]   M. Neilsen. *Quorum Structures in Distributed Systems*. PhD thesis, Dept. Computing and Information Sciences, Kansas State University, 1992.

[NX95]   R. H. B. Netzer and J. Xu. Necessary and sufficent conditions for consistent global snapshots. *IEEE Transactions on Parallel and Distributed Systems*, 6(2):165–169, February 1995.

[Pet82]   G. Peterson. An $o(n \log n)$ unidirectional algorithm for the circular extrema problem. *ACM Transactions on Programming Languages and Systems, 4:758–762*, 1982.

[PK93]   S. L. Peterson and P. Kearns. Rollback based on vector time. In *Proc. 12th IEEE Symposium on Reliable Distributed Systems, October 1993.*

[PKR82]   J. K. Pachl, E. Korach, and D. Rotem. A technique for proving lower bounds for distributed maximum-finding algorithms. In *ACM Symposium on Theory of Computing*, pages 378–382, 1982.

[PSL80]   M. Pease, R. Shostak, and L. Lamport. Reaching agreements in the presence of faults. *Journal of the ACM*, 27(2):228–234, April 1980.

[PW95]   D. Peleg and A. Wool. Crumbling walls: a class of practical and efficient quorum systems. In *Proceedings of the 14th Annual ACM Symposium on Principles of Distributed Computing (PODC '95)*, pages 120–129, New York, August 1995. ACM.

[RA81]   G. Ricart and A. K. Agrawala. An optimal algorithm for mutual exclusion in computer networks. *Communications of the ACM*, 24, 1981.

[Ray88]   M. Raynal. *Distributed Algorithms and Protocols*. John Wiley and Sons Ltd, Chichester, England, 1988.

[Ray89]   K. Raymond. A tree-based algorithm for distributed mutual exclusion. *ACM Transactions on Computer Systems*, 7(1):61–77, February 1989.

[RH90]   M. Raynal and J. M. Helary. *Synchronization and Control of Distributed Systems and Programs*. John Wiley and Sons Ltd, Chichester, England, 1990.

[RST91]   M. Raynal, A. Schiper, and S. Toueg. The causal ordering abstraction and a simple way to implement it. *Information Processing Letters*, 39(6):343–350, July 1991.

[SG01]   A. Sen and V. K. Garg. Automatic generation of compu-
            tation slices for detecting temporal logic predicates. Tech-
            nical Report ECE PDSLAB 2001, University of Texas at
            Austin, Austin, TX, November 2001. Electrical and Com-
            puter Engineering Department.

[SG02]   A. Sen and V. K. Garg. Detecting temporal logic pred-
            icates in the happened before model. In *International
            Parallel and Distributed Processing Symposium (IPDPS)*,
            page to appear. IEEE, 2002.

[SJT95]   S. W. Smith, D. B. Johnson, and J. D. Tygar. Com-
            pletely asynchronous optimistic recovery with minimal
            rollback. In *Intl. Symp. on Fault-Tolerant Computing Sys-
            tems*, pages 361–370, 1995.

[SK85]   I. Suzuki and T. Kasami. A distributed mutual exclu-
            sion algorithm. *ACM Transactions on Computer Systems*,
            3(4):344–349, November 1985.

[SK86]   M. Spezialetti and P. Kearns. Efficient distributed snap-
            shots. In *Proc. of the 6th International Conference on
            Distributed Computing Systems*, pages 382–388, 1986.

[SK92]   Mukesh Singhal and Ajay Kshemkalyani. An efficient im-
            plementation of vector clocks. *Information Processing Let-
            ters*, 43(1):47–52, August 1992.

[Ske82]   D. Skeen. *Crash Recovery in Distributed Database Sys-
            tem*. PhD Dissertation, EECS Department, University of
            California at Berkeley, 1982.

[SL87]   S. Sarin and N. A. Lynch. Discarding obsolete information
            in a replicated database system. *IEEE Transactions on
            Software Engineering*, SE-13(1):39–47, January 1987.

[SP98]   E. Styer and G. L. Peterson. Improved algorithms for dis-
            tributed resource allocation. In *Proceedings of the Seventh
            Annual ACM Symposium on Principles of Distributed
            Computing (PODC '88)*, pages 105–116, New York, Au-
            gust 1998. ACM.

[SS94]   M. Singhal and N. G. Shivaratri. *Advanced Concepts in
            Operating Systems*. McGraw Hill, New York, NY, 1994.

[SS95]   S. D. Stoller and F. B. Schneider. Faster possibility detection by combining two approaches. In *Proc. of the 9th International Workshop on Distributed Algorithms*, pages 318–332, Le Mont-Saint-Michel, France, September 1995. Springer-Verlag.

[SW89]   A. P. Sistla and J. L. Welch. Distributed recovery using message logging. In *Proc. of the Principles of Distributed Computing*, pages 223–238, 1989.

[SY85]   R. E. Strom and S. Yemeni. Optimistic recovery in distributed systems. *ACM Transactions on Computer Systems*, 3(3):204–226, 1985.

[SZ93]   M. Saks and F. Zaharoglou. Wait-free k-set agreement is impossible: The topology of public knowledge. In *Proceedings of the Twenty-Fifth Annual ACM Symposium on the Theory of Computing*, pages 101–110, San Diego, CA, 16–18 May 1993.

[Tay83]   R. N. Taylor. Complexity of analyzing the synchronization structure of concurrent programs. *Acta Informatica*, 19(1):57–84, April 1983.

[Tay89]   K. Taylor. The role of inhibition in asynchronous consistent-cut protocols. In *Workshop on Distributed Algorithms*, pages 280–291. Springer-Verlag, LNCS 392, 1989.

[Tel94]   G. Tel. *Introduction to Distributed Algorithms*. Cambridge University Press, Cambridge, UK, 1994.

[TG93]   A. I. Tomlinson and V. K. Garg. Detecting relational global predicates in distributed systems. In *Proc. of the Workshop on Parallel and Distributed Debugging*, pages 21–31, San Diego, CA, May 1993. ACM/ONR.

[TG94]   A. I. Tomlinson and V. K. Garg. Maintenance of global assertions in distributed systems. In *International Conference on Computer Science and Education*, Bangalore, India, June 1994. Tata McGraw-Hill.

[TG95]   A. I. Tomlinson and V. K. Garg.   Observation of soft-
            ware for distributed systems with RCL. In *Proc. of 15th
            Conference on the Foundations of Software Technology &
            Theoretical Computer Science.* Springer Verlag, December
            1995. Lecture Notes in Computer Science.

[TG97]   A. I. Tomlinson and V. K. Garg. Monitoring functions on
            global states of distributed programs. *Journal for Parallel
            and Distributed Computing,* 1997. a preliminary version
            appeared in Proc. of the ACM Workshop on Parallel and
            Distributed Debugging, San Diego, CA, May 1993, pp.21
            – 31.

[TG98a]   A. Tarafdar and V. K. Garg.   Addressing false causal-
            ity while detecting predicates in distributed programs. In
            *Proc. of the 18th International Conference on Distributed
            Computing Systems,* pages 94 – 101, Amsterdam, The
            Netherlands, May 1998. IEEE.

[TG98b]   A. Tarafdar and V. K. Garg. Predicate control for active
            debugging of distributed programs. In *Proc. of the 9th
            Symposium on Parallel and Distributed Processing,* pages
            763 – 769, Orlando, FL, April 1998. IEEE.

[TG99]   A. Tarafdar and V. K. Garg.   Software fault-tolerance
            of concurrent programs using controlled reexecution. In
            *Proceedings of the 13th International Symposium on DIS-
            tributed Computing (DISC),* pages 210 – 224, Bratislava,
            Slovakia, September 1999.

[Tho79]   R. H. Thomas. A majority consensus approach to concur-
            rency control for multiple copy databases. *ACM Transac-
            tions on Database Systems,* 4(2):180–209, June 1979.

[VD92]   S. Venkatesan and B. Dathan.   Testing and debugging
            distributed programs using global predicates. In *Thirti-
            eth Annual Allerton Conference on Communication, Con-
            trol and Computing,* pages 137–146, Allerton, IL, October
            1992.

[Wan97]   Y. M. Wang. Consistent global checkpoints that contain
            a given set of local checkpoints. *IEEE Transactions on
            Computers,* 46(4), April 1997.

[WDG97]   Y. M. Wang, O. P. Damani, and V. K. Garg. Distributed recovery with k-optimistic logging. In *ICDCS '97; Proceedings of the 17th International Conference on Distributed Computing Systems; Baltimore, Maryland*, pages 60 – 67, Washington - Brussels - Tokyo, June 1997. IEEE.

[Wei82]   M. Weiser. Programmers use slices when debugging. *Communications of the ACM*, 25(7):446–452, 1982.

[YM94]   Z. Yang and T. A. Marsland. Introduction. In Z. Yang and T. A. Marsland, editors, *Global State and Time in Distributed Systems*, Los Alamitos, CA, 1994. IEEE Computer Society Press.

Index

Printed and bound by CPI Group (UK) Ltd, Croydon, CR0 4YY

27/10/2024

14580256-0002